M000093381

Oracle Web
Applications 101

ORACLE®   *Oracle Press*™

Oracle Web
Applications 101

Sten E. Vesterli

Osborne/**McGraw-Hill**

New York   Chicago   San Francisco
Lisbon   London   Madrid   Mexico City
Milan   New Delhi   San Juan
Seoul   Singapore   Sydney   Toronto

Osborne/**McGraw-Hill**
2600 Tenth Street
Berkeley, California 94710
U.S.A.

To arrange bulk purchase discounts for sales promotions, premiums, or fund-raisers, please contact Osborne/**McGraw-Hill** at the above address. For information on translations or book distributors outside the U.S.A., please see the International Contact Information page immediately following the index of this book.

Oracle Web Applications 101

1234567890 CUS CUS 01987654321

ISBN 0-07-213221-3

Publisher
Brandon A. Nordin

Vice President & Associate Publisher
Scott Rogers

Acquisitions Editor
Jeremy Judson

Project Editor
Jennifer Malnick

Acquisitions Coordinator
Ross Doll

Technical Editor
Steve O'Hearn

Copy Editor
Sally Engelfried

Proofreader
Linda Medoff

Indexer
Claire Splan

Computer Designers
Elizabeth Jang, Lauren McCarthy, Roberta Steele

Illustrator
Michael Mueller

Series Design
Jani Beckwith

Cover Design
Will Voss

This book was composed with Corel VENTURA™ Publisher.

To my wife for her love and support
To my children for their understanding
To my parents for teaching me the joy of sharing knowledge

About the Author

Sten E. Vesterli is an expert on Oracle Internet technology who has been working with the Oracle Web/Application server products since version 1.0. An experienced developer and systems architect, he has first-hand experience with almost every Oracle tool or server with Web capabilities.

Mr. Vesterli has been a highly rated speaker at international Oracle conferences in Europe and U.S.A for many years, and also leads seminars and courses on Oracle Web technology.

Though a native Dane, Mr. Vesterli currently lives with his family in southern Germany. He works for IconMedialab, helping clients mainly in Switzerland and Germany implement Oracle Web solutions.

He maintains a Web site on building Oracle Web applications at www.vesterli.com and can be reached at sten@vesterli.com.

About IconMedialab

IconMedialab is the world leader in providing integrated e-business professional services to companies doing business globally. Recognized by the World Economic Forum as one of the world's pioneering new technology companies, IconMedialab helps clients attain competitive advantage and generate long-term value by utilizing the power of emerging technologies to build stronger, more profitable relationships with customers, business partners, employees, suppliers, and shareholders.

IconMedialab delivers on the promise of the network economy with employees deployed in 15 countries throughout Europe, North America, and employees in Asia and in Australia through IconMedialab Asia. As a recognized leader in usability, security, and wireless applications, the company has developed and executed programs for such clients as Stora Enso, Siemens Medical, Föreningssparbanken, Sonera Zed, Ferrari, Sony Computer Entertainment, and Motorola.

Contents at a Glance

PART III
Reference

Contents

PART I
An Introduction to Web Applications

PART II
Building Web Applications

PART III

Reference

Acknowledgements

lthough there is only one name on the cover of this book, many people deserve thanks for their part in making this book possible. First, the people from Oracle Press: Jeremy Judson, my acquisitions editor, who I met over lunch at the IOUG-A Live 2000 in Anaheim; Steve O'Hearn, my technical editor, who provided many insightful comments; Jennifer Malnick and Sally Engelfried, my project editor and copy editor, for improving the text and keeping it consistent; and Ross Doll, the acquisitions coordinator, for keeping the process running smoothly.

Bradley Brown from TUSC also deserve thanks for our discussions at the outset of this project, and for his help choosing the scope of this book.

A great thank you to my current and previous colleagues at TPI, Corebit, and IconMedialab for interesting discussions on how to build Web applications as well as valuable feedback on different chapters of the book: Hans Peter Guldager, Michael Hofmann, Anders Houlberg, Morten Tangaa-Andersen, Lars Bo Vanting, and Sebastian Ziemke. Also, thanks to Henrik Sønderby Petersen for always being willing to download the latest Oracle software so it was ready for me to pick up on a CD. And extra thanks to Morten for building the nice little html2java and html2plsql utilities that save my work every time I hand-build a Web application.

I appreciate the support that IconMedialab has given me, and thank my managers there: Kenneth Linnebjerg, Finn Larsen, and Stig Hølledig.

Also, a warm thanks to my client Profitline, in Switzerland, for accepting the time I had to take off from their projects to write, and for still inviting me to join them on their trip to Morocco, where I wrote this.

Through the wonders of modern communications, I have also had valuable input from Gary Belleville, who was willing to share insights from his evaluation of Web tools for a customer, as well as from John Caputo and Ken Atkins, all of whom I have never met in person, but hope to meet one day. I have also enjoyed the interesting discussions on the ODTUG-WEBDEV-L mailing list, where many of the questions I try to answer in this book have been extensively discussed—thanks to everybody who has asked or answered a question there.

Another important group of people who have helped me and countless other Oracle developers is the many people working in the Oracle user groups—especially those who have made the big IOUG-A and EOUG conferences a recurring success as organizers, speakers, and participants. I thank all the people who have attended my presentations there and asked interesting questions and provided useful comments.

I also have to thank my kids, Michael and Maria, for patiently accepting all the time Daddy has been working and using "their" computer.

Finally, the biggest thank you of all goes to my wife, Lotte, for her love, understanding, and support during this project, and for keeping the family together while I was writing.

Foreword

In 1995, when I was asked to debate whether client/server was dead, I did a tremendous amount of research. I quickly understood that client/server would indeed soon be dead. I started building serious Oracle Web applications in early 1996. I knew that this technology would become important, but could not guess how all-pervasive Web applications would be just five years later. Nor could I have predicted what an impact it would have on my life and those around me.

We have come a long way, but every exciting interactive Web site being built today seems to point the way toward even better Web applications of tomorrow: flexible, personalized, and interactive. We are at the beginning of the Web's lifecycle—in other words, you ain't seen nothing yet. But now is certainly the time for you to get in; the longer you wait, the more difficult it is to enter the Web world.

What's in store? Better development tools and environments (as we're already beginning to see, such as Portal, JSP, and Cherokee), fast access speeds (T3 speeds to the home), better reliability and performance (iAS clearly provides these), software companies becoming service companies (as promised by Larry Ellison of Oracle), improved business-to-business communication (via XML), and so much more!

The collapse of many dot coms has certainly caught the headlines, but behind the sensationalist stories, the Web revolution is quietly continuing. A great many organizations are building and expanding their Web applications, experiencing dramatic improvements in efficiency, sales, revenue, and customer service. The Web isn't simply about the Internet and the ubiquitous connection, but rather it's about a powerful development architecture.

In my own books, most recently in *Oracle8i Web Development*, I and my other colleagues at TUSC have shared the extensive experience we have collected building Web applications with Oracle tools and servers. My prior book, *Oracle Application Server Web Toolkit Reference*, was a fine introduction to Web technology, but this book is even better (and it's current). These highly successful books (and soon *Oracle9i Web Development*, to be published by Oracle Press) contain tips and tricks for the experienced developer to make full use of the many features that the Oracle products offer.

The book you hold in your hands takes a different approach. It is part of the highly successful *101* series from Oracle Press, and is intended to help you start your career building Oracle Web applications. It includes a step-by-step description of how to install all the servers and tools you need, and covers five ways of building Oracle Web applications: by hand using Java or PL/SQL, with Oracle Designer, Oracle Portal, and Oracle Developer.

When I received a copy of this book from Sten, I was very impressed by his easy-to-follow and clear writing style. I really like the way he puts things into analogies, like comparing the client/server architecture with an interesting television arrangement. I found his style to be absolutely wonderful to read. Sten is obviously very dedicated to sharing the knowledge.

This book is a great way to get started in the exciting world of Oracle Web applications. I will recommend this book to new developers in TUSC, and I recommend it to you.

—Bradley D. Brown, Chairman and Chief Architect,
TUSC,The Ultimate Software Consultants;
Author, *Oracle8i Web Development* and
Oracle Application Server Web Toolkit Reference

Introduction

his book is a beginner's guide to building Oracle Web applications—Web applications accessing an Oracle database built using Oracle tools. It explains the choices you face when building Oracle Web Applications and covers the five basic ways of building them:

- Using Java servlets
- Using handwritten PL/SQL
- Using Oracle Designer
- Using Oracle Portal
- Using Oracle Developer: Forms and Reports

The book takes you by the hand as you install all the necessary software and make your first Web applications run using each of the methods. You'll see how to build the same four sample applications in five different ways, letting you follow the entire development process and allowing you to discover for yourself which method fits the your needs.

The software covered in this book includes the Oracle8i Release 3 database, the Oracle9i Application Server, Oracle JDeveloper 3.2, Oracle Designer 6i, Oracle9iAS Portal, and Oracle Developer 6i.

Who is This Book for?

The book is aimed at developers who want to start building Web applications connecting to an Oracle database using the Oracle tools. It will also be useful for system architects or others who want an overview of the Oracle Web technologies. You do not have to know anything about Web technology, but you should be familiar with the basics of SQL and the Oracle database.

Each of the five ways is covered in a chapter that can be read independent of the others—so if you only want to know about Java servlets or Oracle Designer, you can read just those chapters.

Two chapters describe ways of building Web applications "by hand": Chapter 6 on Java servlets, and Chapter 7 on PL/SQL Web applications. These chapters cannot avoid depending a bit on knowledge of the language used, so Chapter 6 assumes a bit of Java knowledge, and Chapter 7 requires some basic PL/SQL knowledge.

How to Read This Book

Chapters 1, 2, and 3 introduce Web applications in general, compare the tools available from Oracle, and explain how they work.

Chapter 4 then contains a step-by-step guideline for installing *all* the Oracle software you need to develop and run Oracle Web applications on a single machine—database, application server, and development tools. Ideally, you'll have a moderately powerful PC available to install the software and play around. It should have Windows/2000 or Windows NT and at least 256 MB of RAM (even though you might get by with 128 MB and a large swap file). The installation instructions walk you through the installation on a Windows/2000 machine, but most of the instructions apply to Linux and other Unix flavors as well.

Chapter 5 describes a general application development methodology that applies to all kinds of handwritten Web applications, whether you choose Java, PL/SQL, or a completely different language.

Chapter 6 then describes how use this method in practice to develop four small sample applications as Java servlets with Oracle JDeveloper; Chapter 7 shows the same using PL/SQL. To allow you to refer to one or the other chapter as needed, some material occurs in both chapters—after all, the approach is the same, even though another programming language is used.

Chapters 8 and 9 describe how to use the two Oracle code-generating tools: Oracle Designer and Oracle Portal. In both chapters, the same four small applications are developed.

Chapter 10 describes how the familiar Oracle client/server development tools, Oracle Forms and Oracle Reports, can be use to develop the same applications and deploy them to the Web.

Chapter 11 lists some tools and utilities that might be useful when developing Oracle Web applications, and Chapter 12 explains the code library used in the examples (the code and all the example from this book is available for download from **www.vesterli.com**).

Chapter 13 finally provides you some pointers to books and Web sites where you can continue your journey toward becoming a master of Oracle Web applications.

Conventions

Many of the code listings show the complete HTML, PL/SQL or Java code to let you see how it all fits together. The part written in **bold** font is the new material that is explained in more detail in the accompanying text:

```
// this is trivial
// but this is explained in detail
// this isn't hard either
```

When some part of the code has already been explained, it might be left out of later listings. This is indicated by the text *[snip]* in bold italic font, like this:

```
// we already know all this stuff
[snip]
// here is where it gets interesting again
```

Upper and Lower Case

Java is case sensitive. All PL/SQL developers please say after me: JAVA IS CASE SENSITIVE. If you are coming to Java from PL/SQL, this will initially cause you many compile errors—but you'll quickly get the hang of it.

To ease the transition, and to make it easier to compare the Java and PL/SQL code, much of the PL/SQL code uses the Upper-lower notation common in Java instead of the all–upper-case notation normally used in PL/SQL. So instead of calling a PL/SQL function START_PAGE, this book might use a name like startPage.

Getting Maximum Benefit From This Book

Whether you want to learn only one of the five ways described in this book, or you want to become an expert on all of them, I encourage you to get your hands on a moderately powerful Windows 2000 or NT computer you can use for learning the material. Then install the software and follow the examples that show the method you are interested in. Each method is shown through the same four small examples, and step-by-step instructions take you through the same four small examples as well as the entire process. If you have a problem, you can download many of the completed applications from **http://www.vesterli**.com. Okay? Let's get started!

PART I

An Introduction to Web Applications

CHAPTER 1

Why Web Applications?

magine a world where each TV set receives only one channel. There is no channel selector; and if you want to watch a program on another station, you need another TV set. You have to sign up for the channel with a TV station, and they send a professional TV set installer by your house to install the customized TV set for that channel. When you decide to watch another channel, yet another professional installer must come by and set up another TV set.

Ridiculous? Yes, of course!

But consider for a moment the way that client/server applications have been built: for each application, someone has been going around installing custom clients at each client workstation; and for every new application, an IT professional has been going around to the users again to install and set up the application.

Web applications are a return to the standards-based approach that works well for TV: if you want to start receiving a new channel, you simply tune in. Now, when you want to use a new Web application, you simply enter the address in your browser, and you have access.

This chapter defines Web applications and explains the difference between intranets, extranets, and the Internet. It then describes the possible range of clients and ends with a discussion of the advantages of writing Web applications.

What Is a Web Application?

A Web application is an application based on the public standards used on the World Wide Web (described in more detail in just a bit). The Internet, and the World Wide Web in particular, has been such a tremendous success that it makes sense to emulate the principles used there, even if your application will never be accessible to the world via the Internet.

All multiuser applications today are client/server applications in one form or another—each user works at a client workstation, and some central server stores the common data. Both the "old-fashioned" client/server applications developed with tools like Oracle Forms and the new Web applications are really client/server applications.

To distinguish between traditional client/server applications and Web applications, we will use another measure: how many layers (or *tiers*) the whole architecture has.

In traditional client/server applications (using tools like Oracle Forms), a client computer handled the user interface, and a database server stored the data. The actual functionality (*business logic*) of the application could reside on the client (as triggers in Oracle Forms) and/or in the databases (as stored procedures). This is a *two-tier* architecture.

Back in 1990, when the World Wide Web was originally conceived at CERN, the European Laboratory for Particle Physics in Geneva, Switzerland, it was intended to serve static files like research papers. The Web thus also originally had two tiers: a browser that needed only to display the file on the screen and a file server (or *Web server*) that delivered the file on request.

This was great; but after a while, Web developers wanted more. They wanted the ability to create dynamic content by running a program that created a customized page on the fly. The Web server was therefore extended with the possibility to call programs through the *Common Gateway Interface (CGI)*.

This was great, but it wasn't long before Web developers wanted to let these programs access databases. This was achieved in many different ways from different programming languages; but because the databases normally resided on other servers than the Web servers, there was now a Web browser on the client side, and two or more layers of servers on the server side. This lead to the terms *three-tier* and *multitier* applications.

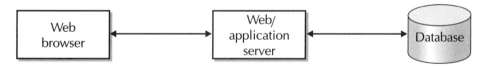

A Web application is thus defined as a multitier application based on the Internet standards, using a Web browser as client.

The Internet Standards

Web applications overcome many of the problems that plague the client/server world, because the communication and presentation of Web pages are based on a number of public standards. The most important standards are listed in Table 1-1.

Standard	Full Name	Applies To
TCP/IP	Transmission Control Protocol/Internet Protocol	Network communication between client and server hardware
HTTP	Hypertext Transport Protocol	Communication between Web server and Web browser
HTML	Hypertext Markup Language	Page definition
XML	Extensible Markup Language	User-specific definition of content
XHTML	Extensible Hypertext Markup Language	Page definition (latest version of HTML)

TABLE 1-1. *Public Standards Used on the Internet*

TCP/IP

The most basic standard is the TCP/IP protocol. This protocol defines the rules for establishing connections between computers, that is, between the client and server hardware.

IP Numbers

Every computer on a TCP/IP network must have a unique *IP number*, written as four groups of numbers where each number lies in the range from 0 to 255, like this: 192.168.27.43.

These numbers can be fixed (that is, defined in the computer configuration), or they can be dynamically assigned. In the case of dynamically assigned numbers, one computer is given a pool of numbers to give out to other computers that request one. The protocol for requesting and receiving a number is called *Dynamic Host Configuration Protocol (DHCP),* and the server that gives out the numbers is called a *DHCP server.*

Server Names

The IP number allows computers to find one another and to communicate; but we humans prefer names, not just numbers. Therefore, every computer can also have a name. This name is written as three or more words, separated by periods, as shown in Figure 1-1.

The rightmost word ("com," in Figure 1-1) is the *top-level domain (TLD)*, and the second word from right is the *second-level domain (SLD).*

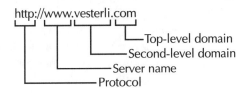

FIGURE 1-1. *Elements of a server name*

Top-level domains are administered by the Internet Corporation for Assigned Names and Numbers (ICANN) and exist in several forms, as listed in Table 1-2. In addition to these, a number of new top-level domains are under consideration at ICANN.

In the generic top-level domains, companies and individuals can register their own second-level domain (Oracle, for example, has oracle.com) with a registrar accredited by the ICANN. Your Internet Service Provider can do this for you.

To register a second-level domain in one of the special top-level domains, your organization must fit in one of the categories, and you must contact the relevant authority.

Type	Domains	Intended For
Generic TLDs	.com	Commercial organizations
	.net	Networking organizations
	.org	Other organizations, including nonprofit
Special TLDs	.edu	Higher education
	.gov	U.S. government
	.int	International organizations
	.mil	U.S. Department of Defense
Country TLDs	.uk	United Kingdom
	.jp	Japan
	.de	Germany
	.dk	Denmark
	and so on	

TABLE 1-2. *Top-Level Domains*

The country top-level domains are handled by local registrars. Each have different rules—some allow you to register a company name as a second-level domain (like Germany, where Oracle is oracle.de); others use the second-level domain to further group the country domain (like the United Kingdom, where Oracle is oracle.co.uk). Also, some countries require that you are a resident of the country or have an office there, and others don't.

From Name to Number

In order for the computer to be able to communicate with a server, it needs to know that server's IP number. In a small, closed network, you can create a file (called a *hosts* file) that contains a list of names and corresponding numbers. However, on the Internet, this is, of course, impossible. Instead, the computer that needs to know the number of another computer will contact a special information server—a *Domain Name System (DNS)* server—that knows about these names and numbers. A DNS server has information about some servers that it is responsible for, and it knows which other servers to contact for information about other servers.

For you as a Web developer, this whole mechanism is transparent—if you can connect to a server by name, the network is set up properly.

HTTP

While the TCP/IP protocol is the standard for low-level communication between two computers, the HTTP protocol is a higher-level protocol that controls the communication between a Web browser and a Web server. You recognize it as the prefix in full Web addresses (refer to Figure 1-1).

When you enter a Web address in a browser, the browser sends an HTTP message to the server, requesting a Web page. If the page can be found, the Web server responds with another HTTP message containing information about the data type it is returning and, of course, the page itself. If the page cannot be found or another error occurs, the Web server returns an HTTP error message.

Note that the occurrence of an HTTP error message indicates that your browser did get through to the Web server, but the Web server was for some reason not able to deliver the page you requested.

HTML

The actual Web page returned by the Web server must conform to the Hypertext Markup Language (HTML) standard. This standard defines the allowed format for Web pages.

HTML was based on older work on *Structured General Markup Language (SGML)*, which is a standard for indicating the structure of documents. Therefore,

HTML was originally intended to model only the structure of a document, not the layout. That's why HTML initially only contained information like "this is a level 2 subheading" and not "this is Times Roman 24 point bold."

In the client/server world, screens were carefully defined with pixel precision, as shown in Figure 1-2. The screen definition, together with all the business logic, was stored in a proprietary file format like the .fmb files used by Oracle Forms.

In the Web world, the layout is not strictly defined pixel by pixel. Instead, the page is defined in HTML, and the browser determines how to display the page on the screen, as in Figure 1-3. The advantage of this is that the browser will automatically try to compensate for smaller or bigger screens. The disadvantage is that the developer has to give up the exact control over the screen layout.

Chapter 5 contains a crash course with enough HTML information to get started; but if you really want to learn HTML, you will need some supplementary information. Refer to Chapter 13 for some Web sites and books that will help you.

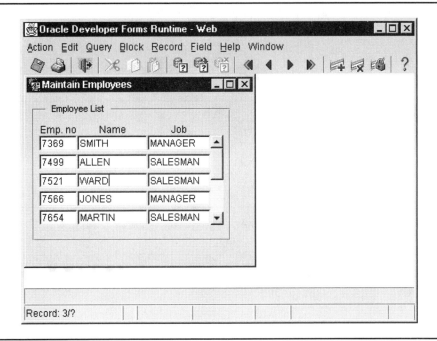

FIGURE 1-2.   *An Oracle Forms page seen in a browser*

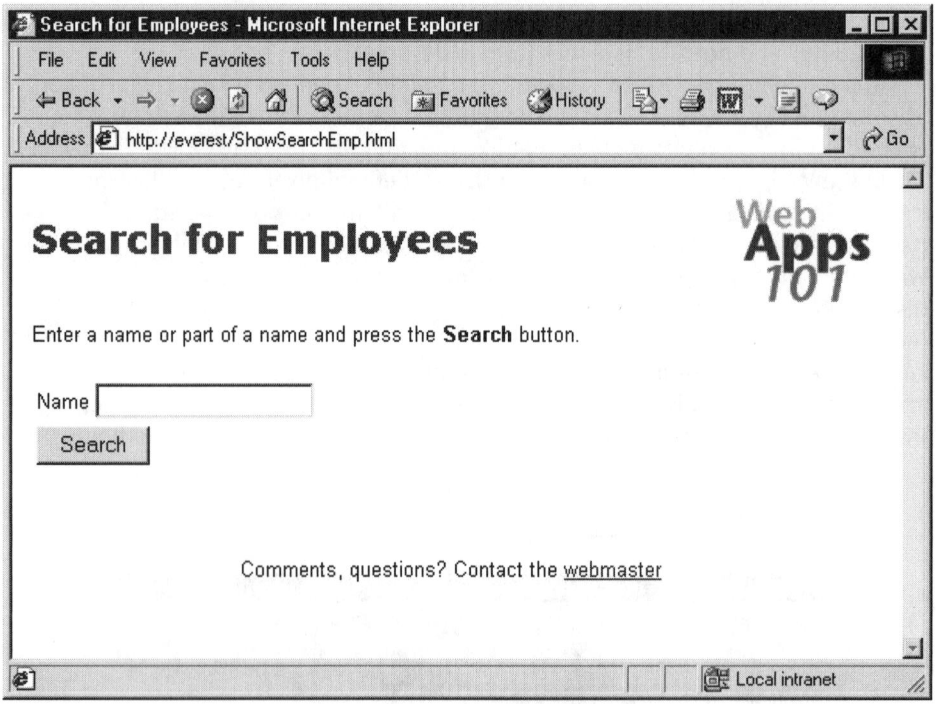

FIGURE 1-3. *An HTML page*

XML

HTML is very useful for creating Web pages, but it suffers from one serious drawback: The HTML format does not provide any information about the content. If a Web page contains the word *Shakespeare*, you don't know if the page contains a text *by* Shakespeare or *about* Shakespeare.

The way to solve this is to expand the library of tags using Extensible Markup Language (XML). This means that the page will not just contain the word *Shakespeare* with some optional formatting instruction; instead, it contains the data and a label indicating what the data is.

HTML Code	XML Code	Displays As
Shakespeare	<author>Shakespeare</author>	Shakespeare

To control how this data displays on the screen, HTML provides basic formatting information like "use bold font." In the XML world, this is handled with Extensible Stylesheet Language (XSL), which allows you to define how to present the data in an XML file to a browser. This allows a clean separation of data values from their presentation.

The XML standard defines the rules for defining new sets of tags; you can consider XML to be a language for describing languages. It is rapidly becoming the standard for all kinds of automatic data exchange between computers—many organizations are using XML to define standard formats for exchanging invoices, orders, and other types of information. Even the latest version of the HTML standard (called *XHTML*) is defined in XML.

XML and XSL are outside the scope of this book, but Chapter 13 points you to some books and Web sites you can refer to for more information.

Intranets, Extranets, and the Internet

The *Internet* is the network of publicly accessible computers running the Internet standard protocol TCP/IP. Many of these computers run Web servers, so you can connect to them using Web browsers. However, many computers do something else (like send and receive e-mail).

An *intranet* is a private network of computers that also uses the TCP/IP protocol. The difference is that an organization can have its own intranet shielded from the Internet through the use of a firewall. Figure 1-4 shows an intranet for the company with the domain company.com.

The firewall controls all traffic to and from the intranet. It can be configured, for example, to allow all clients on the inside to connect to servers on the Internet, maybe barring a few; and it might specify that clients outside on the Internet can access only the server www.company.com, but no others.

An *extranet* is a network of computers connecting an organization with selected partners, suppliers, and/or customers. In Figure 1-4, for instance, the firewall might allow clients belonging to specific partners to access both the server partner.company.com and the public server www.company.com, but not the internal server intranet.company.com.

The Ideal Client

Imagine that you want to purchase an aircraft. A plethora of aircraft is available, from ultra-light aircraft for hobby pilots, to single-engine propeller aircraft, to business jets, to 747s. Each aircraft is optimized for a specific type of flying, and they differ widely in cruise speed, payload, maintenance needs, and many other respects.

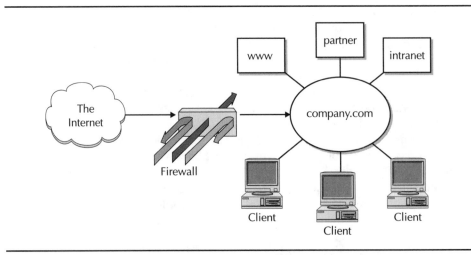

FIGURE 1-4. *Intranets, extranets, and the Internet*

Similarly, when you want to build a Web application, you have a variety of clients available, from ultra-light clients like the Palm Pilot or WebTV, to older PCs and Macintoshes, to the very latest Web browser running on powerful PCs with high-speed Internet connections. Each fulfills a different task, and they differ in processing speed, network connection speed, and graphics capabilities.

And, just as most people would not want to fly from San Francisco to Los Angeles every week in an ultra-light aircraft, you would not want to make a data-entry clerk use a Palm Pilot to enter data all day.

The Trade-off

Why would anybody want to move away from the traditional two-tier client/server approach? After all, the applications can be fast and have sophisticated user interfaces, with intelligent validation and every graphical widget you can imagine.

Well, the problem is that developers were trying to use the same tool for all applications. And, even though each successive generation of client/server development tools were supposedly easier to use, the application development backlog grew: the applications that the business needed could simply not be built fast enough. In addition, more and more infrastructure was needed to support the applications: complicated client-side software installation, powerful client hardware, and so on.

This was like trying to use a 747 as the only aircraft. Obviously, only major routes were worth the effort to establish, and big airports with long runways were needed everywhere.

Web applications are a return to necessary and reasonable flexibility. Because the communication between the client and the server is now guided by published, universal standards, the application developer can choose a client that fits his need. Some applications are primarily self-service applications for casual users—they need fast load times and can manage with a simple user interface. Other applications are used intensively all day—in these cases, a bit of complexity and longer startup time must be accepted in exchange for a more productive user interface.

The main options are shown in Figure 1-5, and they are described in the following sections.

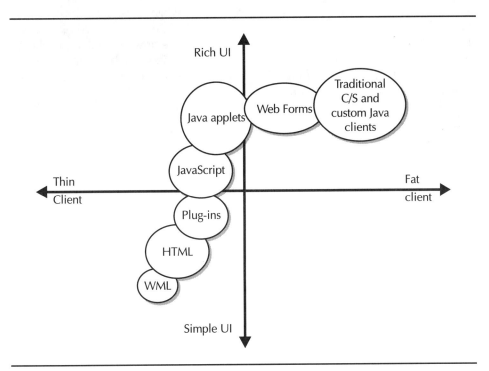

FIGURE 1-5. *Client weight versus user interface capability*

Heavy Clients

At the heavy end of the spectrum lie the custom-built clients. In traditional two-tier client/server computing, the client was the Forms Runtime—an executable program compiled for each platform that had to be installed on each client workstation.

The equivalent approach in a three-tier Web application is the custom-built Java client. This has many of the same advantages and disadvantages as two-tier applications. On the plus side, the developer has full control over the user interface and can use all the features she is used to. On the minus side, an executable program must still be installed (the Java virtual machine that actually executes the Java code), as well as the application itself. And it is probably also necessary to set up the networking in order to access the database.

Browser-Based Java Applications

To avoid most of these problems but still keep the advantages of the rich user interface possible with Java, applications can be developed with browser-based Java using *Java applets*. These are Java programs that are downloaded to the client when the application starts and then executed on the client machine. They have the advantage that the *Java virtual machine (JVM)* is already available, and the network connection is already set up correctly.

However, since nothing is installed on the client, the users will have to wait until the Java applet has been transmitted to the browser and the JVM has started. In addition, the application will have to live with the JVM available on the browser—and the Java language and the JVMs have progressed significantly over the last couple of years. This means that some browsers might not be able to execute the Java applets that you send them.

Writing Your Own

When you write a Java applet application, you are tying together many different components to paint the screen and handle user events. In addition, your applet must communicate with the application server from which it was downloaded to retrieve and transmit data and handle transactions.

Because this can be quite difficult, especially for developers new to the Java language, Oracle provides another option: you can deploy the familiar Forms applications in a browser as Web Forms.

Using Web Forms

In this case, Oracle has written the user interface applet for you; you simply need to configure your server to send the user interface applet to the browser when requested by the client. This applet communicates with a special process (the Forms server) on the Web server. The Forms server then executes the forms and handles the connection to the database just as in client/server, two-tier Forms applications. This gives you the ability to use the familiar Forms development interface and still deploy the application to a Web browser as a Java applet. Figure 1-2 shows a Web Forms screen, and Chapter 10 describes this approach in more detail.

HTML-Based applications

If you want applications that do not need extensive download and initialization before they start, you must limit yourself to applications that use only HTML.

Ultra-Light Clients

In the most extreme case, your Web application will have to cater to extremely lightweight clients like PDAs or smart phones. In this case, you must use especially restricted HTML-like languages such as Wireless Markup Language (WML).

Pure HTML Clients

In classic HTML-based Web applications, the server simply sends HTML pages to the browser and the browser paints the screen. The HTML language has gone through several versions since it was originally developed, and older browsers understand only the older versions of the HTML language. In addition, some enhancements to HTML were invented by Netscape and some by Microsoft; some (but not all) of these enhancements later found their way into a version of the HTML standard.

Therefore, some care is needed to ensure that your pages look as intended on both types of browsers and all the versions you decide to support. And if you want to use the later features of HTML, you must accept that some older browsers will not render your HTML page in the manner you intend.

Browser Plug-Ins

The data returned by the Web server to the browser will normally be in HTML format, and the Web browser will display it on the screen. However, you might sometimes need richer data formats than plain HTML. In this case, you can let the server deliver a file in a different format. This is indicated by the *Multipurpose Internet Mail Extension (MIME)* type information in the HTTP header that precedes the data.

If the browser does not know how to display the data type it receives, it will look for a plug-in program. This is a program created especially for the purpose of handling one or more data types, and normally made freely available for download. Examples of browser plug-ins are the Adobe Acrobat Reader and the Macromedia Flash Player.

Client-Side Scripting

With the help of plug-ins, it is possible to create documents and other types of presentations with a precision not supported by HTML. But for data validation and responding to user events, you need a simple programming language that will execute on the client.

Fortunately, browser manufacturers realized this, and the solution is JavaScript. This is a scripting language that allows you to perform simple tasks such as field-level data validation. JavaScript code is embedded in the HTML code and can read and change the individual page elements.

The JavaScript language has gone through the same rapid evolution as HTML and exists in several different versions. Even more than HTML, JavaScript implementations differ between Microsoft and Netscape browsers. So if you want to use JavaScript extensively in your application, you must carefully test your application in as many different browser versions as possible.

Chapter 13 lists some Web sites and books that can help you with JavaScript.

Can I Have It All?

In traditional design, you choose the application type before you start developing. However, with model-based design as used in Oracle Designer, you can defer the choice of application type until you generate the first-cut application. And if you are willing to accept the limitations of 100 percent generation, you can change application type by simply regenerating.

In theory, you could regenerate to get a different user interface. In practice, this is a major decision not to be undertaken lightly. But, early in the project, you could generate both a Forms application and an HTML-based Web application.

Benefits of Web Applications

Now that you know what a Web application is, let's have a look at some of the benefits they offer.

Free Infrastructure

A major benefit is the fact that the whole infrastructure is already in place. The actual software showing the user interface and communicating with the server is the standard Web browser, and the network communication uses the standard protocols already configured.

This makes it possible to make new applications available to all relevant users immediately—IT support professionals do not have to go around to each client workstation to install the Forms Runtime, install and set up SQL*Net or Net8, or install the application.

Free Upgrades

In addition, when the application resides on the server, new versions will be immediately and simultaneously available to every user. There is no need to distribute updated application files to every user, and everybody always has the latest version.

Interchangeable Components

Because Web applications are based on published standards, it is, in principle, possible to exchange either the server or the browser without breaking the application.

The Browser Wars

Unfortunately, the intense competition in the browser market means that the new versions of the browsers sometimes run before the standards, implementing each feature in different ways. Eventually, the standards catch up; but in the meantime, browser manufacturers add even more features. To make matters worse, sometimes the browser manufacturers simply ignore features specified in the standard.

This means that a Web application has to contend with a very fragmented client base. On an intranet, where everybody is using the standard company browser, this will not be a major problem; but for true Internet applications you will need to check the application in several different browsers on several platforms in several versions.

Java-based applications are very sensitive to bugs in the Java Virtual Machines they run in and will often crash if there is a compatibility problem. This makes it imperative that Java-based applications are extensively tested in all target browsers.

HTML-based applications are much more tolerant and will normally run even in very old browsers. Depending on your application, it might be acceptable for a few error messages to pop up or the page elements to be out of alignment on old browsers—but high-profile public Web sites for big corporations are rightfully expected to run flawlessly across many browsers, versions, and platforms.

You will find a few pointers on basic, widely compatible HTML and JavaScript, and some validation tools, in Chapter 5; for more information, refer to Chapter 13 for books and Web sites. However, if you want to use any Java-based applications or if you have a high-profile site, you should have specialized testing professionals check your site in all common browsers.

High-profile sites normally take a relatively "conservative" approach and eschew the use of the latest features. In addition, such a site might have several versions of each page and use clever techniques to determine the capabilities of the browser to deliver only the sophisticated versions to browsers capable of understanding them.

Focus on Usability

Because Web applications can be made available to everyone with a Web browser, it is no longer practical (or even possible) to gather every user for a training class. The application must be truly self-explanatory.

This, by necessity, leads to a greatly improved focus on the usability of the application. Not that usability testing is new—commercial software developers have been using this for a long while. But for most in-house applications, it was accepted that the user interface might be somewhat clunky—after all, "the users will get used to it." This was not caused by ill will on the side of application developers—they simply did not have the very different skills needed to design an attractive and intuitive user interface.

That is why Web development teams nowadays involve both designers (to make the pages visually attractive) and experts on *Human-Computer Interaction (HCI)*.

This approach normally means more work for the development team in the form of a series of prototypes tested with the users. In effect, because Web applications can have many more users, it pays off to invest some extra development time in order to create a truly useful application.

Summary

Web applications are based on public standards and use a Web browser as the standard client. A wide variety of Web applications is possible—the needs of your users and the clients they have will determine if you will need a fat client running a Java application or a thinner client running an HTML-based application.

But no matter what the approach, you can achieve significant benefits from moving to Web applications: lower infrastructure costs, easier software maintenance, more vendor independence, and an increased focus on creating user-friendly applications.

CHAPTER

2

How to Build
a Web Application

hen you need to get from one place to another in New York City, you have a number of options: you can take a taxi, drive yourself, or take the subway. If you decide to take a taxi, you tell the driver where you want to go, and he takes care of the details. He knows the city and the current traffic and will get you to your destination as quickly as possible. If you are in doubt about the driver's competence, you can try to give him detailed instructions about the route; but this will normally not get you there any faster, and he might misunderstand you and get you both lost.

If you drive yourself, you do all the work. You consider the traffic conditions and decide on the exact route. You might get to the destination more quickly or you might not; but either way, you have full control all the way.

If you go by subway, you must accept that it might get you close but probably not exactly to where you want to be. However, it is cheap and can often be faster than taking a taxi or driving yourself.

You have a similar choice of three approaches when you are going to build a Web application: you can develop an HTML-based application or a Java applet–based application, or use a code-generating tool.

The HTML-based application is like taking the taxi: you give an instruction (an HTML-formatted file) to the driver (a Web browser). The browser then decides how to present that, given your current window size and browser settings. With the latest clever HTML formatting tricks, you can try to give detailed instructions; but if the browser does not understand them, your page might end up garbled.

Java applet–based applications are like driving yourself: you must do all the work and carry the responsibility. You have full control over every pixel on the screen, but you also have the responsibility of deciding in detail what happens when the user presses a button.

Taking the subway is like using a code-generating tool. It will quickly and efficiently take you to a number of standard destinations, but you will have to accept that only the functionality envisioned by the builders of the tool can be realized.

In this chapter, you will see if and where to use Java and how to choose the right tool for your audience and application. You will get a brief overview of HTML-based applications, Java applet–based applications, and code-generated applications, as well as some advice on producing hardcopy output.

Does It Have to Be Java?

For many people, Web applications are synonymous with object-oriented programming in Java. However, this is not really true: a Web application *can* be written in Java, but does not *have* to be. Remember that there are two main types of Web applications:

■   HTML-based

■   Applet-based

In HTML-based applications, the application code resides on the server side (in the Web/application server and/or the database). This code then produces a sequence of HTML Web pages that are sent to the browser to be displayed. There is nothing in this procedure that dictates the server-side programming language—as a matter of fact, you can use almost any programming language.

In applet-based applications, Java applets get downloaded to the client and run there. An applet controls each pixel of the user interface and can react with pixel precision to mouse events and other user interaction.

You can also write full applications in Java. These are similar to applets but are installed on the client and run in a Java virtual machine. This is comparable to writing client applications in C++ or Visual Basic and is outside the scope of this book.

Choose Your Weapon

To decide what development and deployment approach is right for you, you need to consider the needs of your users:

- Who will be using your application? Intranet, extranet, Internet users?

- How complex is the user interface you need?

You need to determine whether your application is only intended for internal (intranet) users, whether you will have a limited number of external users (on an extranet), or whether your application is intended for the general public on the Internet.

You will also need to consider whether you need a rich, full-featured user interface like you find in traditional client/server applications developed with Oracle Forms, or whether an HTML interface will do. If you select an HTML interface, you must also determine if your users can live with a simple standard interface, or you need to use sophisticated HTML programming to realize the application your users need.

The decisions you need to make are documented in the flowchart in Figure 2-1.

Where Are Your Users?

In an ideal world, you would be able to deploy every application to every Web browser and not worry where your users are. Unfortunately, real-world concerns like limited bandwidth and imperfect support for the various Web standards make it necessary that you give some thought to where your users are.

- Intranet

- Extranet

- Internet

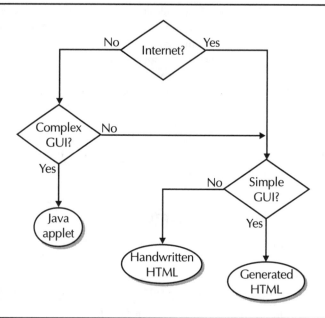

FIGURE 2-1. *The decisions you make about your interface determine how complex your application will be*

On the Intranet

If your application is intended purely for internal use on your organization's intranet, generally all the options will be open to you: you probably have good network connections to every client, and you only have to contend with one browser (or at most, a few different versions). But if some users will be using ultra-light clients like PDAs (personal digital assistants) or smart phones to access your application, you have the limitations of an Internet application.

On an Extranet

If your application is also intended for partners on an extranet, you must carefully consider whether Java is still an option. You have three main points to consider.

What Browser Will My Users Have?   Like most other Internet technologies, the Java language has developed rapidly. Early browsers supported only Java 1.0; later generation browsers have not kept up with the development of the Java language (now in version 1.4) but have concentrated on supporting Java 1.1 adequately (see Table 2-1).

Browser Generation	Microsoft Version	Netscape Version	Supported Java Version
3	3.0	3.0	1.0 (sort of)
4	4.0	4.0	1.1 (almost, but not quite)
5	5.0	4.5+	1.1
6	5.5	6.0	1.1

TABLE 2-1. *Java Versions Supported in Different Browsers*

Sun wants to promote the Java language; but for various reasons, the browser manufacturers have not been keeping up with the latest version of Java. Therefore, Sun has developed Java plug-ins that support the latest version of Java. Such a plug-in can be installed on the browser (even back to third-generation browsers), and the application developer can specify that the application is to use the Java plug-in instead of the built-in Java Virtual Machine (JVM).

Since Java 1.0 lacks a lot of features necessary for serious applications (such as database connectivity!), you do not want to deploy Java applets unless all your users have fifth-generation browsers, like Internet Explorer 5 or Netscape 4.5 or above, or unless you can rely on them to install the Java plug-in.

Can I Get the Applet to My Users?   The first hurdle is that the firewalls used by all your partners must allow the initial download of the applet. This will normally be the case, but very security-conscious firewall administrators might have blocked all applets.

Can My Applet Communicate Back to the Server?   If you are deploying applets outside your own intranet, you must use a standard protocol like HTTP for the communication between the applet and the server. The job of the firewall is to protect against suspicious activity, so all attempts at nonstandard communication will, of course, be blocked.

The Forms Server from Forms version 6.0 can be configured to communicate in this way.

On the Internet
If you are going to deploy your applications to users on the Internet, do not use Java applets. Many browsers do not support Java, or they support only an old version or have bug-ridden, early JVMs. Even if your application would run on the client

browser, Java applets take a long time to start: the applet itself must be downloaded, and then you must wait about a minute for the JVM on the browser to start. Internet users demand an immediate response that Java applets cannot deliver.

What Do Your Users Need?

Another important question for a Web application is how much of their day your users will spend using the application. Will they use it for a few minutes every month to enter expenses? Will they use it for half an hour every week to get the latest product information? Or will they be using your application for several hours daily doing data entry and analysis?

The Need for Speed

For casual users, the most important usability issue is the load time: users have come to expect that Internet applications will be available after a few seconds. In this case, an HTML-based application will be satisfactory.

All the Bells and Whistles

For "heads-down" users who work intensively with the application all day, a startup time of a minute or two is secondary to the productivity possible in the application once it is started. In this case, the advantages of the rich user interface possible in Java outweigh the few minutes it will take to download the applet and start up the JVM of the browser.

Just the Basics

Finally, remember that some basic applications do not need sophisticated HTML or Java applets. A lot of Web applications just need basic query, insert, update, and delete functionality. For this type of application, you can use code-generating tools to reach a standard solution very quickly.

Building Applet-Based Applications

If you have determined that you do need the rich user interface that is only possible with Java, you have two options: use Web Forms or write a Java applet application yourself (see Figure 2-2).

The main factor that will guide your choice is the skills of your developers. If your organization has deep experience developing traditional, two-tier client/server applications using Oracle Forms, it makes sense to capitalize on this knowledge. And, if an existing application must be Web enabled, Web Forms is an obvious choice.

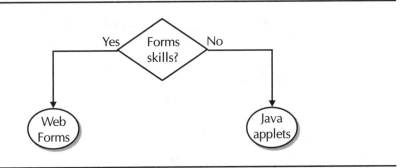

FIGURE 2-2. *Choosing an approach for applet-based applications*

On the other hand, if you are lucky enough to have experienced Java programmers on your team (or the application deadline allows you to learn on the job), developing applets from the bottom up gives you maximum flexibility.

If you have neither and you really need a Java applet–based application, it makes more sense to learn Java than Forms.

Using Web Forms

Web Forms is mainly a deployment option; you use the normal Forms development environment that's familiar from traditional two-tier client/server applications. You do not need to learn any Java—Oracle is providing you with the Forms user interface applet that your users need in order to run the application.

Once your Forms application is ready, you deploy the Forms definition (the .fmb files) to the application server on the middle tier and configure the application server to deliver the user interface applet to the Web browser on the client. The application then runs in the Web browser (see Figure 2-3) and, with a few exceptions, looks and works just as if it were deployed as a traditional, two-tier client/server application.

Chapter 4 describes all the setup necessary to deploy Forms applications as Web Forms, and Chapter 10 shows it in practice.

Using Java Applets

Developing Java applets is like developing a custom client application. It involves significant effort but leaves you in full control of the user interface. This kind of application will look to the user like a traditional client/server application built with a tool like Oracle Forms or PowerBuilder.

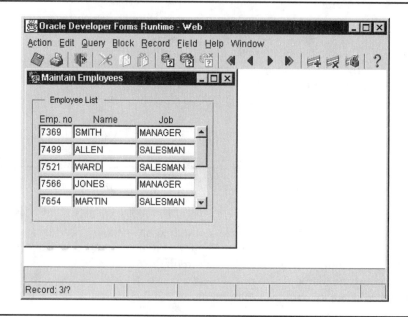

FIGURE 2-3. *A Web Forms application*

If you can only use Java version 1.1 (see Table 2-1), you must use the Java Abstract Windowing Toolkit to paint the screen—this takes a lot of coding. In later versions of Java, the Java Foundation Classes (JFCs) make it somewhat easier to build a functional Java applet showing data from a database.

Nevertheless, no matter what version of Java and what component libraries you have available, it takes a lot of effort to develop applications with Java applets, and this approach will not be covered further in this book. However, Chapter 13 lists some books that can help you get started in this direction.

Building HTML-Based Applications

If have determined that you need to deploy an HTML-based application, or you want the immediacy of an application that is available within a few seconds, your next choice is the language you want to use to realize your HTML-based Web application (see Figure 2-4).

In an HTML-based application, you must write a program that ultimately returns HTML code back to the browser, so that the user will see a series of Web pages. As

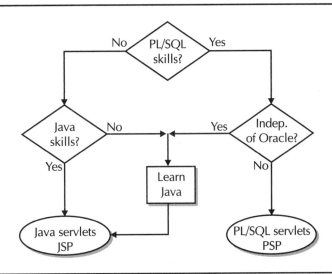

FIGURE 2-4. *Choosing an approach for HTML-based applications*

already mentioned, this can be done in any programming language; and if you know Perl, C++, Python, PHP, or another programming language, you are free to use these. For most Oracle developers, however, the main choice is between Java and PL/SQL.

Remember that Java is a universal programming language—it can be used on the client (in applet-based applications as described in the preceding section) or on the server in the form of Java servlets.

One important consideration when choosing a server-side programming language is how important it is to you to be independent of Oracle—that is, whether you want to maintain the option of moving your Web applications to another Web/application server and database. With Java, you are free to choose among the many Java-capable Web/application servers and can use any database; whereas if you decide to use PL/SQL for your Web applications, you will have to use Oracle databases and application servers.

Server Pages or Servlets

If you choose to use Java or PL/SQL, you have another choice to make: whether to write the whole application as servlets in your chosen programming language or to combine HTML with active components using a server page technology.

Servlets

A *servlet* is a piece of code that returns HTML in a way that the Web/application server can understand. Traditionally, the word *servlet* is used to describe Java servlets, but you could also consider a PL/SQL Web application a PL/SQL servlet.

The following Java code produces the screen in Figure 2-5—the classic "Hello World" example you find in the beginning of any computer book.

```java
import javax.servlet.*;
import javax.servlet.http.*;
import java.io.*;
import java.util.*;

public class hello extends HttpServlet {
  public void doGet(HttpServletRequest request,
      HttpServletResponse response)
      throws ServletException, IOException {
    response.setContentType("text/html");
    PrintWriter out = new PrintWriter (
      response.getOutputStream()
    );
    out.println("<html>");
    out.println("<head>");
    out.println("<title>Hello World</title>");
    out.println("</head>");
    out.println("<body>");
    out.println("<h1>Hello World</h1>");
    out.println("<p>The time is "
        + new Date().toString()
        + "</p>");
    out.println("</body>");
    out.println("</html>");
    out.close();
  }
}
```

Java servlet applications are covered in detail in Chapter 6.
The same functionality would look like this in PL/SQL:

```sql
procedure hello is
begin
  htp.p('<html>');
  htp.p('<head>');
```

```
htp.p('<title>Hello World</title>');
htp.p('</head>');
htp.p('<body>')
htp.p('<h1>Hello World</h1>');
htp.p('<p>The time is '
     || to_char(sysdate, 'hh24:mi:ss yyyy-mm-dd')
     || '</p>'
);
htp.p('</body>')
htp.p('</html>')
end hello;
```

PL/SQL Web applications are discussed in more detail in Chapter 7.

As is clear from even these simple examples, the HTML tags that actually control the appearance of the Web page easily get buried in the code among the business logic. That means that even simple changes to the look of the page can make it necessary to change complicated pieces of code, possibly breaking business logic that didn't even change!

Good programming practice dictates a separation of an application into presentation, business, and data logic, but the servlet approach does not in itself encourage this. A disciplined programmer could, for instance, break up the PL/SQL

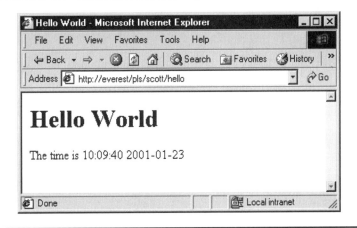

FIGURE 2-5.   *Hello World*

example in a formatting package and a business logic package, leaving the main procedure looking like this:

```
procedure startpage is
begin
  htmlFormat.pageStart('Hello World');
  htmlFormat.para('The time is '
      || htmlFormat.datetime(sysdate)
  );
  htmlFormat.pageEnd;
end hello;
```

When the formatting is taken out, the business logic code gets easier to read and the formatting code can be maintained separately without the risk of breaking the business logic.

Server Pages

The enforcement of this separation is one of the advantages of server page technologies such as Java Server Pages (JSPs) or PL/SQL Server Pages (PSPs). In this chapter, we will use the term *xSP* to mean both JSP and PSP.

In an xSP application, the application code consists of a normal HTML file with occasional special tags to indicate where the business logic goes. The "Hello World" example would look like this as a Java Server Page:

```
<html>
<body>
<h1>Hello World</h1>
<p>The time is <%= new Date() %><p>
</body>
</html>
```

The corresponding PL/SQL Server Page would look like this:

```
<%@ page language="PL/SQL"%>
<%@ plsql procedure="hello" %>
<html>
<body>
<h1>Hello World</h1>
The time is <%= to_char(sysdate, 'hh24:mi:ss yyyy-mm-dd') %>
</body>
</html>
```

This approach cleanly separates the business logic in Java or PL/SQL from the presentation controlled with HTML. This separation also facilitates splitting the development task between Web designers working with an HTML editor, and a programmer working with a Java or PL/SQL programming environment.

Comparison

If your HTML is complicated or will change often, it can be an advantage to use a server page technology. But properly modularized servlet code offers many of the same benefits, and can be easier to write and debug.

Using Java

If you choose Java as the programming language, you have the choice of Java Server Pages (JSPs) or servlets. Both are published standards defined by Sun and part of Java 2 Enterprise Edition (J2EE). Since full J2EE support is considered a must-have feature in Web/application servers, almost all modern Web/application servers (including the Oracle9i Application Server) support both.

The actual combination of the static HTML from the page definition with the output of the Java code can be handled by the Web server when the page is requested by the user, or the Java Server Page can be compiled to a Java servlet in advance.

Developing Web applications with Java servlets is covered in more detail in Chapter 6.

Using PL/SQL

If you choose PL/SQL, you can also write both servlets and server pages. The ability to write PL/SQL servlets has been available for several years through the Oracle Web/application servers, whereas the ability to write PL/SQL Server Pages is new.

Since PL/SQL is a proprietary language used only by Oracle, third-party vendors have not been lining up to support this approach—you will need an Oracle Web/application server and an Oracle database to use it. On the plus side, having the application code execute in the database means fast data access—when the application must work heavily with database data, PL/SQL Web applications show unbeatable performance.

PL/SQL Server Pages are always compiled into PL/SQL servlets, which are stored procedures in the database. This can be achieved using a program that comes with the Oracle database (from version 8.1.6) or using a third-party tool (see Chapter 11).

You can find detailed information about PL/SQL servlets in Chapter 7 and information about the ChangeGroup PL/SQL Server Page product in Chapter 11.

Using Other Programming Languages

If you are programming for the Microsoft platform, you can also use Microsoft's server page technology called *Active Server Pages (ASPs)*. By default, you can write your ASP applications in both a Visual Basic–like language called *VBScript* and in the Microsoft variation of JavaScript.

In most other programming languages, you must, in effect, write servlets that produce the output directly in HTML. But there is nothing stopping you (or anybody else) from writing your own xSP precompiler that will compile an HTML page with special tags into a servlet in your chosen programming language.

This book will not cover ASP or other programming languages.

Generating Applications

When you write servlets or components of server pages, most of your coding effort will go into handling data validation, ensuring transactional integrity, and handling errors. Since this is standard code common to many types of Web applications, it makes sense to try to build as much as possible of this code automatically.

This will get you started quickly; but, of course, you can only generate the types of application functionality that the designers of the tool have thought of.

You can use such tools to generate a "first-cut" application and then modify it by hand. This is not for the faint of heart, however, as the generated code can be very complex and is not intended to be modified; you can easily break the code and accidentally introduce subtle and hard-to-find errors.

The other way to use these tools is to accept the limitations of the tool and stay with 100-percent generated code. "Hardcore" developers will sometimes keep a list of post-generation modifications or even develop scripts that automatically modify the generated code, but this poses the same problems as using a generator to build first-cut applications.

Oracle offers two tools with generating capability: Oracle Portal (which was called WebDB in earlier releases) and Oracle Designer.

Oracle Portal

The Oracle Portal development tool is fully browser based; that is, there is no software to install on the developer workstation. The ability to create applications is only one part of this tool: it also offers content management and can serve as a "portal" to tie together different applications with a single sign-on. However, this book will only cover the application development features of Oracle Portal.

In Oracle Portal, the developer builds application components by filling in a number of forms with information such as what table the component will work on, which fields will be displayed, how they will be formatted, and so on (see Figure 2-6).

The application components can then be collected to form simple applications. Developing applications with Oracle Portal is described in detail in Chapter 9.

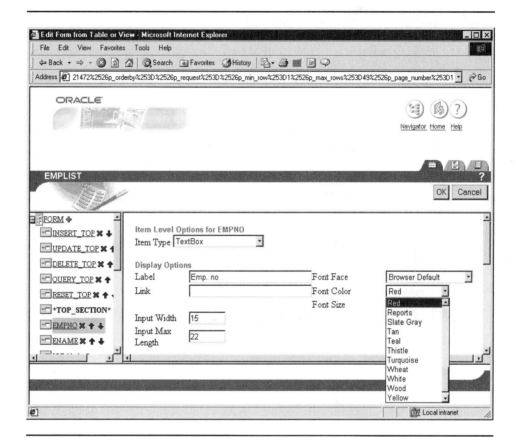

FIGURE 2-6. *Defining an application component in Oracle Portal*

Oracle Designer

Oracle Designer is Oracle's full-featured computer-aided software engineering (CASE) tool. It consists of two parts:

- Developer tools
- A design repository

The developer tools are installed on each developer workstation and are used by the application developers modeling and generating the application.

The Oracle Repository is a collection of tables in an Oracle database that holds the application definition. The developer tools work on the data in the Repository.

The final application does not need the developer tools or the Repository—just an Oracle database and an Oracle Web/application Server.

Oracle Designer is intended for model-driven design and is normally used for medium to large projects. It contains a number of tools (see Figure 2-7) that are intended to be used in the following sequence:

1. Model the data and the functionality using visual tools like the Process Modeler, the Data Flow Modeler, the Function Hierarchy Diagrammer, and the E-R Diagrammer.

2. Generate database design and application modules from the model with the Database Design Transformer and the Application Design Transformer.

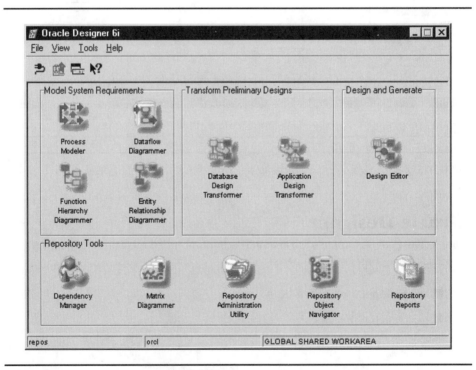

FIGURE 2-7. *Oracle Designer tools*

3. Refine the generated database design and application modules using the Design Editor.

4. Generate the application.

Oracle Designer is not an easy tool to learn, but it has a lot of flexibility; and it can generate high-quality applications with a lot of functionality. It is possible to generate both Forms and PL/SQL Web applications from Designer, although this book will only cover the generation of PL/SQL Web applications. Refer to Chapter 13, which describes how to use Oracle Designer to generate Forms applications.

Could I Have That in Writing?

One problem that HTML-based and applet-based applications have in common is their poor printing capabilities.

The Problems with Printing

Java applets did not support even basic printing before Java 1.1, so only recent browsers (fifth-generation and above) have the option to print from a Java applet. Even so, the relatively primitive drawing capability in Java 1.1 makes it tedious to produce output from a Java applet in this way—not to mention that the security rules for Java applets, by default, forbid them to print!

The printing is much improved in Java 1.2 and 1.3; but to use these versions of the Java language, the user must install the Sun Java plug-in in the browser.

Printing HTML pages is not much better: It is easy for the user to click the Print button; but if the HTML page is wider than the printed page, most browsers will simply cut off everything to the right of the right edge of the paper. In addition, printed Web pages often have problems with alignment, font sizes, and so on.

The Solution

The solution to the problem of printing from Web applications is to provide the users with a separate printable page in Adobe Portable Document Format (PDF). The advantage to this format is that it allows you to specify exactly how your printed page should look. The disadvantage is that the user must have the free Acrobat Reader plug-in installed on his browser. However, the PDF format is already the de facto standard format for distributing white papers, documentation, and marketing brochures via the Internet, so many people can be counted on to have this plug-in. And if you need to distribute reports via the company intranet to a known client software environment, the PDF format is the obvious choice.

Oracle Reports can create printable pages (including graphs) in both HTML and PDF format.

Summary

This chapter has provided you with some guidelines for choosing the right tool for your audience and application: If you are developing for users that will use the application intensively all day on the company intranet, a Java applet application is probably appropriate; but if you are building an application to be deployed on the Internet, you need to stick with an HTML-based application.

You can use either PL/SQL or Java for HTML-based applications: Java is vendor independent and offers the advantages of modern object-oriented programming, while PL/SQL offers unbeatable performance for database-intensive applications.

The next chapter will present an overview of Oracle's product offerings, and Part II will cover how to build an application using the five main approaches to building Oracle Web applications.

CHAPTER
3

Oracle Web
Architecture

s you saw in Chapter 1, a complete Web architecture consists of a Web browser, a Web/application server, and a database server. In addition to these components that are needed to serve the users, you also need development tools and management tools, as shown in Figure 3-1.

Oracle does not directly sell hardware and no longer offers a Web browser (does anybody remember the Oracle PowerBrowser?), but they do offer the rest of what you need: Web/application server software, database software, development tools, and management tools.

The Names of Oracle Products

The Internet changes everything—including all the Oracle product names. The name changing started with the Oracle Web Server, but it has really speeded up lately. If the changing names were not enough to confuse you, Oracle has added a marketing name (for example, Oracle8i Release 3) to some of its products in addition to the version that all software has.

To find the right information in the Oracle documentation, you might need to translate the real version number that the software shows you into an Oracle marketing name. The tables in the following sections show the relationship between the version number and the marketing name of the database and the Web/application server.

Database

The basis of all modern applications is the database used to store all the application data. Oracle is the market leader and sells an excellent (if expensive) database product.

You can use any supported version of the database for your Web applications, and you can even use a non-Oracle database for some approaches, as explained later in this chapter. Like all other Oracle products, the database has many names and versions. Table 3-1 lists some of these.

Development tools		
Web browser	Web/application server	Database
Management tools		

FIGURE 3-1. *A complete Web architecture*

Marketing Name	Version
Oracle 7.3	7.3
Oracle8	8.0
Oracle8i	8.1.5
Oracle8i Release 2	8.1.6
Oracle8i Release 3	8.1.7

TABLE 3-1. *Names and Versions for the Oracle Database*

- **Version 7**   If you have a version 7.3.4 database that is running well, there is no need for you to change that just to be able to run Web applications. But if your database is older than 7.3.4, you should consider an upgrade.

- **Version 8.0**   Version 8.0 of the Oracle database added many features. One is especially interesting in Web applications, even though it is not used in any of the examples in this book: the new UTL_HTTP package allows you to retrieve a Web page from within a PL/SQL stored procedure. For more information on the original Oracle8 version of this package, refer to *Oracle8 Application Developer's Guide Release 8.0.*

  The most recent version of this package (in the 8.1.6 and 8.1.7 database) is described in *Oracle8i Supplied PL/SQL Packages Reference Release 2 (8.1.6).* As with most recent Oracle manuals, both are available for download from the Oracle Technology Network Web site at **http://otn.oracle.com**.

- **Version 8i**   Oracle8i gave us the possibility to execute Java code directly in the database. Among many other new features, some interesting possibilities were added in the form of new built-in packages: the UTL_SMTP package, which allows you to send mail from PL/SQL; and the UTL_TCP package, which lets a stored procedure establish its own network connection.

- **Version 8.1.7 (or Oracle8i Release 3, if you like)**   This comes with the Apache Web server and additional Apache modules developed by Oracle. Together, this lets you build simple Web applications with only a database license. We'll go over exactly what you need to get started with Oracle Web applications in Chapter 4.

Non-Oracle Databases

When an organization decides to use Oracle tools and Web/application servers for their Web applications, it is usually because they already have one or more Oracle databases. But as Table 3-2 shows, some of these approaches are useful even if the underlying database is not from Oracle.

Java servlets use Java Database Connectivity (JDBC) to connect to the database, so they can connect to any database where a JDBC driver exists. In addition, through the JDBC-ODBC bridge driver from Sun, they can connect to any database that comes with an ODBC driver.

Hand-built PL/SQL procedures, as well as Oracle Designer and Oracle Portal, use PL/SQL stored in the database. Because the PL/SQL language is proprietary to Oracle, these approaches depend on an underlying Oracle database.

Applications built with Oracle Developer are almost exclusively built against Oracle databases, but it is possible to access other databases through ODBC.

Web/Application Server

Between the database and the Web browser stands the *Web/application server.* As the name implies, this middle component has two tasks:

- As a *Web server* it communicates with the Web browser.

- As an *application server* it runs applications.

In some architectures, the Web server and the different components of the application server run on different physical machines; and to achieve the performance that big Web sites need, they often have many Web and/or application servers running in parallel.

Approach	Needs Oracle Database	Covered in Chapter
Hand-built Java servlets	No	6
Hand-built PL/SQL procedures	Yes	7
Oracle Designer	Yes	8
Oracle Portal	Yes	9
Oracle Developer	No	10

TABLE 3-2. *Overview of the Five Development Approaches*

The Oracle Web/application server products have been harder hit by name changes than most Oracle products—Table 5-3 lists the different names.

As you can see from the version numbers, the first line of Oracle Web/application servers ended when the OAS 4.0.8 died without leaving any heir. The products in the new line are based on the Apache Web server and new code that was developed from scratch.

The Oracle9i Application Server that is the main focus of this book exists in different *editions* that differ only in how many of the possible components they include. Figure 3-2 shows the main components of the Oracle9i Application Server; the different editions are explained later in this chapter.

The Web Server

The Web server is the component that communicates directly with the Web browser. Because this communication uses the *HyperText Transport Protocol (HTTP)*, a Web server is often also called an *HTTP server*. All of the Oracle Application Servers in the new line use the Apache HTTP server. Apache is a free, open-source Web server and is the unofficial standard on the Internet—more than 50 percent of all Web traffic is delivered from Apache HTTP servers.

NOTE
You can download the Apache HTTP server for free from the Internet, but the Apache developers rate the Apache HTTP server on Windows NT and Windows 2000 as "experimental." However, when you buy it as part of the Oracle HTTP Server, you are also buying Oracle's commitment to support you.

Marketing Name	Version
Oracle Web Server	2.1
Oracle Web Application Server	3.0
Oracle Application Server	4.0
Oracle Internet Application Server	1.0.0
Oracle8i Application Server	1.0.1
Oracle9i Application Server	1.0.2

TABLE 3-3. *Names and Versions for the Oracle Web/Application Servers*

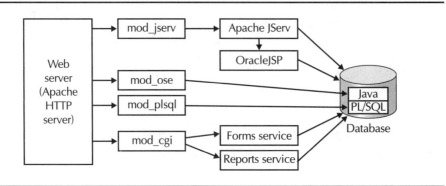

FIGURE 3-2. *The main components of the Oracle9i Application Server*

The Apache HTTP server itself serves all the static files that your Web application uses. These can be HTML files that do not change (for example, help pages for your application), images, style sheets, and so on.

Whenever the Apache HTTP server receives a request that it cannot handle itself, it passes it off to one of its *modules* (or *mods)*. The Apache HTTP server comes with a number of standard modules, and Oracle supplies some additional modules.

The Application Server

The application server part of Oracle9i Application Server has a lot of capabilities and consists of a lot of components. This book covers the basics you need to get started—among the interesting components *not* covered are the advanced caching functions that lend substance to Oracle's claim that your Web site will run three times faster on the Oracle9i Application Server. Refer to the Oracle documentation for more information about other possibilities with the Oracle9i Application Server.

Apache JServ

When the Apache HTTP server receives a request for a Java servlet, by default, it passes it to the mod_jserv module. This module in turn passes the request on to the Apache JServ servlet engine—another piece of open source code that you can use to run your Java servlets.

Oracle Servlet Engine

It is also possible to configure the Apache HTTP server to run your Java servlets inside the Oracle Java Virtual Machine in the database. However, because this can be somewhat tricky to use, this book will describe how to run Java servlets through the Apache JServ component instead.

PL/SQL Gateway

The PL/SQL gateway is an Apache module (mod_plsql) that receives requests from Web browsers and translates them into calls to a stored procedure in the database. This component is needed for all the Web application development approaches that use PL/SQL—that is, hand-built PL/SQL Web applications, as well as applications that were code generated from Oracle Portal or Oracle Designer.

OracleJSP

OracleJSP is an implementation of the Java Server Pages (JSP) standard. It supports all the features of the JSP standard version 1.1, as well as some Oracle-specific enhancements. Just like Microsoft, Oracle would like you to use their enhancements. If you do, it can increase your productivity, but it also ties you to a specific vendor.

CGI Support

One of the standard modules that the Apache HTTP server comes with is the mod_cgi module that adds support for the *Common Gateway Interface (CGI)*. This standard defines how the HTTP server can invoke any external program.

Both the Oracle Forms Service and the Oracle Reports Service are initially invoked through the CGI interface.

Oracle Forms Service

The Oracle Forms Service (occasionally called *Forms Server* in the documentation) allows you to run forms developed with Oracle Forms through a Web browser. It consists of the following:

- A Forms CGI program that responds to the initial request for a Forms application from the Web browser

- A Forms applet that is sent to the Web browser

- A Forms Listener that handles incoming requests from the Forms applet

- A number of Forms Runtime Engines that each handle the session with one user

The way all these components interact is described later in this chapter.

Oracle Reports Service

The Oracle Reports Service makes it possible to run reports developed with Oracle Reports from a Web browser. It consists of the following components:

- A Reports CGI program that receives the request for a report. (The Reports Service also comes with a Java servlet that can replace the CGI program.)

■ A Reports server that handles the request and manages a pool of Reports Runtime Engines.

■ A number of Reports Runtime Engines that connect to the database and produce the report.

Later in this chapter, you'll see how these components work together to deliver a report to a Web browser.

Editions of the Internet Application Server

Oracle Internet Application Server exists in several different editions that contain a different subset of the many components. Unfortunately, these editions have not yet found their final form—Oracle rebundles them occasionally; so even if you download the software and the documentation on the same day, they might still be out of sync.

In general, you are likely to find the following editions:

■ Oracle HTTP Server

■ Standard Edition

■ Enterprise Edition

■ Wireless Edition

You might not find Oracle HTTP Server as a separate edition, but rather as an installation option. In addition, you might find that the Oracle Portal product is not part of what is called Oracle HTTP Server on the Oracle 8i Release 3 CD, but that it *is* part of the Oracle HTTP Server on the Oracle9i Application Server CD.

■ **Oracle HTTP Server** The Oracle HTTP Server is the most basic installation and the one that you will install if you follow the instructions in Chapter 4. It contains the Apache HTTP server with all requisite modules, including Apache JServ, the PL/SQL Gateway, and OracleJSP.

■ **Standard Edition** The Standard Edition contains all the components that are part of the Oracle HTTP Server, as well as the Oracle8i JVM.

■ **Enterprise Edition** The Enterprise Edition contains all the components that are part of the Standard Edition. In addition, it includes the Oracle Database Cache, the Oracle Web Cache, and the Forms and Reports Services.

The Oracle Database Cache can cache data on your application server, but it also gives you the option of running PL/SQL Web applications on the application server.

■ **Wireless Edition** The Wireless Edition has additional personalization features and the ability to define automatic transformation of content to match the requesting client. These features can be used to serve the same content in different formats to different clients—in particular, delivering appropriate content to smart phones and other wireless devices with small screens.

Development Tools

To deploy Web applications to users with Web browsers, you need only a Web/application server and a database server. Before you get that far, however, you need some tools with which to develop the application.

Java Tools

If you want to build your applications with Java servlets, you do not necessarily need a fully integrated Java development environment. A Java compiler that can compile your Java source code into bytecode that the Apache JServ module can execute will work just fine. This Java compiler is freely available as a part of the Java Software Development Kit that you can download from Sun's Web site.

However, your productivity will be much higher if you use a proper tool. The Java tool from Oracle is called Oracle JDeveloper, and it contains an editor with syntax coloring, a compiler, a debugger, and many supporting tools and wizards. You can use this tool to build Java servlets, Java Server Pages, Java applets, and other Java components.

The main strength of Oracle JDeveloper is its integration with the other Oracle products, including the Business Components for Java framework; but if you are already familiar with another Java environment, you can use that.

Chapter 4 describes how to install JDeveloper, and Chapter 6 shows how to use this tool to build four small sample applications as Java servlets.

PL/SQL Tools

If you decide to build your PL/SQL Web application by hand, you can also get by without tools—just write your stored procedures in Notepad or another text editor and use SQL*Plus to compile them.

This is obviously not the most productive way of building applications, so you should consider using a tool. Oracle offers the Procedure Builder tool, and there are a number of third-party tools with syntax coloring, integrated debuggers, and many other features also available.

Chapter 7 shows in detail how to build the same four small applications as built in Chapter 6, only with PL/SQL stored procedures instead of Java. Chapter 11 lists some third-party tools available for writing PL/SQL Web applications, including a PL/SQL editor and a third-party tool for developing PL/SQL Server Pages.

Oracle Designer

The hand-built approach allows you full freedom to choose your tool, even to choose to use only a text editor. But if you want to generate your application code, you must accept the limitations of the generating tool.

To develop applications with Oracle Designer, you need to install the Oracle Designer client software on one or more developer workstations and to install the Oracle Repository in a central database. You can then use the client software to define the model and use the generator tools to build PL/SQL code that can be installed in the database.

Chapter 4 describes how to install both the client software and the repository, and Chapter 8 shows how to build the four sample applications with Oracle Designer.

Oracle Portal

To develop applications with Oracle Portal, you do not need to install any development tools on the client—this approach is purely browser based. Oracle Portal is, in effect, a PL/SQL Web application that you install in an Oracle database and then access through the Oracle HTTP Server.

Chapter 4 describes how to install Oracle Portal, and Chapter 9 describes how to use Oracle Portal to build and run the four sample applications.

Oracle Forms

Oracle Forms is a highly productive environment for developing traditional client/server applications. It offers complete control over the layout of the screen and allows the programmer to control program flow to the smallest detail. At the same time, it contains wizards and default functionality that make it possible to build applications very rapidly.

The development environment for Web applications is exactly the same as for traditional client/server applications—the application developer does not have to worry about whether the application is to be deployed as a traditional client/server application or as a Web application.

Oracle has managed to create almost the exact same user interface when the form is deployed to the Web as when the form is deployed in traditional client/server fashion. They achieve this feat with a Forms applet that runs on the

Web browser while the rest of the functionality is implemented on the server. You'll see an overview of how this works later in this chapter.

Chapter 4 shows how to install Oracle Forms, as well as how to set up all the components necessary to deploy Forms applications to the Web. Two of the four sample applications in Chapter 10 are developed using Oracle Forms.

Oracle Reports

Oracle Reports is a powerful reporting tool with a long heritage in the traditional client/server world. It has a complex layout model that can make it hard for beginners to use, but it allows experienced developers a very high degree of control over the output. Even beginners, however, can use the built-in wizards to create simple reports that will probably cover 80 percent of all requirements.

Reports intended for the Web are developed exactly like reports intended for traditional client/server deployment, using the same tool. When deploying a report to the Web, you can choose from the following output formats at runtime:

■ *HTML format* can be displayed directly in the Web browser, but offers only limited control over the layout.

■ *Adobe Portable Document Format (PDF)* can only be viewed by users who have installed the free Adobe Acrobat reader. This format offers full control over the layout just like when running the report in traditional client/server deployment.

Chapter 4 shows how to install Oracle Reports and how to set up the components necessary to deploy reports to the Web. Two of the four sample applications in Chapter 10 are developed using Oracle Reports.

Management Tools

For managing all the components in your Web architecture, Oracle offers *Oracle Enterprise Manager (OEM)*. This visual administration tool can handle all operations on the database, and monitor and manage many other components.

The only part of the architecture that OEM currently does not handle is configuring the Apache HTTP server—for this task you still need your trusty old text editor.

Running Oracle Web Applications

The HTTP server receives every request from the Web browser, examines it, and uses its configuration information to decide who should handle it.

Static Content

Static content is all the things that do not change, that is, information that can be delivered straight from the file system on the server—for example, static Web pages, images, or style sheets that define the appearance of Web pages.

From the HTTP server's point of view, even the Forms applet is static content: the HTTP server will deliver the exact same file to all Web browsers that ask for it. So, even though the Forms applet described in the upcoming sections will actually execute on the client computer, the HTTP server has only the task of delivering them to the client.

Java Servlets

When the HTTP server determines that the request is for a Java servlet, it passes the request to the JServ component to be executed, as shown in Figure 3-3. The following steps describe how a Java servlet works:

1. The user requests a Web page (by typing in a URL, clicking a link, or pressing a button).

2. The Apache HTTP server determines that the request is for a Java servlet and passes the request to the mod_jserv module.

3. The mod_jserv module passes the request to the JServ servlet engine.

4. The JServ servlet engine loads the requested servlet if it is not already in memory. It then creates a request object, which includes all the information from the request, and a response object, and passes both to the servlet.

5. The servlet class executes, using JDBC to connect to the database if necessary. It writes the output to the response object—usually in HTML code, but the output could also be an Excel spreadsheet or any other type of data.

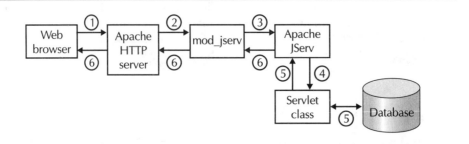

FIGURE 3-3.   *Running a Java servlet*

6. The response is passed back to the Web browser from JServ through mod_jserv and the Apache HTTP server.

Java Server Pages

When the HTTP server determines that the request is for a Java Server Page (JSP), it passes the request via the JServ component to the OracleJSP component. This process is shown in Figure 3-4. The following steps describe how Java Server Pages work:

1. The user requests a Web page.

2. The Apache HTTP server determines that the request is for a Java Server Page and passes the request to the mod_jserv module.

3. The mod_jserv module passes the request to the JServ servlet engine.

4. The JServ servlet engine creates a request object, which includes all the information from the request, and a response object, and passes both to the OracleJSP component.

5. The OracleJSP component converts the JSP file to a servlet and passes the request and response objects to this new servlet.

6. The servlet executes, using JDBC to connect to the database if necessary. It writes the output to the response object— usually in HTML code, but the output could also be a Word document or any other type of data.

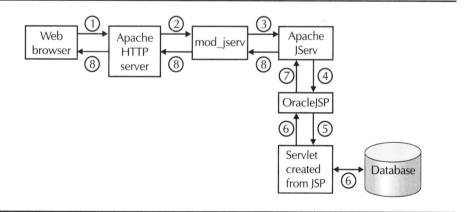

FIGURE 3-4. *Running a Java Server Page*

7. The OracleJSP component returns the response object to the JServ component.

8. The JServ server then returns the output through mod_jserv and the Apache HTTP server to the Web browser.

PL/SQL Web Applications

All types of PL/SQL Web applications, whether hand built or code generated from Oracle Designer or Oracle Portal, work in the same way: the HTTP server passes the request to the mod_plsql module, which invokes the stored procedure in the database, as shown in Figure 3-5. The following steps describe how PL/SQL Web applications work:

1. The user requests a Web page by typing in a URL, and clicking a link or pressing a button.

2. The Apache HTTP server determines that the request is for a PL/SQL stored procedure and passes it to mod_plsql.

3. The mod_plsql module uses the information in the URL along with the configuration information in the Database Access Descriptor to determine to which Oracle user in which database it should connect. It then invokes the procedure in the database.

4. The stored procedure runs, using the procedures in the HTTP package to write output in a buffer.

5. The mod_plsql module returns the output in the buffer through the Apache HTTP server to the Web browser.

PL/SQL Server Pages

PL/SQL Server Pages (PSP) are different from Java Server Pages in that they must be compiled into PL/SQL stored procedures in advance. The Oracle9i Application

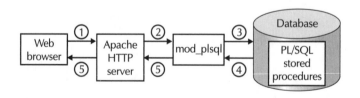

FIGURE 3-5. *Running a PL/SQL Web application*

Server cannot perform this translation on-the-fly as it can for Java Server Pages. Therefore, at runtime, a PL/SQL Server Page is identical to a stored procedure developed in any other way, as described in the preceding section.

Oracle Forms

It is quite easy for a user to start a Web Forms application, but there is a lot happening behind the scenes.

The process occurs in two parts:

■ Getting the Forms applet (and possibly the JInitiator Java plug-in)

■ Running the application through the applet

Starting a Web Forms Application

To start a Web Forms application, you first need to get the Forms applet to the user. This process is shown in Figure 3-6 and described step by step.

1. The user requests the first Web page of the application.

2. The Apache HTTP server determines that the request is for a CGI program and passes the request to the mod_cgi module.

3. The mod_cgi module starts the Forms CGI program.

4. The Forms CGI program reads any parameters that were included in the request, as well as some configuration information that was stored on the application server. It uses this information to produce an HTML page with the right parameters and an instruction to load the Forms applet.

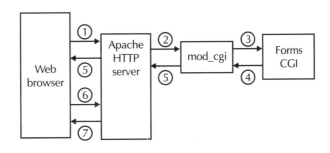

FIGURE 3-6. *Getting the Forms applet to the user*

NOTE
In the configuration on the application server, you specify whether the Forms CGI should build a page that instructs the Web browser to use the default Java Virtual Machine or attempt to download JInitiator (recommended). If you choose to use JInitiator, the browser will automatically prompt the user to download and install this plug-in.

5. The HTML page is passed back to the Web browser through the mod_cgi module and the HTTP server.

6. The Web browser automatically requests the Forms applet from the HTTP server (and the JInitiator Java plug-in if you have configured the Forms CGI program to make the browser request JInitiator).

7. To the HTTP server, the Forms applet (and the JInitiator) is just another static file that is delivered unchanged. Once the Forms applet arrives on the client, the client JVM is started and the applet starts running.

TIP
One of the benefits of JInititator is the caching it offers: once the Forms applet is downloaded, it remains available until you shut down your system. This means that you only have to download it the first time you start a Forms application.

Running a Web Forms Application

Once the Forms applet runs on the client machine, the application can start. The process is shown in Figure 3-7 and described in the following steps:

1. The Forms applet contacts the Forms Listener to start a session. This connection does not involve the Apache HTTP server in any way—it goes straight from the applet to the Forms Listener.

2. The Forms Listener starts a Forms Runtime Engine for that client.

3. The Forms Runtime Engine establishes a connection to the database and to the client applet.

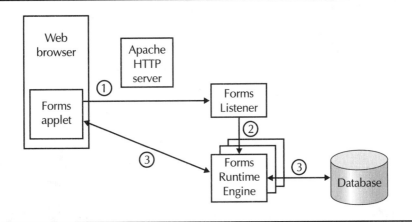

FIGURE 3-7. *Running a Web Forms application*

NOTE
The communication can be a plain TCP/IP connection or can use the HTTP protocol. A plain TCP/IP connection can be used on an intranet; but if there are any firewalls between the client and the Forms Listener, you must use HTTP communication.

When this connection is established, the Forms applet can establish a persistent database session just like when a form is running in traditional client/server mode.

Oracle Reports

When a Web browser requests a report developed with Oracle Reports, the process is as shown in Figure 3-8 and described in the following steps:

1. The user requests the report by typing in a URL or clicking a link.

2. The HTTP server passes the request to the mod_cgi module. (It is also possible to configure the application server so that the request is handled by a Reports servlet.)

3. The mod_cgi module invokes the Reports CGI program.

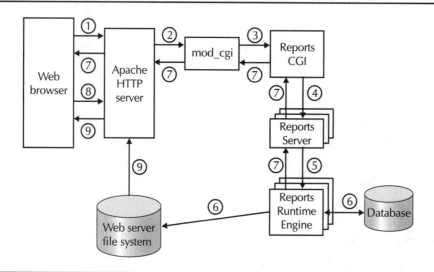

FIGURE 3-8. *Running a report through a Web browser*

4. The Reports CGI or servlet reformats the request and passes it on to the Reports Server.

5. The Reports Server checks whether the desired report already exists in the report cache. If so, it sends a *redirect* instruction back to the browser telling the browser to ask the HTTP server directly for the report. If the report is not in the cache, the Reports Server assigns the report to the next available Reports Runtime Engine.

6. The Reports Runtime Engine connects to the database, retrieves and formats the data, and writes the report in the cache.

7. The Reports Server instructs the requesting Web browser to pick up the report through the HTTP server.

8. The Web browser requests the report from the Web server.

9. The Web server delivers the report.

The report can be produced dynamically on request, but it is always written to disk on the application server. When the report is ready, the Report server sends a *redirect* instruction to the Web browser. The Web browser automatically responds to this message and requests the file—because it is a static file, it can be delivered directly by the HTTP server.

Summary

This chapter showed you that Oracle offers you all the software you need to build Web applications in many different ways. The Oracle9i Application Server is at the core of the Oracle Web architecture, and you learned how its many components work together to deliver content back to a Web browser in different ways.

The next chapter takes you step by step through installing all the Oracle software you need to get started with any (or all) of the five different approaches to building Web applications.

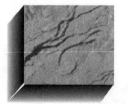

CHAPTER 4

What You Need to Get Started

s you saw in Chapter 3, you need a database server and an application server in order to run a Web application. In the Oracle world, this currently translates into the Oracle 8i database and the Oracle 8i or 9i Application Server. By the time you read this book, there might be new versions of several of the software components mentioned here, but the decisions you need to make will be similar.

This chapter describes how to install enough Oracle software to get you started with Oracle Web applications; and if you are interested in only one or two of the five approaches described in this book, you can install only those tools and components.

Your organization might already have all the CD-ROMs you need; if not, you can get all of them through the *Oracle Technology Network (OTN)*. If you have a fast Internet connection, you can download everything you need from the OTN Web site (**http://otn.oracle.com**), or you can subscribe to a "tech track" to get a quarterly shipment of the latest Oracle software.

This chapter shows you how to install the software on a Windows 2000 Professional machine that is not running any additional software (in particular, a machine that is not running any other Web/application server or database). It assumes that you have such a machine to yourself and that you know the administrator password. All components (database, application server, and development tools) will be installed on this machine to make matters easier. If you want to install the software on a Linux machine, please do! The installation is similar, and the software is likely to perform better. Windows 2000 was chosen for the examples in this book because, despite the rise in popularity of Linux, most people are still more likely to have access to a Windows 2000 machine than to a Linux machine.

How to Install Oracle Software

If you have ever flown in a small aircraft in which you were close enough to the pilot to see what he was doing, you might have noticed that he ran his finger down a check list as he prepared for take-off. That wasn't because he forgot how to fly an airplane (I hope!). It was because he needed to make absolutely sure he performed every action in exactly the right order.

When installing Oracle software, it is also important to take all the steps in the right sequence. Oracle software is complicated machinery, so the folks at Oracle provide you with all the information you need to install it and get it working— I encourage you to use that information. In fact, the number one reason that people sometimes have problems making Oracle software work is that they did not follow the instructions—so it pays to pay attention.

Whenever you install Oracle software, you should

- Find and read the "Release Notes." There is almost always such a document, either in paper or electronic form (if it's electronic, it might be called READMEDOC.htm). This document describes important limitations, things that don't work the way the documentation says it should, and so on. It can be rather large (33 pages for Oracle 8i Release 3), and you probably won't understand most of it. That's OK—simply skip the parts that do not apply to your situation.

- Find the installation guide for *your* operating system and follow it. The documentation looks almost identical for different operating systems and, although you will eventually notice it if you pick up the wrong one, you may as well start off right.

Even if you follow all the instructions carefully, you might run into problems that you have a hard time solving. As long as you are on an experimental machine that you have to yourself and no additional software is running, there is no need to mess around with the settings. Instead, just clean out all the Oracle software (see the section "If Something Goes Wrong" at the end of this chapter), grab a mug of coffee, and reinstall. With practice (and if you are playing around with new Oracle software much, you *will* get practice), you will be able to install all the software from scratch in the course of a day and still handle your normal work.

What You Need

This book covers the five most common ways of building Oracle Web applications:

- With Java servlets
- With hand-built PL/SQL procedures
- With Oracle Designer
- With Oracle Portal
- With Oracle Developer (Oracle Forms and Oracle Reports)

Hardware

The installation guidelines in this chapter assume that you have one machine to play around with and that everything is installed on that machine. The Oracle specifications are, of course, the final word, but all the software used in this book runs nicely together on a laptop with the specifications in Table 4-1.

Specification	Minimum Requirement
Processor	Pentium II 400 MHz
Memory	256MB
Swap file	384MB
Hard disk	6GB

TABLE 4-1. *Sufficient Hardware to Install All the Oracle Software for All Five Approaches*

NOTE
At the time of writing, the Oracle9i Application Server was not supported on Pentium 4 processors.

Partitioning Your Hard Disk

Your Windows 2000 system probably has a C drive that contains the operating system. There is nothing stopping you from installing all your software on this drive, but you'll have better control over your system if you use different drives for different software.

All the examples in this book use the directory C:\web_apps_101 for the examples and a separate O drive for installing the Oracle software. Chapter 11 describes a repartitioning tool, but if you are not familiar with repartitioning your disk and assigning drive letters, don't worry—you can place everything on C—just remember to substitute a *C* for an *O* in all the paths in this book.

Network

It should come as no surprise that you need a network to develop and run Web applications. Your machine does not have to be physically wired to another machine—you don't even need a network card—but you must have TCP/IP software installed.

To check whether the TCP/IP protocol is available, start a command prompt (Start | Programs | Accessories | Command Prompt), type the command **ipconfig**, and press ENTER. You should see some configuration information, including at least one line with the text "IP Address" and an IP number (four groups of numbers 0–255, separated with periods).

Installing Minimum Networking

If the ipconfig command does not exist or show any IP number, you need to install the TCP/IP protocol. This section explains how to do that; but if you are installing on a machine at the office, please check with your network administrator first.

You cannot use the Network Connection Wizard if there is no network card installed in your computer, so you must instead install a *virtual* network card—the Microsoft Loopback Adapter. This is just a piece of software, not a real network card, but it allows Windows 2000 to install the TCP/IP software. Follow these instructions to install the software:

1. Choose Start | Settings | Control Panel, and double-click the Add/Remove Hardware icon.

2. At the Welcome screen, click Next. Choose Add/Troubleshoot a Device and click Next.

3. After the wizard searches for hardware, choose Add a New Device and click Next.

4. Choose No, I Want to Select the Hardware from a List (this is not the default setting) and click Next.

5. Choose Network Adapters and click Next.

6. In the Select Network Adapter dialog box, in the Manufacturers box on the left, scroll down to find Microsoft. The right-hand box automatically changes to the only network adapter from Microsoft: the Microsoft Loopback Adapter. Click Next twice and then Finish.

Now you have a virtual network card on your computer; the TCP/IP protocol was installed at the same time. You should now see an IP number (it doesn't matter which number) when you run the ipconfig command from a command prompt.

TIP
If you have a dial-up connection to the Internet on this computer, installing the Loopback Adapter might make Windows 2000 think that you have a fixed connection to the Internet. If Windows no longer dials your Internet connection, you can temporarily disable the Loopback Adapter by choosing the connection (Start | Settings | Network and Dial-Up Connections), right-click the loopback connection, and choose Disable from the pop-up menu.

Software

If your organization already has licenses for Oracle products, you might have all the software you need in official boxed sets that are complete with CDs and some printed documentation. If you don't have the software you need, however, this section tells you how you can get it and which software to get.

Getting the Software

Fortunately, Oracle has realized that it is important to make the latest software available for developers to play around with. You have several options:

- You can sign up for a free membership of Oracle Technology Network (OTN) and download everything you need. However, you'll need a fast Internet connection, especially if you want the server products—Oracle 8i Release 3 is 598MB, and the Oracle9i Application Server is a whopping 973MB!

- If you have signed up for OTN, you can also subscribe to a "tech track" for a nominal fee to get a quarterly shipment of the latest Oracle software.

- If you participate in Oracle events like the iDevelop conferences, you often get a box of CDs with the latest software.

Determining What You Need

Table 4-2 shows the software you need to follow the examples in Chapters 6–10 in this book.

Approach	Necessary Software	Recommended Additional Software
Java servlets	Oracle8i Release 3	JDeveloper 3.2 Oracle9i Application Server
Hand-built PL/SQL	Oracle8i Release 3	Any PL/SQL programming tool Oracle9i Application Server
Oracle Designer	Oracle8i Release 3 Oracle Designer 6i Release 2	Oracle9i Application Server
Oracle Portal	Oracle8i Release 3 Oracle9i Application Server	
Oracle Developer	Oracle8i Release 3 Developer/Server 6i Release 2	Oracle9i Application Server

TABLE 4-2. *The Minimum and Recommended Software You Need to Build Oracle Web Applications Using Each of the Five Approaches*

NOTE
*Some of the tools and servers require that at least
Service Pack 1 for Windows 2000 is installed. You
should download and install the latest service pack
from Microsoft at **www.microsoft.com** before
installing the Oracle software.*

As you see in Table 4-2, you do not need the Oracle9i Application Server for
many of the approaches—the Oracle8i Release 3 database comes with the Oracle
HTTP Server component, and that is all you need. However, if you can get your
hands on the application server and can find the disk space to install it, you will be
able to install additional components later to explore the many capabilities of this
product.

Documentation

If your Oracle software came in a box from Oracle, you probably received an
Oracle documentation CD. If you don't have such a CD, your download set might
include documentation.

All the Oracle manuals are also available for individual download in PDF format
from the Oracle Technology Network Web site at **http://otn.oracle.com**.

Database

The following instructions describe how to install the Oracle database that you need
for all kinds of Oracle applications. This installation includes a small database and the
features needed for Web applications, but it does not include all the bells and whistles.

You need either to have the Oracle8i Release 3 (version 8.1.7) software on an
Oracle CD or to have downloaded the installation set.

Preparing to Install the Database

What is the first thing to do before installing Oracle software? You guessed it: read
the Release Notes.

Reading the Release Notes

Go to the root of the CD or the installation set, and double-click the file welcome.htm.
The welcome screen in Figure 4-1 appears. From this screen, click Release Notes.
Browse through the file to see if it contains information that you need.

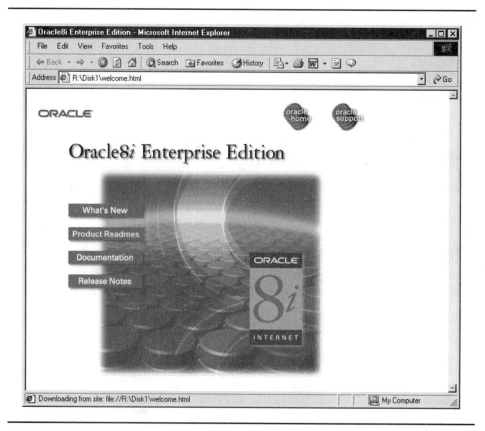

FIGURE 4-1. *The Database Installation Welcome screen*

NOTE
This is a long file, but do browse through it and read all the headings. It describes documentation changes, features that do not work properly or that work with restrictions, potential problems, and many other things. You do not have to read every word, but reading the Release Notes is the mark of the professional.

Reading the Installation Guide

If you do not have a printed installation guide, you should go back to the Welcome screen and click Documentation to get to the documentation page. Choose the installation guide in PDF format, print it, and place it in a binder. If you want to save paper, you don't need Appendixes A through E, but Appendix F gives a nice overview of the available Oracle documentation.

Table 4-3 gives you a bit of guidance on how to read the installation guide.

Setting Up a Drive

As mentioned previously, it is a good idea to keep your Oracle installation separate from the operating system. I usually create a 4GB partition with the drive letter O for this. If your disk is already partitioned, however, you will probably need a third-party tool like Partition Magic (see Chapter 11) to change your partitions. If you are not comfortable with this, just install everything on the C drive.

Chapter	How to Read
1 (Introduction)	Read this nice introduction—it's only a few pages.
2 (Overview)	Skim this—you will need to read about the Top-Level Component Oracle8i Enterprise Edition.
3 (Requirements)	Check that you have what you need for Installation Type Minimal.
4 (Methods)	Skim this chapter briefly. You are going to create a minimum installation without a starter database (you create the starter database later).
5 (Installing)	Read this chapter carefully before you start installing.
6 (Reviewing)	Skim this chapter to see what will be installed on your system. Depending on your knowledge of Oracle databases, this information may or may not make sense to you. Assuming this is an experimental database, you do not need to change the system and other passwords.
7 (Post-installation)	Skim this chapter. Assuming this is an experimental database, there are no essential tasks here.
8 (Deinstalling)	You only need this if something goes wrong. The section "Manually Removing All Oracle Components and Services from Your Computer" describes how to clean out everything Oracle from you machine if you want to start all over.

TABLE 4-3. *How to Read the Oracle8i Installation Guide*

Installing the Database Software Step By Step

When you have read the Release Notes and the Installation Guide, follow the instructions in Chapter 5 of the Oracle8i Installation Guide to install the database. This section suggests some settings and choices that will install the minimum software to run an Oracle database. The Oracle Installer likes to install everything in great big packages with everything and the kitchen sink, but I recommend a more minimalist approach.

Installing the Oracle Database Software

1. Remember to log on to *your machine* with an account that is a member of the Administrators group.

NOTE
If the machine is part of a Windows NT or 2000 domain, you normally log on to the domain in order to access network resources. In order to install software, however, you must log on to the machine as an administrator. If there is a Domain drop-down list in the login dialog box, you can normally select either the domain or the machine.

2. Start the SETUP.EXE program from the root of the CD or the installation set. The Installer Welcome screen appears, as shown in this illustration.

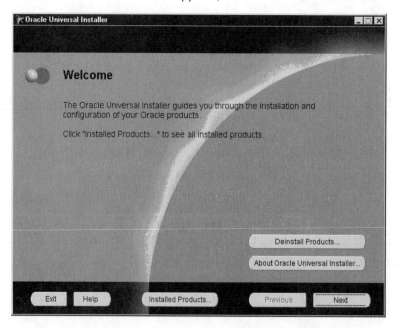

NOTE
The Installer appears in the language that you have selected in Windows. If you run Windows in a foreign language but prefer the Oracle software to show English messages, you should change your language setting to U.S. English before starting the Installer.

3. Click Next to proceed to the File Locations screen, shown in the following illustration. Here you must enter a name for the Oracle home directory for the database (e.g., OraHome81) and choose a directory. If you assigned the drive letter O to your Oracle drive, for instance, you would choose O:\oracle\ora81. Then click Next.

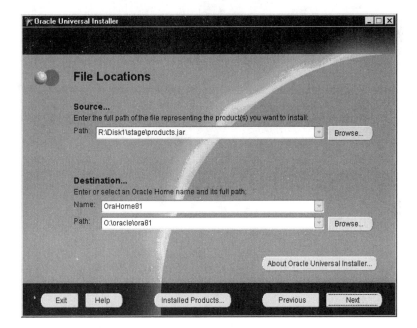

4. The Installer now reads all the products in the installation set and eventually shows the Available Products screen, shown in the next illustration. Choose Oracle 8i Enterprise Edition and click Next.

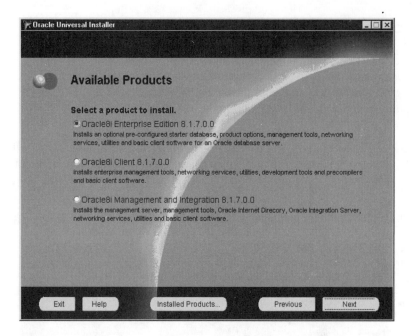

5. The Installation Types screen appears, shown next. Choose Custom and click Next.

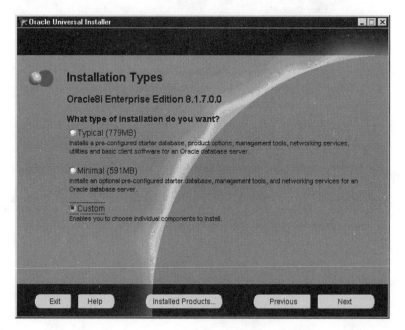

6. The Available Product Components screen appears, shown in this illustration.

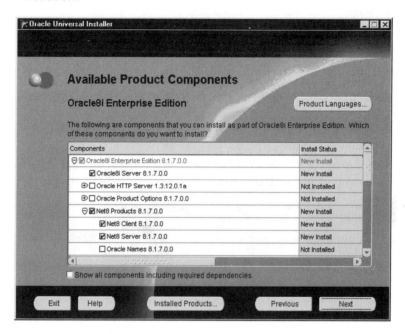

7. On this screen, check the items listed in the following table. If you like to maintain a bit of control over the software installed on your machine (I do), do not select any of the other options unless you have a reason to. When you have made your selection, click Next.

Oracle 8i Server (under Oracle Enterprise Edition)

Net Client (under Net8 Products)

Net8 Server (under Net8 Products)

Oracle Database Utilities (under Oracle Utilities)

SQL*Plus (under Oracle Utilities)

Oracle Database Configuration Assistant (under Oracle Configuration Assistants)

NOTE
*Make sure to deselect the Oracle HTTP Server here,
because this option will get in the way of the later
installation of the Oracle9i Application Server.*

8. The Component Locations screen appears. Click Next to continue.

9. When you are asked if you want to create a database, choose No. When
   using the custom installation option, it is easier to create the database later.
   Click Next.

10. The Installer Summary screen appears, as shown in the following illustration.
    Scroll through this list to see all the products that will be installed for you.
    When you have finished, click Install to start the installation.

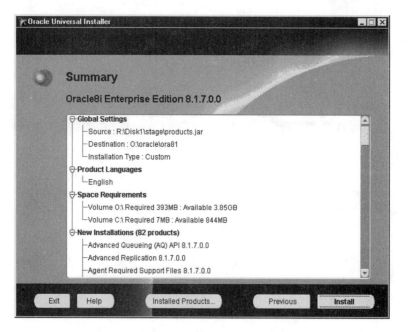

NOTE
*It will take quite a while for the installation to
complete. You do not have to watch the computer
while it works.*

Configuring Networking

When the Oracle software has been installed, the Configuration Tools window appears:

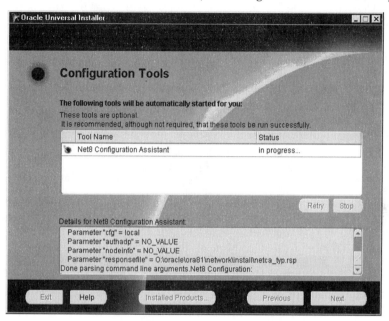

1. The Net8 Configuration Assistant tool starts automatically and shows the Welcome screen, shown next. On this screen, select the Perform Typical Configuration check box and click Next.

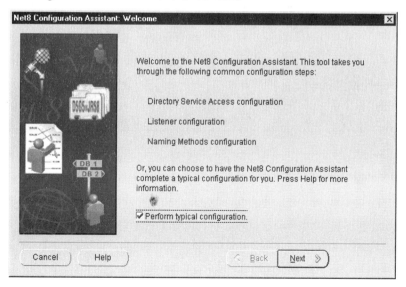

2. The Net8 Configuration Assistant runs to completion and the End of Installation screen appears. Click the Exit button and confirm that you want to leave.

Creating a Database

Now you have installed the Oracle database software, but you do not have a database yet. The database software is just programs sitting on the hard disk—the database itself needs storage on the hard disk somewhere, as well as an NT service that starts the Oracle software when your computer boots. You can have many separate databases on the same machine, but each will take up hard disk, memory, and CPU power.

For the purpose of this book, you need only one database. To build it, you use the Database Configuration Assistant described next.

1. Click Start | Programs | Oracle – OraHome81 | Database Administration | Database Configuration Assistant. The first window of the Database Configuration Assistant appears, as shown here:

2. Choose Create a Database and click Next. You are asked what type of database you want to create, as shown next.

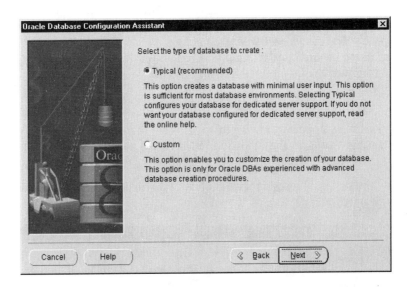

3. Choose Typical and click Next. You are then asked how you want to create the database.

4. Choose Copy Existing Database Files from the CD. This is the fastest and easiest way to create a standard database. Then click Next.

5. On the next screen shown on the following illustration, give your database a global name and System Identifier (SID). For a stand-alone test database, you can use orcl for both. Then click Finish to start the creation of the database and confirm that you want to start building.

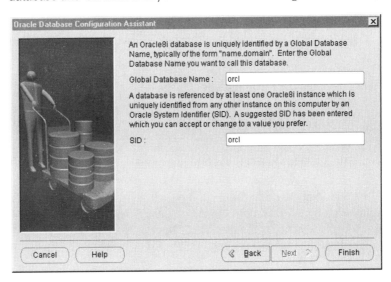

NOTE
In a production system with many databases, the global name should consist of a unique database name followed by the Internet domain name of your organization.

6. A window appears showing the passwords that will be used. Make a note of the passwords for the SYS and SYSTEM users so you will be able to log on to your new database.

7. Write down the passwords and click OK. The configuration tool now starts creating the database, as shown here:

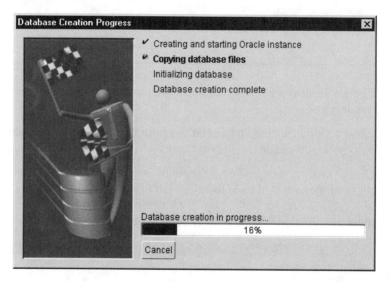

8. A message will tell you that the database has been created. Click OK to leave the Database Configuration Assistant.

Check the Installation

Once you have created the database, you should check that everything runs correctly. You can do this by following these steps:

1. To check that the database is running, choose Start | Programs | Oracle – OraHome81 | Application Development | SQL Plus. At the SQL* Plus login prompt, type **scott** as the username, **tiger** as the password, and **orcl** as the connect string, as shown next.

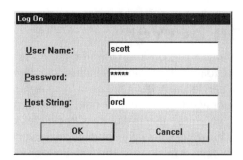

2. When you click OK, you should get to the SQL*Plus command prompt from which you'll be able to work with the database. Try a simple query like **select * from dept** to make sure that the database is running, as shown here:

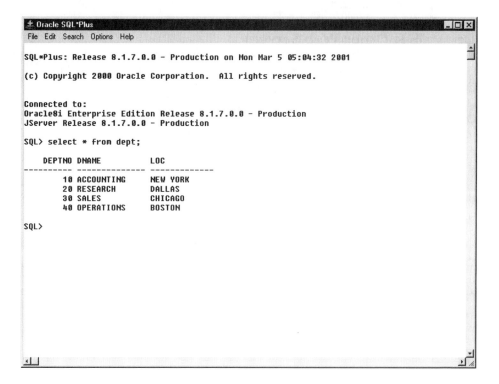

If you can log on and execute the query, the database software has been installed correctly and your database is running. Before you can access it from a Web browser, you'll need to install an Oracle Web/application server, as described in the next section.

Application Server

The Oracle HTTP Server is a precondition for all Oracle Web applications, and this section shows you how to install it. This installation includes Oracle Portal and allows you to run Java servlets and PL/SQL-based Web applications, whether they're hand-built or code-generated from Oracle Portal. To run applications generated from Oracle Designer, you must also install the Oracle Designer Web Toolkit.

You need either to have the Oracle9i Application Server (version 1.0.2) on CD-ROM (2 CDs) or to have downloaded the installation set.

Preparing to Install the Application Server

Before you start installing the Oracle HTTP Server, you should check that there is not already a Web server running on your machine. You should also, as always, check the Release Notes.

Deinstalling Other Web Servers

These days, it seems that everyone wants to foist their own Web server on you. Unless you take precautions, both the Microsoft Windows installation and the Oracle database installation will provide you with a Web server.

Do I Have Other Web Servers Running?   To check whether you have other Web servers running on your machine, start a command prompt (Start | Programs | Accessories | Command Prompt) and type the command **netstat –a –p tcp**. This should show a list like the one in Figure 4-2.

Look in the Local Address column for a line with your servername, a colon, and the text http. If you see such a line, it means that your server is running a network service that is listening on the standard port for HTTP connections—that is, you already have a Web server running.

Do I Have the Oracle HTTP Server Installed?   If there is a network service listening on the http port, check whether it is the Oracle HTTP Server. To do this, choose Start | Settings | Control Panel, and first double-click Administrative Tools, and then Services. Scroll down the list of services until you get to those that start with Oracle.

If you have an OracleHTTPServer service, the Oracle HTTP Server is installed on you machine.

Why Remove the Oracle HTTP Server?   Even if the Oracle HTTP Server is already installed on your system, you should remove it and follow the instructions in this chapter to install the Oracle9i Application Server. A separate application server installation allows you to place the application server in a separate home directory so you can add more components to it later.

```
Command Prompt                                                    _ □ X
C:\>netstat -a -p tcp

Active Connections

  Proto   Local Address              Foreign Address         State
  TCP     everest:epmap              everest:0               LISTENING
  TCP     everest:microsoft-ds       everest:0               LISTENING
  TCP     everest:1028               everest:0               LISTENING
  TCP     everest:1031               everest:0               LISTENING
  TCP     everest:1032               everest:0               LISTENING
  TCP     everest:1034               everest:0               LISTENING
  TCP     everest:1521               everest:0               LISTENING
  TCP     everest:2481               everest:0               LISTENING
  TCP     everest:netbios-ssn        everest:0               LISTENING
  TCP     everest:1032               everest:1521            ESTABLISHED
  TCP     everest:1521               everest:1032            ESTABLISHED
  TCP     everest:netbios-ssn        everest:0               LISTENING
  TCP     everest:1030               everest:0               LISTENING
  TCP     everest:1030               GANDALF:netbios-ssn     ESTABLISHED
  TCP     everest:1748               everest:0               LISTENING
  TCP     everest:1754               everest:0               LISTENING
  TCP     everest:1808               everest:0               LISTENING
  TCP     everest:1809               everest:0               LISTENING

C:\>_
```

FIGURE 4-2. *Network services running*

CAUTION
You cannot install additional Oracle9i Application Server components in the home directory that the Oracle database uses. If you install the Oracle HTTP Server that comes with the database, you are cutting yourself off from adding new features in the future.

Removing the Oracle HTTP Server   Choose Start I Programs I Oracle Installation Products I Universal Installer. The Installer welcome screen appears. Click Deinstall Products to see the Inventory window. Expand the OraHome81 node and then the Oracle8i Enterprise Edition node to see the Oracle HTTP Server node, as shown in Figure 4-3.

Select the check box for the Oracle HTTP Server node, click Remove, and click Yes in the confirmation dialog box.

Removing Other Web Servers   If there is a network service listed on the http port but you do not find the OracleHTTPServer service on the Services list, you have some other Web server installed. It is probably the Microsoft Internet Information Server, but it could also be a "personal" Web server that installed automatically together with some Web page design tool.

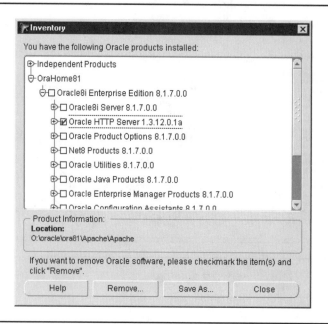

FIGURE 4-3. *Deinstalling the Oracle HTTP Server*

The deinstallation instructions will vary from product to product, but a good place to start is to click Start | Settings | Control Panel and then double-click the Add/Remove Programs icon to see what you have.

Reading the Release Notes
Place disc 1 in your CD drive or change to the disk1 subdirectory of the installation set. Then double-click the file welcome.html. The Welcome screen in Figure 4-4 appears. From this screen, click the Release Notes link. Browse through this file to stay up to date with the latest changes in the Oracle product names and skim through the long list of restrictions to see if anything might be relevant to you.

Reading the Installation Guide
If you do not have a printed Installation Guide, go back to the Welcome screen and click the PDF link in the Installation Guide paragraph. It is a good idea to print this document and place it in the binder with the database installation guide. If you want to save paper, you do not need to print the Appendixes (you can refer to Appendixes A and E online if you need to during the installation of Oracle Portal or if you want to install the Oracle9i Documentation Library).

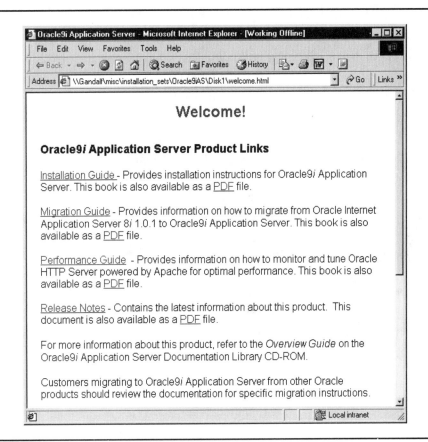

FIGURE 4-4. *The Oracle9i Application Server Welcome screen*

See Table 4-4 for a guide on how to read the Oracle9i Application Server Installation Guide.

Adding a Tablespace for Oracle Portal

The standard database installation comes with a USERS tablespace with enough space for several small applications, but it's not enough for all the tables needed by Oracle Portal. You should create a new tablespace for Oracle Portal of at least 150MB.

Start SQL*Plus (Start | Programs | Oracle – OraHome81 | Application Development | SQL Plus). Type the username **system**, the password **manager**, and

Chapter	How to Read
1 (Requirements)	Check that you have what is needed for an Oracle HTTP Server installation.
2 (Concepts and Preinstallation)	The first section gives an overview of the different editions of the Oracle9i Application Server—you should read this to get a general overview. The rest of this chapter covers the preinstallation tasks—you will be doing an Oracle HTTP Server Only installation, so there are no preinstallation tasks and you can skip the rest of the chapter.
3 (Oracle HTTP Server Only)	Read this chapter carefully before you start installing.
4 (Standard Edition)	You will not be doing this type of installation, so you can skip this chapter.
5 (Enterprise Edition)	You will not be doing this type of installation, so you can skip this chapter.
6 (Deinstallation and Reinstallation)	This chapter explains how to deinstall the Oracle9i Application Server only. If you're having problems and you are working on a machine you have to yourself, it is safer (and probably faster as well) to get rid of all the Oracle software rather than just this portion. Refer to the troubleshooting section at the end of this chapter.

TABLE 4-4. *How to Read the Oracle9i Application Server Installation Guide*

the host string **orcl**. If you installed the standard database on the O drive, enter the following command in SQL*Plus:

```
create tablespace portal
    datafile 'o:\oracle\oradata\orcl\portal01.dbf'
    size 150m;
```

If you did not install your database on the O drive, substitute your own drive letter.

Installing the Internet Application Server Step by Step

After reading the Release Notes (the mark of the professional, remember?) and the Installation Guide, follow the instructions in Chapter 3 of the Oracle9i Application Server Installation Guide to install the application server.

Setting Up the Installation of Oracle9i Application Server

1. Remember to log on to your machine (not the domain) with an account that is a member of the Administrators group.

2. Start the SETUP.EXE program from the first CD-ROM or from the disk1 directory in your installation set. The Oracle Universal Installer Welcome screen appears, as shown previously in Figure 4-4. Click Next to proceed to the File Locations screen shown in this illustration.

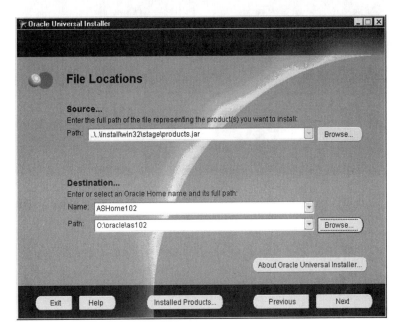

3. Do not install in the existing Oracle home directory where the database was installed. Enter a new name and home directory for the application server. Since the Oracle9i Application Server has the true version number 1.0.2, this example shows a home directory of O:\oracle\AS102 with the name ASHome102. Again, if you don't have an O drive, you can install on any other drive with sufficient space. Then click Next to proceed to the Installation Types screen shown here:

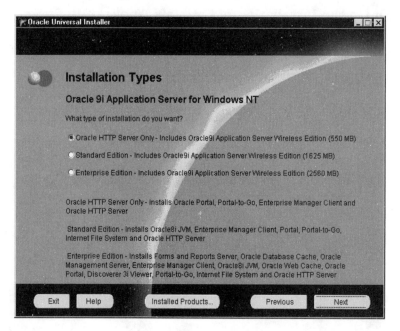

4. Choose Oracle HTTP Server Only, and click Next to start the installation and see the screen shown next.

Chapter 4: What You Need to Get Started **83**

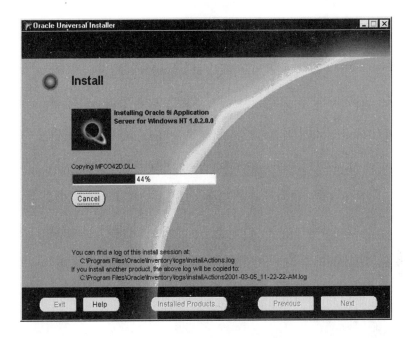

NOTE

*Every option includes the Oracle9i Application
Server Wireless Edition, and there is no custom
installation option. Currently, Oracle insists that you
cannot live without this product; but if you don't
want it, you can leave a couple of fields blank
during the installation, described in the next section.
This will make only that part of the installation fail—
don't worry, the rest will still install correctly.*

The Installation Guide states that the machine should automatically reboot
when the installation of the application server is complete. I have never seen this
happen—the installation program simply terminates without any message. Don't
worry; just reboot your machine manually to continue the installation.

When you log on again, you might be prompted for the location of the installation files, as shown in the following illustration.

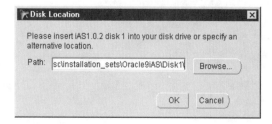

Specify the location and click OK when you are ready to continue with the installation.

Setting Up Oracle Portal Installation

When the installation continues, you will see the database access configuration screen for Oracle Portal, as shown in the following illustration.

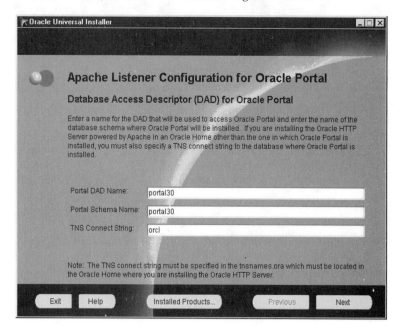

To install Oracle Portal, follow these steps.

1. Leave the Portal DAD Name and Portal Schema Name at their default values of portal30. In the TNS Connect String field, type **orcl** and click Next. The database access configuration screen for the Oracle Portal Login Server appears, as shown here:

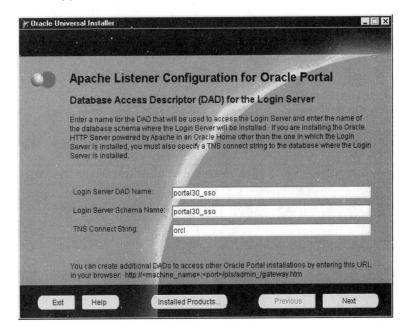

2. Leave the Login Server DAD Name and Login Server Schema Name at their default values of **portal30_sso**. In the TNS Connect String field, type **orcl** and click Next.

Setting Up Installation of Oracle Portal-to-Go
When you have defined the installation parameters for Oracle Portal, the installation program will prompt you for information about Oracle Portal-to-Go. This is a completely separate product that has nothing in common with Oracle Portal but the first part of the name.

NOTE

As part of the general renaming trend, Oracle has renamed Portal-to-Go as well—it's now called Oracle9i Application Server Wireless Edition. At the start of the installation, you saw the Installer use the new name; but here, in the middle of the installation, you still see the old name.

On the next three screens, leave the fields blank—this book does not cover Oracle Portal-to-Go. Click Next until the installation Summary screen in Figure 4-5 appears.

Running the Installation

On the installation Summary screen, click Install to start the installation. The installation progress window (see Figure 4-6) shows the status. The Oracle9i

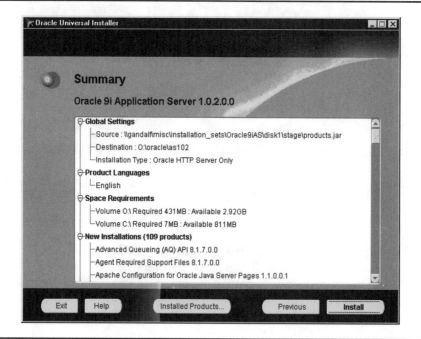

FIGURE 4-5. *Installation Summary screen for Oracle9i Application Server*

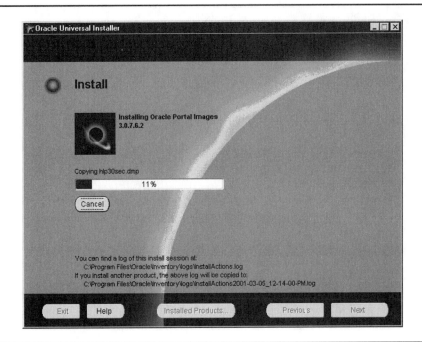

FIGURE 4-6. *The installation in progress*

Application Server software installation will run for up to an hour, and the Oracle Portal installation will take another hour or two.

During the installation, you should check the computer occasionally—it might prompt you for the second disk or the location of the disk2 installation directory.

If you left the Portal-to-Go fields blank in the preceding section, the installation of Portal-to-Go will fail. However, everything else will install correctly. If you see a command prompt with a failed login message, press CTRL-C or ENTER to continue.

Configuring Net8

After the installation itself is complete, the configuration tools start, as shown in Figure 4-7.

The first tool is the Net8 Configuration Assistant shown in Figure 4-8. In this tool, select the Perform Typical Configuration check box and click Next.

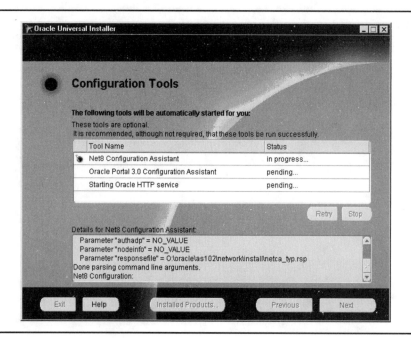

FIGURE 4-7. *The Configuration Tools screen*

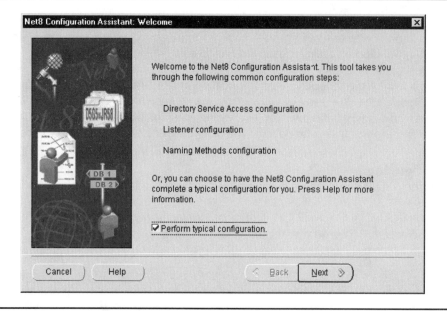

FIGURE 4-8. *The Net8 Configuration Assistant*

Configuring Oracle Portal

Next, the Oracle Portal Configuration Assistant automatically starts and displays this screen:

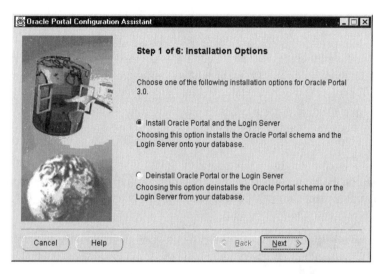

1. Leave the Install Oracle Portal and the Login Server radio button selected and click Next. Step 2 appears, as shown in this illustration.

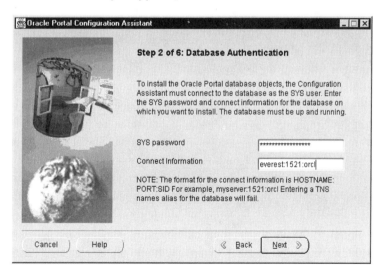

2. If you did not change the SYS password, it is **change_on_install**. The connect information field must be a JDBC-style connect string, *not* an Oracle connect string. This connect string has the format *server:port:sid* where *server* is the TCP/IP name of your computer, *port* is where the Oracle Net8 listener is listening for database connections (**1521** if you chose the typical configuration in the preceding step), and *sid* is the Oracle system identifier you chose when installing the database (**orcl** if you followed the installation guideline in the "Database" section). When you have finished, click Next.

3. In Step 3, leave the Oracle Portal Schema and the Oracle Portal DAD fields at the default value of portal30 and click Next.

4. In Step 4, leave the SSO Schema and the SSO DAD fields at the default value of portal30_sso and click Next.

5. In Step 5, in the Default, Document, and Logging Tablespace drop-down boxes, select the portal tablespace you created in a previous section, as shown in the following illustration. Click Next.

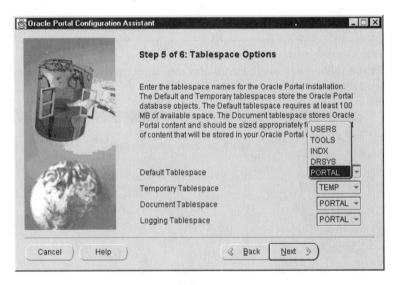

6. Before Step 6, you will probably see a warning that the PL/SQL Web Toolkit is already installed (it is automatically installed when you install the standard database). To be sure that you have the version of the toolkit that is compatible with Oracle Portal, click Yes to replace it. The actual installation of Oracle Portal starts, as shown in the next illustration.

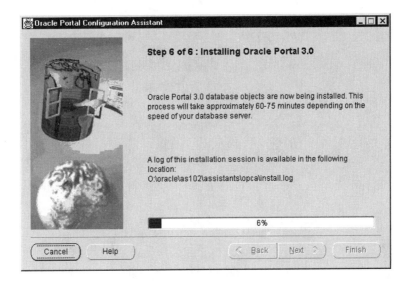

When the Oracle Portal installation finishes, click Finish. The Oracle Portal installation summary shown here appears.

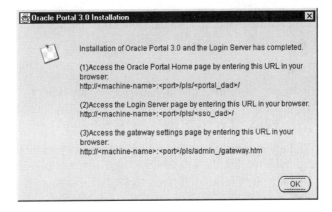

Click OK to end the Oracle Portal installation. The Oracle HTTP Server automatically starts in a Command Prompt window, and the Configuration Tools window is replaced with the End of Installation screen shown in Figure 4-9.

NOTE
The Oracle HTTP Server only runs in a command prompt right after the installation completes. When you reboot your computer, the Oracle HTTP Server will start invisibly as a Windows service.

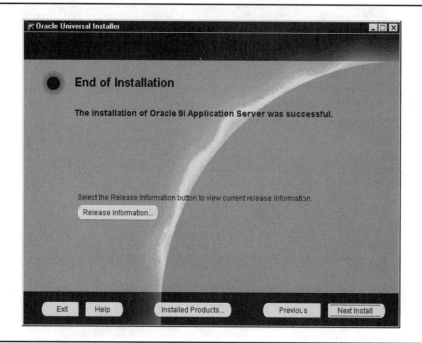

FIGURE 4-9.   *End of the installation of Oracle9i Application Server*

Click the Exit button, confirm that you want to exit, and reboot your computer.

Configuring the Application Server

The Apache HTTP Server, the Apache modules, and the JServ servlet engine are all configured through a hierarchy of configuration files. The root of this hierarchy is the httpd.conf file that you will find in O:\oracle\as102\Apache\Apache\conf.

If you like, open and inspect this file (but make it read only or make a backup first!). You will see that it includes other configuration files that may, in turn, include yet more files. This hierarchy can be a bit complicated to navigate, and Oracle has had to postpone support for Apache in their general administration tool Oracle Enterprise Manager.

The standard documentation provided by the people working on the Apache project can be a bit terse; this chapter shows you how to perform the basic configuration needed to get started. If you are interested in understanding the Apache Web server and the associated modules, refer to the resources listed in Chapter 13.

Setting Up Oracle Networking

All Oracle products that use the Oracle networking products look in a file called TNSNAMES.ORA to translate a connect string into a machine name and database name. By default, each product looks in its own Oracle home directory; the database uses O:\oracle\ora81\network\admin\tnsnames.ora, and the application server uses O:\oracle\as102\network\admin\tnsnames.ora.

This is not very practical, so you should configure all Oracle products to refer to one TNSNAMES.ORA file (the one in the database home directory is a good choice).

To do this, use the REGEDT32 program to add some values to the Windows 2000 Registry.

CAUTION

If you have ever read an article in the Microsoft Knowledge Base that talked about editing the Registry, you will be familiar with the bloodcurdling warnings about doing so. Suffice it to say that if you do anything wrong, your system probably won't work anymore. If you have anything on the system you would like to keep, back up your data and copy it to another machine or to removable media. You should also create a new Emergency Repair Disk and choose Also Back Up the Registry to the Repair Directory before editing the Registry! See Windows Help for more information.

Are you scared yet? It's really not all that hard:

1. Click Start | Run and, in the Open box, type **regedt32**.

2. In the HKEY_LOCAL_MACHINE window, expand the SOFTWARE node and the ORACLE node. If you followed the preceding instructions exactly, you should see two HOMEx nodes (HOME0 and HOME1), as shown in this illustration.

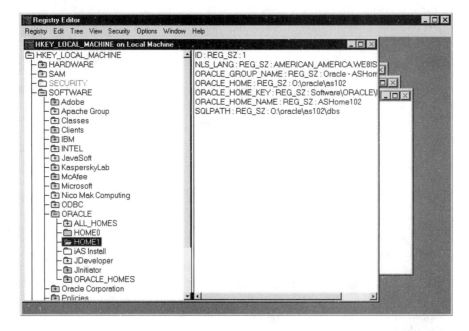

3. Click each HOMEx node in turn and check whether it has a TNS_ADMIN value in the right-hand frame. If it doesn't, choose Edit | Add Value. Enter the value name **TNS_ADMIN** and press ENTER.

4. In the String Editor window that pops up, type the name of the network configuration directory in the Oracle home directory of the database: **O:\oracle\ora81\network\admin**, as shown here:

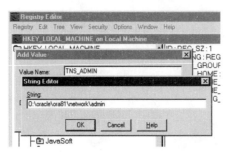

5. Then click OK. The new value should appear in the right-hand side of the window.

6. Close the Registry Editor.

How the HTTP Server Serves Static Files

Two important settings in the httpd.conf file control how static files are delivered by the Apache HTTP server:

- *DocumentRoot* defines where in the file system the HTTP server should start when translating a URL into a specific file location in the file system on the Web server. The default value is O:\oracle\as102\Apache\Apache\htdocs.

- *DirectoryIndex* defines the name of the file that should be used when an index is requested. The default value is index.html.

You don't have to change these. In fact, if you're not interested, skip the rest of this section that briefly explains how these settings control the Apache HTTP server. Refer to the resources in Chapter 13 if you are interested in learning more about Apache.

Serving the Home Page   When a user requests the server home page with a URL in the form http://<servername>, the Web server looks in the DocumentRoot directory for a file with the name DirectoryIndex. In the default installation, this becomes the file O:\oracle\as102\Apache\Apache\htdocs\index.html, as shown in Figure 4-10.

Serving Another Page   When the user provides a *virtual path* as part of the URL, the Web server will look for a corresponding subdirectory under DocumentRoot. For example, if the user requests the page http://<servername>/manual/mod/mod_ssl/ssl_overview.html, the Web server will look for the file ssl_overview.html in a subdirectory manual/mod/mod_ssl under the DocumentRoot. In the default installation, this translates into the file O:\oracle\as102\Apache\Apache\htdocs\manual\mod\mod_ssl\ssl_overview.html.

Directory Browsing   When the user provides a virtual path but no filename, the Web server will look for a file with the name specified by DirectoryIndex in that directory. For example, a request for http://<servername>/demo will show the file O:\oracle\as102\Apache\Apache\htdocs\demo\index.html.

If a file with this name is not found in the directory, the Web server will produce an Explorer-like page that allows the user to browse the directory structure. For example, if the user entered http://<servername>/doc, she would see the page in

FIGURE 4-10. *The Oracle HTTP Server home page*

Figure 4-11 showing the directory structure of the physical directory
O:\oracle\as102\Apache\Apache\htdocs\doc.

Adding Virtual Directories

You can change the DocumentRoot setting to point somewhere else in your file
system, but what if you want your virtual directories arranged in a different order
from the physical file structure?

You have two options:

■ Add aliases to the httpd.conf file.

■ Create symbolic links (called *junctions*) directly in the NTFS file system.

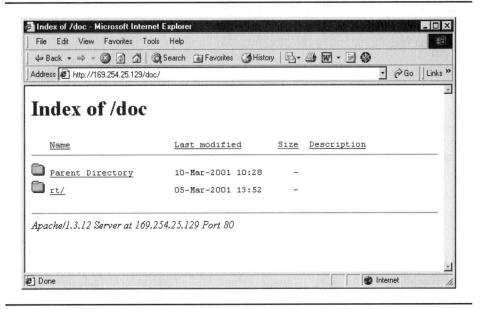

FIGURE 4-11. *Browsing the directory structure*

To create an alias in the file, look at the examples in the file and refer to the resources in Chapter 13.

To create a junction, use the freeware junction tool (see Chapter 11) or the **linkd** utility in the Microsoft Resource Kit. The section "Setting Up the Virtual Directories" later in this chapter shows how to use the junction tool to create the virtual directories needed for Oracle Developer.

Installing the Sample Files
If you want to use the example files shown in this book, first create a sample directory C:\web_apps_101. Then download the file samples.zip from **www.vesterli.com**, unzip it into this directory, and copy the files webstart.css and web_apps_101.gif to O:\oracle\as102\Apache\Apache\htdocs.

Configuring to Run Servlets
Just as you have to tell the HTTP server where to find static files, you have to tell the JServ servlet engine where to find your servlets.

The JServ configuration is split between many files. It can be a bit tricky trying to follow which files include which, but you just need to know that the file O:\oracle\as102\Apache\Jserv\servlets\zone.properties contains the servlet *repositories,* which are directories that the servlet engine searches for servlets. To add the c:\web_apps_101 directory to this list, open the zone.properties file and look for a line starting with repositories=. Add another line so the file reads

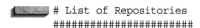

```
# List of Repositories
#######################

# The list of servlet repositories controlled by this servlet zone
# Syntax: repositories=[repository],[repository]...
# Default: NONE
# Note: The classes you want to be reloaded upon modification should be put
#       here.

repositories=O:\oracle\as102\Apache\Jserv\servlets
repositories=C:\web_apps_101
```

When you have performed this change, save the file and reload the OracleHTTPServer service or reboot the machine.

The Apache JServ works with a concept of different *zones*—this can be useful if you have one server serving different applications or Web sites. The preceding configuration just makes your own servlets a part of the default zone. If you are interested in the details, refer to one of the resources in Chapter 13.

Checking the Installation

OK, the Installer told you that everything has been installed correctly—but seeing is believing. Let's check the four features that you need to use any of the five ways of building Oracle Web applications covered in this book:

- Static files

- PL/SQL procedures

- Java servlets

- CGI programs

Checking Static Files

To check that the Apache HTTP Server can deliver static files, type the following URL into your browser:

http://<*servername*>

where <*servername*> is the name of your server. You should see the Oracle HTTP Server home page, as shown previously in Figure 4-10.

NOTE
You can start a Command Prompt (Start | Programs | Accessories | Command Prompt) and type the command **hostname** *to see the name of your computer. As you can see from the screenshots, my machine is called everest.*

Checking PL/SQL Applications

To check that the Apache HTTP Server can invoke a stored procedure in the database through the mod_plsql module, type the following URL in your browser:

http://<*servername*>/pls/portal30/portal30.home

This should produce the screen shown in Figure 4-12.

Why does this demonstrate that the application server can run PL/SQL Web applications? Because the /pls in the URL indicates the mod_plsql module, the /portal30/ indicates a preconfigured Database Access Descriptor connecting to the PORTAL30 user, and the portal30.home indicates the stored procedure HOME in schema PORTAL30. You can use a PL/SQL tool to examine this procedure if you're interested.

Checking Java Servlets

To check that your Oracle Web server is able to run servlets, enter the following URL in your browser:

http://<*servername*>/servlet/IsItWorking

where <*servername*> is the name of your server. In the default installation, the virtual path /servlet/ indicates that the request should be passed to the mod_jserv module that in turn passes it to the JServ servlet engine, as described in Chapter 3.

The IsItWorking servlet is now invoked and produces the screen shown in Figure 4-13.

NOTE
You must type the name IsItWorking *exactly as shown in the code, with uppercase I, I, and W. Java is picky about upper- and lowercase.*

The way JServ is set up by default does not allow you to see the image—don't worry about that; the important part is the "Yes, It's Working!" message.

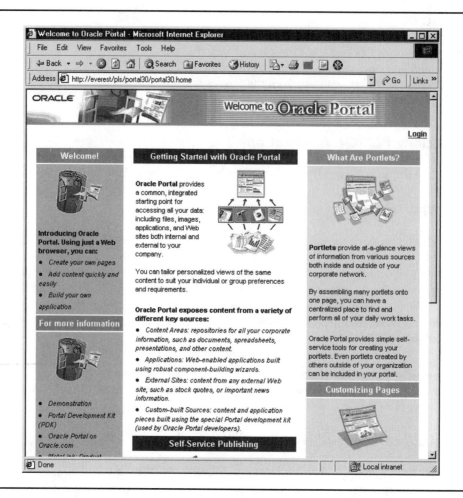

FIGURE 4-12.   *The Oracle Portal public home page*

In case you wondering, though, the image comes from the JServ status servlet that is disabled by default. You can enable it by changing the configuration in jserv.conf. Refer to the Resources in Chapter 13 for more information about Apache.

Checking CGI

To check that you can run CGI programs, type the following URL in your browser:

http://*<servername>*/cgi-bin/printenv

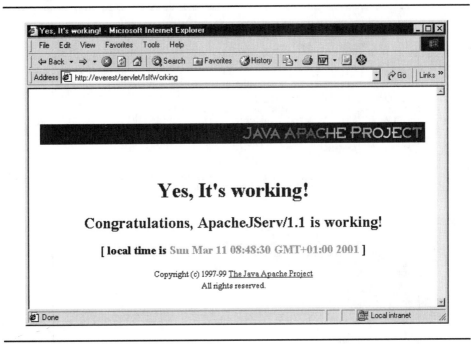

FIGURE 4-13.   *Apache JServ is working*

The default installation maps the /cgi-bin/ directory to the mod_cgi module, and this module will look for a program in the directory O:\oracle\as102\Apache\ Apache\cgi-bin. The printenv program found in this directory runs and produces a screen like the one shown in Figure 4-14.

Web PL/SQL Generator Package Library

After installing the Oracle8i database and the Oracle9i Application Server, you have all you need to run Java servlets, hand-built PL/SQL Web applications, and Oracle Portal applications. You also have almost (but not quite) everything you need to run Oracle Designer applications.

Like hand-built PL/SQL applications or Oracle Portal applications, Oracle Designer applications consist of PL/SQL packages. However, they also make use of a number of PL/SQL packages that come with Oracle Designer that are not installed

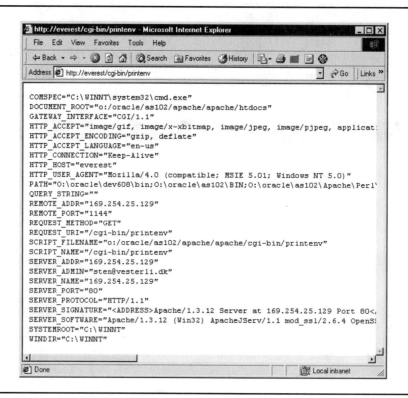

FIGURE 4-14. *Output of a CGI program*

in a default database. These packages are called the Web PL/SQL Generator Package Library.

It is possible to install this library directly from the Oracle Designer installation files, but it is easier to do it from a computer where the Oracle Designer client tools are installed. We'll return to installing this library in the "Preparing for Web Applications" section, later in this chapter.

Developer Services

If you followed the instructions so far, you can now run Java servlets, hand-built PL/SQL Web applications and Oracle Portal applications. But to run forms and reports from a Web browser, you need the Developer Services (Forms Service and Reports Service) as well.

Both are part of Oracle9i Application Server Enterprise Edition; but since this installation installs so many components that are outside the scope of this book (and because it takes up several gigabytes), this section explains how to install just the parts you need to deploy forms and reports to the Web.

You need to have the Oracle Developer 6i Release 2 CD-ROM or to have downloaded the corresponding install set from Oracle Technology Network.

Preparing to Install

In Oracle Developer 6i, Oracle has decided to hide the release notes deep in the install set—so you have to *install* the release notes before you can read about installation!

Reading the Getting Started Guides

If you do not have the Getting Started Guides in hardcopy, download them from the Oracle Technology Network Web site. To do this, go to **http://otn.oracle.com**, click the Documentation bar, click the Forms Developer hyperlink (in the Internet Tools section), and download the guide Forms 6i Getting Started for Windows. Go back to the documentation home page, click Reports Developer (in the Business Intelligence Tools section), and download the guide Reports 6i Getting Started for Windows.

Browse through Chapters 1 and 2 of both guides—note that section 1.6 reveals where you find the missing release notes.

Installing the Release Notes

1. To start the installation, double-click the SETUP.EXE program in the root directory of your CD-ROM or downloaded installation set. The Oracle Installation Settings dialog box appears, as shown in the following illustration. It might already have picked up the company name from a previous installation.

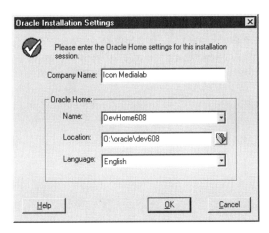

2. Provide a separate home directory—do not use the one where you have
   already installed the database or the application server. For example,
   provide the name DevHome608 and the location o:\oracle\dev608 as
   shown in the previous illustration. Then click OK twice to confirm the new
   home directory. The Installation Options screen shown in the following
   illustration appears.

3. Choose Oracle Forms Server and click Next. The next window appears,
   shown here:

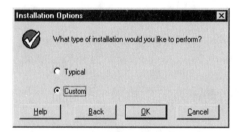

4. Select Custom and click OK. The Software Asset Manager window, shown
   next, appears, displaying all the available software in the left-hand box and
   all the software installed in this home directory in the right-hand box.

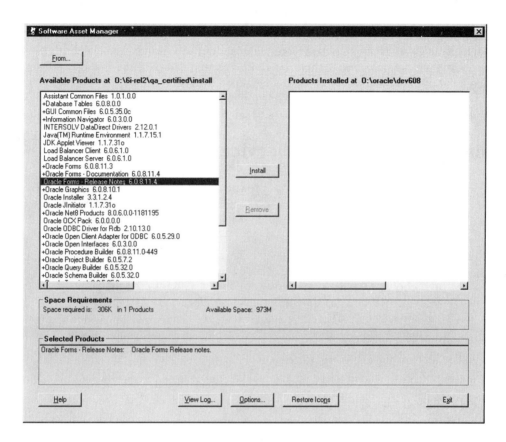

5. Select Oracle Forms Release Notes and click Install.

   For mysterious reasons, Oracle has chosen to make it impossible to install both Forms and Reports in one session—you have to exit the Installer, restart it, choose the home directory you just created, and choose Oracle Reports Server and then Custom to get back to the Software Asset Manager showing the Reports products.

6. Select Oracle Reports Release Notes, and click Install.

7. Exit the Installer.

Reading the Release Notes

To read the Oracle Forms Release Notes, choose Start | Programs | Oracle Forms 6i | Release Notes (choose from either Text or PDF format). Scroll through these notes to see if there is anything that applies to your situation.

Then choose Start | Programs | Oracle Reports 6i | Release Notes (Text or PDF format). Page through these notes as well to see if there is anything you need to know.

Installing the Forms Service

The Forms Service consists of the Forms CGI program, the Forms Server, and the Forms Runtime. All of this is needed on the Web/application server in order to run Forms applications from a Web browser. In addition, you should install the JInitiator (an Oracle-supplied browser plug-in) on the Web/application server so that it is available for the Web browser to download.

1. Start the Installer once more; choose the DevHome608 home directory, and choose Oracle Forms Server and then Custom to see the Software Asset Manager window, as shown in this illustration.

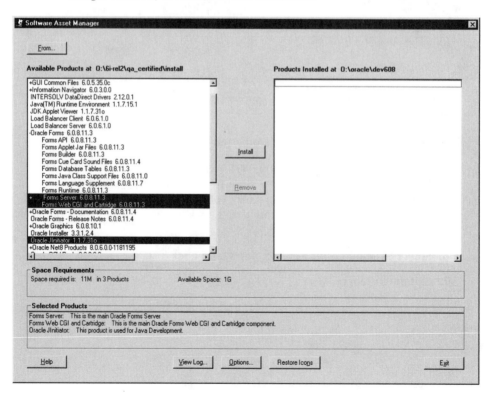

2. Expand the Oracle Forms node and select Forms Server, Forms Web CGI
and Cartridge (hold down the CTRL key while clicking to select multiple
items), and Oracle JInitiator. Then click Install.

3. You might be asked if you want to create and start the Forms Service, as
shown here:

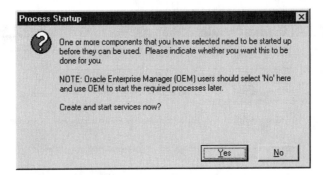

Answer Yes to continue. The Forms Server Parameters screen appears,
shown in this illustration.

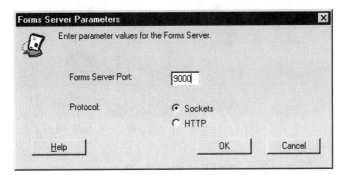

4. For the purposes of this book, leave both settings at their default. In a
production environment, you might want to change the port number to
something else. You also might have to choose HTTP communication
if there is a firewall between your clients and the Forms Listener is
running on the application server.

5. A couple of messages might appear to inform you about the software
components being installed. Read each message, and then click OK to
continue. Eventually, the installation starts.

6. When the installation is completed, a window tells you that the installation has produced a file listing the actions that you need to take before you can use the Forms Service. Click Yes to open this file—it will look something like the following illustration. It will instruct you to reboot your machine and to set up some virtual directory mappings; you'll see how to do this in the next section.

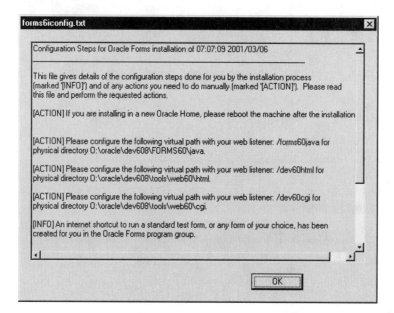

7. When you close the window, a message tells you that the installation was successful. Click OK, close the Oracle Installer, and reboot your computer.

Installing the Reports Service

The Reports Service consists of the Reports Server, the Reports Web CGI, and the Reports Runtime. You need all of these in order to run reports from a Web browser.

1. By now, you should be getting used to restarting the Installer—start it, choose the DevHome608 home directory, choose Oracle Reports Server, and then choose Custom to see the Software Asset Manager window, as shown in the following illustration.

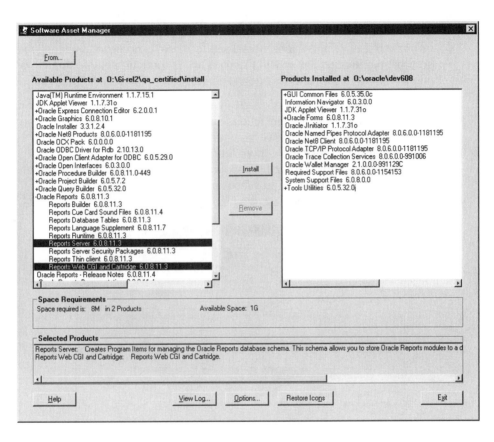

2. Expand the Oracle Reports node and select Reports Server and Reports Web CGI and Cartridge, and then click Install.

3. If you are asked whether you want to create and start the Reports Server, click Yes. The Reports Server Parameters screen appears, shown here:

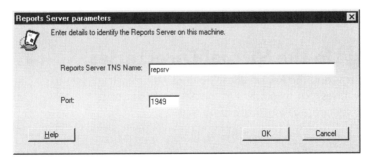

4. In this dialog box, enter a shorter value for Reports Server TNS Name—for example repsrv. In this experimental setting, there is no need to change the port that the Reports Server will listen on (in a production environment, you might want to change this to a nonstandard value). Then click OK.

5. When the installation is completed, a window tells you that the installation has produced a file listing the actions that you need to take before you can use the Forms Service. Click Yes to open this file—it will look something like the following illustration. It will instruct you to reboot your machine and set up some virtual directory mappings, and will give some additional instructions about how to send Web reports directly to a printer. The directory mapping will be described in the next section.

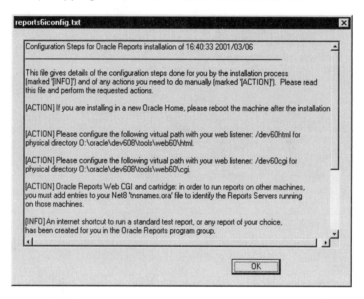

6. When you close the window, a message tells you that the installation was successful. Click OK, close the Oracle Installer, and reboot your computer.

Setting Up the Virtual Directories

Both the Forms and the Reports Service installation instruct you to create specific virtual directories that map URLs to the actual locations of the files on your Web server. This section explains how to do that.

The Virtual Directories You Need

After installing the Developer Services, you will find two files called forms6iconfig.txt and reports6iconfig.txt, respectively, in the directory O:\oracle\dev608\orainst. (All the paths in this section assume that you followed the names suggested earlier.)

These files instruct you to create the virtual directory mappings in Table 4-5.

You can skip the mapping of /dev60cgi to O:\oracle\dev608\tools\web60\cgi. This physical directory is where the Oracle Installer places the Developer CGI programs (see Chapter 3 for an explanation of the Developer CGI program). You do not have to map this directory—instead, just copy the files ifcgi60.exe and rwcgi60.exe from directory O:\oracle\dev608\tools\web60\cgi to the default CGI directory used by the Apache Web server (O:\oracle\as102\Apache\Apache\cgi-bin).

Creating the Virtual Directories

You can create these mappings by adding *aliases* to the Apache configuration file httpd.conf, or you can use the junction utility to create *symbolic links* in the file system, as shown in Figure 4-15.

An alias is an Apache configuration concept—aliases do not exist in the file system. When the Apache HTTP server needs to map the virtual directory in the URL to a physical directory, it reads all the aliases defined in the httpd.conf file to find the right one. Because you also have to configure the access rights to an alias in the configuration file, this method needs a bit of Apache know-how.

Virtual Directory	Physical Directory	Remark
/forms60java	O:\oracle\dev608\forms60\java	For downloading the Forms applet
/dev60html	O:\oracle\dev608\tools\web60\html	
/dev60cgi	O:\oracle\dev608\tools\web60\cgi	Not needed—see the next section
/dev60temp	O:\oracle\dev608\tools\web60\temp	
/jinitiator	O:\oracle\dev608\jinit	Only used for the initial download of JInitiator

TABLE 4-5.   *Virtual Directory Mappings for Oracle Developer*

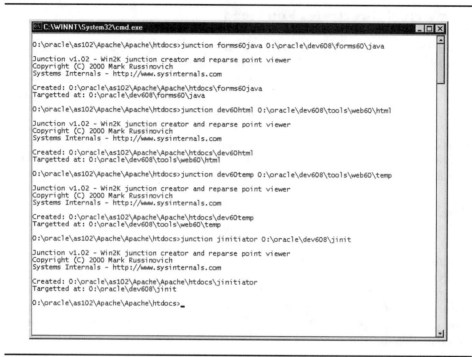

FIGURE 4-15. *Using the junction utility to create symbolic links*

A symbolic link is an entry in the file system that refers to somewhere else. If you know Unix, you are probably already familiar with symbolic links—Microsoft calls them *junction points*, but it's the same thing. A symbolic link appears just like a normal subdirectory to all software—for example, in Windows Explorer, symbolic links look just like directories and work in exactly the same way. The only place you see that they are not normal directories is when you use the **dir** command from a command prompt—there you will see ordinary directories have the type <DIR>, but symbolic links have the type <JUNCTION>. They work just like directories, though, and you can use commands like **cd** to follow a symbolic link just as if you were navigating to a subdirectory.

This section shows how to use the junction utility (refer to Chapter 11 first for the URL from which you can download this small utility).

Start a command prompt (Start | Programs | Accessories | Command Prompt) and change to the directory O:\oracle\as102\Apache\Apache\htdocs. Then enter the following commands:

```
junction forms60java O:\oracle\dev608\forms60\java
junction dev60html O:\oracle\dev608\tools\web60\html
junction dev60temp O:\oracle\dev608\tools\web60\temp
junction jinitiator O:\oracle\dev608\jinit
```

As mentioned, these symbolic links look just like directories when viewed from Windows Explorer; but if you use the **dir** command from a command prompt, you will see the symbolic links shown as the type <JUNCTION>.

Changing the Environment Parameters

Before you start working with the Oracle Developer products, you should configure networking and the search paths.

Setting Up Oracle Networking

Because the Oracle Developer products are installed in their own Oracle home directory, they will, by default, refer to their own TNSNAMES.ORA Oracle network configuration file (O:\oracle\dev608\network\admin\tnsnames.ora). This is not very practical, so you should configure it to refer to the TNSNAMES.ORA file in the database home directory just as you did for the application server.

This must be done by changing the Windows 2000 Registry as you did previously for Oracle networking in the "Configuring Networking" section.

CAUTION
The same warning still applies: Take care when editing the Windows Registry!

1. Click Start | Run and type **regedt32** in the Open box.

2. In the HKEY_LOCAL_MACHINE window, expand the SOFTWARE node and then the ORACLE node. If you followed the preceding instructions exactly, you should now see three HOMEx nodes (HOME0, HOME1, and HOME2).

3. Click each HOMEx node in turn and check whether it has a TNS_ADMIN value in the right-hand frame. If not, choose Edit | Add Value. Enter the value name **TNS_ADMIN** and press ENTER.

4. In the String Editor window that pops up, write the name of the network configuration directory in the Oracle home directory of the database: **O:\oracle\ora81\network\admin**.

5. Click OK. The new value should appear in the right-hand side of the window.

You've set up Oracle Networking, but leave the Registry Editor open—you need to edit a few values, as described in the following section.

Setting Up the Developer Path

When you request a form through the Forms Service, the Forms Runtime will look in the *forms path*. This is a list of directories just like the normal PATH variable that the operating system uses when it looks for an executable program; in Windows it is defined by the Registry value FORMS60_PATH.

Similarly, the Reports Service will look for reports in the *reports path* defined by the REPORTS60_PATH value in the Windows Registry.

For the examples in this book, you will add the example directory (C:\web_apps_101) to both the forms path and the reports path. If you left the Registry Editor open in the previous section, you can now continue as follows:

1. Click the HOME node for Oracle Developer. If you followed the preceding installation guidelines exactly, it is HOME2 (you can easily identify the right one by all the D2K and DEV2000 values).

2. Find the FORMS60_PATH value in the right-hand frame and double-click it. The String Editor window appears. Click at the end of the selected text and add your own directory, C:\web_apps_101, to the end of the string. Then click OK.

3. Find the REPORTS60_PATH value in the right-hand frame and double-click it. The String Editor window appears. Click at the end of the selected text and add your own directory, C:\web_apps_101, to the end of the string. Then click OK.

4. Close the Registry Editor.

Copying the Report Service Configuration

By setting the TNS_ADMIN value in the Registry, you are instructing the Developer Services to refer to the TNSNAMES.ORA configuration in the database home directory. However, as you might have noticed in the message at the end of the installation, the installation program actually wrote some necessary configuration information into the TNSNAMES.ORA file in the Developer home directory.

You must copy this information from one TNSNAMES.ORA file to another. To do that, follow these steps:

1. Open the file O:\oracle\dev608\net80\admin\tnsnames.ora.

2. Scroll down to the bottom of the file and copy the line starting with repsrv.

3. Open the file O:\oracle\ora81\network\admin\tnsnames.ora and add the copied line at the bottom.

Development Tools

If you followed all the preceding instructions, you now have an Oracle8i database, an Oracle9i Application Server, and the Developer Services. With this, you can *run* four out of five application types covered in this book (how to install the Oracle Designer Web Toolkit needed to run Designer applications is described in a few pages). But you still need some additional tools to be able to *develop* the different types of applications.

Table 4-6 shows the tools necessary for the five approaches.

JDeveloper

If you want to use Java (in the form of Java servlets or in any other way), you should install a Java tool. This section describes how to install the tool from Oracle, Oracle JDeveloper version 3.2.2

Reading the Release Notes

The Release Notes for Oracle JDeveloper can be found in the file README.HTM in the root directory of the CD or install set. Read the table of contents and skim through the document reading any section that seems relevant to you.

I recommend always scrolling through the Release Notes before installing any Oracle product, but there is no need for you to read all 42 pages thoroughly.

Reading the Installation Guide

The Installation Guide is found in the INSTALL.HTM file. Browse through this file and make sure your system meets the system requirements.

The following instructions are going to guide you through a *custom* installation to avoid filling up your hard disk with too much chaff. If you later decide that you do

Approach	Development Tool
Java servlets	JDeveloper or another Java tool
Hand-built PL/SQL	Any PL/SQL development tool
Oracle Designer	Oracle Designer
Oracle Portal	Oracle Portal
Oracle Developer	Oracle Developer

TABLE 4-6. *Development Tools for the Different Approaches*

want to play around with Business Components for Java or that you want to build an application using a specific version of Java, you can always run the installation again.

These instructions will tell you how to install HTML Help, not WebHelp. HTML Help has more functionality, but it requires Internet Explorer 4 or above.

You are not going to install support for Oracle Repository.

Installing JDeveloper

1. Double-click SETUP.EXE to start the installation program. On the Welcome screen, click Next to proceed to the Setup Type dialog box, shown in this illustration.

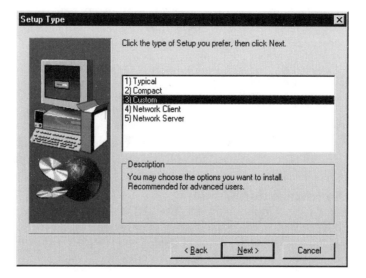

2. Choose Custom and click Next.

3. Click Browse and choose a directory where JDeveloper should be installed.

4. Do not accept the default—it contains a space, which will cause problems down the road. Use something short like o:\oracle\jdev322. Then click Next. The component selection screen appears, shown in the next illustration).

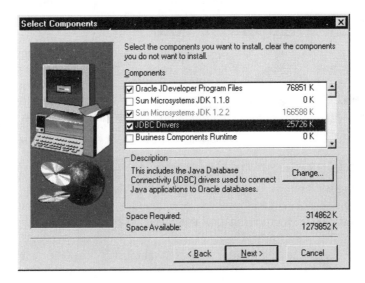

5. Choose the components in the following table.

Oracle JDeveloper Program Files

Sun Microsystems JDK 1.2.2

JDBC Drivers

Documentation—HTML Help

Documentation—JavaDoc

If you are new to Java, you might also want to install the samples.

When you have finished, click Next.

6. Leave the name of the Program Folder at the default value and click Next.

7. At the Start Copying Files window, click Next to start the installation. The installation runs for a few minutes, and the Setup Complete window appears with the option to read the release notes (but you already read those, didn't you?). Just click Finish to end the installation.

In Chapter 6 you will learn how to use Oracle JDeveloper to create four small Java servlets.

PL/SQL Development Tool

For PL/SQL development, Oracle offers you the Procedure Builder that is part of Oracle Developer. If you are not happy with this, there is no reason that you should ever again be stuck with SQL*Plus and Notepad as your development platform—Chapter 11 describes where to get the free version of Tool for Oracle Application Developers (TOAD), and there are several other third-party tools for PL/SQL development.

Oracle Designer 6i Release 2

The following instructions explain how to install Designer 6i Release 2 and the Designer 6i Repository on a computer where the Oracle database version 8.1.7 is already installed. Remember that Oracle Designer has two parts:

■ The Oracle Designer client software that must be installed on all workstations where a developer will use Oracle Designer to develop applications.

■ The Oracle Repository (Oracle tables) that must reside in a central Oracle database.

The installation instructions in this chapter cover how to install both the tools and the repository.

NOTE
Do not attempt to install Oracle Designer 6i Release 1 on an Oracle Database version 8.1.7—you must have Designer Release 2 in order to install on an 8.1.7 database.

Preparing to Install

As always when installing Oracle software, you should refer to the documentation first: double-click the welcome.htm file in the root directory of your Designer 6i CD-ROM or installation set to see the available documentation. Note that the documentation is split in two parts: Oracle Designer 6i (the client part), and Oracle Repository 6i (the server part).

First, click the Oracle Designer 6i Release Notes. Browse through this document to get the latest information on restrictions, limitations, and special procedures. Then go back to the welcome page and click the Oracle Repository 6i Release Notes. This document contains some of the same information as the Designer 6i Release Notes, but also some new information. Browse through this document as well to get an idea of the problem areas and restrictions.

Finally, go back to the welcome page again. Oracle is apparently in the process of separating the Designer product from the Repository product, so this page has two links to installation guides: one behind a link called Oracle Designer 6i Installation Guide, and one behind the link Oracle Repository 6i Installation Guide. However, as of Release 2, they both end at the same manual, called Oracle Repository Designer Installation Guide. Read the instructions in Chapter 1, "Client-Side Installation," and Chapter 2, "Server-Side Installation," before performing the installation in the next sections.

Installing the Designer Tools

The Designer tools must be installed on each workstation where you want to use Designer. To do this, follow the instructions in Chapter 1 of the Installation Guide. Note the following:

- The Installation Guide only talks about version 8.1.6 of the database (but you read in the release notes that 8.1.7 was supported, didn't you?). The release notes are "the last word" and Designer 6i Release 2 does indeed run on the database version 8.1.7.

- Remember to log on to Windows with an Administrator account.

- Remember to shut down all Oracle products: click Start | Settings | Control Panel | Administrative Tools | Services, select each Service where the name starts with Oracle and the status is started, and choose Action | Stop or click the Stop button.

- In the Oracle Installation Settings dialog box, select the home directory where you installed the Forms and Reports service (DevHome608 if you followed the earlier sugestion). Then click OK to continue.

NOTE
As a general rule, you should install each piece of Oracle software in a separate home directory. However, as you can read in the installation guide, Designer must be installed in the same home directory as Developer.

1. At the Oracle Repository and/or Designer Installation Type page, shown next, choose Oracle Repository and Designer Install Wizard.

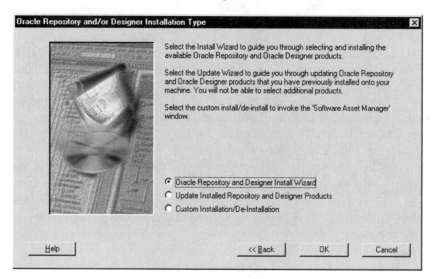

2. On the Package Installation Settings screen, shown in the following illustration, leave the default settings. You can also leave the default settings on the two following Advanced Options screens.

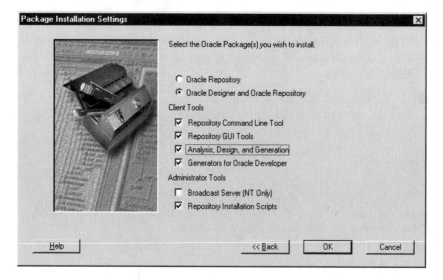

3. On the Oracle Repository 6i Import and Export Tools screen, shown next, deselect the Install Repository 6i Import and Export Tools check box—you already have these tools installed if you installed the database as described in the preceding section.

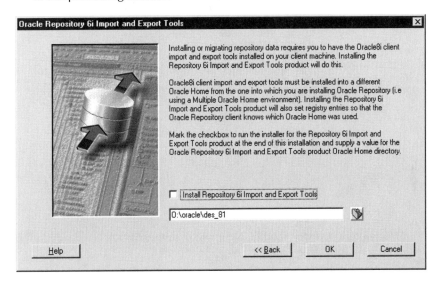

4. If a dialog box appears about Oracle TCP/IP support, it will probably say that the necessary TCP/IP support is already installed. If not, you need to select the check box to allow Oracle to install TCP/IP.

5. Before the actual installation starts, the Installer gives you various messages about software it wants to install. Read each message and then click OK—none of these messages require any other action. After the final confirmation, the Installer runs for a while, installing all the Designer tools.

6. After the software has been installed, you might see a message about a lot of tools you must install to achieve specific functionality—ignore those for now.

7. Near the end of the installation, the Connection Information dialog box, shown in the following illustration, appears.

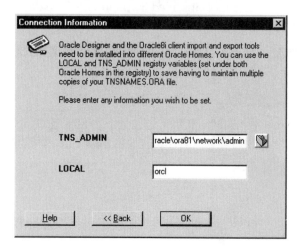

Oracle Networking would be the topic of another book (indeed, it *is* the topic of several, including *Oracle8i Networking 101*, from Oracle Press); for now, set TNS_ADMIN to O:\oracle\ora81\network\admin and LOCAL to orcl.

TNS_ADMIN tells Designer where to look for a configuration file (called TNSNAMES.ORA) that it needs to find the database; LOCAL tells it which database name to assume if you do not provide any database connect string.

8. Finally, you will see a message saying that your system might need an update from Microsoft, most likely followed by a message that your system didn't need this upgrade after all.

9. The installation program then exits. Reboot your computer at this time.

Setting Up the Repository

To store the model of your application, Designer uses a *repository*. This is a collection of tables that must be installed into an Oracle database. You normally need only one repository that can contain many application systems, and can be used by many analysts and developers.

To install the Designer tools, follow the instructions in the Installation Guide, Chapter 2, in the section "Installing a New Repository." This section contains 17 clearly marked steps that you must follow carefully. The following comments apply to each step.

1. Remember to log on to the local machine with an account that is a member of the Administrators group.

2. The instructions for finding the INIT.ORA file are a bit misleading. If you followed the preceding instructions when installing the database, the init.ora file is located in the directory O:\oracle\admin\orcl\pfile. In a default installation, you'll have to add or change the parameters listed in the following table (hash_area_size, optimizer_index_caching, and optimizer_index_cost_adj are new parameters).

Parameter	New Value
compatible	8.1.6
sort_area_size	262144
hash_area_size	1048576
optimizer_index_caching	50
optimizer_index_cost_adj	25
shared_pool_size	32000000
open_cursors	1000

3. To restart the database, choose Start | Settings | Control Panel | Administrative Tools | Services. Select the Service OracleServiceORCL, and choose Action | Restart or click the Restart button.

4. While the Services window is open, check that the service OracleOraHome81TNSListener is running (status is Started). Then close the Services window.

5. Choose Start | Programs | Oracle – OraHome81 | Application Development | SQL Plus. Log on as user **sys** with password **change_on_install** and connect string **orcl**. Create the tablespaces as instructed (you can download some script for the default minimum installation from **www.vesterli.com** if you don't feel like typing all the commands). If you do retrieve these scripts, first run create_des6i_tablespaces.sql and then set_temp_next_256.sql.

6. Create the dedicated rollback tablespace and rollback segment. If you do this by hand, note that the view giving information on the rollback segments is called DBA_ROLLBACK_SEGS (*not*, as the Installation Guide says, DBA_ROLLBACK_SEGMENTS). Alternatively, download and run the script des6i_rbs.sql.

7. Your SYSTEM tablespace in a default installation does not have nearly the space you need. To be on the safe side, add an additional 200MB by hand or use the script system_add200.sql. Using AUTOEXTEND is not recommended; some day you'll suddenly discover that Oracle has filled up your entire disk.

8. Create the repository user. Use the existing tablespace TEMP as temporary tablespace for this user. The script create_repos_user.sql creates a user with the name REPOS and the password REPOS.

9. You are already working at the client workstation—you do not have anything to do in this step.

10. You are already connected as SYS, so there is nothing to do in this step either.

11. You can perform Step 11 in the Installation Guide with the script repos_priv.sql if you followed the default installation and used the preceding script to create the repository user. When the script has completed (or you have entered all the GRANT statements listed in the Installation Guide by hand), exit SQL*Plus.

12. Choose Start | Programs | Oracle Repository 6i – DesHome65 | Repository Administration Utility, and log on with username **repos**, password **repos**, and connect string **orcl**.

13. Click Check Requirements. The check shouldn't show any problems, but you should do it anyway.

14. Click Install. The instructions in the Installation Guide concerning the check boxes in the Repository Installation Options dialog box are not quite clear—leave both selected. Choose Yes to use public synonyms.

15. For this first experience with Oracle Designer, you need only a small repository.

16. Choose all the tablespaces you created in Step 5. When you have finished, this dialog box should look like the following illustration.

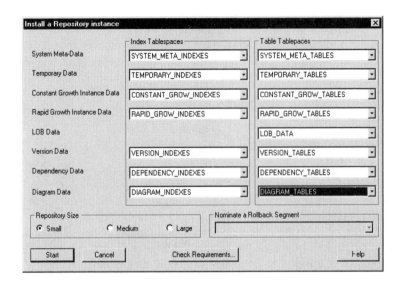

17. The installation runs for more than an hour on most computers. When it's done, check the logs as described in the Installation Guide. If you experienced any problems, refer to the troubleshooting section in the Installation Guide.

Before you close the Repository Administration Utility, click the Compute Statistics button. Leave the default sample size of 20 percent (if you're impatient to get started, you can also choose 10 percent or 5 percent).

When the installation is successfully completed, you can restart your database to bring the standard rollback segments back online (and the special Designer rollback segment offline). If you like, you can now drop the Designer installation rollback segment and the associated tablespace.

NOTE
Even if you drop the tablespace, the corresponding data file in O:\oracle\oradata\orcl must still be deleted manually.

To keep things simple, do not enable version control. As long as you are just playing with Designer, you do not need to create subordinate users either—simply use the REPOS user to log on to all Designer tools.

To check that your repository was created correctly, start any tool and create a few objects. Choose Start | Programs | Oracle Designer – DesHome65 | Oracle Designer. Log on with username **repos**, password **repos**, and connect string **orcl**.

CAUTION
It is not enough to see that the tools start. Until you have created and saved objects, you cannot be sure that everything ran smoothly.

Start a tool. For example, click the Design Editor icon and click OK in the Welcome dialog box to start the Server Model Guide (see Figure 4-16). Choose SYSTEM FOLDER as Context Container and click the Create/Edit Database Objects link.

Create an object with the relevant wizard; for instance, choose Tables and Columns to create a table. If a dialog box called Default Database Implementation appears and asks you about assigning objects to databases, you can choose the option Do Not Assign This Database Object to a Database and Display This Wizard Again.

If you do not see any error messages and your object is visible in the Server Model Navigator in the left-hand side of the Design Editor window, your Designer installation works correctly. Chapter 8 explains how to use Oracle Designer to build Web applications.

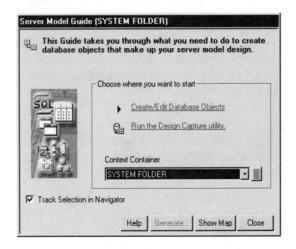

FIGURE 4-16.   *The Server Model Guide*

Preparing for Web Applications

One additional step is necessary in order to generate PL/SQL Web applications from Designer: you must install the Web PL/SQL Generator Package Library.

NOTE
This is not the same as the Web PL/SQL Developer's Toolkit. The Developer's Toolkit is used by all PL/SQL Web applications (whether handwritten or generated from Oracle Designer or Oracle Portal). The PL/SQL generator packages are needed only by Designer-generated PL/SQL applications.

These packages must be installed in some database schema, for example, SYS. Your DBA will argue that they belong to a tool and should not be placed in the SYS schema; on the other hand, Oracle already put the Web PL/SQL Developers Toolkit here.

To install these packages in the SYS schema, choose Start | Programs | Oracle Designer 6i – DesHome65 | Install Web PL-SQL Generator. SQL*Plus starts and prompts for a connect string to the "toolkit user." Type **sys/change_on_install@orcl** and let the script run. It will give you a message about synonyms already existing—this is OK; these are synonyms for the Web PL/SQL Developer's Toolkit that were created when the database was installed.

Oracle Portal

To develop applications with Oracle Portal, you do not need a separate development tool. Indeed, you cannot use any tool other than your Web browser.

Oracle Developer

This section describes how to install the Oracle Developer development tools (Oracle Forms and Oracle Reports). You installed the *server-side* components that are necessary to run an application developed with these tools— this section describes how to install the development tools used by the developer to build the applications.

Preparing to Install

As you noticed when you installed the Developer Services, the Release Notes and Getting Started guides for Oracle Developer cover both the development tools and the services, so you have already read the necessary installation instructions.

Installing Form Builder

To develop applications with Forms, you need the Form Builder tool. To install it, follow these instructions:

1. Double-click the SETUP.EXE program in the root directory of the CD or installation set. The Oracle Installation Settings dialog box that you have seen several times before appears again.

2. Select the home directory that you already used for the Forms Service and the Reports Service, and click OK.

3. In the Oracle Tools Installation Options dialog box, choose Oracle Forms Developer and click OK.

4. In the next window, choose Custom Installation and click OK to proceed to the Software Asset Manager window.

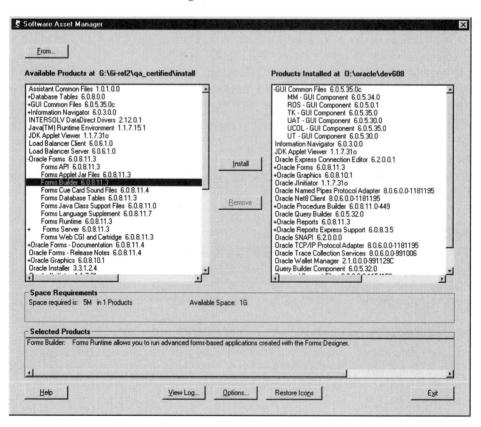

5. Expand the Oracle Forms node and select Forms Builder. Then click Install to start the installation.

6. If you are prompted to stop the Oracle Forms Service, choose Start | Settings | Control Panel, and double-click Administrative Tools and then Services. Scroll down and select the Oracle Forms Server and choose Action | Stop or click the Stop button.

7. After a few minutes, a message informs you that installation is complete. Click OK to return to the Software Asset Manager, and then close the Installer.

NOTE
It might not be very logical, but you cannot install Oracle Reports now. It is simply missing from the box of available software on the left, probably because you chose to install Oracle Forms in an earlier step. When leaving the Installer, you may get a Windows error message saying that orainst.exe has caused an error and will be terminated; that's OK, since that's what you wanted anyway.

Installing Reports Builder
In order to build reports, you need the Report Builder tool. To install it, follow these steps:

1. Once more, double-click the SETUP.EXE program.

2. Select the same home directory once more and click OK.

3. In the Oracle Tools Installation Options dialog box, choose Oracle Report Developer and click OK.

4. In the next window, choose Custom Installation and click OK to proceed to the Software Asset Manager window.

5. Expand the Oracle Reports node and select Reports Builder. Then click Install to start the installation.

6. If you are prompted to stop the Oracle Reports Service, choose Start | Settings | Control Panel, and double-click Administrative Tools and then Services. Scroll down and select the Oracle Reports Server, and choose Action | Stop or click the Stop button.

7. After a few minutes, a message informs you that installation is complete. Click OK to return to the Software Asset Manager, and then close the Installer.

NOTE
It's OK if you see a Windows error when exiting the Oracle Installer.

After installing Oracle Developer, it is a good idea to restart your computer.

If Something Goes Wrong

There can be many reasons why things don't work the way they're supposed to. An experienced DBA or developer might be able to fix the problem; but on a development machine, it is often possible (and simpler) to reinstall all the Oracle software.

You do have a backup of all your source code files and the database, don't you?

Clean Machine

Until recently, the act of cleaning out all Oracle software from a machine was something of a secret—you had to rely on messages in newsgroups or wait in line for Oracle support to get some help.

Fortunately, Oracle realized that things will indeed occasionally go wrong, so they now provide official instructions on how to clean out all Oracle software from a Windows machine. These instructions are in the Windows database installation guide in Chapter 8, in the section "Manually Removing All Oracle Components and Services from Your Computer."

Disk Images

Another useful trick is to create disk images of your system right after installing, while everything is still running smoothly. You need some third-party software for this—see Chapter 11.

If you have a problem, you can simply restore your system disk (C) and the disk that you installed your Oracle software on (for example, O). After reading the images back, everything should be working like it was at the time you created the image.

NOTE
The database will also be the empty startup database—you'll need to read in an export of the database.

Summary

This chapter has taken you step by step through installing all the software you need to try out the five different approaches to Web applications covered in this book: Java servlets, hand-built PL/SQL, Oracle Designer, Oracle Portal, and Oracle Developer.

You learned how to install a database with only the necessary features, how to install the right edition of the application server, and how to install the appropriate development tools.

Part II will show you how to build Oracle Web applications with all five approaches: Chapter 5 introduces HTML-based applications, Chapter 6 covers Java servlets, and Chapter 7 explains hand-built PL/SQL Web applications. Chapter 8 describes how to use Oracle Designer to build Web applications, and Chapter 9 shows how to use Oracle Portal. Finally, Chapter 10 shows how to develop applications with Oracle Developer (Forms and Reports) and to deploy them to the Web.

PART
II

Building Web
Applications

CHAPTER
5

Designing an
HTML Application

epending on the type of Web applications you have chosen, you have more or less freedom in the design of your application (see Figure 5-1). If you have chosen Java applet applications, you are free to control every aspect of the application. Building applets from the bottom up is an advanced topic that is outside the scope of this book; but building applet-based applications by deploying Oracle Forms to the Web is covered in Chapter 10.

If you have chosen to generate your application, you must respect the limitations that the generation tool sets. Oracle Portal is fast and easy to learn but has rather limited capabilities (see Chapter 9). Oracle Designer is powerful and flexible but is quite a bit more challenging to get started with (see Chapter 8).

Finally, if you have chosen hand-built HTML-based Web applications, you have much freedom, but remain subject to the limitations inherent in the Web standards (HTTP, HTML, and so on). This chapter describes an efficient process for developing all kinds of hand-built HTML-based Web applications (whether based on Java, PL/SQL, or any other programming language) and serves as an introduction to the following two chapters:

■ Chapter 6 will provide you with all the details you need in order to build HTML-based Web applications using Java servlets.

■ Chapter 7 will provide you with the knowledge you need to build HTML-based Web applications using PL/SQL stored procedures.

Overview

Say you want to open a restaurant. You start out small with a little diner: people come up to the counter and order food, you go prepare it and bring it back, and the customer pays.

Business is good; you can hire an assistant. But since both of you can handle each complete transaction yourself (receive orders, prepare food, bring food, and receive payment), you don't need any coordination mechanism between you.

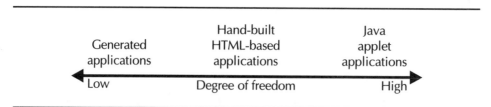

FIGURE 5-1.   *Degrees of freedom in Web applications*

Now you want to increase customer loyalty by offering free coffee to customers who bought a meal. But you need to distinguish between the customers who just bought a bagel (and won't get free coffee) and those who bought a meal. Since it might be your assistant bringing the food and you bringing the coffee, you agree to place a cookie on the counter in front of a customer to indicate that the person gets free coffee. This will work unless the customer eats the cookie . . .

Your customers are happy, so you decide to start offering a menu of the day: a starter, a main course, and coffee. Simply placing a cookie in front of the customer is not going to be enough anymore: there must be a continual flow of information between the customer and your employees to allow them to serve the right thing at the right time. You decide on the following work process for all your employees:

1. When a customer signals, go to her. If she has no order slip in front of her, write the order down on a new order slip. If the customer has an order slip, take it. Go back to the kitchen.

2. In the kitchen, read the order slip to determine what the next course is for that customer. Read the menu of the day to determine which course will follow the current one; write the next course on the order slip. Go back to the customer with the food and the updated order slip.

This is the way Web applications work:

- A number of requests arrive anonymously at the server.

- The server executes instructions and delivers the requested page.

- Information about what comes next can be included with each page.

This type of application is somewhat different from a traditional client/server application in which you have the same waiter guide you through the whole meal. Web applications thus need more careful planning of the communication process between client and server. To ensure this, the following four-step approach is recommended:

1. Application design

2. Page design

3. Conversion

4. Business logic

Application Design

Because HTML-based Web applications use the HTTP protocol, they suffer from some limitations inherent in HTTP. Remember, the World Wide Web was originally built to distribute research papers. Well, to deliver a research paper, the system really did not need to know exactly who asked for it. Any concept of a "session" and a user "logging on" was unnecessary overhead.

Of course, if you have visited a modern Internet site like Amazon or E*Trade, you have noticed that with a bit of thought it is indeed possible to establish sessions with logins just as in traditional client/server applications. The limitations of HTTP simply mean that a bit more thought is needed in the application design.

The Flow of a Web Application

A Web application always alternates between two states:

- User has a Web page to work on.

- User is waiting for the next page while the server works.

The Web server will be idle (or serving another user) while the user is reading or manipulating data in his browser, or it will be working on producing the next page for the user. When the user has finished with a page, he will click a button or a hyperlink to invoke the next program module that will process the information entered and generate the next screen.

This means that before and after every Web screen displayed to the user, some of your application code will run to

- Process the data received from the previous Web page.

- Produce the next Web page.

This means that each code module in the application is connected to the preceding and following module via a Web screen that the user sees (see Figure 5-2).

If the application will allow the user to enter the name of an employee, you might want to use the following code to produce the Web page:

```
// Java servlet to display form for entering a new employee
import javax.servlet.*;
import javax.servlet.http.*;
import java.io.*;
import java.util.*;
public class showNewEmp extends HttpServlet {
```

```
public void doGet(HttpServletRequest request,
    HttpServletResponse response)
    throws ServletException, IOException {
  response.setContentType("text/html");
  PrintWriter out = new PrintWriter (response.getOutputStream());
  out.println("<html>");
  out.println("<head><title>Enter new employee</title></head>");
  out.println("<body>");
  out.println("<form method=\"get\" action=\"processNewEmp\">");
  out.println("<p>Name: <input type=\"text\" name=\"empname\"></p>");
  out.println("<p><input type=\"submit\" value=\"Create\"></p>");
  out.println("</form>");
  out.println("</body></html>");
  out.close();
  }
}
```

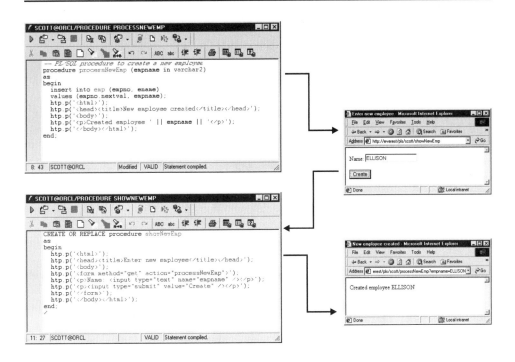

FIGURE 5-2. *The flow between code and Web screens*

or in PL/SQL:

```
-- PL/SQL procedure to display form for entering a new employee
procedure showNewEmp
as
begin
  htp.p('<html>');
  htp.p('<head><title>Enter new employee</title></head>');
  htp.p('<body>');
  htp.p('<form method="get" action="processNewEmp">');
  htp.p('<p>Name: <input type="text" name="empname" /></p>');
  htp.p('<p><input type="submit" value="Create" /></p>');
  htp.p('</form>');
  htp.p('</body></html>');
end;
```

This will generate the following HTML:

```
<html>
<head><title>Enter new employee</title></head>
<body>
<form method="get" action="processNewEmp">
<p>Name: <input type="text" name="empname" /></p>
<p><input type="submit" value="Create" /></p>
</form>
</body></html>
```

and it looks like this on the screen:

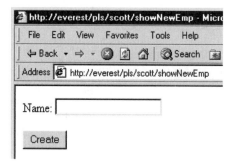

There are four important elements of this code to take note of:

- The **action** attribute of the <form> tag defines *where* to send the data entered or changed in the Web page. In the example, the data will be sent to the processNewEmp module.

- The **method** attribute of the <form> tag defines *how* to send the data. In the example, use the get method, which is explained in the following section.

- The **name** attribute of the <input > tag defines the name of the parameter that the input tag represents. The data entered in the field is associated with this parameter name when it is passed to the following module (defined by the **action** attribute just described). In the example, the module processNewEmp must be prepared to receive a parameter named **empname**.

- The Submit button is where the user must click to actually send the content of the input field to the destination specified by the **action** attribute.

The Action Attribute

The **action** attribute defines the URL or Web address of the procedure that must process the data entered on the page. You can give a full Web address (starting with http://), an absolute address (starting with /), or a relative address (all others).

A Full Address   A full address such as **http://server2.anothercompany.com/ app5/plsql/processNewEmp** allows you to send the data to any Web server accessible to the user.

An Absolute Address   An absolute address is used to send data from one application to another on the same server. The browser will automatically prefix the address you give with the server name; so if a module has the URL **http:// server1.company.com/app1/servlet/showNewEmp** and the <form> tag has a method of **/app2/cgi-bin/processNewEmp**, the browser will send the data to the procedure with the URL **http://server1.company.com/app2/cgi-bin/ processNewEmp**.

A Relative Address   A relative address such as **processNewEmp** is most frequently used. Here, the browser will automatically prefix the address with all the information from the current URL. For example, if the preceding example had the full URL **http://server1.company.com/app1/servlet/showNewEmp**, the browser would translate a relative address of **processNewEmp** to **http:// server1.company.com/app1/servlet/processNewEmp**.

NOTE
Nobody dictates that all parts of your application must be in the same programming language. The parameter passing is defined in the HTTP standard, so you could use a Java servlet to create a Web page and let a PL/SQL stored procedure receive the data from it.

The Method Attribute

The **method** attribute specifies how the data will be transferred. The HTTP protocol defines two methods: get and post.

Get   This will transfer the data by placing the name/value pairs at the end of the URL in a special format:

1. Between the end of the real URL and the first parameter name is a question mark (?).

2. The name of the first parameter, an equal (=) sign, and the value of the first parameter follows.

3. If you are transferring more than one parameter pair, an ampersand (&) is placed before each following pair.

For example, if you want to transfer the value BLACK as parameter **empname** to the procedure processNewEmp, the end of your URL would look like this: processNewEmp?empname=BLACK. If you were then to pass an employee number of 1234 as parameter **empno**, the URL would end in processNewEmp?empname=BLACK&empno=1234.

This format can be good for debugging, but it should not be used in a real application running in production for several reasons:

- You are disclosing the inner working of your program (maybe even confidential data) in the URL.

- If the user bookmarks the page, the whole URL, including parameters, is stored. This means that the user might accidentally try to return to the middle of your application that was not designed to be an entry point.

- URLs cannot have an arbitrary length. Depending on your operating system, problems will occur somewhere between 200 and 1,000 characters.

While surfing the Internet, you will often see long, unintelligible URLs that indicate this type of parameter passing; however, for the reasons just stated, you should avoid creating them yourself.

Post   This will pass the data to the Web server on the standard input stream. The data is hidden and in principle not subject to any limitations. This is the normal way of passing parameters from one Web page to the next.

Parameter Names

All parameters defined in the form using <input> tags will be passed to the next module in the form of name/value pairs. You can pass any number of parameters to the next module of your Web application—each gets passed as a name/value pair.

NOTE
*In the example, the <input type="submit"> tag does not have a **name=** attribute, so it does not get passed to the next module. If you were to define a tag such as <input type="submit" name="submit_button" value="Create">, the name/value pair submit_button / Create would be passed to the next module in addition to any other <input> tags you define. This lets you use several Submit buttons on a form; the following module can determine which button the user clicked by examining the name/value pairs passed.*

It is up to the Web/application server to translate the parameters and make them available to the application, whether they are received through get or post.

■   In a Java servlet, the parameters are made available to the servlet through the getParameter() and getParameterValues() methods of the HttpServletRequest class. Java servlets are described in Chapter 6.

■   In a Web application that uses PL/SQL stored procedures, the parameters are passed as input parameters to call the following stored procedure. The parameter names must match the definition of the following procedure exactly. PL/SQL Web applications are described in Chapter 7.

The procedure processNewEmp that receives the parameter **empname** would look like this in Java:

```
import javax.servlet.*;
import javax.servlet.http.*;
import java.io.*;
import java.util.*;
public class processNewEmp extends HttpServlet {
  public void doGet (HttpServletRequest request,
      HttpServletResponse response)
      throws ServletException, IOException {
    response.setContentType("text/html");
    PrintWriter out = new PrintWriter (response.getOutputStream());
    String empName = new String(request.getParameter("empname"));
    out.println("<html>");
    out.println("<head><title>Enter new employee</title></head>");
    out.println("<body>");
    // insert statement not included in this example
    out.println("<h1>One row created with name " + empName + "</h1>");
    out.println("</body></html>");
    out.close();
  }
}
```

Notice the following places in the code:

■ The doGet() method means that this servlet will respond only to get requests.

■ The request.getParameter() line reading the **empname** parameter.

The parameter-passing mechanism in Java servlets is robust; it can gracefully handle missing or double parameters.

■ If a parameter is missing, the getParameter() method will simply return a null value.

■ If the same parameter name is submitted multiple times, the getParameter() method will take one of them (the Web server is free to choose any one).

■ If your application uses multiple parameters with the same value, you should instead use the method getParameterValues() that returns an array of String objects.

In PL/SQL, the parameters are passed in the procedure specification, so the same functionality would look like this in PL/SQL:

```
-- PL/SQL procedure to create a new employee
procedure processNewEmp (empname in varchar2)
as
begin
  insert into emp (empno, ename)
  values (empno.nextval, empname);
  htp.p('<html>');
  htp.p('<head><title>New employee created</title></head>');
  htp.p('<body>');
  htp.p('<p>Created employee ' || empname || '</p>');
  htp.p('</body></html>');
end;
```

Unfortunately, PL/SQL is rather picky about the parameter passing: Unless the parameter names exactly match the procedure specification, the Web server will not run your procedure and will instead display an error message. If, for instance, you mistakenly defined your processNewEmp procedure to take a parameter **ename** instead of **empname**, you would see an error screen like the one in Figure 5-3.

The first lines in this error message show

- The parameters passed that were not in the procedure definition (in this case, EMPNAME).

- The parameters in the procedure that did not have a default value and did not receive a value from the Web page (in this case, ENAME).

You should always define your parameters as **VARCHAR2** with **DEFAULT NULL** to avoid as many problems as possible:

- By defining parameters as **VARCHAR2** instead of **NUMBER** or **DATE**, you are sure that the parameter value is accepted by your procedure. If the parameter is really a number, you can convert it once your procedure has accepted it; this lets you handle any errors gracefully.

- By defining parameters as **DEFAULT NULL**, you make sure that your procedure starts even if one or more parameters are not supplied. Once your procedure runs, you can make decisions and show your own error messages if a mandatory parameter is missing.

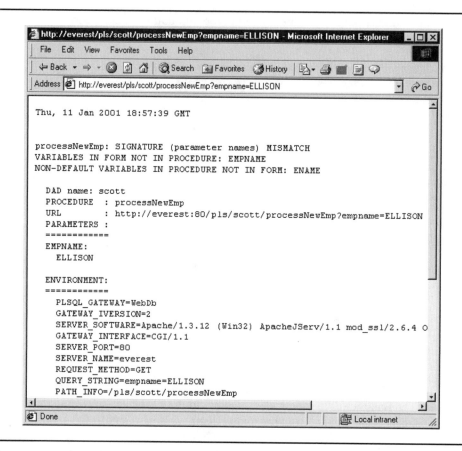

FIGURE 5-3. *Error message when PL/SQL parameters don't match*

Creating a Storyboard

When designing Web applications, you must carefully consider the screens you
want to show to the users as well as the navigation between them. Web designers
call this high-level view of your Web site or Web application a *storyboard* or a *site
map*. This section will show all the steps in building such a storyboard; for a simple
application that allows you to query, insert, update, and delete a single table, the
high-level storyboard could look like the one in Figure 5-4.

You can use this storyboard to discuss the workflow in the Web application with
your users and possibly with a user interface expert.

When your users have signed off on the high-level storyboard, you know which
screen you are going to need. With this knowledge, you can start building detailed
storyboards like the one in Figure 5-5 for each main part of your application.

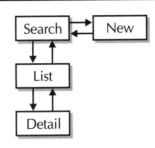

FIGURE 5-4. *A high-level storyboard*

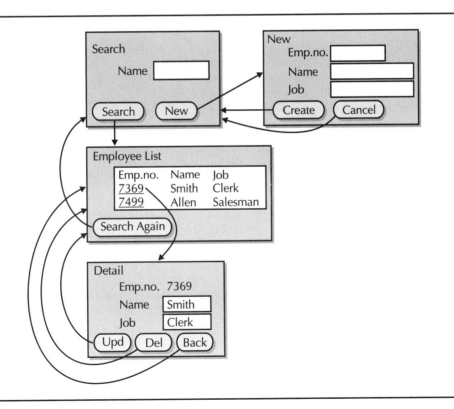

FIGURE 5-5. *A detailed storyboard*

The detailed storyboard must contain all the elements that the users can click to go to a different page. It is not important to show each and every data field—you just need enough to give an idea of the task performed on each page. However, all the buttons and hyperlinks must be included.

From each way out of a Web page, you draw an arrow to the screen that that button or hyperlink navigates to. The resulting web of arrows defines all possible flows through your application.

Application Flow Diagram

From the detailed storyboard, you know exactly which screens you need and how they are interconnected. The next step is now to document what information will flow between the screens and the program modules. This can be done with an application flow diagram, as shown in Figure 5-6.

In this diagram, program modules are shown as square boxes, and the Web pages displayed to the user are shown as parallelograms. Arrows show which modules generate which screens, as well as which screens can invoke which modules.

NOTE

Normally, a square box (a server-side code module) will always lead to a parallelogram (a screen), and a parallelogram will always lead to a square box. If your drawing shows something else, you should check it carefully to see if it might be an error.

Drawing an Application Flow Diagram

To draw an application flow diagram, draw a parallelogram for the first screen and give it a name (for instance, SearchEmp for the screen to search for employees). Then draw a square box for the procedure before the screen and an arrow leading from the procedure to the screen. This procedure has the task of producing the screen and will be called show*XXX* where *XXX* is the name of the screen it produces (for instance, showSearchEmp).

Now look at the detailed storyboard to find a screen following the screen you are working on. (In the example, both the NewEmp and the EmpList screen follow the SearchEmp screen.) Draw the next screen (for example, NewEmp) and the preceding module (for example, ShowNewEmp). Then add an arrow from the first screen to the show module for the following screen. (In the example, this arrow goes from the SearchEmp screen to the ShowNewEmp module).

Repeat this process until you have covered all screens and navigation on your storyboard. When you've finished, you will have an application flow diagram like the one in Figure 5-6.

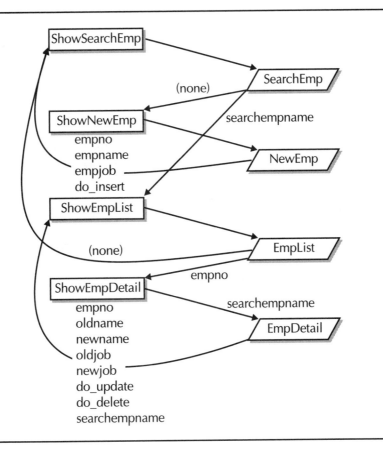

FIGURE 5-6. *An application flow diagram*

Adding Parameters

The next task is to write the parameters that get passed next to each arrow to document the parameter names your application will use.

Receiving Data from the Web Page   For a field where the user can enter or change a value, decide on a parameter name and write it on the line leading from the screen to the following module. For instance, the SearchEmp screen has a field to enter an employee name. This becomes the parameter **searchempname** on the arrow leading from the SearchEmp screen to the ShowEmpList module.

When a screen can call a module without passing any parameters, write **(none)** on the application flow diagram to show that you did consider the link.

For all arrows leading from hyperlinks, decide on a parameter to pass. Consider, for instance, the arrow from each line on the EmpList screen to the showEmpDetail: this link becomes the parameter **empno**.

Handling Updates   Because Web applications do not have sessions, they cannot lock records when a user starts an update. This makes them vulnerable to *lost update*, where one user's change overwrites another's.

This can be avoided by passing the old values as well as the new to the process module; the module can then check that the values in the database are unchanged and, if so, effect the update. If the values in the database are different from the old values passed in from the Web page, someone else has changed the record and the update must be refused.

In the example, this means that in addition to the **newname** and **newjob** parameters passed from the EmpDetail screen to the ShowEmpList module, you need to pass **empno** (to identify the record to update) as well as **oldname** and **oldjob**.

Using the Application Flow Diagram

When you have finished with your application flow diagram, you can see all the parameters that must be passed into every module of your application. You will use this information in two places:

- When designing your example pages, make sure that the **name** attribute of every screen element matches the name you have defined on the arrow leading from that screen to the corresponding process module.

- When creating the skeleton of your Web application, make sure that each module accepts the exact parameter names you have defined on the arrow leading into the module.

Building the Skeleton

Armed with the application flow diagram, you can build the skeleton of your application. If you want to build your application using Java servlets, you can use standard code templates or a JDeveloper wizard to define all servlets in the application, including the code to accept the parameters passed to each servlet. If you want to build the application with PL/SQL, you can write the package specifications for all screens with the correct procedure definitions matching the parameters passed to each procedure.

For example, you could use the following template for all your Java servlets:

```
package package1;

import javax.servlet.*;
import javax.servlet.http.*;
import java.io.*;
import java.util.*;

public class ServletTemplate extends HttpServlet {
  public void doGet (HttpServletRequest request,
    HttpServletResponse response)
    throws ServletException, IOException {
    doPost(request, response);
  }

  public void doPost(HttpServletRequest request,
      HttpServletResponse response)
      throws ServletException, IOException {
    String empName = request.getParameter("empname");
    response.setContentType("text/html");
    PrintWriter out = new PrintWriter (response.getOutputStream());
    out.println("Output from the Servlet template");
    out.println("<p>Parameter empname=" + empName + "</p>");
    out.close();
  }
}
```

You need to change this template in the following places:

■ In the first line, change package1 to the name of your package.

■ In the first line of the servlet definition itself, change ServletTemplate to the name of your servlet (remember that this name must match the filename exactly, including the use of upper- and lowercase).

■ The lines getting the parameters must be changed to read whatever parameters your application flow diagram specifies. For instance, the ShowSearchEmp servlet must take the three parameters **empno**, **empname**, and **empjob** coming from the NewEmp screen.

Note the whole doGet() method. This method does nothing but call doPost() so that your servlet will run whether you call it from the address line in the browser (with a get request) or from an HTML form on a preceding page (with a post request). Once your application is ready to go into production, you can remove unnecessary methods and leave in only those that your application design calls for.

If you intend to build your Web application with PL/SQL, you could use a template like this:

```
create or replace package package1
as
  procedure templateProcedure(empName in varchar2);
end package1;
/
create or replace package body package1
as
  procedure templateProcedure(empName in varchar2)
  is
  begin
    htp.p('Output from the PL/SQL Web template');
    htp.p('<p>Parameter empname=' || empName || '</p>');
  end;
end package1;
/
```

You need to change this template in the following places:

■ Change package1 to the package name you want to use.

■ Change templateProcedure to the name of your procedure.

■ Change the procedure head to accept the exact parameters your application flow diagram specifies. For instance, the ShowSearchEmp procedure must have the three input parameters **empno**, **empname**, and **empjob** coming from the NewEmp screen.

In a PL/SQL Web application, you do not need to distinguish between post and get requests—both are automatically handled by the Oracle Web server.

NOTE
Java is case sensitive, while PL/SQL is not. For easier comparison between the PL/SQL and Java examples in this book, upper/lowercase notation is also used for PL/SQL.

Page Design

When you have finished with the application design, it's time to start with the detailed design of the Web pages. You should start by creating examples of all the pages that your storyboard shows, using sample data. At this point, the issue is primarily the layout, not the data that form the content of the pages.

You need to design HTML pages whether you are developing Java servlets, PL/SQL stored procedures, or Server Pages.

An HTML Crash Course

If you are going to hand-build an HTML-based Web application, you need to know a little bit of HTML. This section will provide you with enough knowledge to get you started, but remember that Web design is an art form in itself. After reading this book, you will be able to produce simple Web pages for internal use, but public Web applications intended for the Internet are often developed by professional graphic artists and coded in HTML by expert HTML programmers.

Chapter 13 contains some pointers to books and Web sites that can help you further if you are interested in HTML programming.

Flavors of HTML

Like most other Web-related standards, HTML has undergone a dramatic evolution. The latest version of the HTML standard is XHTML version 1, which was published in December 2000. This is really a reformulation of HTML 4 in XML, a cleaner specification that weeds out some of the unclear and browser-specific practices that have become common in HTML pages.

With a bit of care, it is possible to write XHTML that displays correctly in browsers that support HTML 4, including Internet Explorer 4 and Netscape Navigator 4; one of these two browsers (version 4 and later) is used by approximately 99 percent of all Web users.

All the examples in this book are compatible with XHTML—that is, they are written in valid XHTML, but they will display correctly in fourth-generation browsers. I encourage you to use this approach to get the best of two worlds: well-formed Web pages that can easily be rendered on next-generation Web browsers, but at the same time display correctly in the common browsers today. Chapter 13 lists the Web address of some guidelines for producing compatible XHTML.

What Is an HTML page?

An HTML page is a normal text file. It usually contains only ASCII characters and has the extension .htm or .html to allow Web servers and browsers to recognize it.

NOTE
*What if you want to use non-ASCII characters like
ä or å? Don't worry—the HTML standard provides
for special characters through the concept of
entities. These start with & (an ampersand) and end
with ; (a semicolon) with the middle part normally
being some kind of mnemonic abbreviation or a
decimal number. For instance, ä or ä
means "the letter a with an umlaut" (the two dots
that appear over certain vowels in some languages).
Many Web sites (refer to Chapter 13) include a
complete table of non-ASCII characters, and most
HTML editors can automatically replace non-ASCII
characters with the corresponding HTML entity.*

The page consists of *tags* and content. Tags always start with a < character
and end with a >character. Everything between these two characters is part of the
tag; everything outside is the content of the page. All tags are shown in bold; the
rest is content. The screen shown in Figure 5-7 was produced from the following
XHTML code:

```
<?xml version="1.0" encoding="UTF-8"?>
<!DOCTYPE html
    PUBLIC "-//W3C//DTD XHTML 1.0 Transitional//EN"
    "DTD/xhtml1-transitional.dtd">
<html xmlns="http://www.w3.org/1999/xhtml" xml:lang="en" lang="en">
<head>
<title>Welcome</title>
</head>
<body>
<h1>Welcome</h1>
<p>This is a sample page</p>
<p>The time is: <br /> 2:32:14 p.m.</p>
</body>
</html>
```

The XHTML Header   This consists of the <?xml> tag (XML declaration), the
<!DOCTYPE> tag (specifies document type definition), and the <html> tag (starts
the page and indicates the XML namespace). These lines are required at the top of
every page to make it a strictly conforming XHTML document (if your document
is not in English, you should replace the EN codes in the preceding code with the
corresponding two-letter ISO code for your language. For brevity, the remaining
examples in this book do not show this header (just the <html> tag).

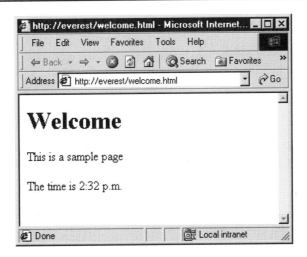

FIGURE 5-7. *An example HTML page*

Tags   Notice that some tags have a slash after the leading <. The version without the slash is the *start tag*, and the version with the slash is the *end tag*. For example, the <h1> tag starts a level-one heading and the </h1> ends it.

Tags can be nested within one another, to produce bold and italic text, for example:

```
<b><i>This is bold and italic</i></b>
```

Letting the tags overlap is not valid XHTML—in the preceding example, the <b> tag comes before the <i> tag, so it is the "outer" start tag. Correspondingly, the </b> tag should come after the </i> tag. Most browsers are able to display the text correctly even if you overlap the tags, but that is no reason not to write proper XHTML.

A few tags (like the <br/> tag that indicates a line break) are *empty elements*— they do not have an end tag.

So, what if you want to display a < character in your content? Not a problem— there are entities for these as well. For instance, < means *less than* (<). Table 5-1 lists a few examples, and you can find more on the Web (refer to Chapter 13 for a URL) or in any book on HTML design.

File Types   When you have an HTML file on your disk with the extension .htm or .html, you can double-click it to open it in the Web browser. Based on the extension, Windows recognizes it as an HTML file.

Entity	Numeric Code	Displays As
"	"	"
&	&	&
<	<	<
>	>	>
		(space)
©	©	©
®	®	®

TABLE 5-1. *Some Useful Entities*

When a Web browser requests a file from a Web server using the HTTP protocol, the Web server will look at the file extension and send the browser information about the file type in the HTTP header that precedes the page. The file type (also known as the Multipurpose Internet Mail Extension or *MIME* type) will usually be text/html; the browser recognizes that this is a file type that it can display and displays the file in the browser window. But many other file types are possible; a few examples are listed in Table 5-2.

When a Web page is delivered by a program running on the Web/application server, the program can set the MIME type. This can be used, for example, to tell the browser that the page is in Microsoft Excel format. When the browser receives information that the file is in Excel format, it will check the browser configuration

MIME Type	Description
text/html	Normal HTML Web page
text/plain	Text file
application/vnd.ms-excel	Microsoft Excel file
application/vnd.ms-word	Microsoft Word file

TABLE 5-2. *Some Common MIME Types*

information to see if it has a plug-in or a helper program registered to handle the Excel MIME type. If it does, it will automatically open Excel and place the page content in the Excel worksheet.

NOTE
If you have Microsoft Internet Explorer and Excel installed on a PC, this configuration should happen automatically. In Netscape, you might have to associate the Excel MIME type with the Excel program yourself.

If the browser has no plug-in or helper program available, it will normally display a dialog box asking what you want to do with the file.

The complete list of MIME types is very long—you'll find the URL of the complete list in Chapter 13.

Structure of an HTML page

An HTML page must begin with an <html> tag and end with the corresponding </html> end tag. Between these tags, the page consists of a *head* followed by a *body*.

The Head   This part starts with a <head> tag immediately following the <html> tag. This part of the HTML file defines all the elements of a page that do not get shown in the work area of the browser, such as the title of the page (displayed in the browser title bar) and instructions describing the content of the page (for instance, search words to help Web search engines find relevant pages). The head ends with a </head> tag.

The Body   This part starts with a <body> tag immediately after the </head> tag. Following the <body> comes everything that will be displayed in the browser window, and the content ends with a </body> tag just before the </html> tag that ends the whole page.

The Standard Tags

The HTML standard contains many tags, but with just a few standard tags you can create the basics, as shown in Figure 5-8.

Headings   These are marked with tags <h1> through <h6>, with <h1> being the highest level. The heading tags only indicate the structure of the document and do not specify the font—that is for the browser to decide. Most Web applications use only levels 1, 2, and maybe 3.

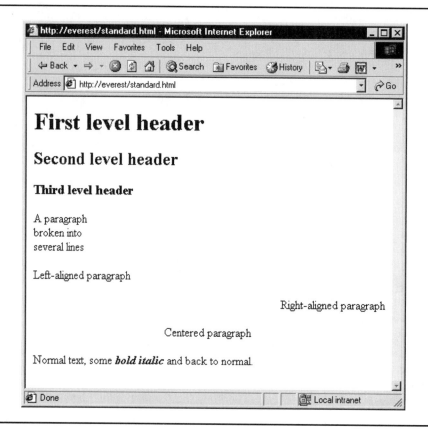

FIGURE 5-8. *A Web page using the standard tags*

Paragraphs These are enclosed between a <p> and a </p> tag. The browser will normally place a blank line between paragraphs (you can achieve a different spacing using Cascading Style Sheets).

Paragraphs can be aligned left (the default), centered, or aligned right. This is achieved by placing an **align** attribute in the tag, like this:

```
<p align="left">Left-aligned paragraph</p>
<p align="right">Right-aligned paragraph</p>
<p align="center">Centered paragraph</p>
```

Line Breaks These are indicated with a <br /> tag. This tag makes the browser end the current line and start a new line without adding a blank line.

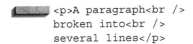

```
<p>A paragraph<br />
broken into<br />
several lines</p>
```

NOTE
*The space before the slash is not strictly required
by XHTML, but it ensures that the tag is correctly
understood by today's browsers.*

Bold and Italics   You can specify this with the <b> and <i> tags, respectively. If
you want both bold and italic, remember that you should nest one tag within the
other, that is, if the bold start tag (<b>) appears before the italic start tag (<i>), the
bold end tag (</b>) should appear after the italic end tag (</i>), like this:

```
Normal text, some <b><i>bold italic</i></b> and back to normal.
```

Hyperlinks   These are created using the <a> tag. This tag has the form

<a href="*url*">*link text*</a>

where *url* is the destination of the link and *link text* is the text displayed for the user
to click. Note that these two elements are completely separate—hard-to-find errors
can occur when you cut and paste links and forget to change either the url or the
link text. Also take care to remember the </a> tag at the end; if you forget it, all text
until the next </a> tag will be considered link text by the browser.

The <a> tag can also be used to set bookmarks (called *anchors* in HTML) in the
text in this way:

<a id="anchor name" name="anchor name">

where the *anchor name* is the name of the anchor.

NOTE
*The id attribute is the real XHTML anchor **name**
attribute, but to ensure that your code works in older
browsers as well, you can place a **name** attribute in
the tag as well.*

To refer to such a bookmark, you use an <a href="*page#anchor name*"> tag (see
Table 5-3). Note that you can leave out the *page* if you want to link to another place
on the same page. You should not use a # character in name of the anchor—this

Link	Function
<a href="*page*">	Jump to top of page
<a href="#*anchor*">	Jump to anchor on current page
<a href="page#*anchor*">	Jump to anchor on the specified page

TABLE 5-3. *Hyperlinks*

character only serves to separate the page name from the anchor name when *referring* to an anchor.

Named anchors can be used for instance to create a table of contents, as seen in Figure 5-9, which contains the following HTML code:

```
<html>
<body>
<a id="top" name="top"><h1>Information Sources</h1></a>
<p>There are many sources for information about
Oracle Web applications </p>
<ul>
<li><a href="#oracle">Oracle</a></li>
<li><a href="#iouga">IOUG-A</a></li>
</ul>

<a id="oracle" name="oracle"><h2>Oracle</h2></a>
<p>The <a href="http://www.oracle.com">main site</a>
contains mostly marketing information while the
technical stuff is found on
<a href="http://technet.oracle.com">Oracle
Technology Network</a></p>
<p><a href="#top">Back to top</a></p>

<a id="iouga" name="iouga"><h2>International Oracle
User's Group - Americas</h2></a>
<p>The <a href="http://www.ioug.org">IOUG-A</a>
is a well-run user group.</p>
<p><a href="#top">Back to top</a></p>
</body>
</html>
```

If you click the Oracle hyperlink at the top, the page will scroll to the Oracle heading (if it is not already visible), and clicking the IOUG-A hyperlink similarly

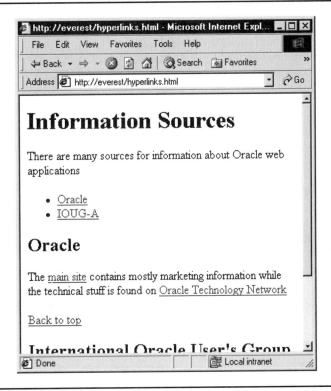

FIGURE 5-9. *Examples of hyperlinks*

scrolls to the International Oracle User's Group—Americas heading. Both of the
Back to Top links will cause the browser to scroll back to the top of the page.

NOTE
*If the destination of the link is already visible in the
browser window, nothing will happen.*

Images   These are included in a Web page using the <img> tag like this:

<img src="*image url*" **alt=**"*description*">

where the *image url* is the complete Web address of the image file and *description* is a textual description of the image. The browser will first load the HTML file and then start to download all the images one by one.

The **alt** attribute was optional in HTML, but is mandatory in XHTML. It is useful for users who for some reason cannot or will not view the images:

- Users on slow links might turn images off to make the page load faster.

- Users on ultra-light devices like smart phones or PDAs might choose not to display the images to conserve screen space.

- Visually impaired users might use screen reader technologies to have the page read out to them.

In addition, many browsers will show this as a tooltip-style pop-up when you point to the image.

All browsers support the GIF and JPEG formats (.gif and .jpg file extensions), so you are advised to use only these for the time being.

- JPEG files are appropriate for medium and large photos because they can have as many colors as you like. They are compressed using *lossy* compression—this means that they will lose details as you increase the compression. But because you can choose the compression yourself with an image-editing program, you can find the right trade-off between image file size and image quality.

- GIF files are appropriate for everything else (including small photos like the "mug shots" used on many intranets). GIF images can only have 256 colors and are automatically compressed. It is possible for your image-editing program to choose a separate palette of 256 colors for each image; but, because your users might have their computer screens set to only 256 colors in total, you should use a standard palette for all images. Many image-editing programs call this standard palette the *browser safe* colors.

The <img> tag has a number of additional attributes that you should always use:

<img alt = "*description*" src = "url" border = "0" width = "w" height = "h">

The **border** attribute removes the invisible border that normally surrounds an image. If you don't remove this border by setting it to 0, a blue border will surround all images that you place inside hyperlinks.

The **width** and **height** attributes tell the browser how many pixels the image will occupy once it is loaded. You should always provide this information so that the browser can place the text correctly right away. If you do not provide this information, the browser must reformat the page every time an image finishes loading, which makes the text jump.

Creating images for Web use is a science of its own—refer to Chapter 11 for an image-editing tool and to Chapter 13 for some references.

Lists   The HTML standard supports both ordered lists and unordered lists.

- Unordered lists start with a <ul> tag and end with a </ul> tag and are normally shown as bulleted lists.

- Ordered lists start with an <ol> tag and end with an </ol> tag and are normally shown numbered (1, 2, 3 . . .). However, it is up to the browser to decide exactly how to display a numbered list as long as the sequence of the items is clear.

Within the <ol> or <ul> tags, each list item starts with an <li> tag and ends with an </li> tag. The preceding hyperlink example used an unordered list to create the bullets you saw in Figure 5-9.

Controlling Appearance

The first versions of the HTML standard were only concerned with indicating the structure of the content—it was supposed to be up to the browser to decide on the exact screen appearance based on the available screen area and the fonts available on the computer where the browser is running.

Fonts   Web page authors were not really happy with this lack of control, so version 3 of the HTML format (supported from third-generation browsers) supported a <font> tag that allowed the Web designer to specify the font details. Because each client computer might have different fonts installed, the <font> tag allows the Web developer to specify a list of fonts that the browser should use.

Using the <font> tag makes it possible to create screens like this:

Unfortunately, littering the HTML code with specific <font> tags can make the page quite a bit heavier as the code for the preceding example shows:

```
<html>
<body>
<p><font face="Verdana, Arial, Helvetica, sans-serif" size="5"><b>
Welcome to this page</b></font></p>
<p><font face="Arial, Helvetica, sans-serif">We would like to control the
<font face="Courier New, Courier, mono">fonts</font>
   carefully here</font></p>
<p><font face="Arial, Helvetica, sans-serif" size="-1">Even though the
result isn't very <font size="4">pretty</font>.</font></p>
</body>
</html>
```

In addition, users who do not have any of the fonts listed in the <font> tag available will see a default font.

Generally, you should avoid using <font> tags and instead control the appearance of your Web page with style sheets as described in the following.

Style Sheets   If your users belong to the 99 percent of the Web users who have fourth-generation browsers or above, a better option than individual <font> tags is available: Cascading Style Sheets (CSS).

A style sheet is a text file (either included directly in the HTML page or referenced) that defines a number of *styles*. These can either redefine standard tags like <h1> or they can be custom styles that the HTML file must explicitly refer to. Complex style sheets are tedious to write by hand, so it is a good idea to use some kind of tool (for example, TopStyle from Bradbury—see Chapter 11 for more information).

Figure 5-10 shows the same page with and without using the following style sheet.

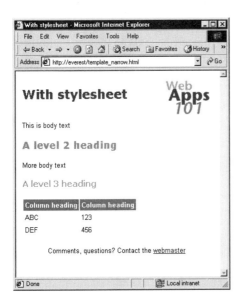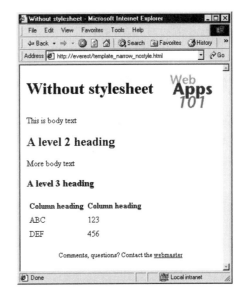

FIGURE 5-10. *An example page with and without using a style sheet*

```
h1 {
     font-family: Verdana, Arial, Helvetica, sans-serif;
     font-size: 18pt;
     font-weight: bold;
     color: #990033
}
h2 {
     font-family: Verdana, Geneva, Arial, Helvetica, sans-serif;
     font-size: 14pt;
     font-weight: bold;
     color: #FF6633
}
h3 {
     font-family: Verdana, Geneva, Arial, Helvetica, sans-serif;
     font-size: 12pt;
     font-weight: bold;
     color: #cc9900
}
body, td {
     font-family: Arial, Helvetica, sans-serif;
     font-size: 10pt;
```

```
}
a  {
      font-family: Arial, Helvetica, sans-serif;
      color: blue
}
a:hover {
      text-decoration: underline;
      color: Red;
}
th {
      font-family: Arial, Helvetica, sans-serif;
      background-color: #FF3333;
      color: White;
      font-size: 10pt;
      font-weight: bold;
      text-align: left
}
```

A Web page can include style information like this between <style> and </style> tags in the header (that is, between the <head> and </head> tags), or it can contain a style inclusion tag like this:

```
<link rel="stylesheet" href="/webstart.css" type="text/css">
```

This type of reference instructs the Web browser that the appearance of the page is controlled by the style sheet indicated by the **href** attribute. This attribute can point to any URL—even a style sheet on a completely different server. In the preceding example, the browser will look for a style sheet called webstart.css in the root directory on the Web server.

Using Cascading Style Sheets makes it easy to control the appearance of a whole Web site with just one style sheet—you can simply include a line like this one in the header of every Web page. Any change to the CSS file will automatically be reflected in all pages of the whole site.

Tables

HTML's roots as a markup language are clear in the lack of formatting tags; there are tags to identify the structure of the document, but not the layout. But fortunately, the HTML standard provides for *tables* that can be used to achieve many formatting tasks.

A simple table looks like this:

```
<table border=1>
   <tr>
     <th>Name</th>
     <th>Job</th>
   </tr>
```

```
<tr>
  <td>SCOTT</td>
  <td>ANALYST</td>
</tr>
<tr>
  <td>KING</td>
  <td>PRESIDENT</td>
</tr>
</table>
```

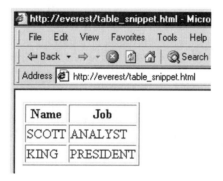

The <table> Tag   This starts a table, and the </table> tags ends it. Tables can be nested within one another, but don't go overboard with this feature: HTML code with nested tables is hard to read and takes longer for the browser to display on the screen.

The <table> tag can contain a **border** attribute that specifies the border in pixels—use border=0 to create an invisible table for controlling the layout.

NOTE
Keep the border displayed while you work on your Web page, and set the border width to zero once everything looks right.

The <tr> Tag   This starts a table row; the </tr> tags ends it.

The <th> and <td> Tags   These start a table header cell (normally displayed in bold font) and a normal table cell, respectively. Both end with a corresponding </th> or </td> tag.

Empty Cells   If your table has a border and contains empty cells, place a   (nonbreaking space) entity in these cells. This will ensure that they display properly—otherwise, the cell will "collapse" and have a width of zero, making your table look strange.

HTML Forms

Delivering Web pages showing data already in the database is only half the story—you also need to allow the users to send information back. For this purpose, HTML offers the concept of *HTML Forms.*

An HTML Form is a part of a Web page between a <form> and a </form> tag. A Web page can contain a form but does not have to. A page can contain many HTML Forms if it makes sense for your application.

In HTML Forms (that is, between the start tag and end tag), you can place a number of form elements defined in the HTML standard. Most (but not all) of these are variations on the <input> tag with different values for the **type** attribute.

The good news is that all commonly used browsers understand all the form elements; the bad news is that you have only this rather limited set of user interface elements available. To create all possible form elements, as shown in Figure 5-11, you could use the following HTML code:

```
<form method="post" action="some_procedure">
<p>User name:
<input type="text" name="username" value="SCOTT" /></p>
<p>Password:
<input type="password" name="passwd" maxlength="8" size="10" /></p>
<p>Message:<br />
<textarea name="msg" cols="40" rows="5">You can type
some text here</textarea></p>
<p>Sex:
<input type="radio" name="sex" value="1" checked="checked" />Female
<input type="radio" name="sex" value="2" />Male</p>
<p>Skills:
<input type="checkbox" name="plsql" checked="checked" />PL/SQL
<input type="checkbox" name="java" value="java" />Java
<input type="checkbox" name="vb" />Visual Basic </p>
<p>Job:
<select name="job">
  <option value="dba" />DBA
  <option value="dev" selected="selected" />Developer
  <option value="arch" />Architect
  <option value="pm" />Project Manager
</select></p>
<p>Databases:<br />
<select name="db_vers" size="4" multiple>
  <option />6 and earlier
  <option selected="selected" />7.x
```

```
  <option selected="selected" />8.0
  <option />8i
  <option />9i
</select></p>
<p>
<input type="submit" name="do_it" value="Do something" />
<input type="button" value="Do something else"
    onClick="alert('hello')" />
<input type="reset" /></p>
</form>
```

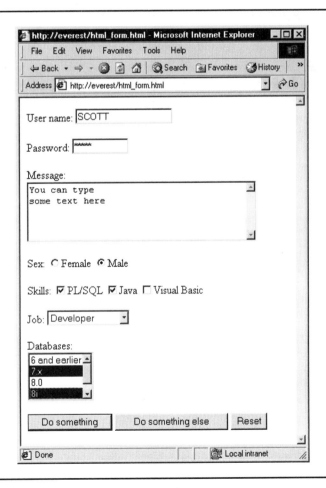

FIGURE 5-11. *All possible HTML Form elements*

The <form> Tag   This was described in the preceding section. It has an **action** attribute that specifies the procedure that is to receive *all* the data on this form when the user submits the form, and a **method** attribute that specifies how the data is transmitted. Each HTML Form can only send data to one destination.

NOTE
While debugging, it can be informative to set all your HTML Forms to transfer their data using the get method: this causes all the parameter names and values to show up in the browser location field. In production applications, you should almost always use post.

One-Line Text Entry Fields   These exist both as normal type **text** and in a variation of type **password** that displays only asterisks (***) when the user enters text. Both should have a **name** attribute to identify the value when passing it on to the next procedure and can have a value that serves as the default value when the form is displayed.

You can add the **maxlength** attribute to limit the number of characters that can be entered in the field and the **size** attribute to control the size of the field as shown on the screen.

NOTE
In HTML 4, numeric attribute values can be written without the quotes, but XHTML requires quotes.

Multiline Text Entry Field   These are created with the <textarea> tag. Like most other tags, this should have a name and can have **cols** and **rows** attributes to indicate the size of the field. Text areas can have scroll bars and do not have a maximum number of characters.

While the <input> fields are empty elements that end immediately with />, the <textarea> tag has a real closing tag: all the text between the starting and ending tag is used as default value for the text. This includes spaces and line breaks—note the line breaks after the word *type* in the example because the HTML code contains a line break here.

NOTE
Be aware that the user can press the ENTER key while typing text in the box. This causes a line break on the screen that the user sees; however, different browsers handle this line break differently. Some browsers will ignore the line break, some will send an ASCII character 10 (a line feed), some will send an ASCII 10 and a 13 (line feed and carriage return), and so on. Make sure that your program checks for ASCII 10 and 13 in the text and handles them consistently.

Radio Buttons   These have type **radio** and are used to select among mutually exclusive options. All the radio buttons that have the same **name** attribute belong together in a group; whenever the user selects one radio button in a group, all other radio buttons in the group are automatically deselected.

You can specify which radio button in the group is initially chosen by adding the **checked="checked"** attribute to that button.

NOTE
*HTML 4 allows you to minimize attributes (for example, entering **checked** to indicate that a radio button is selected). This is not supported by XHTML; you should therefore use the **checked="checked"** form just shown. This works correctly in all HTML 4–compliant browsers.*

The information sent to the processing program from a radio button group is always a single name/value pair. The parameter name comes from the **name** attribute and the parameter value comes from the **value** attribute of the selected radio button.

A page can contain several radio button groups—just ensure that each group has a separate name.

Check Boxes   These have type **checkbox**. A check box must have a **name** and can have a **value**. If the check box is not selected when the form is submitted, no value is passed. If the check box is selected, the corresponding **value** will be passed or, if no **value** is defined, the default value is "on." You can specify that a check box is initially checked by adding the **checked="checked"** attribute to the check box.

Select Lists   These start with a <select> tag, contain one or more options between <option> and </option> tags, and end with a </select> tag. The basic form of the select tag has just a **name** and is shown as a drop-down list where the user can choose one value. If the corresponding <option> tag contains a **value**, this value is passed with the name from the <select> tag; if no value is specified, the content (displayed value) of the option is passed.

You can add the attribute **size** to make the select list expand to a list box showing multiple values. If you also add the attribute **multiple** to the <select> tag, the user is allowed to select several values. In this case, all values are passed with the same **name** (from the <select> tag), so the receiving module must be able to handle multiple values.

By adding the attribute **selected="selected"** to an option, you can make that option a default value, that is, the option will already be selected when the page loads.

Submit, Reset, and Other Buttons   The **submit** type is used to create a button that submits the HTML Form, that is, sends all parameter name/value pairs to the module specified in the **action** attribute of the <form> tag. You can provide a **value** that is displayed as the button label. For this tag, the **name** attribute is optional. If you provide a name like in the preceding example, a parameter with the name do_it and the value "Do something" will be passed to the following code module. As you will see in the examples in Chapters 6 and 7, you can use several Submit buttons with different names if you want the following code to take some action based on which button the user clickes.

The **button** type doesn't do anything by itself—it does not submit the HTML Form. To make a button do anything, you need to add some JavaScript code to it in the form of an onClick event like in the preceding example. This is a flexible and powerful feature, but it needs a certain level of JavaScript skills.

The **reset** button simply sets every input item on the whole form back to the default value: text and password fields return to the **value**, text areas to the text between the <textarea> and </textarea> tags, check boxes and radio buttons to the **checked** choices, and select lists to the **selected** items.

JavaScript

An HTML page is basically static—once it has been delivered to the browser, it cannot change. It can contain a few active elements like a drop-down list box, but, for example, it does not support any kind of field-level validation.

This limitation can be overcome with client-side scripting in JavaScript or the equivalent Microsoft language Jscript.

NOTE
JavaScript has only the name in common with Java. Java is a full-featured programming language that can be used for client- or server-side code, whereas JavaScript is a simple scripting language normally used only on the client side.

Among other things, JavaScript can read and change all elements in an HTML form on a Web page and can pop up warnings informing the user of errors in data entered without having to go to the server for validation.

You can use JavaScript in several places on your page:

- In the header of your page to define functions that you can call from other JavaScript code. You can either write the code directly in the page between <script> and </script> tags, or use a <script src="*URL*"> tag to include a JavaScript file stored on the Web server.

- In the body of your page between <script> and </script> tags or using a <script src="URL"> tag. This code is executed immediately when the page loads.

- Inside a specific tag in an event handler. This code only gets executed when the event happens—for example, one of the buttons in the preceding example looked like this:

```
<input type="button" value="Do something else"
    onClick="alert('hello')" />
```

This code defines that in response to the Click event (when the user clicks the button) the code "alert('hello')" should be executed (displaying a dialog box with the text "hello").

Refer to the references in Chapter 13 for more information about JavaScript, including the events you can respond to. If you have a bit of Java experience, you should be able to read and understand JavaScript without too much difficulty.

A Few Tips on Web Design

- Leave it to the pros. If you are a skilled programmer, you need only enough HTML knowledge to get by—you do not have to spend time becoming an HTML wizard. Your organization might already have HTML wizards, or you can have a contractor produce your HTML.

- Know your users. Decide which browsers you want to support, and test your pages in these (or get someone to do it for you).

- Give the users what they want right away. Don't start with a welcome page that has no information—make your application start with the first useful page. And don't make people scroll down on the page—research shows that 85 percent never do.

- Don't use too many images, and keep all graphics light (a Web design expert or a good Web graphics book will tell you how—see the resources in Chapter 13). Provide **height** and **width** attributes as well as an **alt** text for all images and set **border="0"** for all images used as links.

- Use drop-down list boxes, radio buttons, and check boxes to limit the user to valid entries. Remember that all the data has to go back to the server for validation—try to exclude user input errors as much as possible by using the right user interface elements.

- Keep text readable. Most text is black on a white or only slightly colored background. Don't use background images—they make the text hard to read.

- Do not use blinking text. Do not use moving images unless the movement conveys information.

- Ensure that your text lines do not expand to an unreadable length if the user maximizes the browser window. One way to do this is by putting all your text inside invisible HTML tables.

Choosing a Tool

While it is completely possible to write all your HTML in Notepad, it is faster and more convenient to use a specialized HTML editor. These come in two main flavors:

- Visual editors like Macromedia Dreamweaver or FrontPage

- Code editors like Allaire HomeSite

Many HTML professionals prefer to work in a pure code editor to maintain complete control over the HTML code. But, if you are not going to be writing much HTML, it might be easier for you to use a visual tool.

Bear in mind, though, that as a Web application developer, you have different needs from pure HTML designers: You need a tool that produces understandable HTML. A normal Web page designer can allow herself to be happy with a Web page if it looks nice in her target browser and does not contain many kilobytes of unnecessary HTML tags. But a Web application developer needs to be able to take the HTML code apart to insert business logic in the right places—and for that, you need clear and understandable HTML.

Before choosing a visual HTML tool, get a trial version and check that the HTML result of your visual editing is clear and understandable. Many visual editors produce almost incomprehensible HTML code full of unnecessary complexity—you want to avoid these. Chapter 11 lists some tools: of these, Dreamweaver from Macromedia is an excellent choice, FrontPage is not as good, and Word is not at all good at producing understandable HTML.

Conversion

If you have chosen to use Java servlets or PL/SQL stored procedures, you need to convert your example HTML pages to code in your chosen programming language. The result of this step is program code that contains a hard-wired Web page—it will always produce the same sample page no matter what data you have in your underlying tables. This section shows you how to manually convert the following Web page to a Java servlet or a PL/SQL stored procedure, as well as how to use a couple of small utilities to achieve this.

If you have chosen Java Server Pages, this step is extremely simple: simply rename your .htm file with a .jsp extension. If your Web/application server is set up correctly, it will automatically recognize the .jsp extension and convert your Java Server Pages into Java servlets the first time they are invoked.

If you have chosen to use PL/SQL Server Pages, you do not need to convert your HTML page. You do, however, currently need to convert them into PL/SQL stored procedures yourself. This is a final step only needed for PL/SQL server pages and can be achieved with the loadpsp program supplied by Oracle or a third-party utility.

All the following examples show how to convert the page shown in Figure 5-12 into Java servlets, PL/SQL stored procedures, and Server Pages. The static HTML code for this page looks like this:

```
<html>
<head>
<title>Search for Employees</title>
<link rel="stylesheet" href="/webstart.css"
    type="text/css" />
</head>

<body bgcolor="#FFFFFF">
<table width="550">
  <tr>
    <td>
```

```
      <h1>Search for Employees</h1>
    </td>
      <td align="right">
      <img src="/web_apps_101.gif" alt="Web Apps 101 logo"
          width="90" height="69" />
    </td>
  </tr>
</table>
<table width="550"><tr><td>
<p>Enter a name or part of a name and press the
<b> Search </b>button. </p>
<form method="post" action="maintainemp.ShowEmpList">
<table>
  <tr>
    <td>Name</td>
    <td>
      <input type="text" name="empname" />
    </td>
  </tr>
  <tr>
    <td colspan="2">
      <input type="submit" value=" Search " />
    </td>
  </tr>
</table>
</form>
<p> </p>
<p align="center">
<font size="-1">
  Comments, questions? Contact the
  <a href="mailto:sten@vesterli.dk">webmaster</a>
</font></p>
</td></tr></table>
</body>
</html>
```

Converting HTML to Java

To convert this example HTML page to Java, you need to wrap each line of HTML in Java servlet print statements. Since both Java and HTML use double quotes to delimit strings, all the " signs in the HTML must be prefixed with a backslash to tell the Java compiler that the " is part of the string to print and does not end the string. For example the HTML tag <input type="text"> becomes out.println("<input type=\"text\">").

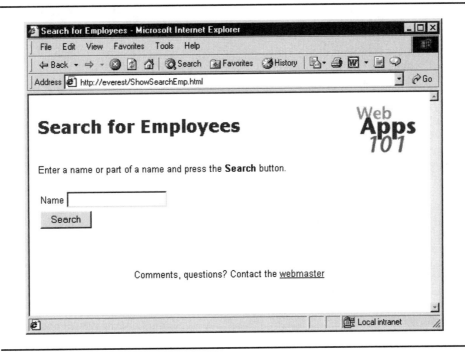

FIGURE 5-12. *Show Search screen in pure HTML*

Manual Conversion

A manual conversion involves

1. Replacing all occurrences of double quotes (") with a backslash and a double quote (\").

2. Placing the string **out.println("** before each line and **");** after each line using a macro or replace options. Be sure to insert a number of spaces before the **out.println** statement to achieve proper indentation.

When you have performed these steps, you can cut and paste the newly created Java code into one of the skeleton Java servlets created in the previous step. For example, if you created a skeleton for the ShowSearchEmp servlet in the preceding step and then added the converted HTML code, your Java servlet could look like the following code.

```
package maintainemp;

import javax.servlet.*;
import javax.servlet.http.*;
import java.io.*;
import java.util.*;

public class ShowSearchEmp extends HttpServlet {
  public void doGet(HttpServletRequest request,
    HttpServletResponse response)
    throws ServletException, IOException {
    doPost(request, response);
  }

  public void doPost(HttpServletRequest request,
      HttpServletResponse response)
      throws ServletException, IOException {
    String empNo = request.getParameter("empno");
    String empName = request.getParameter("empname");
    String empJob = request.getParameter("empjob");
    response.setContentType("text/html");
    PrintWriter out = new PrintWriter (response.getOutputStream());
    out.println("<html>");
    out.println("<head>");
    out.println("<title>Search for Employees</title>");
    out.println("<link rel=\"stylesheet\" href=\"/webstart.css\" ");
    out.println("    type=\"text/css\" />");
    out.println("</head>");
    out.println("");
    out.println("<body bgcolor=\"#FFFFFF\">");
    out.println("<table width=\"550\">");
    out.println("  <tr>");
    out.println("    <td> ");
    out.println("      <h1>Search for Employees</h1>");
    out.println("    </td>");
    out.println("    <td align=\"right\">");
    out.println("      <img src=\"/web_apps_101.gif\" "
        + "alt=\"Web Apps 101 logo\"");
    out.println("        width=\"90\" height=\"69\" /> ");
    out.println("    </td>");
    out.println("  </tr>");
    out.println("</table>");
    out.println("<table width=\"550\"><tr><td>");
    out.println("<p>Enter a name or part of a name and press the "
        + "<b> Search </b>button. </p>");
    out.println("<form method=\"post\" "
        + "action=\"maintainemp.ShowEmpList\">");
    out.println("<table>");
    out.println("  <tr> ");
```

```
    out.println("    <td>Name</td>");
    out.println("    <td> ");
    out.println("       <input type=\"text\" name=\"empname\" />");
    out.println("    </td>");
    out.println("  </tr>");
    out.println("  <tr> ");
    out.println("    <td colspan=\"2\">");
    out.println("       <input type=\"submit\" value=\" Search \" />");
    out.println("    </td>");
    out.println("  </tr>");
    out.println("</table>");
    out.println("</form>");
    out.println("<p> </p>");
    out.println("<p align=\"center\">");
    out.println("<font size=\"-1\">");
    out.println("  Comments, questions? Contact the ");
    out.println("  <a href=\"mailto:sten@vesterli.dk\">"
        + "webmaster</a>");
    out.println("</font></p> ");
    out.println("</td></tr></table>");
    out.println("</body>");
    out.println("</html>");
    out.close();
  }
}
```

The next chapter describes in detail how to use Oracle JDeveloper to enter, test, and edit Java servlets in this way.

Using the html2java Utility

The first two steps can be handled automatically by a small unsupported freeware utility called html2java (available from **www.vesterli.com**; see Chapter 11) that takes the name of an HTML file as input and produces Java code to be included in a Java servlet. For instance, to convert the file showSearchEmp.html, from a command prompt, simply enter:

```
C:>html2java showSearchEmp.html
```

This produces a file, showsearchemp.java, that looks like this:

```
    out.println("<html>");
    out.println("<head>");
    out.println("  <title>Search for Employees</title>");
    out.println("</head>");
    out.println("<body bgcolor=\"#FFFFFF\">");
    out.println("<h1>Search for Employees</h1>");
[snip]
```

You can simply cut and paste this text into the correct skeleton Java servlet.

Converting HTML to PL/SQL

To convert the same example page to a PL/SQL procedure, you simply need to wrap each line of HTML in a call to the HTP.P procedure. Fortunately, PL/SQL uses single quotes to delimit strings and HTML uses double quotes, so it is not necessary to convert the quotes as it is for Java servlets.

Manual Conversion

To convert the HTML file manually, you can use an editor macro or search and replace to place the string **htp.p('** before each line and **');** after each line. You can then cut and paste this text into your skeleton package.

For example, if you created a skeleton for the ShowSearchEmp procedure in the preceding code and then added the converted HTML code, your PL/SQL package would look like this:

```
create or replace package maintainemp
as
  procedure showSearchEmp(
    empno in varchar2
  , empname in varchar2
  , empjob in varchar2
  );
end maintainemp;
/
create or replace package body maintainemp
as
  procedure showSearchEmp(
    empno in varchar2
  , empname in varchar2
  , empjob in varchar2
  ) is
  begin
    htp.p('<html>');
    htp.p('<head>');
    htp.p('<title>Search for Employees</title>');
    htp.p('<link rel="stylesheet" href="/webstart.css" ');
    htp.p('    type="text/css" />');
    htp.p('</head>');
    htp.p('');
    htp.p('<body bgcolor="#FFFFFF">');
    htp.p('<table width="550">');
    htp.p('  <tr>');
    htp.p('    <td> ');
```

```
   htp.p('        <h1>Search for Employees</h1>');
   htp.p('      </td>');
   htp.p('        <td align="right">');
   htp.p('        <img src="/web_apps_101.gif" '
         || 'alt="Web Apps 101 logo"');
   htp.p('              width="90" height="69" /> ');
   htp.p('      </td>');
   htp.p('   </tr>');
   htp.p('</table>');
   htp.p('<table width="550"><tr><td>');
   htp.p('<p>Enter a name or part of a name and press the '
         || '<b> Search </b>button. </p>');
   htp.p('<form method="post" action="maintainemp.ShowEmpList">');
   htp.p('<table>');
   htp.p('   <tr> ');
   htp.p('      <td>Name</td>');
   htp.p('      <td> ');
   htp.p('        <input type="text" name="empname" />');
   htp.p('      </td>');
   htp.p('   </tr>');
   htp.p('   <tr> ');
   htp.p('      <td colspan="2">');
   htp.p('        <input type="submit" value=" Search " />');
   htp.p('      </td>');
   htp.p('   </tr>');
   htp.p('</table>');
   htp.p('</form>');
   htp.p('<p> </p>');
   htp.p('<p align="center">');
   htp.p('<font size="-1">');
   htp.p(' Comments, questions? Contact the ');
   htp.p(' <a href="mailto:sten@vesterli.dk">webmaster</a>');
   htp.p('</font> ');
   htp.p('</td></tr></table>');
   htp.p('</body>');
   htp.p('</html>');
  end;
end maintainemp;
/
```

Chapter 7 describes this procedure in more detail.

Using html2plsql

The act of wrapping every line of HTML in calls to HTP.P can be handled
automatically by a small unsupported freeware utility called html2plsql (available
from **www.vesterli.com**; see Chapter 11). This utility takes the name of an HTML

file as input and wraps each line in a call to HTP.P. For example, to convert the file showSearchEmp.html, from a command prompt, simply enter:

```
C:>html2plsql showSearchEmp.html
```

This produces a file showsearchemp.pls that looks like this:

```
htp.p('<html>');
htp.p('<head>');
htp.p('  <title>Search for Employees</title>');
htp.p('</head>');
htp.p('<body bgcolor="#FFFFFF">');
htp.p('<h1>Search for Employees</h1>');
[snip]
```

Just as when converting manually, you can cut and paste this code snippet into the correct PL/SQL skeleton.

Using WebAlchemy

WebAlchemy is another free, unsupported tool that does everything you need to convert an HTML page to a PL/SQL stored procedure. It was written by an Oracle employee, but this is *not* an Oracle tool—so don't call Oracle support about it. You can find the URL from which to download it in Chapter 12.

Unfortunately, WebAlchemy has not been updated since 1996, so it has a few problems converting XHMTL pages (and even plain HTML 4):

- It doesn't understand the <!DOCTYPE> tag required by XHTML.

- It doesn't understand the <html> tag with an xmlns attribute.

- It generates an invalid call to the for <link rel> tag.

Of course, you can still use this tool—just remember that you will need to fix a few things before you can use the output.

To use this tool, start it, open a file (choose "All Files" to see files with the .html extension), and press CTRL-G to generate PL/SQL code (see Figure 5-13).

The WebAlchemy tool tries to use the right procedure from the full content of the PL/SQL Web Toolkit; it does not simply wrap everything in a call to the HTP.P package.

Running WebAlchemy on the example file generates the following PL/SQL:

```
CREATE OR REPLACE PROCEDURE showsearchemp AS
BEGIN
  htp.htmlOpen;
```

```
htp.headOpen;
htp.title( 'Search for Employees');
htp.linkRel( curl => '/webstart.css');
htp.headClose;
htp.bodyOpen(  cattributes => ' bgcolor="#FFFFFF"' );
htp.tableOpen(  cattributes => ' width="550"' );
htp.tableRowOpen;
htp.tableData( htf.header( 1, 'Search for Employees'));
htp.tableData( htf.img( '/web_apps_101.gif', calt =>
        'Web Apps 101 logo', cattributes =>
        ' width="90" height="69" /'), calign => 'right');
htp.tableRowClose;
htp.tableClose;
htp.tableOpen(  cattributes => ' width="550"' );
htp.tableRowOpen;
htp.tableData( htf.para ||
   'Enter a name or part of a name and press the  ' ||
   htf.bold( 'Search ') ||
   'button. ' ||
   htf.formOpen( curl => 'maintainemp.ShowEmpList',
                 cmethod => 'post') ||
   htf.tableOpen ||
   htf.tableRowOpen ||
   htf.tableData( 'Name') ||
   htf.tableData( htf.formText( cname => 'empname',
       cattributes => ' /')) ||
   htf.tableRowClose ||
   htf.tableRowOpen ||
   htf.tableData( htf.formSubmit( cvalue => ' Search ',
       cattributes => ' /'), ccolspan => '2') ||
   htf.tableRowClose ||
   htf.tableClose ||
   htf.formClose ||
   htf.para ||
   ' ' ||
   htf.paragraph( calign => 'center') ||
   '<FONT size="-1">' ||
   'Comments, questions? Contact the  ' ||
   htf.anchor( 'mailto:sten@vesterli.dk', 'webmaster') ||
   '</FONT>');
  htp.tableRowClose;
  htp.tableClose;
  htp.bodyClose;
  htp.htmlClose;
END;
/
```

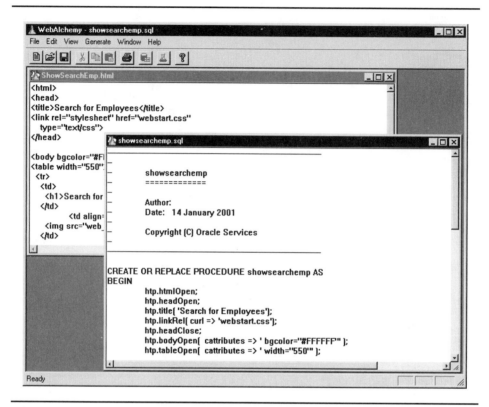

FIGURE 5-13. *Using WebAlchemy*

This procedure is functionally equivalent to the one where everything is wrapped in HTP.P calls—which you use is a matter of personal preference. The WebAlchemy style is a bit more compact, but the "pure" HTP.P style is easier for HTML programmers to read.

Modularization

This conversion is all you need in order to build a functional application; but to build a *maintainable* application, you must also separate the presentation properly from the business logic.

If you split the HTML formatting part from the actual logic, it becomes much easier to change the layout consistently. In addition, your business logic becomes much simpler, easier to read, and less bug prone.

A Format Class or Package

Every HTML page normally starts and ends with the same HTML code; instead of embedding this code in every PL/SQL procedure or Java servlet, you can move this to a separate Format Java class or PL/SQL package. Other blocks of code can also be taken out and placed in this application-specific Format class or package.

This process is described in detail in Chapters 6 and 7 on Java servlets and handwritten PL/SQL Web applications.

A Web Application Toolkit

While the Format class or package contains the HTML formatting that is specific to one or a few applications, other components can be reused in almost every Web application.

For example, you will often create a <select> list based on a specific table in the database or to produce an HTML table containing the result of a specific query. Tasks like these can be placed in a general Web Application Toolkit.

Chapter 12 describes a PL/SQL and Java Web Application Toolkit that you can download from **www.vesterli.com** to get started—but remember that a toolkit is most useful when you continually refine it and add new tools to it.

The following examples and the next two chapters on Java and PL/SQL Web applications will use functions from this toolkit.

Business Logic

At this point, you have a static Server Page file or servlet—executable code that can be tested through the Web server. It will always produce the same result, of course, so now you need to add the real business logic.

Adding Business Logic to Server Pages

If you intend to use Java Server Pages or PL/SQL Server Pages, the split between presentation and business logic is given in the HTML file: you leave all the HTML formatting tags and static parts unchanged, add the business logic for database access and program flow, and replace the example data with corresponding Java or PL/SQL code.

All the following examples show how to add the logic for inserting a new employee to the ShowSearchEmp module. Remember that the application flow diagram (refer to Figure 5-6) showed that the SearchEmp screen comes after the NewEmp screen. The task of actually inserting a record entered on the NewEmp screen thus falls to the ShowSearchEmp module.

Java Server Pages

Java Server Pages do not automatically have database access, so you must explicitly add the code to establish a database connection. If you want to add the ability to actually insert a record to the ShowSearchEmp page using Java Database Connectivity (JDBC) to connect to the database, your Java Server Page might look like this:

```
<%@ page import="java.sql.*" %>
<html>
<head>
<title>Search for Employees</title>
<link rel="stylesheet" href="webstart.css"
    type="text/css" />
</head>

<body bgcolor="#FFFFFF">
<table width="550">
  <tr>
    <td>
      <h1>Search for Employees</h1>
    </td>
      <td align="right">
      <img src="Web_apps_101.gif"
          alt="Web Apps 101 logo" width="90" height="69" />
    </td>
  </tr>
</table>
<%
String empNo = request.getParameter("empno");
String empName = request.getParameter("empname");
String empJob = request.getParameter("empjob");
int empNumber = 0;
try {
  empNumber = Integer.parseInt(empNo);
} catch (Exception e) {}

/* only proceed if we got at least empNo and empName */
if (empNumber != 0 && empName.length() > 0) {
  int recordsInserted = 0;
  try {
    DriverManager.registerDriver(
        new oracle.jdbc.driver.OracleDriver());
    Connection conn = DriverManager.getConnection(
        "jdbc:oracle:thin:@everest:1521:ORCL", "scott", "tiger");
    PreparedStatement pStmt = conn.prepareStatement(
        "insert into emp (empno, ename, job) values (?, ?, ?)");
    pStmt.setInt(1, empNumber);
    pStmt.setString(2, empName);
```

```
      pStmt.setString(3, empJob);
      recordsInserted = pStmt.executeUpdate();
%>
<hr />
<%= recordsInserted %> records created
<hr />
<%
   } catch (SQLException e) {
      if (e.getErrorCode() == 1) {
        /* ORA-00001 means empno already exists */
%>
<hr />
Employee number <%= empNo %> already exists
<hr />
<%
      } else {
        /* something serious is wrong */
%>
<hr />
SQL Error <%= e.getMessage() %>
<hr />
<%
      }
   }
}
%>
<table width="550"><tr><td>
<p>Enter a name or part of a name and press the
<b> Search </b>button. </p>
<form method="post" action="maintainemp.ShowEmpList">
<table>
  <tr>
    <td>Name</td>
    <td>
      <input type="text" name="empname" />
    </td>
  </tr>
  <tr>
    <td colspan="2">
      <input type="submit" value=" Search " />
    </td>
  </tr>
</table>
</form>
<p> </p>
<p align="center">
<font size="-1">
  Comments, questions? Contact the
```

```
   <a href="mailto:sten@vesterli.dk">webmaster</a>
</font></p>
</td></tr></table>
</body>
</html>
```

Notice all the Server Page instructions (everything that's not HTML) start with the special <% tag and end with %>. You can think of this as an HTML file in which everything between the <% and %> tags is executed before the page is returned, and everything between <%= and %> tags is included as part of the HTML that is returned.

NOTE
Technically, it's the other way around: the Web server converts the page to a Java servlet by leaving everything between these tags unchanged and placing all the HTML in Java output calls.

The first line of Java code is the import statement at the top of the page that you need in order to be able to create the objects needed for the database connection. Because not all servlets connect to the database, the automatic conversion to a Java servlet does not provide this.

The next block of Java code reads the parameters, converts the string parameter **empNo** to the int **empNumber**, establishes the connection, creates a SQL insert statement, binds the variables in the statement to the parameters, and executes it (Chapter 6 describes this procedure in more detail).

If everything goes well, the value of the Java variable recordsInserted is used in a message next to normal HTML. Then follows some conditional logic that handles different error conditions and, in each case, "leaves" the Java code (with %>) to return some normal HTML as an error message and then "starts" Java code again (with <%).

The final server page code closes all the brackets so the Java code is valid.

Chapter 6 will describe the functionality of this application in more detail—what you should note here is the separation of HTML layout and Java code by the use of <% and %> tags.

PL/SQL Server Pages

In PL/SQL Server Pages, the database connection has already been established. You simply need to add an insert statement and appropriate error handling to the static "showSearchEmp" page. The finished PL/SQL Server Page might look like this:

```
<%@ page language="PL/SQL"%>
<%@ plsql procedure="showSearchEmp" %>
<%@ plsql parameter="empno" %>
<%@ plsql parameter="empname" %>
<%@ plsql parameter="empjob" %>
<html>
<head>
<title>Search for Employees</title>
<link rel="stylesheet" href="webstart.css"
     type="text/css" />
</head>

<body bgcolor="#FFFFFF">
<table width="550">
  <tr>
    <td>
      <h1>Search for Employees</h1>
    </td>
      <td align="right">
      <img src="/Web_apps_101.gif"
          alt="Web Apps 101 logo" width="90" height="69">
    </td>
  </tr>
</table>
<%
begin
  insert into emp(empno, ename, job)
  values (empno, empname, empjob);
%>
<hr />
One record inserted
<hr />
<%
exception
  when others
  then
    if sqlcode = -1
    then
%>
<hr />
Employee number <%= empno %> already exists
<hr />
<%
    else
%>
<hr />
```

```
SQL Error <%= sqlerrm %>
<hr />
<%
    end if;
end;
%>
<table width="550"><tr><td>
<p>Enter a name or part of a name and press
the <b> Search </b>button.</p>
<form method="post" action="maintainemp.ShowEmpList">
<table>
  <tr>
    <td>Name</td>
    <td>
      <input type="text" name="empname" />
    </td>
  </tr>
  <tr>
    <td colspan="2">
      <input type="submit" value=" Search " />
    </td>
  </tr>
</table>
</form>
<p> </p>
<p align="center">
<font size="-1">
  Comments, questions? Contact the
  <a href="mailto:sten@vesterli.dk">webmaster</a>
</font> </p>
</td></tr></table>
</body>
</html>
```

Just as with Java Server Pages, all the PL/SQL Server Page instructions are enclosed in the special <% and %> tags. Similarly, you can consider this an HTML file where everything between the <% and %> tags is executed before the page is returned, and everything between <%= and %> tags is included as part of the returned HTML.

NOTE
Just as with Java Server Pages, technically, it's the other way around: when loading the PL/SQL Server Page into the database as a stored procedure, the loader converts it by leaving everything between these tags unchanged and placing all the HTML in HTP.P statements.

The first server page tag is the language directive that tells the loader that this page is intended for conversion into a PL/SQL Server Page.

The next line is needed to tell the loader the stored procedure name to use when loading the Server Page into the database.

The next three lines declare the parameters that the page will receive (**VARCHAR2** is the default).

Then comes the actual insert statement, followed by a confirmation message in HTML.

If anything goes wrong, this is caught in the following PL/SQL EXCEPTION block that displays an appropriate error message.

Chapter 7 describes Web applications using PL/SQL stored procedures in detail; this example is intended only to demonstrate this step in application development when using PL/SQL Server Pages.

Adding Business Logic to Servlets

If you intend to use Java servlets or PL/SQL stored procedures, you are going to be adding business logic to the converted servlets to build your application.

Remember that you should take out most (or all) of your HTML-generating code and place it in a separate Format package to achieve a consistent user interface and more readable (and maintainable) code.

The following examples show how to add the logic for inserting a new employee to the ShowSearchEmp module. You can refer back to the application flow diagram in Figure 5-6 to see why the task of inserting a record entered on the NewEmp screen falls to the ShowSearchEmp module, as well as the parameters passed.

Java Servlets

The business logic that you need for this example must establish a database connection and perform the update, as well as handle any errors that might occur.

If you started from a modularized Java servlet, you might already have created your own separate Format class that will produce the application-specific HTML. In addition, you can use methods from a general helper class HtmlForm from the Web Application Toolkit in Chapter 12 to produce HTML Form elements. Your Java servlet might look like this:

```
package maintainemp;

import javax.servlet.*;
import javax.servlet.http.*;
import java.io.*;
import java.util.*;
import java.sql.*;
import com.vesterli.webstart.*;

public class ShowSearchEmp extends HttpServlet {
```

```
/**
 * Process the HTTP Get request
 */
public void doGet(HttpServletRequest request,
    HttpServletResponse response)
    throws ServletException, IOException {
  doPost(request, response);
}

/**
 * Process the HTTP Post request
 */
public void doPost(HttpServletRequest request,
    HttpServletResponse response)
    throws ServletException, IOException {
  String empNo = request.getParameter("empno");
  String empName = request.getParameter("empname");
  String empJob = request.getParameter("empjob");
  int empNumber = 0;
  try {
    empNumber = Integer.parseInt(empNo);
  } catch (Exception e) {}

  response.setContentType("text/html");
  PrintWriter out = new PrintWriter(response.getOutputStream());
  StringBuffer page = new StringBuffer();
  int recordsInserted = 0;    // for the return code from the INSERT

  page.append(Format.pageStart("Search for Employees"));

  /* only proceed if we got at least empNo and empName */
  if (empNumber != 0 && empName.length() > 0) {
    try {
      DriverManager.registerDriver(new
          oracle.jdbc.driver.OracleDriver());
      Connection conn = DriverManager.getConnection(
          "jdbc:oracle:thin:@everest:1521:ORCL", "scott", "tiger");
      PreparedStatement pStmt = conn.prepareStatement(
          "insert into emp (empno, ename, job) values (?, ?, ?)"
      );
      pStmt.setInt(1, empNumber);
      pStmt.setString(2, empName);
      pStmt.setString(3, empJob);
      recordsInserted = pStmt.executeUpdate();
      if (recordsInserted == 1) {
        page.append(Format.message("One record created"));
      } else {
        /*
```

```
         * if not exactly one record inserted, something is
         * seriously wrong. Ask user to contact support and
         * terminate
         */
        out.println(Format.errorPage(recordsInserted
          + " records created.<br>Expected exactly one."));
        out.close();
      }
    } catch (SQLException e) {
      if (e.getErrorCode() == 1) {
        /* ORA-00001 means empno already exists */
        page.append(Format.message("Employee number "
            + empNo
            + " already exists."
        ));
      } else {
        /* something serious is wrong */
        out.println(Format.errorPage("SQL Error: " + e.getMessage()));
        out.close();
      }
    }
  }
}

    page.append(Format.introText("Enter a name or part of a name "
        + "and press the <b> Search </b>button. "));
    page.append(HtmlForm.start("maintainemp.ShowEmpList"));
    page.append(HtmlForm.textField("Name", "searchempname"));
    page.append(HtmlForm.buttonsStart());
    page.append(HtmlForm.submitButton("Search"));
    page.append(HtmlForm.button("New", "maintainemp.ShowNewEmp"));
    page.append(HtmlForm.buttonsEnd());
    page.append(HtmlForm.end());
    page.append(Format.pageEnd());

    out.println(page);
    out.close();
  }
 }
}
```

Notice that this Java servlet does not contain any HTML code at all—it's all business logic and calls to methods in the Format and HTML Form classes. This makes it easy to change the HTML format without affecting the business logic in the servlet.

This servlet contains two extra import lines at the top to provide access to the objects you need for the database connection and to the helper class from the Web Application Toolkit used to create HTML Form elements.

The parameters are retrieved just as with a Java Server Page, including the try/catch block to convert the empNo string to the int variable **empNumber**. Note that the exception handler is empty—in case of an error, the **empNumber** variable is simply left at the initial value.

The logic to establish a database connection and perform the insert is also similar to the Java Server Page solution.

After the insert, the Server builds the SearchEmp page by calling methods of the Format and HtmlForm classes:

- The Format class (that you write for each application in the conversion step) contains the application-specific formatting and produces the HTML to start and stop pages.

- The HtmlForm class (from the Web Application Toolkit) contains methods that can be used to produce the HTML code for standard Form elements.

Both the Format and HtmlFormat classes used in this example are covered in the detailed discussion of how to create Java servlet applications in the next chapter, and the free Web Application Toolkit is described in Chapter 12.

PL/SQL Stored Procedures

The business logic for this example is simpler in PL/SQL, because the database connection is already given—just add the insert and do any applicable error handling.

Starting from a modularized PL/SQL package, you might already have created your own Format package to produce application-specific HTML. You can also use the functions from the HtmlForm package of the Web Application Toolkit to produce HTML form elements. The body of your PL/SQL package code might look like this:

```
create or replace package body maintainemp
as
  procedure showSearchEmp(
    empno in varchar2
  , empname in varchar2
  , empjob in varchar2
  ) is
  begin
    htp.p(format.pageStart('Search for Employees'));
    begin
      insert into emp(empno, ename, job)
      values (empno, empname, empjob);
```

```
    exception
      when others
      then
        if sqlcode = -1
        then
          htp.p(format.message('Employee number '
              || empno
              || ' already exists'
          ));
        else
          htp.p(format.errorpage('SQL Error ' || sqlerrm));
        end if;
    end;

    htp.p(format.introtext('Enter a name or part of a name and press '
        || 'the <b> Search </b>button.'));
    htp.p(htmlform.formStart('maintainemp.ShowEmpList'));
    htp.p(htmlform.textField('Name', 'searchempname'));
    htp.p(htmlform.submitbuttonrow(' Search '));
    htp.p(htmlform.formEnd);
    htp.p(format.pageEnd);
  end;
end maintainemp;
/
```

The procedure contains hardly any HTML code—all the application-specific formatting has been moved to the separate Format and HTML Form packages. Just as with Java servlets, this makes it easier to maintain the HTML without the risk of breaking the business logic.

The PL/SQL code is as simple here as it is in the PL/SQL Server Page example—because the database connection is already available, you need only add the insert statement and appropriate error handling.

After the insert, the procedure builds the SearchEmp page using functions in the Format package (that you write in the conversion step) and in the HtmlForm package that is part of the free Web Application Toolkit.

The procedure of producing the Format package and using the HtmlForm package is covered in more detail in Chapter 7, and the Web Application Toolkit is described in Chapter 12.

Summary

This chapter has shown you the four steps in developing a handwritten Web application: application design, page design, conversion, and business logic.

You saw how to use storyboards and application flow diagrams first to define the application structure. Then you saw how to build Web pages with HTML, and how to use different tools and approaches to convert these pages to code in your chosen programming language. Finally, you saw several examples of small applications complete with all necessary business logic.

The next two chapters explain in detail how to use this approach. Chapter 6 describes how to use Java servlets with JDeveloper, and Chapter 7 describes how to build Web applications with PL/SQL stored procedures.

CHAPTER

6

Using Java

nlike C++, Visual Basic, or PL/SQL, the Java language was positioned as a Web programming language from the very beginning, and it is supported by appropriate standards and frameworks. This makes it a very good choice for Web applications. This chapter describes how to use server-side Java in the form of Java servlets. It is rather more complicated to develop applications using Java on the client side; Chapter 10 describes how to use Java on the client for Forms applications deployed to the Web, and Chapter 13 points you to some resources for more information about developing Java client applications.

Getting Started

Now it's time to get started with Java Web applications. If you do not know anything about Java programming, you can read through the complete code examples in this chapter to get a feeling for how Java Web applications look and work, but you should also have a look at some of the resources in Chapter 13 that explicitly aim at teaching you Java.

Compiling Java Code

Java is a compiled language, that is, your Java source file must be compiled before it can be executed. But Java differs from other compiled programming languages in that the result of the compilation is not native machine code but something called *bytecode*.

Other programming languages must be compiled for each target system because the compiler produces specialized code that can be executed directly by the central processor. In addition, the program uses specific libraries provided by the operating system vendor to perform common tasks like reading from disk or writing on the screen. Together, this means that a program compiled for an Intel system running Windows won't run on any other processor or operating system.

Java code, on the other hand, is compiled to an intermediate form called *bytecode*. Bytecode cannot be executed directly by any processor but is instead interpreted at runtime by software called a *Java virtual machine (JVM)*. It is the task of the JVM to translate the bytecode to native machine code that the processor can execute. Since the JVM has the task of translating from bytecode (that's portable) to native code for a specific processor and operating system, it is, of course, operating system–specific. You can download a reference JVM implementation from Sun for your operating system and processor (for example, for Windows on Intel), or you can use another JVM like the one in the Oracle database.

Finding Java Code

Because Java is an object-oriented language, all Java code makes extensive use of objects defined elsewhere. The Java language itself defines a number of packages that are always available (like java.lang, java.util, and so on), but your application can also use objects defined in other packages. Java servlets use other packages; every Java servlet extends the generic HttpServlet class that is found in the javax.servlet.http package.

To enable the JVM to find these packages, you must set an environment variable called *CLASSPATH*. This variable works just like the normal *PATH* variable used for finding executable code in many computer systems, and defines a list of directories and/or libraries where the JVM must search for Java code.

Packages and Paths

As in PL/SQL, Java code can be collected in packages. A *package* is a group of Java classes that the programmer chooses to combine in a package, similar to packages in PL/SQL. A package normally has a name consisting of a number of words separated with periods (for instance oracle.jdbc.driver). Sun recommends that the first part of a package should be the Internet domain of the organization in reverse, that is, Oracle should name their packages com.oracle. However, Oracle and others have decided to leave out the "com," so all packages from Oracle simply start with "oracle."

When a JVM is looking for a class in a package, it will look in each directory in the CLASSPATH for a subdirectory structure matching the package name. If, for instance,

```
CLASSPATH = c:\jdk12;o:\ora81\jdbc\lib
```

the JVM will look for the class oracle.jdbc.driver.OracleDriver in the following directories:

```
c:\jdk12\oracle\jdbc\driver
o:\ora81\jdbc\lib\oracle\jdbc\driver
```

These directories do not have to be real directories; they can just as well be Zip files containing directory information. As a matter of fact, the Oracle JDBC (Java Database Connectivity) driver is found in a Zip file called *classes12.zip* (together with many other classes).

NOTE
If the JVM cannot find a class that is on your CLASSPATH but is in a Zip file, try to unzip the file. This shouldn't be necessary, but occasionally a JVM doesn't handle Zip files correctly.

Running Java in JDeveloper

Oracle JDeveloper 3.2 installs two versions of the Sun JVM: versions 1.1.8 and 1.2. By default, it executes all code using the version 1.2 JVM.

When you run Java code in JDeveloper, the code is automatically compiled and then executed through the JVM.

You do not set the CLASSPATH explicitly in JDeveloper but instead add libraries to the project. A *library* is a collection of one or more packages—JDeveloper comes with a number of libraries already defined. The JDeveloper wizards will normally add all the necessary libraries, but you can right-click a project and choose Properties to see and change the libraries:

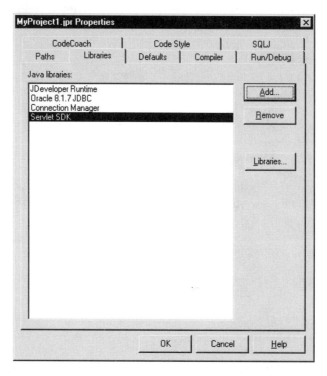

Running Java Through the Oracle HTTP Server

HTML-based Java Web applications consist of either servlets or Java Server Pages (JSPs) that automatically get converted to servlets by the Web server. The Apache Web server has a module (mod_jserv) that passes requests for Java servlets to the JServ engine that is a separate process.

NOTE
This is standard Apache functionality and does not use any Oracle JVM or special Oracle packages.

The JServ servlet engine supports, the concept of multiple *zones* that can be used to separate servlets from one another, but, for simplicity, you can add your servlets to the default zone that is installed with the server.

Like all other configuration settings for the Apache Web server and associated code, the CLASSPATH for the JServ servlets engine is controlled from a configuration file. If you have followed the default installation in Chapter 4, the configuration file for the default zone is

```
O:\oracle\ora81\Apache\Apache\JServ\zone.properties
```

At the top of this file is a section called "Repositories" that looks something like this:

```
# List of Repositories
#######################

# The list of servlet repositories controlled by this servlet zone
# Syntax: repositories=[repository],[repository]...
# Default: NONE
# Note: The classes you want to be reloaded upon modification should be put
#       here.

repositories=O:\oracle\ora81\Apache\Jserv\servlets
```

To add your own servlets to the CLASSPATH, simply add an extra line for each directory where you are storing servlets. For instance, you can create a directory C:\web_apps_101\servlets for your servlets and insert the following line under the existing "repositories" line:

```
repositories=C:\web_apps_101\servlets
```

When you have done this, you must reload the Oracle HTTP Server service. To do this, choose Start | Settings | Control Panel, and double-click Administrative Tools and then Services to see the Services window in Figure 6-1.

Choose the OracleOraHome81HTTPServer service (your service will have another name if you installed in a different Oracle Home directory) and click the Restart button.

To check that your Oracle HTTP server restarted correctly and is (still) able to serve servlets, enter the following URL in your browser:

```
http://<server>/servlet/IsItWorking
```

where *<server>* is the name of your server. This should produce a screen like that shown in Figure 6-2.

NOTE
You must type the name IsItWorking *exactly as shown in the code, with uppercase I, I, and W. Java is picky about upper- and lowercase.*

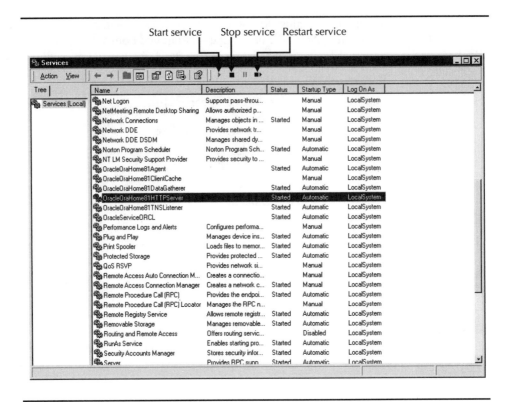

Start service   Stop service   Restart service

FIGURE 6-1. *The Services window*

Don't worry if you get a "broken image" link at the top of the page—the important part is that you see the "Yes, It's Working!" message.

If you get an error message, you have probably accidentally introduced an error in the JServ configuration file. Check the JServ log files:

```
O:\oracle\ora81\Apache\Jserv\logs\jserv.log
O:\oracle\ora81\Apache\Jserv\logs\mod_jserv.log
```

Running Java in the Oracle JVM
The Oracle database and the Oracle Application Server also contain an efficient JVM that supports all the features of Java 2 Enterprise Edition (J2EE), including version 2.2 of the Java servlet specification. Oracle also supplies a module (mod_ose) for the Apache Web server that routes requests for servlets to the Oracle JVM.

However, getting your code loaded into the Oracle JVM and calling it through mod_ose is not a trivial task and falls outside the scope of this book.

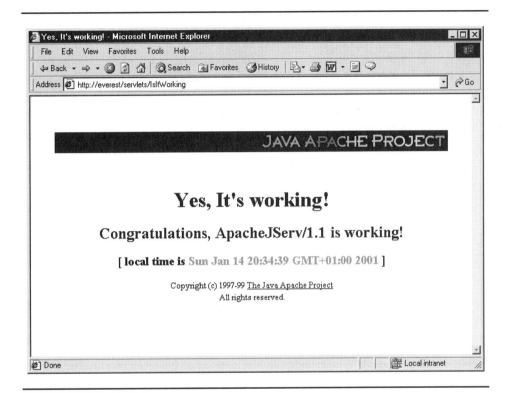

FIGURE 6-2. *Apache JServ is working*

Starting JDeveloper

When you first start JDeveloper, the welcome screen appears (see Figure 6-3).

Setting the Defaults

By default, JDeveloper proposes to keep all your code in subdirectories under the
directory in which you installed JDeveloper. It is generally not a good idea to store
your own code and data together with installed applications, so you should choose
somewhere else. To do this, choose Tools | Default Project Properties. If the Paths
tab (see Figure 6-4) is not in front, click it to bring it forward. If necessary, you can
click the small arrows at the top right corner of the dialog box to scroll through the
tabs until you see "Paths."

For simplicity, you can use the same path for all directory fields:

- Source root directory (where your Java source goes)
- Output root directory (where your compiled Java bytecode goes)

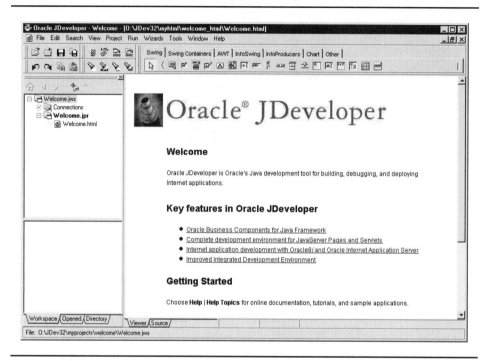

FIGURE 6-3.   *The JDeveloper Welcome screen*

■ Run/Debug working directory (used by JDeveloper)

■ HTML root directory (for any HTML files used or generated by your project)

Notice that clicking the Edit button next to the Source root field does not bring up a normal directory dialog box as you would expect. Instead, you get a dialog box like this:

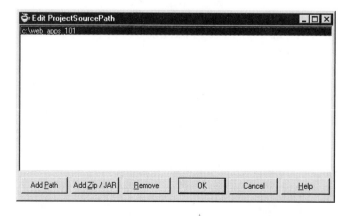

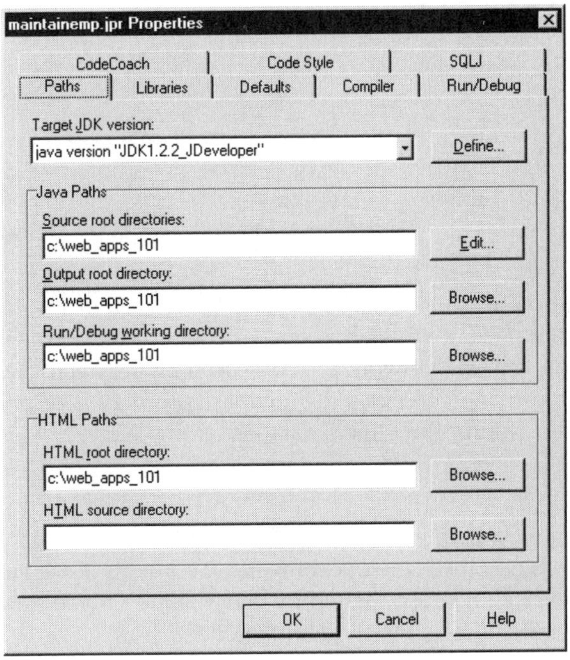

FIGURE 6-4.   *Setting project default properties*

This dialog box allows you to select multiple directories. In this case, though, you can just click the Remove button to remove the JDeveloper default directory and then click Add Path to add your own project directory.

Connecting to the Database

If you are used to developing traditional two-tier client/server applications using tools like Oracle Forms, you are probably taking the database connection for granted. When a user starts up an application developed with Oracle Forms, the Forms client will automatically load the necessary drivers and prompt the user for connect information. The application normally does not run if a connection to the database cannot be established.

In an HTML-based three-tier Java application, the client program is a Web browser. The Web browser does not need a database connection, so it does not automatically load a driver or prompt the user for connection information. These tasks fall to the application code (the Java servlets) running on the middle tier.

JDBC Drivers

JDBC drivers come in several types:

- Thin
- Thick
- JDBC-ODBC bridge

Thin Driver

A *thin driver* is also known as a *native-protocol pure Java driver*. It is called *thin* because it does not need anything but its own code to work. This driver converts JDBC calls directly into the network protocol used by the database, so the client can call the database directly. Since the database protocol is proprietary, you need to install the thin driver for the Oracle database from Oracle.

Thick Driver

A *thick driver* is also known as a *native-API partly Java driver* and is called *thick* because it depends on other network software. *It* converts JDBC calls into calls to the Oracle network client, so the right version of the Oracle network client for the operating system must be installed on the client.

JDBC-ODBC Bridge

The JDBC-ODBC bridge passes JDBC calls on to an ODBC (open database connectivity) driver. Similar to a thick driver, this means that an ODBC driver must be installed on the client. Because all calls pass through first the JDBC bridge and then the ODBC driver, this solution is somewhat slow and is normally only used if a thin or a thick driver is not available from the database vendor.

What to Choose?

In a Web application with a Java client running on the browser, you must use a thin driver, because this driver is self-contained and does not need any operating system–specific code to be installed on the browser machine.

In an HTML-based Web application with Java servlets running on the middle tier, you can choose the driver that suits you. Since you have control over the Web server, you can ensure that an Oracle Net8 Network Client is installed and configured correctly. However, there seems to be little or no performance improvement over the thin driver; so unless you want to use your existing Net8 configuration, I generally recommend that you use the thin Oracle driver.

Mapping SQL Data Types to Java

Because data types in SQL and data types in the Java programming language are not identical, data must be converted when read from or written to the database:

- When data is retrieved from the database, the methods on the ResultSet class return Java types.

- When data is bound to *bind variables* in a SQL statement, the methods on the PreparedStatement class take Java types as parameters.

- When calling a PL/SQL stored procedure that has **OUT** parameters, the CallableStatement class has methods to return these parameters as Java types.

Because there is some overhead involved in this conversion, Oracle provides special objects in the oracle.sql package that can be used to store database values in a Java program without conversion.

However, tasks that process a lot of database data are probably handled better in a PL/SQL stored procedure than in Java.

Creating a Connection from JDeveloper

Several of the JDeveloper tools and wizards use database connections, and all are defined through the Connection Editor.

To invoke the Connection Editor, right-click the Connections node at the top of the Navigator pane and choose Connections. . . from the pop-up menu. The window in Figure 6-5 appears. Fill in this dialog box as follows:

Connection Name   A name you choose for the connection.

Username   Enter a username authorized to access to the database.

Password   Enter the password of the specified username for access to the server database. An asterisk (*) appears for each character you type in this field.

Include Password in Deployment Archive   Select this check box to store the password for this connection. If you are only going to use the connection inside JDeveloper (for instance, to validate SQLJ, as described in the next section), you can safely check it to avoid having to enter a password every time you need to connect to the database.

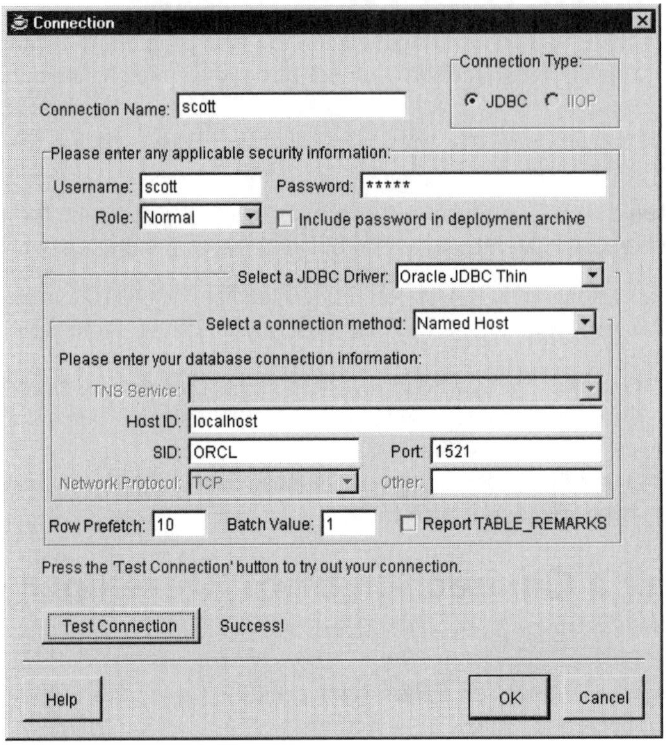

FIGURE 6-5. *The Connection Editor*

On the other hand, if you are going to use the connection in an application developed with JDeveloper and you intend to make the users log on to the database, you should not select this check box.

In addition, the password will, of course, be stored in a JDeveloper settings file; so in a high-security environment, you should not select this box.

Select a Connection Method   Leave this at Named Host to use a standard URL of the form jdbc:oracle:thin:<USERNAME/PASSWORD>@<HOSTID>:<PORT>:<SID>.

TNS Service   When the connection method is Named Host, this box is grayed out and you do not have to enter anything.

Host ID   Identifies the machine running the Oracle server. Enter either an IP address or a host name that can be resolved by TCP/IP. If the database is on your development machine, you can leave this setting at the default localhost.

SID   Identifies the unique system identifier (SID) of the Oracle database instance you want to connect to. You were prompted for this value when you installed the database—if you followed the instructions in Chapter 4, this value should be left at the default ORCL.

Port   Identifies the TCP/IP port to connect to. Unless you have set up your TNS Listener to a nonstandard port, leave this at the default value of 1521.
    When you have finished, click the Test Connection button to test the connection. After a while, you should see the message "Success!" next to the button.
    If the test does not succeed, you can try the following:

- Try to ping the Host ID you use: from a command prompt, type **ping** *host* where *host* is the entry you wrote in the Host ID field. If you do not get a response, and your database is on the same machine as the Web server, try using localhost as the Host ID.

- Try to tnsping your database: from a command prompt, type **tnsping** ***connect_string*** where *connect_string* is the connection string for your Oracle database as defined in your TNSNAMES.ORA file. If you followed the installation instructions in Chapter 4, the installer has created a database ORCL for you, so you could type **tnsping ORCL** to confirm that your database and listener are running (see Figure 6-6). If you do not get an OK message, check that your database and listener service are running.

Connecting to Oracle databases is a big topic—for more information, including troubleshooting, you can refer to *Oracle Networking 101* by Oracle Press or another book on Oracle networking.

Using JDBC

The basic procedure for using JDBC to connect to the database consists of six steps:

1. Load the driver.
2. Establish a connection.
3. Create a statement.
4. Execute the statement.
5. Fetch the result.
6. Close the connection.

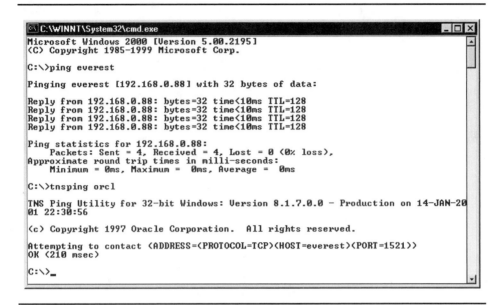

FIGURE 6-6. *Using ping and tnsping to check the connection to the database*

An Example of JDBC

The following servlet shows all these steps and the sections following the code explain some of the details.

```
package myservlets;

import javax.servlet.*;
import javax.servlet.http.*;
import java.io.*;
import java.util.*;
import java.sql.*;

public class DeptListJdbc extends HttpServlet {
  /**
   * Process the HTTP Get request
   */
  public void doGet(HttpServletRequest request,
      HttpServletResponse response)
      throws ServletException, IOException {
    response.setContentType("text/html");
    PrintWriter out = new PrintWriter (response.getOutputStream());
```

```
  out.println("<html>");
  out.println("<head><title>EmpList</title></head>");
  out.println("<body>");
  out.println("<h1>Department list</h1>");

  Connection con = null;
  Statement stmt = null;
  ResultSet rs = null;
  try {
    /* Step 1: Load the driver */
    Class.forName("oracle.jdbc.driver.OracleDriver");
    /* Step 2: Establish a connection */
    con = DriverManager.getConnection(
        "jdbc:oracle:thin:@localhost:1521:orcl",
        "scott", "tiger");
    String stmtString = new String("select deptno, dname, loc "
        + "from dept order by deptno");
    /* Step 3: Create a statement */
    stmt = con.createStatement();
    /* Step 4: Execute the statement */
    rs = stmt.executeQuery(stmtString);
    /* Step 5: Fetch the result */
    while(rs.next()) {
      out.println("<p>");
      out.println(rs.getInt("deptno"));
      out.println(rs.getString("dname"));
      out.println(rs.getString("loc"));
      out.println("</p>");
    }
  } catch(ClassNotFoundExcep
    out.println("<p>Could not load database driver: "
        + e.getMessage() + "</p>");
  } catch(SQLException e) {
    out.println("<p>SQLException caught: "
        + e.getMessage() + "</p>");
  }   finally { // close connection no matter what
      try {
      if (con != null) {
        /* Step 6: Close the connection */
        con.close();
      }
      } catch (SQLException ignored) {}
  }
out.println("</body></html>");
out.close();
  }
}
```

Import java.sql   This statement makes it easier to use the objects that are needed for database connections. Remember that Java import statements are simply typing aids—this line means that you can type just **ResultSe**t instead of having to type **java.sql.ResultSet**.

The Objects You Need   To establish a connection, execute a SQL statement, and retrieve the results, you need a Connection object, a Statement object, and a ResultSet object.

Loading the Driver   The Class.forName() method is used to load the Oracle JDBC driver.

Establishing a Connection   The DriverManager.getConnection() method can take a JDBC connect string, the username, and the password as parameters. You can use localhost as in this example if your database is on the same machine as the Web server; otherwise, you must give the TCP/IP name of the machine here. Your should probably leave the 1521 (this is the default port used by Oracle Net8) and, if necessary, change the last part (orcl) to the Oracle system identifier (SID) of your database.

Defining the SQL Statement   This is a normal Java String object.

Creating a Statement Object   This object is created with the CreateStatement() method of the Connection object.

Executing the Query   The query is executed with the executeQuery() method, and the result is placed in the ResultSet object. In the case of an update, you use the executeUpdate() method instead.

Retrieving the Results   The results are fetched by looping through the ResultSet object using the next() method as your loop condition. This method advances the pointer to the next row and returns a Boolean value indicating whether there are any more rows to get.

     For each row, you can then use the relevant methods of the ResultSet object to retrieve strings, numbers, and so on. There are many of these *getXXX*() methods— Table 6-1 lists some of the most common ones.

If Anything Goes Wrong   If there is any problem, Java throws an exception. This means that all your SQL statements must be inside a **try** block, and you must use a **catch** clause to catch any exceptions.

Finally   When you have finished with the connection, it must be closed. The **finally** part of a **try/catch** block is guaranteed to be executed whether an exception occurs or

Method	Returns
getDate()	java.sql.Date (object)
getDouble()	double
getFloat()	float
getInt()	int
getLong()	long
getString()	String (object)

TABLE 6-1.   *Getting the Values from a ResultSet*

not, so it is a good place for cleanup operations. Since even closing a connect could possibly return an error, the close() method must be put inside a **try/catch** block (but the exception is ignored—the application is terminating anyway).

The Problems of JDBC

As you can see, it takes some code to retrieve data using JDBC; and even though much of this code is standard, there is always a risk of errors creeping in.

One especially error prone place is the SQL statement itself. When you compile the preceding JDBC example, the Java compiler does not know anything about the database, so it will not complain about errors in your SQL syntax. These errors will not occur until runtime, making the development of JDBC applications somewhat tedious because of the continual cycle of correct, compile, run, and correct again.

Using SQLJ

To overcome some of the limitations of pure JDBC, you can use SQLJ (SQL in Java). This is an emerging standard for embedding SQL statements directly in Java using a special syntax and then using a *precompiler* to convert all the special SQLJ statements into standard JDBC statements. This means that the precompiler can connect to the database to check the syntax of your SQL statements and catch any errors at compile time.

NOTE
If you are familiar with the Oracle family of precompilers, such as Pro*C and Pro*Cobol, you can consider SQLJ to be a kind of "Pro*Java."

When you compile a file with the .sqlj extension in JDeveloper, the precompiler is automatically invoked to convert all the SQLJ statements to JDBC calls before the normal Java compiler is called. The code produced by the precompile, also uses some Oracle-supplied code (the SQLJ Runtime) to simplify the resulting Java source file.

An Example of SQLJ

A SQLJ application that shows all the records in the DEPT table might look like this:

```
package myservlets;

import javax.servlet.*;
import javax.servlet.http.*;
import java.io.*;
import java.util.*;
import java.sql.*;
import oracle.sqlj.runtime.*;

public class DeptListSqlj extends HttpServlet {
  /**
   * Process the HTTP Get request
   */
  public void doGet(HttpServletRequest request,
      HttpServletResponse response)
      throws ServletException, IOException {
    response.setContentType("text/html");
    PrintWriter out = new PrintWriter (response.getOutputStream());
    out.println("<html>");
    out.println("<head><title>DeptList</title></head>");
    out.println("<body>");
    out.println("<h1>Department list</h1>");

    /* connect to database */
    try {
      Oracle.connect("jdbc:oracle:thin:@localhost:1521:orcl"
                     "scott", "tiger");
      #sql iterator DeptIter (int deptno, String dname, String loc);
      DeptIter dept = null;
      #sql dept = { select deptno, dname, loc
              from    dept
              order by deptno };
      while(dept.next()) {
        out.println("<p>");
        out.println(dept.deptno());
        out.println(dept.dname());
        out.println(dept.loc());
```

```
        out.println("</p>");
        }
    } catch(SQLException e)  {
        out.println("<p>SQLException caught: "
          + e.getMessage() + "</p>");
    }
        out.println("</body></html>");
        out.close();
    }
}
```

Importing the SQLJ Support Classes   To use SQLJ, you need the oracle.sqlj.runtime package that the new **import** statement specifies. This is necessary because the Oracle SQLJ precompiler generates code that calls supporting classes found in this package.

Establishing a Connection to the Database   This method uses the same format connect string as JDBC.

The Iterator Type   In a SQLJ query, you need an *iterator* to represent the results you will retrieve from each row. You first define the iterator type in the **#sql iterator** statement that defines a DeptIter object type corresponding to the specific data types returned by the query.

The Actual Iterator   You must then create the actual iterator (the object dept) as an instance of the DeptIter class just defined. Use normal Java syntax: DeptIter dept = null. This object is similar to the record in a cursor FOR loop in PL/SQL. In SQLJ, however, the record must be explicitly defined (in PL/SQL, the cursor record is implicitly defined in the FOR statement).

The SQL Statement   The **#sql** statement defines the SQL statement and assigns the result of the query to the dept object just created.

The Results   You can retrieve the results by looping through all the resulting records just as in JDBC. The dept object as produced by the precompiler has a next() method like the ResultSet used in JDBC, and the precompiler makes one method available for each column in the query to get the value for the current record. Because the iterator included an *int* variable with the name *deptno*, the generated code contains a method deptno() that returns an int. Similarly, the *String dname* variable in the iterator defines a method dname() returning a String object, and the *loc* variable defines a method loc().

If Anything Goes Wrong   Java throws a SQLException if there is any problem executing the SQL, so all the SQLJ code must be inside a try block, and you must use a catch clause to catch this exception.

Setting Up a Project for SQLJ Checking

By default, JDeveloper will not check your SQLJ code at runtime—you must set this up yourself. To do so, right-click the project and choose Properties to bring up the project Property dialog box, and then click the SQLJ tab to bring up the window shown in Figure 6-7.

To enable compile-time checking of the SQL syntax, select the Check SQL Semantics Against Database Schema check box and choose a database connection from the Connection Name drop-down list. If you do not have any connections available, the Connection Name drop-down shows only <No connection>—you must click the New Connection button to invoke the JDeveloper Connection Editor. Create a database connection as described in the earlier section "Creating a Connection from JDeveloper."

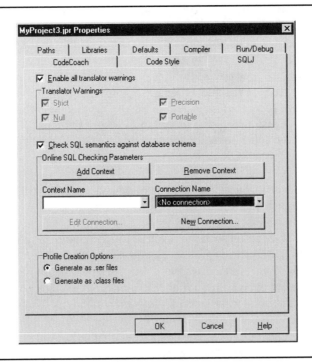

FIGURE 6-7.   *Setting SQLJ properties for a project*

JDBC or SQLJ?

As you can see in Table 6-2, JDBC and SQLJ each have their own advantages and disadvantages.

Because many applications need dynamic SQL somewhere, and I like to have all my database access code use the same technology, I almost always use "pure" JDBC. But if you do not have any dynamic SQL in your application or you are willing to accept two different types of database code, there are distinct advantages to the compile-time checking that SQLJ offers.

Java Servlets

Java servlets is the basic technology used for HTML-based Web applications written in Java. In a Java servlet, you have one piece of Java code (the servlet) that explicitly produces all the HTML that gets sent back to the browser. This is different from the related technology of Java Server Pages, where the programmer produces an HTML format file with embedded Java code. You'll find examples of both approaches with code samples in Chapter 5.

■   If the HTML changes regularly (like on a public Web site that sees smaller or bigger redesigns every few weeks), use Java Server Pages. This allows an HTML designer to use an HTML design tool to change the look of the application without affecting the code.

■   If the HTML design is fairly static (like on an intra- or extranet where the focus is on the functionality), you can use Java servlets. Developing and debugging applications is simpler when all the code can be handled well in the Java development environment.

	Advantages	Disadvantages
JDBC	Supports dynamic SQL Standard	More code Errors in SQL not found until runtime
SQLJ	Fewer lines of code and thus fewer bugs Syntax checking at compile time	Doesn't support dynamic SQL Evolving standard (that is, not yet a standard) Needs Oracle SQLJ Runtime

TABLE 6-2.   *Comparison of JDBC and SQLJ*

Hello World

The first servlet example is (you guessed it!) the classic Hello World application. This section shows how to use JDeveloper 3.2 to build and test this most basic of servlets and assumes that you have already set up an Oracle Web server (the Oracle HTTP Server or Oracle9i Application Server) and have installed JDeveloper 3.2 as described in Chapter 4. If you have not installed and set up an Oracle Web server, you can still follow most of the material in this chapter, as long as you have JDeveloper installed.

The goal is a Java servlet that produces a simple Web page showing the current date and time. The focus is on working with the JDeveloper tool—the following examples will follow the real-world method described in Chapter 5.

Building the Project

The first time you start JDeveloper, it shows the Welcome workspace with a bit of information about JDeveloper and building Oracle Web applications.

A JDeveloper workspace keeps track of the projects and environment settings you use while you are developing your Java program. When you open JDeveloper, it usually opens the last workspace you used so you can continue where you left off. Workspaces are stored in files with the extension .jws. You don't edit these workspace files directly—they get updated automatically when you save the files in the workspace.

You can only have one workspace open at a time; but within the workspace, you can have one or more *projects* open. Projects consist of files and have *project properties* that describe, among other things, where the Java source code and the compiled bytecode is stored on the file system. The current project is always shown in bold font.

To close the Welcome workspace and open a new one, choose File | New Workspace. Then choose File | New Project to start a new project. If the Welcome screen of the Project Wizard appears, click Next to go to the first step in creating a project. On this screen, give your project file a name and choose to create a new project containing an HTTP servlet, as shown in Figure 6-8.

The project file stores project-wide settings but not any of your code. The option A Project Containing a New . . . simply tells JDeveloper to start another wizard once the Project Wizard is done. When finished, click Next to go to Step 2 of the Project Wizard (see Figure 6-9).

On this screen, you can provide a default package name that JDeveloper will then suggest as default for all code you create in the project. By convention, Java packages are named in all lowercase letters.

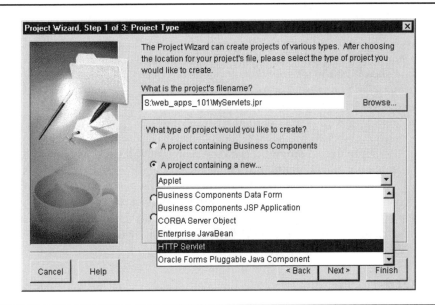

FIGURE 6-8. *Step 1 of creating a new project*

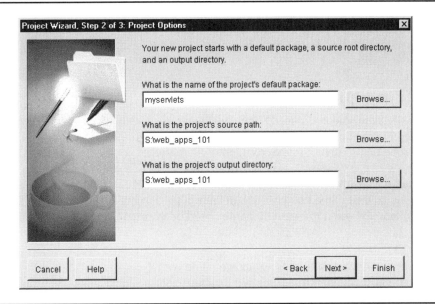

FIGURE 6-9. *Step 2 of creating a new project*

NOTE
*If you are writing code for general use, you should
follow the naming standard proposed by Sun to
avoid naming conflicts. The first part of the package
name should be the internet domain name of your
organization in reverse. For example, my domain
name is vesterli.com, so all my publicly available
packages start with com.vesterli.*

You are not forced to provide a package name, but all code without a package
name is implicitly placed in the default package together with all other objects
without a package name that your Java virtual machine can find. This can lead to
strange behavior, so it is a good idea to always provide a package name.

Enter a package name (for example, myservlets) and click Next through the
remainder of the wizard, or simply click Finished right away to start the HTTP
Servlet Wizard.

NOTE
The project *is a JDeveloper term used for a number
of files that belong together. The* package *is a Java
term for some Java code that the programmer has
indicated has some kind of relationship. One project
can contain many packages; but to keep things
simple, keep the code of one package in one
project, and give the package and the project the
same name.*

Building the Servlet

If the Welcome screen of the HTTP Servlet Wizard appears, click Next to go to the
first step in creating your HTTP servlet, as shown in Figure 6-10.

On the first screen of this wizard, enter the name of your servlet in the Class
field, for example, HelloWorld. By convention, servlets and other classes are named
in mixed case with the first letter in uppercase. The Package field is already filled in
with the package name you chose as default in the Project Wizard, and the File field
is automatically set to the right filename based on your package and class name.

NOTE
*The filename consists of the package name with
each part converted to a directory structure (as
described in the previous section), followed by
the class name with the extension .java.*

FIGURE 6-10. *Step 1 of creating an HTTP servlet*

When finished, click Next to continue to Step 2 (see Figure 6-11). On this screen, you can specify which methods the wizard is to generate for you—in this example, you can deselect the doPost() method and leave only doGet() selected.

NOTE
The doPost() and doGet() methods correspond to the two ways that parameters can be passed to a Web application. This is described in detail in Chapter 5.

When you have finished, click Next through the remainder of this wizard or click Finished right away to end the wizard.

The wizard now creates the HelloWorld.java source file and displays it in the top left frame in the JDeveloper main window.

Looking Around in JDeveloper

When you double-click this file, you will probably see something like Figure 6-12.

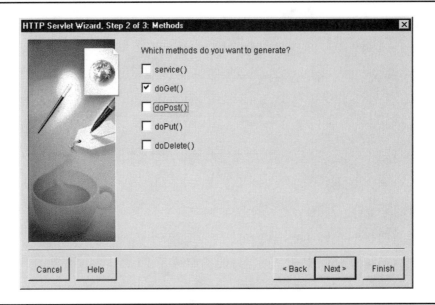

FIGURE 6-11. *Step 2 of Creating an HTTP servlet*

NOTE
This is the default placement of the different windows—you can move all of them around and JDeveloper will remember where you put them next time you start JDeveloper. If you accidentally close a window and want to display it again, choose it from the View menu.

The left side of the JDeveloper window is the Navigator window. It can be moved around or closed if you want to have more space for your code. To hide or display the Navigator window, choose View | Navigator or press ALT-Z.

The Navigator window has two general areas:

■ The upper section is the Navigation pane from which you can navigate through project-related files.

■ The lower section is the Structure pane, in which you can view and browse into the selected file's structure (methods, variables, and so on).

The behavior of these panes depends on which tab is selected at the bottom of the window and which type of node is selected in the Navigation pane.

Structure
pane

Navigation
pane

Save All button

Run button

Source window

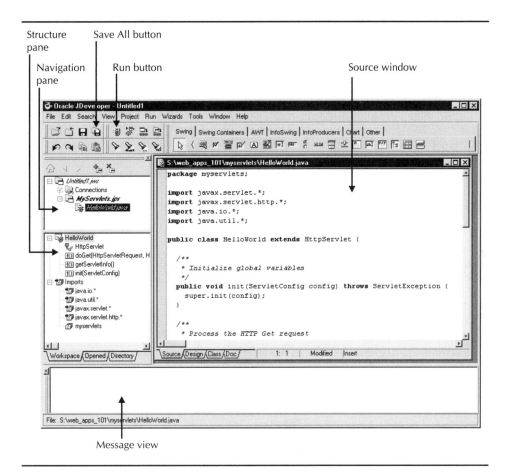

Message view

FIGURE 6-12.   *The JDeveloper main window showing the HelloWorld servlet*

NOTE
*All filenames shown in italics in the top left frame
contain unsaved changes. Make a habit of clicking
the Save All button regularly.*

The bottom part of the screen is the Message view. This window shows errors
and warnings from the compiler as well as console output (what your classes write
using the System.out.println() method). To hide or display this window, choose
View | Message View or press ALT-M.

The right-hand side of the JDeveloper window is used for Source windows. You
can have as many source files open as you like and arrange them with the commands

on the Window menu. At the bottom of each Source window, there are a number of tabs (depending on the file type). For server-side Java code, you generally need only the Source tab.

Now would be a good time to click the Save All button to save the files you have created. When you click this button, you are prompted for a filename for your workspace.

As just described, the workspace contains information about open projects and files, the placement of any open windows, and so on. Give your workspace a name and click Save. You might notice that all the italicized names in the Navigation pane change to a regular font, indicating that there are no longer any unsaved changes.

Running Your First Servlet

Before you run this first servlet, scroll down through the code in the Source window until you come to the following line:

```
out.println("<body>Hello From HelloWorld doGet()");
```

Replace the text with some of your own, for instance:

```
out.println("<body><h1>Hello World</h1><p>The time is "
    + new Date().toString() + "</p>");
```

This code creates the Hello World message as an HTML heading, creates a new Date object with the current date and time, and converts this object to a string.

Click the Run button (the green stoplight) or press F9 to run your servlet within the JDeveloper environment. JDeveloper automatically compiles your Java source code into bytecode, starts up a lightweight Java Web server to execute it, and starts your default Web browser to display the results. If everything goes smoothly, you should see the screen in Figure 6-13.

If there is a problem with your code, JDeveloper will highlight the offending line, and show the errors and warnings in the Message View window at the bottom of the screen. If, for example, you accidentally delete the closing quote, you'll see the error message shown in Figure 6-14. Fix the error and try again.

What Did JDeveloper Build for You?

If you scroll through the code that JDeveloper has generated, you will see that JDeveloper uses 38 lines just to say "Hello World." Fortunately, only about half of this code is strictly necessary, so let's look at the essentials first. The same example pared down to the bone looks like this:

```
1: package myservlets;
2:
3: import javax.servlet.*;
4: import javax.servlet.http.*;
5: import java.io.*;
6: import java.util.*;
7:
8: public class HelloWorldShort extends HttpServlet {
9:    public void doGet(HttpServletRequest request,
          HttpServletResponse response)
          throws ServletException, IOException {
10:       response.setContentType("text/html");
11:       OutputStreamWriter osw =
             new OutputStreamWriter(response.getOutputStream());
12:       PrintWriter out = new PrintWriter (response.getOutputStream());
13:       out.println("<html>");
14:       out.println("<head><title>Hello World</title></head>");
15:       out.println("<body><h1>Hello World</h1><p>The time is "
             + new Date().toString() + "</p>");
16:       out.println("</body></html>");
17:       out.close();
18:    }
19: }
```

■ **The package statement**   This must be the very first line in your servlet
   (apart from any initial comments); it defines which package your servlet
   is part of.

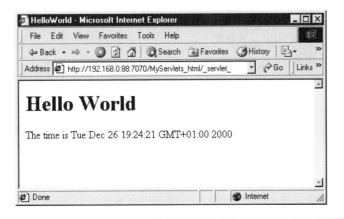

FIGURE 6-13.   *Hello World servlet*

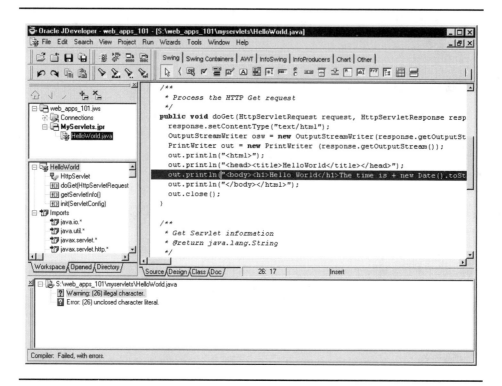

FIGURE 6-14. *Hello World servlet with an error*

- **The import statements** Lines 3–6 define the packages that your servlet will use. This does not include these packages in your code—they must still be available to the Java virtual machine at runtime for your servlet to work. But they make the job of the programmer easier (and the code easier to read) because the compiler knows that you want to use classes from these packages. The code could still work without any import statements, but then you would have to type the full name of the class every time you use it—and typing **HttpServletRequest** is much more convenient than typing **javax.servlet.http.HttpServletRequest** every time.

- **The servlet is defined** This happens in line 8. All servlets that you write *extend* the class HttpServlet (that is part of the javax.servlet.http class just imported). The idea of extending existing classes is one of the cornerstones of object-oriented programming, but you don't really have to know about this. Just note that this line must be used to start all servlets.

■ **The doGet() method**   This method is defined in line 9. A method in a Java class is similar to a function or procedure in a traditional programming language like PL/SQL: you call it with some parameters and optionally receive a return value.

The doGet() method is called by the servlet Web server when the user requests a page. The Web server provides two objects—an HttpServletRequest object and an HttpServletResponse object—and expects nothing returned (thus the keyword *void*, which means "no return value"). The names *request* and *response* are part of your program—you can change them if you like, but this is the default generated by JDeveloper.

This *signature* (HttpServletRequest and HttpServletResponse objects in, nothing out) is part of the *contract* between the Web server and your servlet. The servlet standard specifies this contract that defines which methods of your Java servlet will get called with which parameters at what times.

■ **The response type**   Line 10 defines the response type. All Web applications will call the setContentType() methods of the HttpServletResponse object to set the MIME type of the reply. This is almost always text/html as just shown, but you could set it to some other value like application/ vnd.ms-excel if you want to instruct the Web browser that this servlet produces output that should be handled by Microsoft Excel. There is more information about MIME types in Chapter 5.

■ **The output destination**   This is set in lines 11–12. These two lines create a new PrintWriter object that refers to an output stream that belongs to the HttpServletResponse object (called *response*). This establishes the connection between your servlet code and the Web server that will pass your output back to the Web browser.

You don't have to understand the intricacies of Java data streams and writers to write servlets: consider these lines a necessary incantation to get an object to write output to.

■ **The page content**   The page is finally created and sent to the Web server in lines 13–16. You can consider all the code up to this point to be a standard preamble necessary for all servlets; lines 13–16 are the payload.

To write a line of HTML output, simply call the println() method of the out object that you created. Line 15 creates a new Date object containing the current date and immediately converts it to a string that is appended to the static string.

■ **Closing the page**   This happens in line 17 with a call to the close() method of the out object.

NOTE

If you forget to close the page, as in line 17, you won't see any output!

The Rest of What JDeveloper Built

The previous section covered the basics needed to output HTML from a servlet, but JDeveloper built some more code. The complete code built by JDeveloper looks like this:

```
 1: package myservlets;
 2:
 3: import javax.servlet.*;
 4: import javax.servlet.http.*;
 5: import java.io.*;
 6: import java.util.*;
 7:
 8: public class HelloWorld extends HttpServlet {
 9:
10:    /**
11:     * Initialize global variables
12:     */
13:    public void init(ServletConfig config) throws ServletException {
14:      super.init(config);
15:    }
16:
17:    /**
18:     * Process the HTTP Get request
19:     */
20:    public void doGet(HttpServletRequest request,
            HttpServletResponse response)
            throws ServletException, IOException {
21:      response.setContentType("text/html");
22:      OutputStreamWriter osw =
            new OutputStreamWriter(response.getOutputStream());
23:      PrintWriter out = new PrintWriter (response.getOutputStream());
24:      out.println("<html>");
25:      out.println("<head><title>Hello World</title></head>");
26:        out.println("<body><h1>Hello World</h1>"
                + "<p>The time is " + new Date().toString() + "</p>");
27:      out.println("</body></html>");
28:      out.close();
29:    }
30:
```

```
31:   /**
32:    * Get Servlet information
33:    * @return java.lang.String
34:    */
35:   public String getServletInfo() {
36:     return "myservlets.HelloWorld Information";
37:   }
38: }
```

- **javadoc Comments**   The comments in lines 10–12, 17–19, and 31–34 are comments—that is, the Java compiler ignores them because they are enclosed in /* and */. But because they start with the special /** marker, they can also be recognized as documentation comments by the javadoc utility. This is a tool that Sun offers with the Java development kit that generates code documentation in HTML format; the documentation of the Java API itself was generated with javadoc. JDeveloper has a wizard on the Wizards menu that can call this tool—see Chapter 11.

- **The init() method**   This is another part of the contract defined by the servlet standard: the Web server must call the init() method first when a servlet is loaded (lines 13–15). If you have an init() method, it's important that it contain the super.init(config) command as in line 14 to ensure that your own initialization supplements (and does not replace) the standard initialization for servlets.

  JDeveloper automatically generates this method; but, to save space, it will not be shown in any of the following examples.

- **The getServletInfo() method**   Lines 35–37 are intended for management tools that might ask the servlet to describe itself. A well-behaved servlet should provide this information, but, it is not required. JDeveloper automatically generates this method; but, to save space, it will not be shown in the following examples.

Testing Your Code Through the Web Server

If you have set up an Oracle Web server as described in Chapter 4 and at the beginning of this chapter, you can also run your Java servlet through the Web server by typing the following URL into your browser:

   http://<server>/servlet/<package>.<servlet>

where <server> is the TCP/IP name of your server, <package> is the name of the package that you just selected, and <servlet> is the name of your servlet class. Note that the servlet name is case sensitive: if you use upper- or lowercase in your servlet name, you must use it in the URL as well.

List of All Employees

Now that you have your first servlet running, it is time to move on to a servlet that connects to the database and lists all the employees from the EMP table. In this example, you will follow the steps outlined in Chapter 5:

1. Application design

2. Page design

3. Conversion

4. Business logic

Application Design

In this step, you develop the storyboard and the application flow diagram for your application. For this simple application, you have only one screen, leading to the simplest possible storyboard, as shown in Figure 6-15.

Since there is only one screen involved that does not take any parameters and is followed by no other screen, it does not make sense to produce an application flow diagram—all the necessary information is now available to build the skeleton of the ShowEmpList servlet.

Building the Skeleton

Let's include this servlet in the existing project. Choose File | New and select the Web Objects tab. The following screen appears:

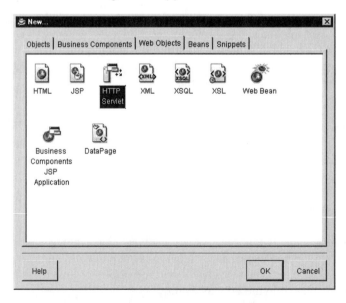

```
Employee List

Emp.no.   Name    Job
7369      Smith   Clerk
7499      Allen   Salesman
7521      Ward    Salesman
7566      Jones   Manager
```

FIGURE 6-15.   *A one-screen storyboard*

Choose HTTP Servlet and click OK to start the HTTP Servlet Wizard. If the welcome page appears (it keeps coming until you remove the check mark next to Display This Page Next Time), click Next to go to the first step in creating your HTTP servlet.

Give this servlet the name ShowEmpList and click Next. In the next step, leave both the doPost() and doGet() methods selected. Click Finished to end the wizard.

The wizard now creates the ShowEmpList.java source file for you and adds it to the project in the JDeveloper Navigation pane. Double-click the file to open it and replace the content of the doGet() method with a call to doPost(), like this:

```java
/**
 * Process the HTTP Get request
 */
public void doGet(HttpServletRequest request,
    HttpServletResponse response)
    throws ServletException, IOException {
  doPost(request, response);
}
```

This ensures that the same code runs whether you call the servlet through the get or post method. Remember that get allows you to pass parameters as part of the URL and is useful for testing, while post is usually used to pass parameters from preceding Web pages.

So far, this servlet can only say "Hello"; you will add your HTML and the business logic in later steps.

Page Design

The second step is to produce an example HTML page. This could look like Figure 6-16 and have the following HTML code:

```html
<html>
<head>
<title>Employee List</title>
```

```
<link rel="stylesheet" href="/web_apps_101.css" type="text/css" />
</head>

<body bgcolor="#FFFFFF">
<table width="550">
  <tr>
    <td>
      <h1>Employee List</h1>
    </td>
      <td align="right">
      <img src="/web_apps_101.gif"
          alt="Web Apps 101 logo" width="90" height="69" />
    </td>
  </tr>
</table>
<table width="550"><tr><td>
<p>This list shows all employees</p>
<table border cellpadding="4">
  <tr>
    <th>Emp. no.</th>
    <th>Name</th>
    <th>Job</th>
  </tr>
  <tr>
    <td>7369</td>
    <td>Smith</td>
    <td>Clerk</td>
  </tr>
  <tr>
    <td>7499</td>
    <td>Allen</td>
    <td>Salesman</td>
  </tr>
  <tr>
    <td>7521</td>
    <td>Ward</td>
    <td>Salesman</td>
  </tr>
  <tr>
    <td>7566</td>
    <td>Jones</td>
    <td>Manager</td>
  </tr>
</table>
<p align="center">
<font size="-1">
  Comments, questions? Contact the
  <a href="mailto:sten@vesterli.dk">webmaster</a>
</font></p>
```

```
</td></tr></table>
</body>
</html>
```

Make sure that all references to other files (such as style sheets and images) start with a forward slash. This indicates a site-relative URL that will work unchanged in both an HTML file and a Java servlet (no matter what the URL of the HTML file or Java servlet is).

NOTE
Beware of references (such as src= or href=) that do not start with a forward slash. References starting with file:// refer to files delivered straight to your browser from the hard disk of your development machine—this will not work for other users accessing your pages through the Web server. References starting with something other than "/" are relative to the current page—these references will break if you move your HTML file from one directory to another and definitely won't work once you convert your HTML to Java servlets.

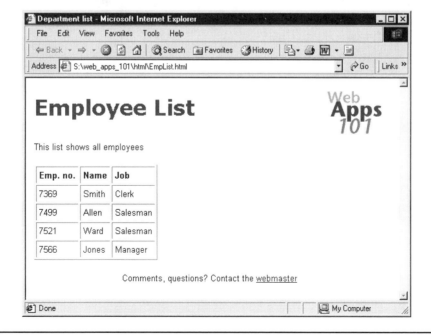

FIGURE 6-16.   *An example Web page showing an employee list*

When you are satisfied with your HTML page, you can test it in your target browsers, run it through a validation tool or service (see resources in Chapter 13), and present it to your users for feedback and approval.

Conversion

The third step is to convert the static HTML file to Java source code and, optionally, modularize the code.

Converting to Java

To convert the HTML to Java, you need to "escape" all the double quotes in the HTML code (add backslashes as a prefix) and wrap each line in a call to out.println().

You can achieve this with the html2java utility that also allows you to specify that a four-character indent would match nicely with the Java servlet (see Figure 6-17).

In JDeveloper, open the generated emplist.java file, and cut and paste the entire contents into your ShowEmpList servlet, replacing all of the out.println() statements

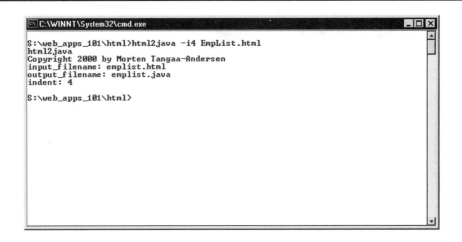

FIGURE 6-17. *Using the html2java utility*

in the doPost() method. Your complete servlet (less the init() and getServletInfo() methods) should then look something like this:

```
package myservlets;

import javax.servlet.*;
import javax.servlet.http.*;
import java.io.*;
import java.util.*;

public class ShowEmpList extends HttpServlet {
[snip]
/**
   * Process the HTTP Get request
   */
  public void doGet(HttpServletRequest request,
      HttpServletResponse response)
      throws ServletException, IOException {
    doPost(request, response);
  }

  /**
   * Process the HTTP Post request
   */
  public void doPost(HttpServletRequest request,
      HttpServletResponse response)
      throws ServletException, IOException {
    response.setContentType("text/html");
    OutputStreamWriter osw =
        new OutputStreamWriter(response.getOutputStream());
    PrintWriter out = new PrintWriter(osw);
    out.println("<html>");
    out.println("<head>");
    out.println("<title>Department list</title>");
    out.println("<link rel=\"stylesheet\" "
        + "href=\"/web_apps_101.css\" type=\"text/css\" />");
    out.println("</head>");
    out.println("");
    out.println("<body bgcolor=\"#FFFFFF\">");
    out.println("<table width=\"550\">");
```

```
    out.println("   <tr>");
    out.println("      <td>");
    out.println("        <h1>Employee List</h1>");
    out.println("      </td>");
    out.println("<td align=\"right\">");
    out.println("         <img src=\"/ web_apps_101.gif\" "
        + "alt=\"Web Apps 101 logo\" "
        + "width=\"90\" height=\"69\" /> ");
    out.println("      </td>");
    out.println("   </tr>");
    out.println("</table>");
    out.println("<table width=\"550\"><tr><td>");
    out.println("");
    out.println("<p>This list shows all employees</p>");
    out.println("<table border cellpadding=\"4\">");
    out.println("   <tr> ");
    out.println("      <th>Emp. no.</th>");
    out.println("      <th>Name</th>");
    out.println("      <th>Job</th>");
    out.println("   </tr>");
    out.println("   <tr> ");
    out.println("      <td>7369</td>");
    out.println("      <td>Smith</td>");
    out.println("      <td>Clerk</td>");
    out.println("   </tr>");
[snip]
    out.println("</table>");
    out.println("<p align=\"center\">");
    out.println("  <font size=\"-1\">");
    out.println("  Comments, questions? Contact the "
        + "<a href=\"mailto:sten@vesterli.dk\">webmaster</a>");
    out.println("  </font></p> ");
    out.println("</td></tr></table>");
    out.println("</body>");
    out.println("</html>");
    out.println("</html>");
    out.close();
  }
[snip]
}
```

After pasting the HTML-generating code in, you must remove the emplist.java file from your project (File | Remove File). If you do not do this, JDeveloper will try to compile the emplist.java file; but because this file is only a code snippet and not a valid Java file, your project will not compile.

Next, run the ShowEmpList servlet from JDeveloper to make sure that the conversion was successful and that your servlet contains only valid Java code.

If you have problems with the images or fonts, your Web browser probably cannot find the style sheet or the images. Check that all your hypertext references start with a forward slash. Remember that when running a servlet through JDeveloper, JDeveloper only runs the servlet; it does not serve the style sheets and images that your page might refer to. If all your image and style sheet references start with a slash (such as /web_apps_101.gif), these static files will be served by your Web server so your page looks correct.

If you can't make it work perfectly through JDeveloper, don't worry. Try to run your servlet through the Web server instead, as described in the previous example— if that works, don't waste too much time trying to make everything run in JDeveloper.

Modularization

Before you start adding the business logic to this servlet, it is important to notice that your servlet is full of HTML formatting tags. If you add your business logic to the servlet as it looks now, you'll be mixing database operations and logic with the presentation that's controlled by the HTML tags. This will not affect the functionality of the application, but it *will* make the application harder to maintain.

It is good programming practice to separate the presentation of data from the business logic, so you should now examine your HTML code a bit more closely. It consists of different types of content:

- **The page header (static text, logo, and so on)**   This is the same on every screen in the application.

- **Introductory text**   This text is different on the different screens in the application, but should have the same font and other formatting. It is independent of the database values—every time a screen is produced, the introductory text is the same.

- **A table of results**   This is dynamic data retrieved from the database.

- **The end of the page (static text)**   This is the same on every screen in the application.

Ideally, every piece of HTML code should be removed and placed in a separate Format class that every module in your application can call. This will neatly separate the presentation (so if someone wants to change the look of the application without changing the logic, she can just change the Format class) and has the added advantage of ensuring consistency when all code modules call the same method to start a Web page.

To create such a Format class, choose File | New and double-click the Class icon. This brings up the Class Wizard (see Figure 6-18) that helps you create a new class. You will now be creating a standard Java class, not a servlet. This is simply a helper module that will only be called by your servlets.

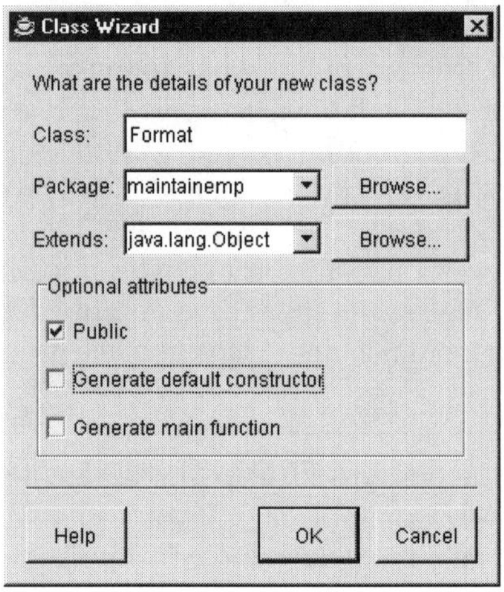

FIGURE 6-18. *The Class Wizard*

Give the class the name "Format" and remove the check mark next to Generate Default Constructor. If you are familiar with Java terminology, you will notice that this new class is not going to be instantiated—we will only be defining and using class methods from this class. When you click OK, JDeveloper builds the Format class for you and adds it to the Navigation pane in the top left corner of the JDeveloper window.

Open this file and add three methods to it:

- A pageStart() method that takes the page title as a String parameter

- An introText() method that takes the introductory text as a String parameter

- A pageEnd() method that takes no parameters

All three methods should return a String object. The skeleton of your class might look like this:

```
package maintainemp;

public class Format extends Object {
  public static String pageStart(String title) {
    String s = new String();
    return s;
  }
```

```
    public static String introText(String text) {
      String s = new String();
      return s;
    }

    public static String pageEnd() {
      String s = new String();
      return s;
    }
}
```

Just to make sure the syntax is right, press CTRL-F9 to recompile the project.

Next, copy the HTML-generating Java code from your ShowEmpList servlet to this new class. Read through the code to find all the places where static values should be replaced by parameter values, and replace them so that your class looks something like this:

```
package maintainemp;

public class Format extends Object {
  public static String pageStart(String title) {
    String s = null;
    s =    "<html>\n"
        + "<head>\n"
        + "<title>" + title + "</title>\n"
        + "<link rel=\"stylesheet\" "
        + "href=\"/ web_apps_101.css\""
        + "type=\"text/css\" />\n"
        + "</head>\n"
        + "\n"
        + "<body bgcolor=\"#FFFFFF\">\n"
        + "<table width=\"550\">\n"
        + "   <tr>\n"
        + "      <td>\n"
        + "         <h1>" + title + "</h1>\n"
        + "      </td>\n"
        + "      <td align=\"right\">\n"
        + "         <img src=\"../images/web_apps_101.gif\" "
        + "alt=\"Web Apps 101 logo\" "
        + "width=\"90\" height=\"69\" /> \n"
        + "      </td>\n"
        + "   </tr>\n"
        + "</table>\n"
        + "<table width=\"550\"><tr><td>"
      ;
    return s;
  }
```

```
public static String introText (String text) {
  String s = null;
  s ="<p>" + text + "</p>";
  return s;
}

public static String pageEnd() {
  String s = null;
  s =    "<p align=\"center\">\n"
      + "<font size=\"-1\">\n"
      + "  Comments, questions? Contact the "
      + "  <a href=\"mailto:sten@vesterli.dk\">webmaster</a>\n"
      + "</font></p> \n"
      + "</td></tr></table>\n"
      + "</body>\n"
      + "</html>"
   ;
  return s;
}
}
```

While you do this, occasionally press CTRL-F9 to check the syntax. When you have finished, replace all the HTML-generating code in your ShowEmpList servlet with calls to the three methods in your new Format class. Your servlet should then look something like this:

```
package maintainemp;

import javax.servlet.*;
import javax.servlet.http.*;
import java.io.*;
import java.util.*;

public class ShowEmpList extends HttpServlet {
[snip]
  /**
   * Process the HTTP Post request
   */
  public void doPost(HttpServletRequest request,
      HttpServletResponse response)
      throws ServletException, IOException {
    response.setContentType("text/html");
    OutputStreamWriter osw =
        new OutputStreamWriter(response.getOutputStream());
    PrintWriter out = new PrintWriter(osw);
    out.println(Format.pageStart("Employee List"));
    out.println(Format.introText("This list shows all employees"));
    out.println("<table border cellpadding=\"4\">");
```

```
      out.println("   <tr> ");
      out.println("      <th>Emp. no.</th>");
      out.println("      <th>Name</th>");
      out.println("      <th>Job</th>");
      out.println("   </tr>");
      out.println("   <tr> ");
      out.println("      <td>7369</td>");
      out.println("      <td>Smith</td>");
      out.println("      <td>Clerk</td>");
      out.println("   </tr>");
      out.println("   <tr> ");
      out.println("      <td>7499</td>");
      out.println("      <td>Allen</td>");
      out.println("      <td>Salesman</td>");
      out.println("   </tr>");
      out.println("   <tr> ");
      out.println("      <td>7521</td>");
      out.println("      <td>Ward</td>");
      out.println("      <td>Salesman</td>");
      out.println("   </tr>");
      out.println("   <tr>");
      out.println("      <td>7566</td>");
      out.println("      <td>Jones</td>");
      out.println("      <td>Manager</td>");
      out.println("   </tr>");
      out.println("</table>");
      out.println(Format.pageEnd());
      out.close();
  }
}
```

Try to run this servlet from JDeveloper to make sure that it still produces the example HTML page that you started from.

Business Logic

The fourth and final step is to add the business logic. In this case, this involves replacing the static example data on the page with dynamic content retrieved from the database. This example shows how to use JDBC for the database connection, but you could just as well use SQLJ—see the"Using JDBC" section, earlier in the chapter.

Getting Data with JDBC

Do you remember the six steps to get data from the database with JDBC?

1. Load the driver.

2. Establish a connection.

3. Create a statement.

4. Execute the statement.

5. Fetch the results.

6. Close the connection.

A Code Example

To perform the six steps, your code will look very similar to the preceding JDBC example at the beginning of this chapter—something like this:

```
package maintainemp;

import javax.servlet.*;
import javax.servlet.http.*;
import java.io.*;
import java.util.*;
import java.sql.*;

public class ShowEmpList extends HttpServlet {
[snip]
  /**
   * Process the HTTP Post request
   */
  public void doPost(HttpServletRequest request,
      HttpServletResponse response)
      throws ServletException, IOException {
    response.setContentType("text/html");
    OutputStreamWriter osw =
        new OutputStreamWriter(response.getOutputStream());
    PrintWriter out = new PrintWriter(osw);
    out.println(Format.pageStart("Employee List"));
    out.println(Format.introText("This list shows all employees"));
    /* check for database connectivity */
    Connection con = null;
    Statement stmt = null;
    ResultSet rs = null;
    try {
      Class.forName("oracle.jdbc.driver.OracleDriver");
      con = DriverManager.getConnection(
          "jdbc:oracle:thin:@localhost:1521:orcl",
          "scott", "tiger");
      String stmtString = new String("select empno, ename, job " +
          "from emp order by ename");
      out.println("<table border cellpadding=\"4\">");
      out.println("  <tr> ");
```

```
        out.println("    <th>Emp. no.</th>");
        out.println("    <th>Name</th>");
        out.println("    <th>Job</th>");
        out.println("  </tr>");

        /* start getting the data from the table */
        stmt = con.createStatement();
        rs = stmt.executeQuery(stmtString);
        while(rs.next()) {
          out.println("  <tr> ");
          out.println("    <td>" + rs.getInt("empno") + "</td>");
          out.println("    <td>" + rs.getString("ename") + "</td>");
          out.println("    <td>" + rs.getString("job") + "</td>");
          out.println("  </tr>");
        }
        out.println("</table>");
    } catch(ClassNotFoundException e) {
        out.println("<p>Could not load database driver: "
            + e.getMessage() + "</p>");
    } catch(SQLException e) {
        out.println("<p>SQLException caught: " +
            + e.getMessage() + "</p>");
    } finally { // close connection no matter what
        try {
          if (con != null) {
            con.close();
          }
        } catch (SQLException ignored) {}
    }
    out.println(Format.pageEnd());
    out.close();
  }
[snip]
}
```

Import java.sql   This statement makes it easier to use the objects that are needed for database connections. Remember that Java import statements are simply typing aids—this line means that you can type **ResultSet** instead of typing **java.sql.ResultSet**.

The Objects You Need   To establish a connection, execute a SQL statement, and retrieve the results, you need a Connection object, a Statement object, and a ResultSet object.

Loading the Driver   The Class.forName() method is used to load the Oracle JDBC driver.

Establishing a Connection   The DriverManager.getConnection() method can take a JDBC connect string, the user name, and the password as parameters. You can use localhost as in this example if your database is on the same machine as the Web server; otherwise, you must give the TCP/IP name of the machine here. You should probably leave the 1521 (this is the default port used by Oracle Net8), and, if necessary, change the last part (orcl) to the Oracle system identifier (SID) of your database.

Defining the SQL Statement   This is a normal Java String object.

Creating a Statement Object   This object is created with the CreateStatement() method of the Connection object.

Executing the Query   The query is executed with the executeQuery() method, and the result is placed in the ResultSet object. In case of an update, use the executeUpdate() method instead.

Retrieving the Results   The results are fetched by looping through the ResultSet object using the next() method as your loop condition. This method advances the pointer to the next row and returns a Boolean value indicating whether there are any more rows to get.

For each row, you can then use the getString(), getInt(), and other getXXX() methods of the ResultSet object to retrieve strings, numbers, and so on. Refer back to Table 6-1 for the most common of these getXXX() methods.

If Anything Goes Wrong   If there is any problem, Java throws an exception. This means that all your SQL statements must be inside a try block and you must use a **catch** clause to catch any exceptions.

Finally   When you have finished with the connection, it must be closed. The "finally" part of a try/catch block is guaranteed to be executed, so it is a good place for cleanup operations. Since even then closing a connect could possibly return an error, the close() method call must be put inside a try/catch block (but the exception is ignored—the application is terminating anyway).

List with Restriction

Showing a list of all employees demonstrated how to establish a connection to the database and retrieve data. However, not many applications show all the data— you'll need to add some kind of restriction. The next example expands on the previous by adding a page where the user can enter part of a name to search for.

This example includes two new features: how to read parameters from a Java servlet and how to use the PreparedStatement class for SQL queries with bind variables.

Once more, the process goes through the same four steps:

1. Application design

2. Page design

3. Conversion

4. Business logic

Application Design

The storyboard (see Figure 6-19) now shows two screens: one in which to enter the search criteria and one in which to view the results.

In this simple application, a little bit of information is passed from the SearchEmp screen to the ShowEmpList screen: the employee name to search for. You can picture this as the very simple application flow diagram shown in Figure 6-20.

As you saw in Chapter 5, this diagram shows the screens as parallelograms (SearchEmp and EmpList, in this example) and the code modules as square boxes. The flow of the application is a zigzag line between code modules and Web pages. As a naming convention, you can let the name of each module that produces a Web page start with Show (for example, ShowSearchEmp and ShowEmpList).

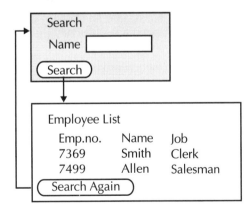

FIGURE 6-19. *A two-screen storyboard*

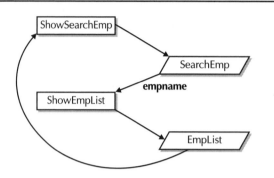

FIGURE 6-20. *A simple application flow diagram*

On the arrows, the names of the parameters passed between modules and screens is written. In this example, the SearchEmp screen is going to pass a parameter called **empname** to the ShowEmpList module that produces the EmpList Web page.

The finished diagram now shows the two servlets you need, and the one parameter (**empname**) is passed into the ShowEmpList servlet.

Creating the Skeleton Servlets

Let's create a new project for this application: choose File I New Project, give a project file name (for example, c:\web_apps_101\maintainemp.jpr), and choose A Project Containing a New HTTP Servlet. Provide a default package name (for example, maintainemp), and choose a source and output directory (for example, c:\web_apps_101). Click Finish to end the Project Wizard and proceed to the HTTP Servlet Wizard.

Create the first servlet with the name ShowSearchEmp, both a doPost() and doGet() method, and no parameters.

When finished, start the HTTP Servlet Wizard again by selecting File I New, choose the Web Objects tab, and choose to create a new HTTP servlet. Give the servlet the name ProcessSearchEmp, leave both doPost() and doGet() checked, and click Next to proceed to the third step in the HTTP Servlet Wizard:

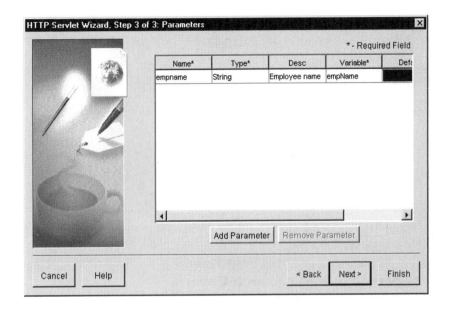

Here you want to add a parameter **empname** to the doPost() method. To do this, click each field in sequence and provide the following values:

■ **Name**   Enter the servlet parameter name (**empname**).

■ **Type**   Select the servlet parameter type (String).

■ **Description**   Enter a description of the servlet parameter (Employee name).

■ **Variable**   Enter the name of the Java variable to which you want to assign this parameter value (empName).

■ **Default**   Leave blank.

■ **Method**   Select the method to which this parameter applies (doPost()).

When you have finished, click Finish. The wizard now creates the ShowEmpList.java source file for you and adds it to the project in the JDeveloper Navigation pane.

Open both servlets and replace the entire content of the doGet() method with a call to doPost(). This leaves the doGet() method in both servlets looking like this:

```
public void doGet(HttpServletRequest request,
    HttpServletResponse response)
    throws ServletException, IOException {
  doPost(request, response);
}
```

Run both servlets from JDeveloper to check that you did not accidentally delete too much or leave extra lines of code in.

Page Design

The next step is to produce static HTML Web pages to determine the HTML that the application must produce.

A New Screen to Enter Search Criteria

For this application, you need an extra screen in which the user can enter the search criteria. It could look like Figure 6-21 and have the following HTML:

```
<html>
<head>
<title>Search for Employees</title>
<link rel="stylesheet" href="/webstart.css"
    type="text/css" />
</head>

<body bgcolor="#FFFFFF">
<table width="550">
  <tr>
    <td>
      <h1>Search for Employees</h1>
    </td>
      <td align="right">
      <img src="/web_apps_101.gif"
          alt="Web Apps 101 logo" width="90" height="69" />
    </td>
  </tr>
</table>
<table width="550"><tr><td>
<p>Enter a name or part of a name and press
the <b> Search </b>button. </p>
<form method="post" action="maintainemp.ShowEmpList">
<table>
  <tr>
```

```
      <td>Name</td>
      <td>
        <input type="text" name="empname" />
      </td>
    </tr>
    <tr>
      <td colspan="2">
        <input type="submit" value=" Search " />
      </td>
    </tr>
</table>
</form>
<p> </p>
<p align="center">
<font size="-1">
  Comments, questions? Contact the
  <a href="mailto:sten@vesterli.dk">webmaster</a>
</font></p>
</td></tr></table>
</body>
</html>
```

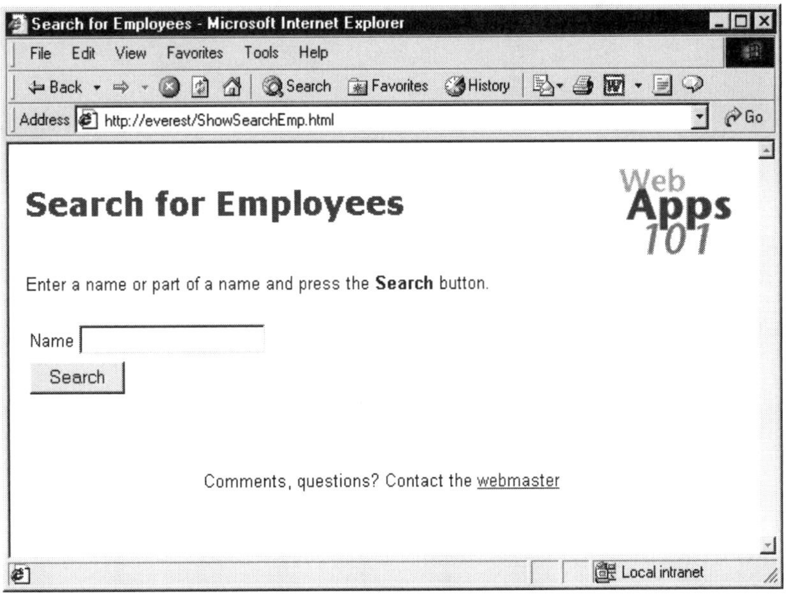

FIGURE 6-21.   *An example search form*

The Action This attribute in the <form> tag specifies where the data on this form is sent (to the servlet maintainemp.ShowEmpList). Remember that this can be any program anywhere on the net—whether written in Java, PL/SQL, or something else.

The Text Field The name attribute of the text field has the value **empname,** so the value entered in this field will be passed to the ShowEmpList servlet with the name **empname.**

The Submit Button This button is used to submit the HTML form, that is, to send the value of the text field to the URL specified in the action attribute of the <form> tag.

Adding a Button to the Employee List

In addition to the new page, you also need to make a change to the Employee List page: it needs a button to go back to the Search screen, as shown in Figure 6-22. This can be done with an HTML form, even though you do not have any fields in which the user can enter anything. The HTML code looks like this:

```
<html>
<head>
<title>Department list</title>
<link rel="stylesheet" href="/web_apps_101.css" type="text/css" />
</head>

<body bgcolor="#FFFFFF">
[snip]
<table width="550"><tr><td>
<p>This list shows all employees</p>
<table border cellpadding="4">
  <tr>
    <th>Emp. no.</th>
    <th>Name</th>
    <th>Job</th>
  </tr>
[snip]
  <tr>
    <td>7566</td>
    <td>Jones</td>
    <td>Manager</td>
  </tr>
</table>
<form method="post"
    action="maintainemp.ShowSearchEmp">
  <input type="submit" value=" Search Again " />
</form>
[snip]
```

```
</td></tr></table>
</body>
</html>
```

The action attribute in this simple HTML form contains the instruction to go to the URL maintainemp.ShowSearchEmp whenever the user submits the form by clicking the Submit button. And the only content of the form is the Submit button with the label Search Again.

The example HTML pages are now ready to be shown to your users.

Conversion

The next step is converting the HTML and incorporating it into your Java servlets.

Converting to Java

Once more, you can convert your HTML by hand, or use a utility such as html2java (with the -i4 option to indent four spaces) to convert both SearchEmp.html and the updated EmpList.html to corresponding snippets of Java source code.

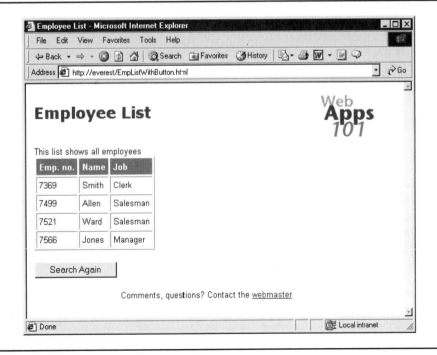

FIGURE 6-22. *The Record List screen with the Search Again button*

In JDeveloper, open the searchemp.java file that you just built and place its entire content into the ShowSearchEmp servlet, replacing all the existing out.println lines in the doPost() method. Similarly, place the content of the emplist.java file into the ShowEmpList servlet. When you've finished, use File | Remove to remove both the searchemp.java and the emplist.java files from the project (they are not complete Java source files, so the project will not compile if you leave them as part of the project).

Now it should be possible for you to run both the ShowSearchEmp and the ShowEmpList servlets from JDeveloper. You should always test your servlets after the conversion to check that your basic Java code is correct before you start adding the business logic.

NOTE

If you get a "Hello from doGet()" message or a blank screen with the correct page title, you probably forgot to replace the automatically generated content of the doGet() method with a call to doPost().

Formatting

Just as in the preceding example, you should split the presentation logic (the HTML tags) from the business logic.

Since you created an application-specific Format class for the previous example, you already have the code you need. By reusing this class, you automatically ensure that your HTML is consistent through the application.

Using HTML Forms

Looking at the converted HTML code, you also quickly realize that it contains quite a lot of code that produces the HTML for elements of HTML forms (elements such as input fields, Submit buttons, and so on).

This code should also be taken out of the servlet before it gets mixed up with the business logic. You could put it in the application-specific Format package together with the HTML to start and end pages, but HTML code for creating HTML forms elements isn't really application specific and is unlikely to change.

Because this code is usually identical or very similar in many projects, it makes sense to create a global class that handles HTML form elements. You can write your own package from scratch, or you can use a prebuilt one like the HtmlForm class of the com.vesterli.webstart package. (This package is described in more detail in

Chapter 12, and is available for download from **www.vesterli.com** together with an example Format class and all the code examples).

After modularizing your code fully using both your project-specific Format class and the HtmlForm package, the code for the ShowSearchEmp servlet might look like this:

```
package maintainemp;

import javax.servlet.*;
import javax.servlet.http.*;
import java.io.*;
import java.util.*;
import com.vesterli.webstart.*;

public class ShowSearchEmp extends HttpServlet {
[snip]
  /**
   * Process the HTTP Post request
   */
  public void doPost(HttpServletRequest request,
      HttpServletResponse response)
      throws ServletException, IOException {
    response.setContentType("text/html");
    OutputStreamWriter osw = new
        OutputStreamWriter(response.getOutputStream());
    PrintWriter out = new PrintWriter(osw);
    out.println(Format.pageStart("Search for Employees"));
    out.println(Format.introText("Enter a name or part of "
    out.println(HtmlForm.formStart("maintainemp.ShowEmpList");
    out.println(HtmlForm.textField("Name", "empname"));
    out.println(HtmlForm.submitButton(" Search "));
    out.println(HtmlForm.linkButton(" New ",
        "/servlet/maintainemp.ShowNewEmp"));
    out.println(HtmlForm.formEnd());
    out.println(Format.pageEnd());
    out.close();
  }
[snip]
}
```

Notice how much simpler and more easy to read the code becomes with proper modularization!

Business Logic

In this application, the two servlets must cooperate, as shown earlier in the application flow diagram (refer to Figure 6-20). The diagram shows that the application goes through the following states:

1. The ShowSearchEmp servlet is called and produces the Web page SearchEmp.

2. When the user clicks the button on this page, the **empname** parameter is sent to the ShowEmpList servlet.

3. The ShowEmpList servlet produces the EmpList Web page.

4. When the user clicks the button on this page, the application continues from step 1.

This application needs business logic added in two places:

■ The ShowEmpList servlet must read the **empname** parameter.

■ The ShowEmpList servlet must connect to the database and loop through all the records that match the search criteria.

When you have finished, your ShowEmpList servlet will look like this:

```
package maintainemp;

import javax.servlet.*;
import javax.servlet.http.*;
import java.io.*;
import java.util.*;
import java.sql.*;

public class ShowEmpList extends HttpServlet {
[snip]
  /**
   * Process the HTTP Post request
   */
  public void doPost(HttpServletRequest request,
     HttpServletResponse response)
     throws ServletException, IOException {
   //Employee name
   String empName = "";
   try {
     empName = request.getParameter("empname");
```

```java
    } catch (Exception e) {
      e.printStackTrace();
    }
    if (empName == null) {
      empName = "%";
    } else {
      empName = "%" + empName + "%";
    }
    response.setContentType("text/html");
    OutputStreamWriter osw =
        new OutputStreamWriter(response.getOutputStream());
    PrintWriter out = new PrintWriter(osw);
    out.println(Format.pageStart("List of Employees"));
    out.println(Format.introText("This list shows the "
        + "employees that satisfy the search criteria."));

    /* check for database connectivity */
    Connection con = null;
    PreparedStatement stmt = null;
    ResultSet rs = null;
    try {
      Class.forName("oracle.jdbc.driver.OracleDriver");
      con = DriverManager.getConnection(
          "jdbc:oracle:thin:@localhost:1521:orcl",
          "scott", "tiger");
      String stmtString = new String("select empno, ename, job " +
          "from emp where upper(ename) like ? " +
                    "order by ename");
      stmt = con.prepareStatement(stmtString);
          stmt.setString(1, empName.toUpperCase());
      rs = stmt.executeQuery();

      out.println("<table border cellpadding=\"4\">");
      out.println("  <tr> ");
      out.println("    <th>Emp. no.</th>");
      out.println("    <th>Name</th>");
      out.println("    <th>Job</th>");
      out.println("  </tr>");
      while(rs.next()) {
        out.println("  <tr> ");
        out.println("    <td>" + rs.getInt("empno") + "</td>");
        out.println("    <td>" + rs.getString("ename") + "</td>");
        out.println("    <td>" + rs.getString("job") + "</td>");
        out.println("  </tr>");
```

```
      }
      out.println("</table>");
    } catch(ClassNotFoundException e) {
      out.println("<p>Could not load database driver: "
          + e.getMessage() + "</p>");
    } catch(SQLException e) {
      out.println("<p>SQLException caught: "
          + e.getMessage() + "</p>");
    } finally { // close connection no matter what
      try {
        if (con != null) {
          con.close();
        }
      } catch (SQLException ignored) {}
    }
    out.println(Format.pageEnd());
  }
}
```

Getting the Parameter

At the very start of the doPost() method in the ShowEmpList servlet, JDeveloper
generates a few lines of code to get the parameter from the first comment to the
end of the try/catch block after the e.printStackTrace() method call.

The HTTP protocol always passes parameters as strings, so the getParameter()
method returns a String object. In this simple case you wanted a String, so no
conversion was necessary and the try/catch block is really superfluous. But if you
specify a parameter of another type, such as an int, JDeveloper generates the code
to convert the parameter value, including handling any errors if the parameter data
cannot be converted to the desired data type.

You do not need to make any changes to this code: JDeveloper has generated
all the code you need to access the value entered by the user on the preceding
Web page as the Java String variable *empname*. But you do need to add the SQL
wildcard characters and a bit of logic to handle the case in which the user does not
enter any search criteria.

Building a Prepared Statement

The second place business logic code is needed is the database connection. The
connection is established as in the previous example; but because the statement now
needs to use a variable, another Java object is appropriate: the PreparedStatement.

A PreparedStatement differs from a normal Statement in that it uses *bind
variables*. These are marked with question marks in the SQL statement text, and they
must be *bound*—that is, given a value—before you execute the query. This is done

with different set methods, depending on the object type. In this example, you need to assign a String value, so you use the setString() method—if you wanted to assign an *int* variable, you would use the setInt() method, and so on.

Why would you want to use another way of building statements? Couldn't you just create a SQL statement with normal string concatenation like this:

```
String stmtString = new String("select empno, ename, job "
    + "from emp where upper(ename) like "
    + empName
    + " order by ename");
```

Well, yes, the functionality is the same. But when the Oracle database prepares to execute a statement, it first checks to see whether that statement has been executed recently; if so, it can save some processing time.

If you query for "smith" and "jones" with a string concatenation, the database sees this as two different statements:

```
select empno, ename, job from emp where upper(ename) like '%JONES%'
select empno, ename, job from emp where upper(ename) like '%SMITH%'
```

Because they are different statements, the database must do the full processing each time.

If you query with bind variables, the Oracle database considers both statements to be of the form

```
select empno, ename, job from emp where ename like :1
```

This allows the database to only parse the statement the first time. This saves time and means that you get your result faster. Therefore, your application should use bind variables whenever relevant.

Maintaining Employees

The final example shows a small application that handles all operations (query, insert, update, and delete) on the EMP table by expanding on the previous example and adding code to handle inserts, updates, and deletes in a safe manner.

Once more, the process goes through the same four steps:

1. Application design

2. Page design

3. Conversion

4. Business logic

Application Design

The storyboard (see Figure 6-23) now shows four screens:

■ The Search screen with an added button to call the NewEmp screen.

■ The EmpList screen with an added hyperlink from each employee number to the detail screen for that employee.

■ A new screen, NewEmp, in which to enter a new employee.

■ A new screen, EmpDetail, in which to show and update the record details. After filling in the fields on this screen, the user is returned to the EmpList screen.

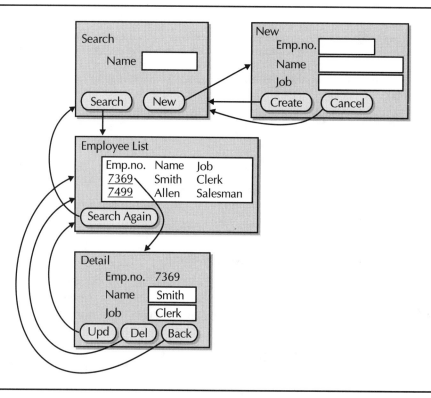

FIGURE 6-23. *A four-screen storyboard*

This application now passes quite a bit more information around:

■ New data from the NewEmp screen

■ Potentially updated data from the EmpDetail screen

■ Instructions to delete records from the EmpDetail screen

All of this data has been written next to the navigation lines on the application flow diagram in Figure 6-24 to show which code modules have to receive and handle the data.

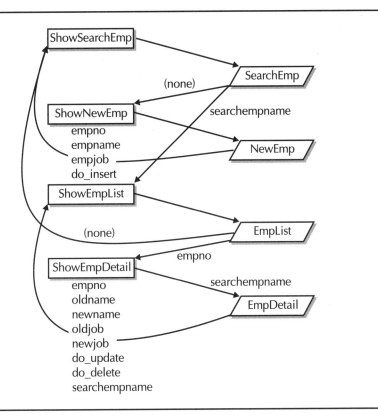

FIGURE 6-24. *A more complicated application flow diagram*

This diagram shows a few things that might be surprising:

- The ShowEmpList servlet must now perform the query to show the EmpList screen *and* perform any database operations resulting from an update or a delete.

- The ShowSearchEmp has gotten the additional task of performing a database insert when the user enters data for a new record.

- The ShowEmpDetail servlet must receive the searchempname. This allows the application to "remember" the last search—see the upcoming section "Creating a Session."

Table 6-3 summarizes all the parameters that each servlet must handle.

Using Buttons

Note the **do_insert**, **do_update**, and **do_delete** parameters. These are used by the code in the following modules to determine which button the user pressed.

Servlet	Parameters
ShowSearchEmp	**empno** **empname** **empjob** **do_insert**
ShowNewEmp	(none)
ShowEmpList	**empno** **oldname** **newname** **oldjob** **newjob** **do_update** **do_delete** **searchempname**
ShowEmpDetails	**searchempname** **empno**

TABLE 6-3. *Parameters Each Servlet Must Receive*

For example, the NewEmp screen has two buttons: Create and Cancel. By producing two buttons of the Submit type and giving the Create button the name **do_insert**, the following servlet can determine what button the user clicked: if the **do_insert** parameter has a value, the user clicked Create; if not, the user clicked Cancel.

Similarly, the EmpDetail module has three Submit buttons; of these, the Update and Delete buttons have a value. The ShowEmpList module then knows that if the **do_update** parameter has a value, the user clicked the Update button; if the **do_delete** parameter has a value, the user clicked the Delete button; and if neither has a value, the user clicked Back.

Because the path from the SearchEmp screen to the ShowNewEmp module does not pass any parameters, this connection can be handled by a simple HTML link—see the HTML code on the next page.

Creating a Session
The specification states that the next Web page after the EmpDetail screen is the EmpList. It is reasonable for the user to expect to return to the same employee lis; but because the HTTP protocol doesn't have sessions, the Web server has forgotten which query the user executed earlier.

One solution to this problem is to pass the searchempname value *through* the EmpList screen in the form of a *hidden field* (refer to Chapter 5 if you don't remember this HTML form element). The ShowEmpList servlet can thus store the search parameter in the EmpList screen for the ShowEmpDetail servlet to receive. The ShowEmpDetail servlet, in turn, stores this value in the EmpDetail screen for the ShowEmpList servlet to retrieve so it can repeat the same query.

NOTE
There are other ways of handling this (with cookies or using an HttpSession object), but that is an advanced topic outside the scope of this book.

Building the Application
To build this application, you can either build all four servlets from scratch or expand the two existing servlets from the last example.

If you build the application from scratch, use the JDeveloper HTTP Servlet Wizard to build all four servlets, referring to Figure 6-24 and Table 6-3 as needed to add the parameters. Then open each servlet and replace the entire content of the doGet() method with a call to doPost(), as in the previous example. Finally, try to run each servlet individually from JDeveloper just to check that the code is valid and runs.

Page Design

You need two new pages:

- NewEmp to allow the user to enter a new employee number, name, and job (for simplicity, leave out the database sequence and trigger that normally provides the employee number for a new employee).

- EmpDetail to allow the user to change the name and job of an existing employee.

In addition, the EmpList page should have hyperlinks that allow you to "drill down" to the detailed information about an employee.

Using a Button Without Submitting the Form

Note on the application flow diagram that the path from the SearchEmp screen to the ShowNewEmp module does not pass any parameters. Only the ShowEmpList module needs to receive the **searchempname** parameter entered on the SearchEmp screen. This makes it possible to have an HTML Form with a Submit button that goes to the ShowEmpList servlet and a separate button that simply jumps to the ShowNewEmp servlet when clicked. The HTML might look like this:

```
<form method="get" action="maintainemp.ShowEmpList">
<table border=0>
  <tr>
    <td>Name</td>
    <td><input type="text" name="searchempname" /></td>
  </tr>
  <tr>
    <td colspan="2">
      <input type="submit" value=" Search " />
      <input type="button" value=" New "
        onClick="document.location.href='maintainemp.ShowNewEmp'" />
    </td>
  </tr>
```

The Search button is an HTML form Submit button that sends the data on the form (the value of the <input> field) to the servlet specified in the **action** attribute of the <form> tag.

The New button is a normal button that does not submit the HTML Form. In fact, normal buttons do nothing by themselves; that's why you use the onClick method that contains JavaScript code to jump to another page without passing any data. (JavaScript programming is outside the scope of this book—refer to the resources in Chapter 13 if you want to learn JavaScript programming. For this example, the preceding JavaScript statement fulfills our need.)

Using Multiple Submit Buttons

The storyboard shows that there are three ways from the EmpDetail screen back to the EmpList screen:

■ Do an update

■ Do a delete

■ Do nothing

Whenever you see this type of layout with several different ways of calling the same module, you can use multiple Submit buttons like this:

```
<input type="submit" name="do_update" value=" Update ">
<input type="submit" name="do_delete" value=" Delete ">
<input type="submit" value=" Back ">
```

These are all three HTML Form Submit buttons that send all the data on the page to the destination specified in the **action** attribute of the <form> tag:

■ The Update button has the name **do_update**; so when the user clicks this button, **the do_update** parameter has the value " Update " (and the **do_delete** parameter does not have a value). This allows the ShowEmpList servlet to detect that an update was requested.

■ The Delete button has the name do_delete; so when the user clicks on this button, **the do_delete** parameter has the value " Delete "(and the **do_update** parameter does not have a value). This allows the ShowEmpList servlet to detect that a delete was requested.

■ The Back button does not have a value. When the user clicks this button, neither the **do_update** nor the **do_delete** parameter has a value, so the ShowEmpList servlet knows to leave the data unchanged.

Adding Data to Hyperlinks

The application flow diagram shows that you must pass the parameters **empno** and **searchempname** from the EmpList screen to the ShowEmpDetail screen. It's possible (but cumbersome) to create a complete HTML form for every record on the EmpList screen to pass these parameters like the other screens in this application.

But it is easier to create a hyperlink for every record and embed the parameter values in the hyperlink. Chapter 5 explains the special format for this kind of parameter passing; in this example, if the user previously searched for the string **mi,** every employee hyperlink would look similar to this:

```
<a href="ShowEmpDetail?empno=7566&searchempname=mi">7566</a>
```

The empno is both used as part of the **href** attribute and as the actual link text. When the user clicks this link, the parameter **empno** with the value 7566 and the parameter **searchempname** with the value mi is passed to the ShowEmpDetail servlet.

Conversion

Once more, you need to convert the HTML and place it in your Java servlets. This involves converting the HTML to Java code (manually or using a tool like html2java) and placing this code in your skeleton servlets.

You should also take out the HTML elements that occur first and last on every screen page, and place them in methods in a special Format class. If you are really thorough about this step, you will move *all* HTML tags out of your application servlets and place this code in the Format class. In addition, you can use a class like the HtmlForm class to handle all elements you use in HTML Forms.

Business Logic

The program has business logic added in three places:

- Inserting new records
- Performing updates
- Deleting records

Handling New Records

As is clear from the application flow diagram, the data for a new employee record is entered on the NewEmp screen and passed to the ShowSearchEmp screen. This means that the ShowSearchEmp servlet must actually do the insert. The code could look something like this:

```
package maintainemp;
[snip]
  public class ShowSearchEmp extends HttpServlet {
[snip]
  /**
   * Process the HTTP Post request
   */
  public void doPost(HttpServletRequest request,
```

```
  HttpServletResponse response)
  throws ServletException, IOException {
String empNo = request.getParameter("empno");
String empName = request.getParameter("empname");
String empJob = request.getParameter("empjob");
int empNumber = 0;
try {
  empNumber = Integer.parseInt(empNo);
} catch (Exception e) {}

response.setContentType("text/html");
PrintWriter out = new PrintWriter(response.getOutputStream());
StringBuffer page = new StringBuffer();
int recordsInserted = 0;    // for the return code from the INSERT

page.append(Format.pageStart("Search for Employees"));

/* only proceed if we got at least empNo and empName */
if (empNumber != 0 && empName.length() > 0) {
  try {

      DriverManager.registerDriver(neworacle.jdbc.driver.OracleDriver());
      Connection conn = DriverManager.getConnection(
          "jdbc:oracle:thin:@everest:1521:ORCL", "scott", "tiger");
      PreparedStatement pStmt = conn.prepareStatement(
          "insert into emp (empno, ename, job) values (?, ?, ?)"
      );
      pStmt.setInt(1, empNumber);
      pStmt.setString(2, empName);
      pStmt.setString(3, empJob);
      recordsInserted = pStmt.executeUpdate();
      if (recordsInserted == 1) {
        page.append(Format.message("One record created"));
      } else {
        /*
         * if not exactly one record inserted, something is
         * seriously wrong. Ask user to contact support and
         * terminate
         */
        out.println(Format.errorPage(recordsInserted
          + " records created.<br>Expected exactly one."));
        out.close();
      }
  } catch (SQLException e) {
    if (e.getErrorCode() == 1) {
      /* ORA-00001 means empno already exists */
      page.append(Format.message("Employee number "
          + empNo
          + " already exists."
```

```
                ));
            } else {
              /* something serious is wrong */
              out.println(Format.errorPage("SQL Error: " + e.getMessage()));
              out.close();
            }
          }
        }

      page.append(Format.introText("Enter a name or part of a name "
      + "and press the <b> Search </b>button. "));
      page.append(HtmlForm.start("maintainemp.ShowEmpList"));
      page.append(HtmlForm.textField("Name", "searchempname"));
      page.append(HtmlForm.buttonsStart());
      page.append(HtmlForm.submitButton("Search"));
      page.append(HtmlForm.button("New", "maintainemp.ShowNewEmp"));
      page.append(HtmlForm.buttonsEnd());
      page.append(HtmlForm.end());
      page.append(Format.pageEnd());

      out.println(page);
      out.close();
    }
[snip]
}
```

Reading the Parameters   The three getParameter() method calls read the **empno**, **empname**, and **empjob** parameters into Java variables. The Integer.parseInt() method is used to convert the String object **empNo** into the Java int **empNumber**.

Inserting a Row   This only happens if the servlet received a valid employee number and a name. If so, the servlet connects to the database, prepares a statement, and binds the supplied parameters to the statement.

It executes the statement and, if the result is that exactly one row is created, adds a feedback message to the Web page shown to the user.

If a SQL exception occurred, the servlet checks for an ORA-00001 (Primary Key violated) and handles this problem gracefully by adding a message to the Web page. If it encounters any other problem, the application terminates with an error message.

Handling Updates and Deletes

The application flow diagram also shows that the ShowEmpList servlet follows the EmpDetail screen. Therefore, the tasks of performing both updates and deletes falls to this servlet. The code could look something like this:

```
package maintainemp;
[snip]
  public class ShowEmpList extends HttpServlet {
[snip]
  /**
   * Process the HTTP Post request
   */
  public void doPost(HttpServletRequest request,
      HttpServletResponse response)
      throws ServletException, IOException {
    //Employee name for search
    String searchEmpName = "%";
    try { searchEmpName = request.getParameter("searchempname"); }
        catch (Exception e) { e.printStackTrace(); }
    //Employee no. (PK for update)
    int empNo = 0;
    try { empNo = Integer.parseInt(request.getParameter("empno")); }
        catch (Exception e) { e.printStackTrace(); }
    //Old Employee name
    String oldName = "";
    try { oldName = request.getParameter("oldname"); }
        catch (Exception e) { e.printStackTrace(); }
    //New Employee name
    String newName = "";
    try { newName = request.getParameter("newname"); }
        catch (Exception e) { e.printStackTrace(); }
    //Old Employee job
    String oldJob = "";
    try { oldJob = request.getParameter("oldjob"); }
        catch (Exception e) { e.printStackTrace(); }
    //New Employee job
    String newJob = "";
    try { newJob = request.getParameter("newjob"); }
        catch (Exception e) { e.printStackTrace(); }
    //Instruction to perform an update
    String doUpdate = "";
    try { doUpdate = request.getParameter("do_update"); }
        catch (Exception e) { e.printStackTrace(); }
    //Instruction to do delete
    String doDelete = "";
    try { doDelete = request.getParameter("do_delete"); }
        catch (Exception e) { e.printStackTrace(); }

    response.setContentType("text/html");
    OutputStreamWriter osw = new
        OutputStreamWriter(response.getOutputStream());
```

```
PrintWriter out = new PrintWriter(osw);
StringBuffer page = new StringBuffer();
int recordsProcessed = 0;  // for the return code from the UPD/DEL

/* connect to database */
Connection conn = null;
try {
  Statement stmt = null;
  ResultSet rs = null;
  DriverManager.registerDriver(new oracle.jdbc.driver.OracleDriver());
  conn = DriverManager.getConnection(
      "jdbc:oracle:thin:@everest:1521:ORCL", "scott", "tiger");

  page.append(Format.pageStart("Employee List"));

  /*
   * if user requested an update and changed the name or job
   * or the user requested a delete, get and lock the row
   */
  if (((doUpdate != null) &&
      (!(oldName.equals(newName) && oldJob.equals(newJob))))
      ||
      (doDelete != null)) {
   try {
     /* must set autocommit off to keep lock */
     conn.setAutoCommit(false);
     /* read and lock what's in the database now */
     PreparedStatement readStmt = conn.prepareStatement(
         "select empno, ename, job from emp where empno = ? "
         + "for update nowait"
     );
     readStmt.setInt(1, empNo);
     rs = readStmt.executeQuery();
     if (rs.next()) {
       /* record is still there */
       if (doUpdate != null) {
         /* read the old database values */
         String dbJob = new String();
         dbJob = rs.getString("job");
         dbJob = (dbJob == null) ? "" : dbJob;
         if ((rs.getString("ename").equals(oldName))
             && (dbJob.equals(oldJob))) {
           /* record was unchanged, so proceed with the update */
           PreparedStatement updStmt = conn.prepareStatement(
               "update emp set ename = ?, job = ? "
               + "where empno = ?"
           );
```

```
            updStmt.setString(1, newName);
            updStmt.setString(2, newJob);
            updStmt.setInt(3, empNo);
            recordsProcessed = updStmt.executeUpdate();
          } else {
            /* Record changed since detail page was produced */
            page.append(Format.message(
                "The record has been changed by another user"
            ));
          }
      } else {
        /* if it wasn't insert, do the delete */
        PreparedStatement delStmt = conn.prepareStatement(
            "delete from emp where empno = ?");
        delStmt.setInt(1, empNo);
        recordsProcessed = delStmt.executeUpdate();
      }
    } else {
      /* Record gone: deleted since detail page was produced */
      page.append(Format.message(
          "The record has been deleted by another user"
      ));
    }
    conn.commit();
    if (recordsProcessed == 1) {
      page.append("1 record processed");
    } else {
      /*
       * if not exactly one record processed, something is
       * seriously wrong. Ask user to contact support and
       * terminate
       */
      out.println(Format.errorPage(recordsProcessed
        + " records updated.<br>Expected exactly one."));
      out.close();
      return;
    }
  } catch (SQLException e) {
    if (e.getErrorCode() == 54) {
      /* ORA-000054 means record locked by other user */
      page.append(Format.message("Record has been locked by "
          + "another user. Please try again later."));
    } else {
      /* Some fatal error; propagate out to next block */
      throw e;
    }
  }
}
```

```
/* do a query */
Vector labels = new Vector();
labels.add("Name");
labels.add("Job");
if (searchEmpName == null) {
  searchEmpName = "";
}
String query = new String(
    "select empno, ename, job from emp where upper(ename) "
    + " like '%"
    + searchEmpName.toUpperCase()
    + "%' order by ename"
);
String resultTable = new String();
resultTable = DatabaseUtility.htmlTable(
  conn,
  query,
  labels,
  1,              /* the column to use as link */
  /* the link text. pass search text as well */
  "maintainemp.ShowEmpDetails?searchempname="
  + searchEmpName
  + "&empno="
);
if (resultTable.length() != 0) {
  /* found some data */
  page.append(Format.introText("This list shows the employees that "
      + "satisfy the search criteria. Click on an employee number "
      + "to see the details."));
  page.append(resultTable);
} else {
  /* no data found */
  page.append(Format.introText("No data satisfy the search "
      + "criteria"));
}
page.append(HtmlForm.start("maintainemp.ShowSearchEmp"));
page.append(HtmlForm.submitButtonRow("Search Again"));
page.append(HtmlForm.end());
page.append(Format.pageEnd());
} catch (SQLException e) {
/* Some fatal error; clear page and add error message */
page.setLength(0);
page.append(Format.errorPage("SQL Error: " + e.getMessage()));
} finally {
if (conn != null) {
  try {
    conn.close();
```

```
        } catch (SQLException ignored) {}
      }
    }
    out.println(page);
    out.close();
  }
[snip]
}
```

Reading the Parameters   This example shows the code that the JDeveloper HTTP Servlet Wizard builds for you to read the parameters. By adding error handling even to **String** parameters (that do not throw any exceptions), the code gets a bit longer, but the end result is the same as the preceding: all the parameters passed to the servlet are read into corresponding Java variables.

Establishing a Database Connection   This is done in the normal manner as you have seen several times before.

Locking the Record   If the user requests an update and provides a new name or a new job, or if the user requests a delete, you will need to establish a lock on the record to be deleted or updated. JDBC, by default, has AutoCommit enabled (so an implicit commit is executed after each statement); but, in this case, you must disable this.

Then you use a prepared statement to retrieve and lock the relevant record.

In case the record is no longer found in the database, the else branch adds a message to the Web page.

If the record could not be locked, an exception occurs and is captured by the catch clause (see the following).

Performing an Update   When the user requests an update, the servlet compares the values in the database with the "old" values passed from the preceding Web page.

You must check this to prevent a lost update. For example, if John clicks on a link and receives a Detail record and then leaves for lunch, it is possible that Sue will have updated the record in the database when John comes back. To prevent John's update from overwriting Sue's, you must check that the value in the database is still the same as it was when John got the original details from the database.

If this problem does not occur, the servlet prepares an update statement and executes it.

Performing a Delete   To delete the locked record, the servlet prepares a statement and executes it.

If Something Goes Wrong   If there is a problem, the servlet produces a relevant error message. The servlet explicitly catches an ORA-00054 error (record locked by another user) to provide a message to the user and allow the application to continue. In case of serious errors (multiple records updated or deleted, as well as other SQL errors), the application has a serious problem and must display an error message and terminate.

Producing the Record List   In this case, the actual HTML table with the results is produced by calling the DatabaseUtility.htmlTable() method. This method is part of the Web Application Toolkit (see Chapter 12), and simply takes a SQL query and a connection as parameters and returns an HTML table. If you don't want to use this toolkit, you can use code similar to the previous examples to create and execute a statement and loop through the results.

Summary

In this chapter, you learned how to use Java to build Web applications from the bottom up as Java servlets. The Java language is well suited for Web applications; and even if you are not familiar with Java, the examples should give you a feeling for what it takes to build a Java Web application.

As you have also seen from the examples, it takes quite a bit of code to write robust and maintainable Java Web applications. This is the price that you have to pay for the full flexibility that you get from a completely handwritten application. The next chapter describes the same approach using PL/SQL as the programming language, and the following chapters cover Oracle tools that offer somewhat less flexibility in return for increased productivity.

CHAPTER
7

Handwritten PL/SQL

his chapter shows how to use PL/SQL to write Web applications. PL/SQL is an Oracle-proprietary language used in the Oracle database and in some of the Oracle development tools. As the name *Procedural Language/SQL* indicates, this language is an extension to SQL and is intended for data-intensive tasks that cannot be handled with normal SQL.

To get the full benefit from this chapter, you should have a working knowledge of basic PL/SQL. However, PL/SQL is an easily read language, so you should be able to read and understand the examples even if you are not familiar with the language.

PL/SQL is especially well suited for data-intensive tasks, for example, code that handles data from the database. Therefore, most organizations using Oracle should have someone who understands PL/SQL to write the data-handling logic.

However, if you only need to develop Web applications and must choose a language to learn, Java might be a better choice. See Table 7-1 for a comparison of Java and PL/SQL.

Getting Started

Writing PL/SQL Web applications is normal PL/SQL programming:

- You can use any tool you normally use to develop PL/SQL procedures.

- You use the PL/SQL Web Toolkit when you need to produce output that will be sent back to the browser.

PL/SQL Programming Tool

You can use any tool you normally use for your PL/SQL development—even Notepad and SQL*Plus. Most of the screens in this chapter show the tool T.O.A.D.

	Advantages	Disadvantages
PL/SQL	Very fast access to database data	Proprietary—Oracle only
Java	General-purpose language	Slower database access

TABLE 7-1. *Comparison of PL/SQL and Java*

(Tool for Oracle Application Developers) from Quest. This tool exists in a freeware version—see Chapter 11.

The PL/SQL Web Toolkit

In order to write PL/SQL Web applications, you need the PL/SQL Web Toolkit. This Oracle-supplied code is automatically installed if you followed the installation instructions in Chapter 4. To verify that these packages are available, log on to your database and check that you have the HTP package installed (see Figure 7-1).

The HTP package is an essential package, as it contains the procedure P that allows you to send output back to the Web browser. The other packages are

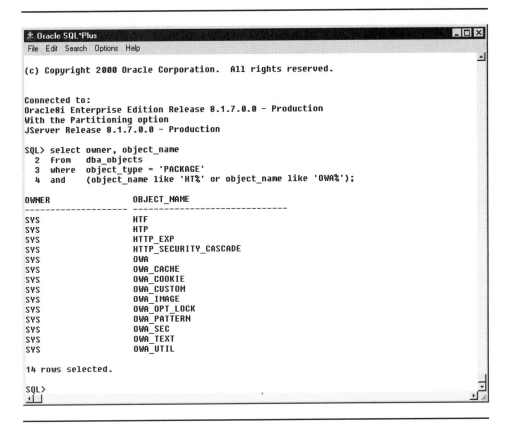

FIGURE 7-1. *Checking that the PL/SQL Web Toolkit is installed*

described in the Oracle documentation (unfortunately, not in the Oracle 9i Application Server documentation—you have to pick up the documentation for an older version from the Oracle Technology Network Web site).

Creating a Database Access Descriptor

A unique feature of Oracle Web/application servers like Oracle9i Application Server is the ability to translate a URL entered in a browser into a call to a specific stored procedure in the database. To do this, you need a *Database Access Descriptor (DAD),* a piece of configuration information that tells the Oracle Web/application server how to translate the URL into a database connection.

Other Web/application servers can also connect to the database, but only Oracle offers the connection directly to a PL/SQL procedure.

Adding a Database Access Descriptor

If you did not change the **DocumentRoot** parameter in your Apache configuration file, you can enter the address **http://*yourserver*** in your browser, where ***yourserver*** is the name of the machine on which the Oracle HTTP server is installed. This will show the Oracle HTTP Server introduction screen in Figure 7-2.

To add or change Database Access Descriptors, you configure the mod_plsql module. When you click the mod_plsql link, the Gateway Configuration Menu screen shown in Figure 7-3 appears.

Click the Gateway Database Access Descriptor Settings link. The Database Access Descriptors page shown in Figure 7-4 appears.

Click Add Default to create a simple DAD suitable for the basic examples in this chapter. The Create DAD Entry page (see Figure 7-5) appears.

Enter a name for your DAD (for example, **scott**), the Oracle user name (**scott**), the password (**tiger**), and the connect string (**orcl**, if you followed the installation instructions in Chapter 4). Then click the OK button. You should be returned to the

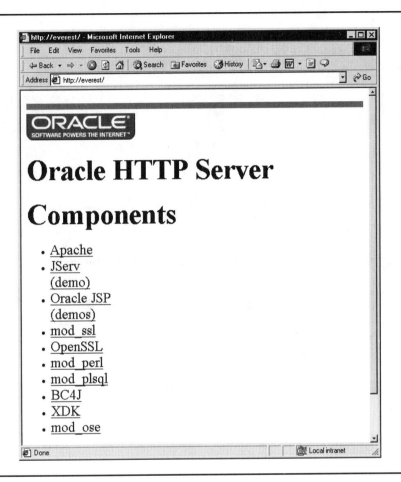

FIGURE 7-2. *The Oracle HTTP Server Welcome page*

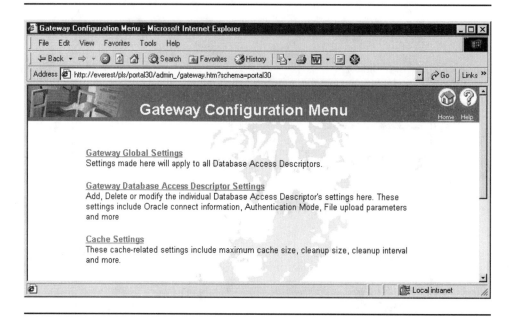

FIGURE 7-3. *Gateway Configuration page*

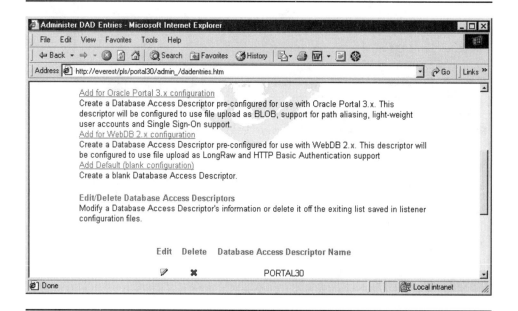

FIGURE 7-4. *Database Access Descriptor administration*

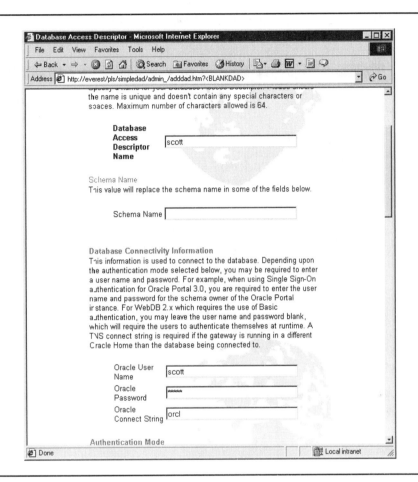

FIGURE 7-5.   *Creating a Database Access Descriptor*

Database Access Descriptor Administration page, shown next, with the message "The changes have been successfully made!"

You can click the Close button to return to the previous screen, or close your Web browser.

If you followed the previous procedure, you should now be able to run stored procedures in the Scott schema through URLs like this:

http://<*yourserver*>/pls/scott/<*procedure*>

where <*yourserver*> is the full name of the machine on which the Oracle HTTP Server is running, and <*procedure*> is the name of your procedure. If the procedure is part of a PL/SQL package, use the normal PL/SQL notation of <*package name*>.<*procedure name*>. The following examples show how to invoke stand-alone procedures, as well as procedures in packages from the address line of a Web browser.

NOTE
Good PL/SQL practice dictates that you should not fill your database schemas with individual procedures and functions, but rather collect them into packages.

Hello World

When you are handwriting Web applications in PL/SQL, Oracle does not provide any wizards or other tools to help you. But you can (and should), of course, use some standard code templates so you don't start from scratch every time.

Writing the Application

The most basic Web application (once more, the classic Hello World) could look like this:

```
create or replace procedure hello
as
begin
  htp.p('<html>');
  htp.p('<head><title>Hello World</title></head>');
  htp.p('<body>');
  htp.p('<h1>Hello World</h1>');
  htp.p('<p>The time is '
        || to_char(sysdate, 'hh24:mi:ss yyyy-mm-dd')
        || '</p>'
  );
  htp.p('</body></html>');
end;
```

Running the Application

If you set up a Database Access Descriptor as described in the preceding section, you can now invoke this PL/SQL procedure through the following URL:

http://*<yourserver>*/pls/scott/hello

where *<yourserver>* is the full name of the machine on which the Oracle HTTP Server is running, including domain. If you are not sure of the name of your machine, you can open a command prompt (Start | Accessories | Command Prompt), type the command **hostname**, and press ENTER. This shows the TCP/IP name of your computer.

If the Web browser is on this machine, you can use the text localhost as server name.

If everything works correctly, you see the picture in Figure 7-6.

List of All Employees

Now you have seen how easy it is to write Web applications using PL/SQL and have tested to see that your configuration works. The next example is a PL/SQL procedure

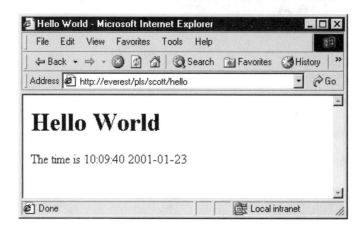

FIGURE 7-6. *Hello World from a PL/SQL Web procedure*

that connects to the database and lists all the employees from the EMP table. In this example, you will follow the method from Chapter 5:

1. Application design

2. Page design

3. Conversion

4. Business logic

Application Design

In this step, you develop the storyboard and application flow diagram for your application. This simple application has only one screen, leading to the simplest possible storyboard, shown in Figure 7-7.

Since there is only one screen involved that does not take any parameters and is followed by no other screen, it does not make sense to produce an application flow diagram. All the necessary information is already available to build the skeleton of the ShowEmpList PL/SQL package.

In PL/SQL, the template is the package specification (produced in this step), and the actual content that produces the Web page is the package body (produced in step 3 and refined in step 4).

Employee List		
Emp.no.	Name	Job
7369	Smith	Clerk
7499	Allen	Salesman
7521	Ward	Salesman
7566	Jones	Manager

FIGURE 7-7. *A one-screen storyboard*

For this application, the package specification looks like this:

```
create or replace package mypackage
as
  procedure ShowEmpList;
end mypackage;
```

NOTE
*In PL/SQL Web applications, the Oracle HTTP
Server automatically invokes the procedure whether
the user used the post or get method to call it. This is
different from Java Web applications where you can
(indeed, must) explicitly specify what kind of
requests your application should serve.*

Page Design

The second step is to produce an example HTML page. This could look as shown in
Figure 7-8 and have the following HTML code:

```
<html>
<head>
<title>Employee List</title>
<link rel="stylesheet" href="/webstart.css" type="text/css" />
</head>

<body bgcolor="#FFFFFF">
<table width="550">
```

```
    <tr>
      <td>
        <h1>Employee List</h1>
      </td>
      <td align="right">
        <img src="/web_apps_101.gif"
            alt="Web Apps 101 logo" width="90" height="69" />
      </td>
    </tr>
</table>
<table width="550"><tr><td>
<p>This list shows all employees</p>
<table border cellpadding="4">
  <tr>
      <th>Emp. no.</th>
      <th>Name</th>
      <th>Job</th>
  </tr>
  <tr>
      <td>7369</td>
      <td>Smith</td>
      <td>Clerk</td>
  </tr>
  <tr>
      <td>7499</td>
      <td>Allen</td>
      <td>Salesman</td>
  </tr>
  <tr>
      <td>7521</td>
      <td>Ward</td>
      <td>Salesman</td>
  </tr>
  <tr>
      <td>7566</td>
      <td>Jones</td>
      <td>Manager</td>
  </tr>
</table>
<p align="center">
<font size="-1">
  Comments, questions? Contact the
```

```
  <a href="mailto:sten@vesterli.dk">webmaster</a>
</font></p>
</td></tr></table>
</body>
</html>
```

Make sure that all references to other files (such as style sheets and images) start with a forward slash. This indicates a site-relative URL that will work whether it is used in an HTML file or in PL/SQL code called through the Web server.

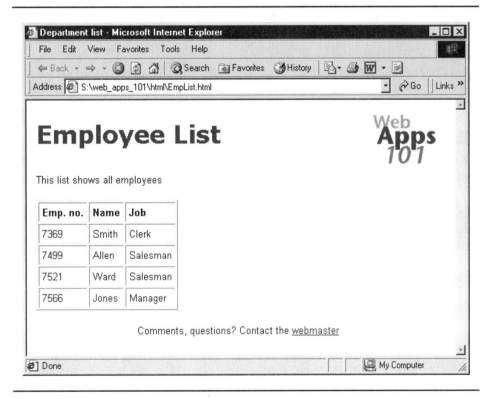

FIGURE 7-8. *An example Web page showing an Employee List*

NOTE
Beware of references that do not start with a forward slash (for example, src= or href=. References starting with file:// refer to files delivered straight to your browser from the hard disk of your development machine—this will, of course, not work for other users accessing your pages through the Web server. References starting with something other than / are relative to the current page— these references will break if you move your HTML file from one directory to another and definitely won't work once you convert your HTML to a PL/SQL stored procedure.

When you are satisfied with your HTML page, you can test it in your target browsers, run it through a validation tool or service (see resources in Chapter 13), and present it to your users for feedback and approval.

Conversion

The third step is to convert the static HTML file to PL/SQL code and, optionally, to modularize the code.

Converting to PL/SQL

Fortunately, HTML uses double quotes and PL/SQL uses single quotes, so you do not have to worry about double quotes as you must in Java. All you need to do to convert HTML to PL/SQL is to wrap each line of HTML in a call to the HTP.P procedure.

You can achieve this manually, for example using an editor macro, or you can use a tool such as html2plsql or WebAlchemy.

html2plsql   The html2plsql is a small utility program that takes an HTML file as input and produces a file where each line is wrapped in HTP.P calls. You can optionally specify an indent so that the code matches the indentation you use in your PL/SQL package.

To run html2plsql, open a command prompt and invoke the utility, as shown in Figure 7-9.

The result of the conversion is a file with the extension .pls that you can paste into the body of your PL/SQL package.

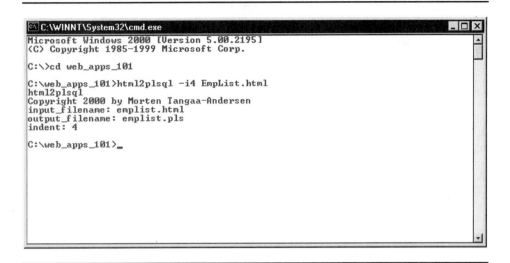

FIGURE 7-9. *Running html2plsql*

WebAlchemy   You can also use a tool such as WebAlchemy (see Figure 7-10). This tool does not only wrap your HTML in HTP.P calls, it uses all the procedures and functions available in the HTF and HTP packages.

The result of a WebAlchemy conversion can be pasted into the body of your PL/SQL package. It might need a bit of post-processing, especially if you are writing strictly conforming XHTML:

- If you have a <link rel> tag in your page, WebAlchemy builds an invalid HTP call. Simply place an HTP.P call with the complete line from your HTML source.

- If your HTML source is a strictly conformant XHTML document, you have a <!DOCTYPE> tag. Since WebAlchemy doesn't understand this tag and ignores it, you must add it in an HTP.P call.

- If your HTML source is a strictly conformant XHTML document, you must specify an XML namespace in the <html> tag. WebAlchemy understands only plain <html> tags, so you must add your <html> tag inside an HTP.P call.

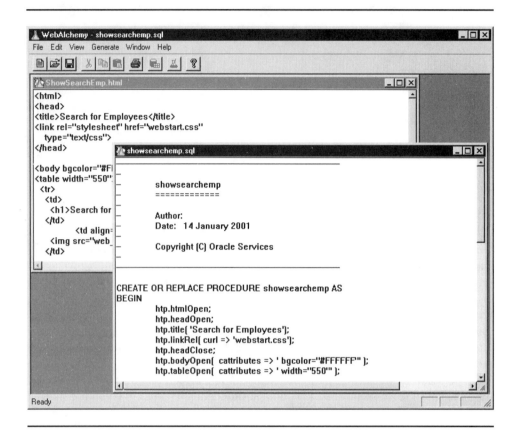

FIGURE 7-10. *Using WebAlchemy*

NOTE
Chapter 5 shows the standard header that every page needs in order to be strictly conformant XHTML version 1.

The Result of the Conversion   When you have finished with the conversion and have placed the converted HTML into the body of your package, it could look like this:

```
create or replace package body mypackage
as
  procedure ShowEmpList
  is
```

```
begin
  htp.p('<html>');
  htp.p('<head>');
  htp.p('<title>Employee List</title>');
  htp.p('<link rel="stylesheet" href="/webstart.css"
      type="text/css" />');
  htp.p('</head>');
  htp.p('');
  htp.p('<body bgcolor="#FFFFFF">');
  htp.p('<table width="550">');
  htp.p('  <tr>');
  htp.p('    <td>');
  htp.p('      <h1>Employee List</h1>');
  htp.p('    </td>');
  htp.p('    <td align="right">');
  htp.p('      <img src="/web_apps_101.gif" '
      || 'alt="Web Apps 101 logo" width="90" height="69" /> ');
  htp.p('    </td>');
  htp.p('  </tr>');
  htp.p('</table>');
  htp.p('<table width="550"><tr><td>');
  htp.p('<p>This list shows all employees</p>');
  htp.p('<table border cellpadding="4">');
  htp.p('  <tr> ');
  htp.p('    <th>Emp. no.</th>');
  htp.p('    <th>Name</th>');
  htp.p('    <th>Job</th>');
  htp.p('  </tr>');
  htp.p('  <tr> ');
  htp.p('    <td>7369</td>');
  htp.p('    <td>Smith</td>');
  htp.p('    <td>Clerk</td>');
  htp.p('  </tr>');
[snip]
  htp.p('</table>');
  htp.p('<p align="center">');
  htp.p('<font size="-1">');
  htp.p('  Comments, questions? Contact the ');
  htp.p('  <a href="mailto:sten@vesterli.dk">webmaster</a>');
  htp.p('</font></p> ');
  htp.p('</td></tr></table>');
  htp.p('</body>');
  htp.p('</html>');
  end ShowEmpList;
end mypackage;
```

If you converted with WebAlchemy, your code will look different but will be functionally identical.

Now test the package through your Web browser—you should see exactly the same file when you call the procedure through the URL **/pls/scott/ mypackage.ShowEmpLis**t as when you double-click your example HTML file in the file system.

If your page looked correct as an HTML file but you have problems with the images or fonts now, your Web browser probably cannot find the style sheet or the images. Check that all your references start with a forward slash. Only the PL/SQL code itself is run from the database—any style sheets or images must be served by the Web server.

- If a reference from a page to an auxiliary file such as an image or a style sheet starts with a slash (for example, /web_apps_101.gif or /images/ logo.gif), the Web browser will look for that file starting in the root directory on the same server.

- If a reference from a page to an auxiliary file does not start with a slash (for example, web_apps_101.gif), your Web browser will look for the auxiliary file in the "same" place as the page that refers to it. So, if a procedure with the URL /pls/scott/mypackage.ShowEmpList refers to a file web_apps_101.gif, the Web browser will try (and fail) to retrieve /pls/scott/web_apps_101.gif.

Modularization

Before you start adding the business logic to this procedure, it is important to notice that your PL/SQL procedure is full of HTML formatting tags. If you add your business logic to the procedure as it looks now, you will be mixing database operations and logic with the presentation that's controlled by the HTML tags. This will not affect the functionality of the application, but it *will* make the application harder to maintain.

It is good programming practice to separate the presentation of data from the business logic, so you should now examine your HTML code a bit more closely. It consists of several different types of content:

- **The page header (static text, logo, and so on)**   This is the same on every screen in the application.

- **Introductory text**   This text is different on the different screens in the application but should always have the same font and other formatting. It is independent of the database values—every time a screen is produced, the introductory text is the same.

■ **A table of results**   This is dynamic data retrieved from the database.

■ **The end of the page (static text)**   This is the same on every screen in the application.

Ideally, every piece of HTML code should be removed and placed in a separate format package that every module in your application can call. This will neatly separate the presentation (so if someone wants to change the look of the application without changing the logic, they can just change the format package) and has the added advantage of ensuring consistency when all code modules call the same function to start a Web page.

If you decide to separate the formatting in this way, your format package could contain three functions returning HTML as **VARCHAR2**:

■ A pageStart function that takes the page title as a **VARCHAR2** parameter

■ An introText function that takes the introductory text as a **VARCHAR2** parameter

■ A pageEnd function method that takes no parameters

The package specification should look like this:

```
create or replace package format
as
   function pageStart(title in varchar2) return varchar2;
   function introText(text in varchar2) return varchar2;
   function pageEnd return varchar2;
end format;
```

Then create the package body and copy the HTML-generating PL/SQL code from your ShowEmpList procedure to the functions in this new package. Read through the code to find all the places where static values should be replaced by parameter values, and replace them, so your package looks something like this:

```
create or replace package body format
as
   function pageStart(title in varchar2) return varchar2
   is
     retval varchar2(32767);
   begin
     retval := '<html>'
       || '<head>'
```

```
      || '<title>' || title || '</title>'
      || '<link rel="stylesheet" href="/webstart.css" '
      || ' type="text/css" />'
      || '</head>'
      || ''
      || '<body bgcolor="#FFFFFF">'
      || '<table width="550">'
      || '   <tr>'
      || '      <td>'
      || '         <h1>' || title || '</h1>'
      || '      </td>'
      || '      <td align="right">'
      || '         <img src="/web_apps_101.gif" '
      || 'alt="Web Apps 101 logo" width="90" height="69" /> '
      || '      </td>'
      || '   </tr>'
      || '</table>'
      || '<table width="550"><tr><td>'
   ;
   return retval;
 end pageStart;

 function introText(text in varchar2) return varchar2
 is
 begin
   return('<p>' || text || '</p>');
 end introText;

 function pageEnd return varchar2
 is
   retval varchar2(32767);
 begin
   retval := '<p align="center">'
      || '<font size="-1">'
      || '   Comments, questions? Contact the '
      || '   <a href="mailto:sten@vesterli.dk">webmaster</a>'
      || '</font></p> '
      || '</td></tr></table>'
      || '</body>'
      || '</html>'
   ;
   return retval;
 end pageEnd;
end format;
```

When you have finished, replace all the HTML-generating code in your
ShowEmpList procedure with calls to the three functions in the new format package.
The body of your PL/SQL package should then look something like this:

```
create or replace package body mypackage
as
  procedure ShowEmpList
  is
  begin
    htp.p(format.pageStart('Employee List'));
    htp.p(format.introText('This list shows all employees'));
    htp.p('<table border cellpadding="4">');
    htp.p('  <tr> ');
    htp.p('    <th>Emp. no.</th>');
    htp.p('    <th>Name</th>');
    htp.p('    <th>Job</th>');
    htp.p('  </tr>');
    htp.p('  <tr> ');
    htp.p('    <td>7369</td>');
    htp.p('    <td>Smith</td>');
    htp.p('    <td>Clerk</td>');
    htp.p('  </tr>');
    htp.p('  <tr> ');
    htp.p('    <td>7499</td>');
    htp.p('    <td>Allen</td>');
    htp.p('    <td>Salesman</td>');
    htp.p('  </tr>');
    htp.p('  <tr> ');
    htp.p('    <td>7521</td>');
    htp.p('    <td>Ward</td>');
    htp.p('    <td>Salesman</td>');
    htp.p('  </tr>');
    htp.p('  <tr>');
    htp.p('    <td>7566</td>');
    htp.p('    <td>Jones</td>');
    htp.p('    <td>Manager</td>');
    htp.p('  </tr>');
    htp.p('</table>');
    htp.p(format.pageEnd);
  end ShowEmpList;
end mypackage;
```

When you have finished implementing the calls to the functions in the format
package, run your PL/SQL procedure again to make sure that it still produces the
example HTML page you started from.

Business Logic

The fourth and final step is to add the business logic. In this case, this involves replacing the static example data on the page with dynamic content retrieved from the database.

Getting Data in PL/SQL

Because the code is a stored procedure running in the database, you do not have to worry about loading drivers and establishing a connection. And because of the tight integration of PL/SQL and SQL, you do not have to go through the whole create/execute/fetch cycle needed for Java Database Connectivity.

A Code Example—The FOR Loop Cursor

You can add a cursor FOR loop to loop through all records in the EMP table; your code could look like this:

```
create or replace package body mypackage
as
  procedure ShowEmpList
  is
    cursor cuEmp
    is
      select empno, ename, job
      from   emp
      order by ename;
  begin
    htp.p(format.pageStart('Employee List'));
    htp.p(format.introText('This list shows all employees'));
    htp.p('<table border cellpadding="4">');
    htp.p('  <tr> ');
    htp.p('    <th>Emp. no.</th>');
    htp.p('    <th>Name</th>');
    htp.p('    <th>Job</th>');
    htp.p('  </tr>');
    for crEmp in cuEmp loop
      htp.p('  <tr> ');
      htp.p('    <td>' || crEmp.empno || '</td>');
      htp.p('    <td>' || crEmp.ename || '</td>');
      htp.p('    <td>' || crEmp.job || '</td>');
      htp.p('  </tr>');
    end loop;
    htp.p('</table>');
```

```
    htp.p(format.pageEnd);
  end ShowEmpList;
end mypackage;
```

The Cursor   This defines the result set: three columns and all rows are retrieved.

The Loop Statement   This statement implicitly defines the cursor record crEmp and loops though all records in the cursor.

The Cursor Record   This variable contains all the columns defined in the cursor.

List with Restriction

Showing a list of all employees demonstrated how to retrieve data from the database. However, not many applications show all the data—you need to add some kind of restriction. The next example expands on the previous by adding a page on which the user can enter part of a name to search for. In PL/SQL, this is simple: you need only add the parameter to the procedure header and a WHERE clause to the cursor.

Once more, the process goes through the same four steps:

1. Application design

2. Page design

3. Conversion

4. Business logic

Application Design

The storyboard (see Figure 7-11) now shows two screens, one to enter the search criteria and one to view the results.

In this simple application, a little bit of information is passed from the SearchEmp screen to the ShowEmpList screen: the employee name to search for. You can picture this in a very simple application flow diagram, as shown in Figure 7-12.

As you saw in Chapter 5, this diagram shows the screens as parallelograms (SearchEmp and EmpList, in this example) and the code modules as square boxes. The flow of the application is a zigzag line between code modules and Web pages.

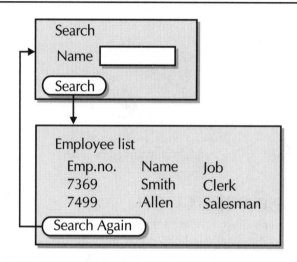

FIGURE 7-11. *A two-screen storyboard*

As a naming convention, you could, for example, let the name of each module that produces a Web page start with Show. . . (like ShowSearchEmp and ShowEmpList).

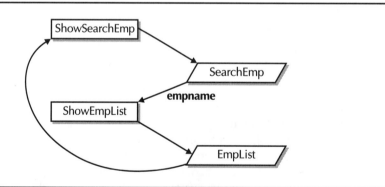

FIGURE 7-12. *A simple application flow diagram*

On the arrows, the names of the parameters passed between modules and screens is written. In this example, the SearchEmp screen is going to pass a parameter called **empname** to the ShowEmpList module that produces the EmpList Web page.

The finished diagram now shows the two PL/SQL procedures you need and the one parameter (**empname**) passed into the ShowEmpList procedure. Your package specification could look like this:

```
create or replace package maintainemp
as
  procedure ShowSearchEmp;
  procedure ShowEmpList(empname in varchar2 default null);
end maintainemp;
```

Page Design

For this application, you need an extra screen on which the user can enter the search criteria. It could look like Figure 7-13 and have the following HTML:

```
<html>
<head>
<title>Search for Employees by Department</title>
<link rel="stylesheet" href="/webstart.css"
    type="text/css" />
</head>

<body bgcolor="#FFFFFF">
<table width="550">
  <tr>
    <td>
      <h1>Search for Employees</h1>
    </td>
    <td align="right">
      <img src="/web_apps_101.gif"
          alt="Web Apps 101 logo" width="90" height="69" />
    </td>
  </tr>
</table>
<table width="550"><tr><td>
<p>Enter a name or part of a name and press
the <b> Search </b>button. </p>
<form method="post"
    action="maintainemp.ShowEmpList">
<table>
  <tr>
    <td>Name</td>
```

```
    <td>
      <input type="text" name="empname" />
    </td>
  </tr>
  <tr>
    <td colspan="2">
      <input type="submit" value=" Search " />
    </td>
  </tr>
</table>
</form>
<p> </p>
<p align="center">
<font size="-1">
  Comments, questions? Contact the
  <a href="mailto:sten@vesterli.dk">webmaster</a>
</font></p>
</td></tr></table>
</body>
</html>
```

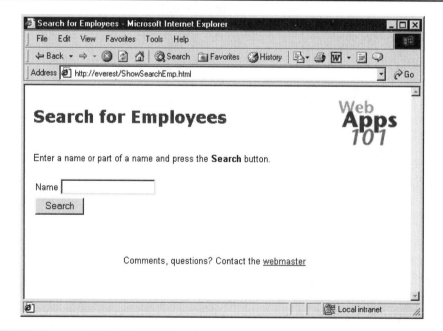

FIGURE 7-13. *An example search form*

The Action   This attribute in the <form> tag specifies where the data on this form is sent (in this case, to the procedure maintainemp.ShowEmpList). Remember that this can be any program anywhere on the Internet that accepts the parameters delivered from the form.

The Text Field   The **name** attribute of the text field has the value **empname**, so the value entered in this field will be passed to the ShowEmpList procedure with the name **empname**.

The Submit Button   This button is used to submit the HTML form, that is, to send the value of the text field to the URL specified by the action attribute of the <form> tag.

In addition to the new page, you also need to make a change to the Employee List page: it needs a button to go back to the Search screen, as shown in Figure 7-14. This means that you need an HTML form, even though you do not have any fields in which the user can enter anything. The HTML code that will make this change looks like this:

```
<html>
<head>
<title>Department list</title>
<link rel="stylesheet" href="/webstart.css" type="text/css" />
</head>

<body bgcolor="#FFFFFF">
[snip]
<table width="550"><tr><td>
<p>This list shows all employees</p>
<table border cellpadding="4">
  <tr>
    <th>Emp. no.</th>
    <th>Name</th>
    <th>Job</th>
  </tr>
[snip]
  <tr>
    <td>7566</td>
    <td>Jones</td>
    <td>Manager</td>
  </tr>
</table>
<form name="form1" method="post"
    action="maintainemp.ShowSearchEmp">
  <input type="submit" value=" Search Again " />
```

```
</form>
  [snip]
</td></tr></table>
</body>
</html>
```

The **action** parameter in this simple HTML form contains the instruction to call the procedure maintainemp.ShowSearchEmp whenever the user submits the form by clicking the Submit button. The only content of the form is the Submit button with the label Search Again.

The example HTML pages are now ready to be shown to your users and revised if necessary.

Conversion

The next step is converting the HTML and creating the body of the PL/SQL package matching the specification created in the first step.5

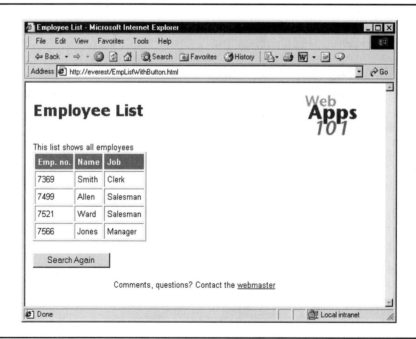

FIGURE 7-14. *The Employee List screen with Search button*

Converting to PL/SQL

Once more, you can either convert the HTML to PL/SQL by hand or use a utility like html2plsql or WebAlchemy. Convert both SearchEmp.html and the updated EmpList.html to corresponding snippets of PL/SQL code.

When you have pasted the converted code into your package body, it should be possible for you to run both the ShowSearchEmp and the ShowEmpList procedures from your Web browser. You should always test your code after the conversion to check that your basic PL/SQL is correct before you start adding the business logic.

Formatting

Just as in the preceding example, it is a good idea to split the presentation (the HTML tags) from the business logic.

If you created an application-specific Format package for the previous example, you already have the code you need. By reusing this package, you automatically ensure that your HTML is consistent throughout the application.

Using HTML Forms

If you look at the converted HTML code, you will quickly realize that it contains quite a lot of code that produces the HTML for elements of HTML Forms, such as input fields, Submit buttons, and so on.

This code should also be taken out of the main PL/SQL procedure before it gets mixed up with the business logic. You could place it in the application-specific Format package together with the HTML to start and end pages, but HTML code for creating HTML form elements isn't really application specific and is unlikely to change.

Because this code is usually identical or very similar in many projects, it makes sense to create a global package to handle HTML form elements. You can use the HtmlForm package from the WebStart toolkit described in Chapter 12, or you can build your own. (This toolkit can be downloaded from **www.vesterli.com** along with all the other code examples.)

After modularizing your code fully using both your project-specific Format package and the HtmlForm package, the code for the ShowSearchEmp procedure could look like this:

```
CREATE OR REPLACE package body maintainemp
as
  procedure ShowSearchEmp
  is
  begin
    htp.p(format.pageStart('Search for Employees'));
    htp.p(format.introText('Enter a name or part of a name and press '
      || 'the <b> Search </b>button. '));
    htp.p(htmlform.formStart('maintainemp.ShowEmpList'));
```

```
      htp.p(htmlform.textField('Name', 'empname'));
      htp.p(htmlform.SubmitButtonRow('Search'));
      htp.p(htmlform.formEnd);
      htp.p(format.pageEnd);
    end ShowSearchEmp;
[snip]
end maintainemp;
```

By removing all the HTML formatting, the code becomes much simpler to read.

Business Logic

In this application, two PL/SQL procedures must cooperate, as shown in the application flow diagram in Figure 7-12. The diagram shows that the application goes through the following states:

1. The ShowSearchEmp procedure is called and produces the Web page SearchEmp.

2. When the user clicks the button on this page, the **empname** parameter is sent to the ShowEmpList procedure.

3. The ShowEmpList procedure creates the EmpList Web page.

4. When the user clicks the button on this page, the application continues from step 1.

The Necessary Business Logic

This application only needs business logic added in one place: the ShowEmpList procedure must loop through all the records that match the search criteria. (A Java servlet would need code to read the parameter, but this happens automatically in PL/SQL when the parameter is defined as an input parameter to the procedure.)

A Code Example—ShowEmpList

When you have finished, your ShowEmpList PL/SQL package will look like this:

```
create or replace package body maintainemp
as
  procedure ShowSearchEmp
  is
  begin
    htp.p(format.pageStart('Search for Employees'));
    htp.p(format.introText('Enter a name or part of a name and press '
        || 'the <b> Search </b>button. '));
```

```
      htp.p(htmlform.formStart('maintainemp.ShowEmpList'));
      htp.p(htmlform.textField('Name', 'empname'));
      htp.p(htmlform.SubmitButtonRow('Search'));
      htp.p(htmlform.formEnd);
      htp.p(format.pageEnd);
   end ShowSearchEmp;

   procedure ShowEmpList(empname in varchar2)
   is
      cursor cuEmpByName(empname in varchar2)
      is
        select empno, ename, job
        from   emp
        where  upper(ename) like empname;
   begin
      htp.p(format.pageStart('Employee List'));
      htp.p(format.introText('This list shows all employees'));
      htp.p('<table border cellpadding="4">');
      htp.p('  <tr> ');
      htp.p('    <th>Emp. no.</th>');
      htp.p('    <th>Name</th>');
      htp.p('    <th>Job</th>');
      htp.p('  </tr>');
      for crEmp in cuEmpByName('%' || upper(empname) || '%') loop
        htp.p('  <tr> ');
        htp.p('    <td>' || crEmp.empno || '</td>');
        htp.p('    <td>' || crEmp.ename || '</td>');
        htp.p('    <td>' || crEmp.job || '</td>');
        htp.p('  </tr>');
      end loop;
      htp.p('</table>');
      htp.p(format.pageEnd);
   end ShowEmpList;
end maintainemp;
```

The Cursor   Notice that the cursor now takes an input parameter used in the WHERE condition of the query. PL/SQL does not consider SQL statements with parameters different from other statements, so the code change necessary in Java (from a Statement object to a PreparedStatement object) is not necessary.

The Loop Statement   This statement now passes the parameter to the cursor (wrapped in % to match substrings and converted to uppercase to make the query case insensitive). As before, the cursor record crEmp is implicitly defined, and the procedure loops though all records satisfying the WHERE condition in the cursor.

The Cursor Record   As in the previous example, the cursor record is used to retrieve the columns for the current row.

Maintaining Employees

The final example shows a small application that handles all operations on the EMP table, that is, query, insert, update, and delete. It expands on the previous example by adding code to handle inserts, updates, and deletes in a safe manner.

Once more, the process goes through the same four steps:

1. Application design

2. Page design

3. Conversion

4. Business logic

Application Design

The storyboard now shows four screens (see Figure 7-15):

■ The Search screen with an added button to call the NewEmp screen.

■ The EmpList screen with an added hyperlink from each employee number to the detail screen for that employee.

■ A new screen NewEmp in which to enter a new employee.

■ A new screen EmpDetail in which to show and update the record details. After filling in the fields on this screen, the user is returned to the EmpList screen.

This application now passes quite a bit more information around:

■ New data from the NewEmp screen

■ Potentially updated data from the EmpDetail screen

■ Instructions to delete records from the EmpDetail screen

All of this data has been written next to the navigation lines on the application flow diagram in Figure 7-16 to show which code modules have to receive and handle the data.

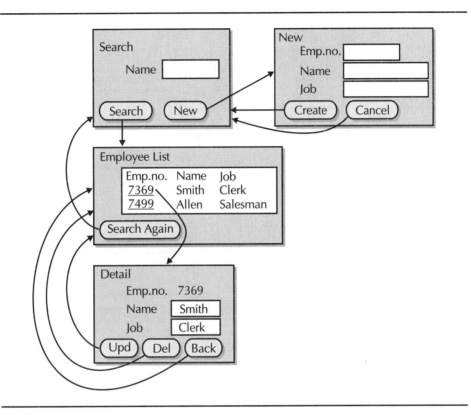

FIGURE 7-15. *A four-screen storyboard*

The diagram in Figure 7-16 shows a few things that might be surprising:

■ The ShowEmpList procedure must now perform the query to show the EmpList screen *and* perform any database operations resulting from an update or a delete.

■ The ShowSearchEmp has the additional task of performing a database insert when the user enters data for a new record.

■ The ShowEmpDetail procedure must receive the **searchempname**. This allows the application to "remember" the last search—see the upcoming section "Creating a Session."

Table 7-2 summarizes the parameters that each PL/SQL procedure must handle.

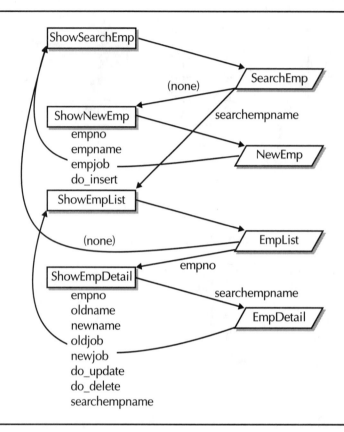

FIGURE 7-16. *A more complicated application flow diagram*

Using Buttons

Note the **do_insert**, **do_update**, and **do_delete** parameters. These are used by
the code module to determine which button the user pressed. For example, the
NewEmp screen has two buttons: Create and Cancel. By producing two buttons of
the Submit type and giving the Create button the name **do_insert**, the following
procedure can determine what button the user clicked: if the **do_insert** parameter
has a value, the user clicked Create; if not, the user clicked Cancel.

Similarly, the EmpDetail module has three Submit buttons, of which the Update
and Delete buttons have a value. The ShowEmpList module then knows that if the

Procedure	Parameters
ShowSearchEmp	**empno** **empname** **empjob** **do_insert**
ShowNewEmp	(none)
ShowEmpList	**empno** **oldname** **newname** **oldjob** **newjob** **do_update** **do_delete** **searchempname**
ShowEmpDetails	**searchempname** **empno**

TABLE 7-2. *The Parameters Each Procedure Must Receive*

do_update parameter has a value, the user clicked the Update button; if the **do_delete** parameter has a value, the user clicked the Delete button; and if neither has a value, the user clicked Back.

Because the path from the SearchEmp screen to the ShowNewEmp module does not pass any parameters, this connection can be handled by a simple HTML link—see the HTML code in the upcoming "Building the Application" section.

Creating a Session

The specification states that the next Web page after the EmpDetail screen is the EmpList. It is reasonable for the user to expect to return to the same employee list; but because the HTTP protocol doesn't have sessions, the Web server has forgotten which query the user executed earlier.

One solution to this problem is to pass the searchempname value *through* the EmpList screen in the form of a *hidden field* (refer to Chapter 5 if you don't remember this HTML form element). The ShowEmpList procedure can thus store the search parameter in the EmpList screen for the ShowEmpDetail procedure to receive. The ShowEmpDetail procedure, in turn, 5 stores this value in the EmpDetail screen for the ShowEmpList procedure to retrieve so it can repeat the same query.

NOTE
There are other ways of handling this (with cookies), but that is an advanced topic outside the scope of this book.

Building the Application

With this information, you can create the package specification, including all procedures and necessary parameters. It will look like this:

```
create or replace package maintainemp
as
  procedure ShowSearchEmp(
    empno in varchar2 default null
  , empname in varchar2 default null
  , empjob in varchar2 default null
  );
  procedure ShowNewEmp;
  procedure ShowEmpList(
    searchempname in varchar2 default null
  , empno in varchar2 default null
  , oldname in varchar2 default null
  , newname in varchar2 default null
  , oldjob in varchar2 default null
  , newjob in varchar2 default null
  , do_update in varchar2 default null
  , do_delete in varchar2 default null
  );
  procedure ShowEmpDetails(
    searchempname in varchar2 default null
  , empno in varchar2 default null
  );
end maintainemp;
```

Page Design

You need two new pages:

- NewEmp to allow the user to enter a new employee number, name, and job (for simplicity, leave out the database sequence and trigger that would normally provide the employee number for the new employee)

- EmpDetail that allows the user to change the name and job of an existing employee

In addition, the EmpList page should have hyperlinks that allow you to "drill down" to the detailed information about an employee.

Using a Button Without Submitting the Form

Note on the application flow diagram that the path from the SearchEmp screen to the ShowNewEmp module does not pass any parameters. Only the ShowEmpList module needs to receive the **searchempname** parameter entered on the SearchEmp screen. This makes it possible to have an HTML Form with a Submit button that goes to the ShowEmpList procedure and a separate button that jumps to the ShowNewEmp procedure when clicked. The HTML could look like this:

```
<form method="get" action="maintainemp.ShowEmpList">
<table border=0>
  <tr>
    <td>Name</td>
    <td>
      <input type="text" name="searchempname" />
    </td>
  </tr>
  <tr>
    <td colspan="2">
      <input type="submit" value="  Search  " />
      <input type="button" value="  New  "
        onClick="document.location.href='maintainemp.ShowNewEmp'" />
    </td>
  </tr>
```

The Search button is an HTML Form Submit button that sends the data on the Form (the value of the <input> field) to the procedure specified in the **action** attribute of the <form> tag.

The New button is a normal button that does not submit the HTML Form. In fact, normal buttons do nothing by themselves; therefore, the onClick method that contains JavaScript code jumps to some other page without passing any data. (JavaScript programming is outside the scope of this book—refer to the resources in Chapter 13 if you want to learn JavaScript programming. For this example, however, the one JavaScript statement fulfills our need.)

Using Multiple Submit Buttons

The storyboard shows that there are three ways from the EmpDetail screen back to the EmpList screen:

- Do an update.

- Do a delete.

- Do nothing.

Whenever you see this type of layout with several different ways of calling the same module, you can use multiple Submit buttons, like this:

```
<input type="submit" name="do_update" value=" Update " />
<input type="submit" name="do_delete" value=" Delete " />
<input type="submit" value=" Back " />
```

These are all three HTML Form Submit buttons that send all the data on the page to the destination specified in the **action** attribute of the <form> tag:

- The Update button has the name do_update; so when the user clicks this button, the **do_update** parameter has the value 'Update' (and the **do_delete** parameter does not have a value). This allows the ShowEmpList procedure to detect that an update was requested.

- The Delete button has the name do_delete; so when the user clicks this button, the **do_delete** parameter has the value " Delete " (and the **do_update** parameter does not have a value). This allows the ShowEmpList procedure to detect that a delete was requested.

- The Back button does not have a value. When the user clicks this button, neither the **do_update** nor the **do_delete** parameter has a value, so the ShowEmpList procedure knows to leave the data unchanged.

Adding Data to Hyperlinks

The application flow diagram shows that you must pass the parameters **empno** and **searchempname** from the EmpList screen to the ShowEmpDetail screen. It would be possible (but cumbersome) to create a complete HTML form for every record on the EmpList screen to pass these parameters like the other screens in this application.

It is easier to create a hyperlink for every record and embed the parameter values in the hyperlink. Chapter 5 explains the special format for this kind of parameter passing; in this example, if the user previously searched for the string **mi**, every employee hyperlink would look similar to this:

```
<a href="ShowEmpDetail?empno=7566&searchempname=mi">7566</a>
```

The empno is used both as part of the **href** attribute and as the actual link text. When the user clicks this link, the parameter **empno** with the value 7566 and the parameter **searchempname** with the value **mi** is passed to the ShowEmpDetail procedure.

Conversion

Once more, you need to convert the HTML and place it in your PL/SQL package. This can be done by hand or with an editor macro, or you can use a tool such as html2plsql or WebAlchemy to convert the HTML to PL/SQL code. Then place the converted code in a package body matching the specification created during the application design.

You can also now take out the HTML elements that occur first and last on every screen page, and place them in methods in a special Format package.

If you are really thorough about this step, you will move *all* HTML tags out of your PL/SQL package and place this code in the Format package. In addition, you can use a toolkit package such as HtmlForm to handle all elements you use in HTML forms.

After a full conversion, the code for the ShowNewEmp PL/SQL procedure could look like this (the complete package code is available on **www.vesterli.com**):

```
create or replace package body maintainemp
as
[snip]
  procedure ShowNewEmp
  is
  begin
    htp.p(Format.pageStart('Create new Employee'));
    htp.p(Format.introText('Enter the data for a new employee and '
        || 'press the <b>Create</b> button. '));
    htp.p(HtmlForm.formStart('maintainemp.ShowSearchEmp'));
    htp.p(HtmlForm.textField('Emp. No.','empno'));
    htp.p(HtmlForm.textField('Name','empname'));
    htp.p(HtmlForm.textfield('Job','empjob'));
    htp.p(HtmlForm.buttonsStart);
    htp.p(HtmlForm.submitButton(name=>'do_insert', label=>'Create'));
    htp.p(HtmlForm.submitButton(label=>'Cancel'));
    htp.p(HtmlForm.buttonsEnd);
    htp.p(HtmlForm.formEnd);
    htp.p(Format.pageEnd);
  end;
[snip]
end maintainemp;
```

Business Logic

The program has business logic added in three places:

- Inserting new records
- Performing updates
- Deleting records

Handling New Records

As it is clear from the application flow diagram, the data for a new employee record is entered on the NewEmp screen but passed to the ShowSearchEmp screen. This means that the ShowSearchEmp procedure must actually do the insert. The code could look something like this:

```
create or replace package body maintainemp
as
  procedure ShowSearchEmp(
    empno in varchar2 default null
  , empname in varchar2 default null
  , empjob in varchar2 default null
  , do_insert in varchar2 default null
  ) is
    page varchar2(32767);
    empNumber emp.empno%type;
begin
begin
      empNumber := to_number(empno);
    exception
      when others
      then
        empNumber := 0;
    end;
    page := Format.pageStart('Search for Employees');
    /* only proceed if we got at least empNo and empName */
    if (do_insert is not null and empnumber != 0 and empname is not null
    then
      begin
        insert into emp (empno, ename, job)
        values (empNumber, empname, empjob);
        page := page || Format.message('One record created');
      exception
        when others
        then
          if sqlcode = -1
          then
            /* ORA-00001 means empno already exists */
            page := page || Format.message('Employee number '
              || empNumber
            || ' already exists.'
          );
          else
          /* something serious is wrong */
          htp.p(Format.errorPage('SQL Error: ' || sqlerrm));
          return;
        end if;
```

```
      end;
   end if;
   page := page || Format.introText('Enter a name or part of a name '
      || 'and press the <b> Search </b>button.');
   page := page || HtmlForm.formStart('maintainemp.ShowEmpList');
   page := page || HtmlForm.textField('Name', 'searchempname');
   page := page || HtmlForm.buttonsStart;
   page := page || HtmlForm.submitButton('Search');
   page := page || HtmlForm.button('New', 'maintainemp.ShowNewEmp');
   page := page || HtmlForm.buttonsEnd;
   page := page || HtmlForm.formEnd;
   page := page || Format.pageEnd;
   htp.p(page);
 end;
[snip]
end maintainemp;
```

The empno Parameter   The parameter is received as a **VARCHAR2** to allow the procedure to start even if the parameter value is not a valid number. Remember that if you define an **IN** parameter to a PL/SQL procedure as a NUMBER and there is any error converting it, your PL/SQL procedure is never invoked and the user sees only an ugly error message from the Oracle HTTP Server.

In this case, a **BEGIN/EXCEPTION/END** block (the PL/SQL parallel to the **try/catch** found in Java) is used to attempt the conversion to the local NUMBER variable empNumber.

Inserting a Row   This only happens if the PL/SQL procedure received a valid employee number, a name, and the **do_insert** parameter:

- If this procedure is called *without* the **do_insert** parameter, it means that the user clicked the Cancel button on the NewEmp screen. Because the HTML tag for the Cancel button does not have a **name** parameter, no value is sent.

- If the procedure is called *with* a **do_insert** parameter, it means that the user clicked the Create button on the NewEmp screen. Because the HTML tag for the Create button has a **name** parameter, the value (the string "Create") is sent to the procedure.

If an insert is called for, the PL/SQL procedure executes the insert and adds feedback to the Web page.

All errors are caught with a WHEN OTHERS exception handler. This checks for an ORA-00001 error (meaning that the primary key constraint was violated); if this error occurred, the procedure shows a message that the **empno** is already in use. If any other error occurs, the procedure produces an error page.

Handling Updates and Deletes

The application flow diagram also shows that the ShowEmpList procedure follows the EmpDetail screen, so the tasks of doing both updates and deletes falls to this procedure. The code could look something like this:

```
CREATE OR REPLACE package body maintainemp
as
[snip]
  procedure ShowEmpList(
    searchEmpName in varchar2 default null
  , empno in varchar2 default null
  , oldname in varchar2 default null
  , newname in varchar2 default null
  , oldjob in varchar2 default null
  , newjob in varchar2 default null
  , do_update in varchar2 default null
  , do_delete in varchar2 default null
  )
  is
    page varchar2(32767);  -- the HTML page being built
    empNumber emp.empno%type;  -- the empno converted to correct format
    dummy number; -- dummy variable selected into for locking
    dbEname emp.ename%type;  -- the empname stored in the db
    dbJob emp.job%type;  -- the job stored in the db
    labels DatabaseUtility.labelTable; -- column labels for the results
    searchCriteria varchar2(255) := '%'; -- restriction for the query
    queryString varchar2(2000); -- SQL statement to execute
    resultTable varchar2(32767); -- the HTML table with the emp list
  begin
    page := Format.pageStart('Employee List');
    begin
      empNumber := to_number(empno);
    exception
      when others
      then
        empNumber := 0;
    end;

    /*
     * if user requested an update and changed the name or job
     * or the user requested a delete, get and lock the row
     */
    if (((do_update is not null)
        and (not(oldName = newName and oldJob = newJob))))
        or (do_delete is not null)
    then
      begin
```

```
    select ename, job
    into   dbEname, dbJob
    from   emp
    where  empno = empNumber
    for update nowait;

    /* no exception: record is still there and could be locked */
    if do_update is not null
    then
      if dbEname = oldName and dbJob = oldJob
      then
        /* record was unchanged, so proceed with the update */
        update emp
        set    ename = newName
        ,      job = newJob
        where  empno = empNumber;
      else
        /* Record changed since detail page was produced * 
        page := page || Format.message(
              'The record has been changed by another user');
      end if;
    else
      /* if it wasn't insert, do the delete */
      delete from emp
      where  empno = empNumber;
    end if;
    commit;
    page := page || Format.message('1 record processed');
  exception
    when no_data_found
    then
      /* Record gone: deleted since detail page was produced */
      page := page || Format.message(
            'The record has been deleted by another user');
    when others
    then
      if sqlcode = -54
      then
        /* ORA-000054 means record locked by other user */
        page := page || Format.message('Record has been locked by '
              || 'another user. Please try again later.');
      else
        /* Some fatal error */
        htp.p(Format.errorPage('SQL Error: ' + sqlerrm));
      end if;
  end;
end if;
```

```
/* do a query */
labels(1) := 'Name';
labels(2) := 'Job';
if searchEmpName is not null
then
  searchCriteria := searchCriteria || searchEmpName || '%';
end if;
searchCriteria := upper(searchCriteria);
queryString := 'select empno, ename, job '
  || 'from    emp '
  || 'where   upper(ename) like '''
  || searchCriteria
  || ''' order by ename'
;
resultTable := DatabaseUtility.htmlTable(
  queryString
, labels
, 1              /* the column to use as link */
  /* the link text. pass search text as well */
, 'maintainemp.ShowEmpDetails?searchempname='
  || searchEmpName || '&empno='
);
if length(resultTable) > 0
then
  /* found some data */
  page := page
    || Format.introText('This list shows the employees that '
      || 'satisfy the search criteria. Click on an employee '
      || 'number to see the details.')
    || resultTable
  ;
else
  /* no data found */
  page := page
    || Format.introText('No data satisfy the search criteria');
end if;
page := page || HtmlForm.formStart('maintainemp.ShowSearchEmp');
page := page || HtmlForm.submitButtonRow('Search Again');
page := page || HtmlForm.formEnd;
page := page || Format.pageEnd;
htp.p(page);
end;
```

```
[snip]
end maintainemp;
```

The empno Parameter   As in the ShowSearchEmp procedure, the **empno** parameter is received as a **VARCHAR2**; it is similarly converted to a local NUMBER variable in a begin/exception/end block.

Locking the Record   If the user requests an update and provides a new name or a new job, or if the user requests a delete, you must retrieve and lock the relevant record with a SELECT FOR UPDATE.

Performing an Update   Before performing a requested update, the procedure compares the values in the database with the old values passed from the preceding Web page.

This check is necessary to prevent a lost update. For example, if John clicks on a link and receives a Detail record and then leaves for lunch, it is possible that Sue has updated the record in the database when John comes back. To prevent John's update from overwriting Sue's, you must check that the value in the database is still the same as it was when John got the original details from the database.

If this problem does not occur, the procedure executes the update.

If the database values are different from the old values passed to the procedure, the procedure adds a message to this effect to the page and does not perform the update.

Performing a Delete   To delete a record, the procedure executes the relevant DELETE statement.

If Something Goes Wrong   If there is a problem, processing continues in the EXCEPTION block:

- In case the record is no longer found in the database, a NO_DATA_FOUND exception occurs. The code adds a message to the page saying that the record has been deleted by someone else.

- The procedure explicitly catches any ORA-00054 errors (record locked by another user), provides a message to the user, and allows the application to continue.

■ In case of other errors, the application has a serious problem and must display an error message and terminate.

Retrieving the Data   In this case, the record list is produced by calling the DatabaseUtility.htmlTable function. This function is part of the Web Application Toolkit (see Chapter 12) and takes the following parameters:

■ A SQL query statement

■ A table of column labels

■ An index number for a link column (A 1 means that the first item in the query should be used as key in a hyperlink)

■ A link URL to use for the key-based hyperlink

The function returns an HTML table with hyperlinks to all the details. If you don't want to use this toolkit, you can use code similar to the previous examples to create and execute a statements, and loop through the results.

Summary

In this chapter, you saw how to use PL/SQL to hand-build Web applications. The PL/SQL language offers a very good integration with the database and is well suited for database-intensive Web applications.

As you have also seen from the examples, it takes quite a bit of code to write robust and maintainable PL/SQL Web applications. This is the price that you must pay for the flexibility that a completely handwritten application offers. The next chapter describes how to use Oracle Designer to generate PL/SQL code, sacrificing a little flexibility in return for vastly improved productivity.

CHAPTER

8

Designer Applications

ay you wanted to create a model of a bear for a child. If you were a skilled craftsman, you could pick up a block of wood and use a small selection of carving tools to create a detailed, lifelike bear model. It would take you a long time, and would require a lot of skill, but you could get exactly the result you were looking for.

If you are not particularly adept at woodworking, you have to look for another approach. You might decide to build a bear from Lego bricks. This would not take as long, and you would not need many years of experience before you could create a good result. But, of course, your bear is going to be a little less lifelike; after all, you can't create the same types of surfaces with Lego bricks that you can with wood.

You face a similar choice when building Web applications. The preceding two chapters described the craftsman's approach: using only simple tools, you can hand-build any application you want, but it takes skill and much time to achieve a satisfactory result.

This chapter will describe generating an application with Oracle Designer, which is like building something with Lego bricks: much faster and reasonably flexible, but limited to the available bricks.

The Designer Approach

Oracle Designer is a computer-aided software engineering (CASE) tool. It uses a *model* of your application stored in a *repository* and *generates* your application code at the push of a button.

The Designer Tools

Designer has many tools that work on the same model in the repository. This means that if you make a change to a table in one tool, that change is immediately available in all other tools. Figure 8-1 shows the Designer main screen with all the tools; Table 8-1 gives a brief overview of all the tools.

If you have not already installed the Designer tools and set up the Oracle Repository in a database, you can refer to Chapter 4 for step-by-step instructions.

Using Designer

There are many ways to use Designer, from the comprehensive Information Engineering (IE) approach to the light-weight Rapid Application Development (RAD) approach.

In the IE approach, most of the Designer tools are used as the development flows down a number of successive stages from analysis to design to generation. This is a more careful, formal approach well suited for big, complex, or critical systems. Oracle has developed a methodology called *Oracle CDM Advantage* with well-defined deliverables and supporting tools for this approach.

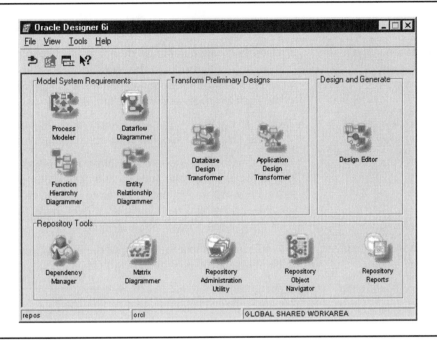

FIGURE 8-1. *The Designer main screen*

Tool	Description
Process Modeler	Used to model the business processes in the organization.
Dataflow Diagrammer	A modeling tool that lets you create diagrams that show how data flows through the organization.
Function Hierarchy Diagrammer	A modeling tool used to refine business processes into more detailed functions that become the basis of the application.
Entity Relationship Diagrammer	Used to create an entity-relationship model (a *logical* model) showing the information that the organization needs.

TABLE 8-1. *An Overview of the Tools in Oracle Designer*

Tool	Description
Database Design Transformer	Used to create a database design (a *physical* model) from an entity model in the repository. This tool can add primary and foreign-key columns to implement the logical model as database tables.
Application Design Transformer	Used to create first-cut application modules based on the functions modeled with the modeling tools.
Design Editor	Along with the generators, allows you to refine the preliminary database and module design produced by the transformers and to generate code to create tables and program code (for example, in the form of PL/SQL Web application modules).
Dependency Manager	A support tool to analyze dependencies between elements in the repository.
Matrix Diagrammer	A support tool that can create many forms of cross-referencing tables that can be used for quality assurance.
Repository Administration Utility	A support tool to administer the Oracle Repository.
Repository Object Navigator	A support tool to work with elements in the repository, including creating, editing, and deleting repository elements; exporting objects to files; and controlling access.
Repository Reports	Contains a lot of predefined reports that you can run to document the contents of the repository.

TABLE 8-1. *An Overview of the Tools in Oracle Designer* (continued)

In the RAD approach, the focus is on using the Design Editor for iterative development where prototypes can rapidly be built and refined. This approach is best suited for smaller applications, or where the requirements are changing or unclear.

In addition, Designer can be used to capture existing databases and Oracle Forms applications for documentation or further development.

Building Web Applications with Designer

This book covers the RAD approach that is suitable for small, prototype-driven projects. If you are interested in other approaches, you can refer to the excellent help that Designer offers, or you can refer to one of the books mentioned in Chapter 13.

Building the Database

When building the database, the end result is the same: tables in the database. But you have two ways of getting there: you can either start with an Entity-Relationship model in the E-R modeler or go directly to the Design Editor. Each has advantages and disadvantages, as shown in Table 8-2.

If you decide to use the E-R Diagrammer, you can concentrate on modeling the "real" data that your application will need and can let the Database Design Transformer add the necessary columns for primary and foreign keys.

If you use only the Design Editor, you save the step of transforming and work directly with the server model with all details from the beginning.

Capturing a Design

Designer offers very good tools for building a new database, but many Web applications are not built from scratch. Instead, they are based on tables used in existing systems, maybe with the addition of a few new tables or columns.

To support this situation, Designer offers Design Capture tools to read the existing database and create a Server Model from it. You can then refine the table design with the Design Editor and generate scripts to implement the changes.

Method	Advantages	Disadvantages
Using the E-R Diagrammer	Focus on logical design	Several tools involved
Using the Design Editor	Entire design in one step	Must explicitly code primary and foreign-key columns

TABLE 8-2. *Comparing the E-R Diagrammer with the Design Editor*

Capturing EMP and DEPT

As an example of this situation and in preparation for the following code examples, capture the EMP and DEPT tables into Designer from the existing SCOTT schema in the database.

This task involves the following steps:

1. Choose Start | Programs | Oracle Designer 6i—DesHome608 | Oracle Designer. Log on with the user name **repos**, password **repos**, and connect string **orcl**. The Designer main screen (refer to Figure 8-1) appears.

2. Click the Design Editor icon to start the Design Editor. If this is the first time you have started Designer, the Designer Editor Welcome screen appears:

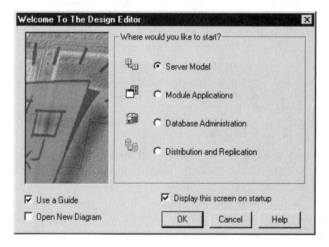

When you become familiar with the Design Editor and want to get rid of this dialog box and the guide that follows, you can deselect the two selected check boxes.

3. Leave the Server Model radio button enabled and click OK to start the Server Model Guide shown in the following illustration. (If you have deselected the Use a Guide check box, you can choose Tools | Server Model Guide to start this guide.)

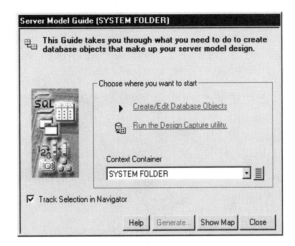

4. Choose SYSTEM FOLDER from the Context Container drop-down list and click the Run the Design Capture Utility link. The Capture Server Model from Database dialog box appears, shown here:

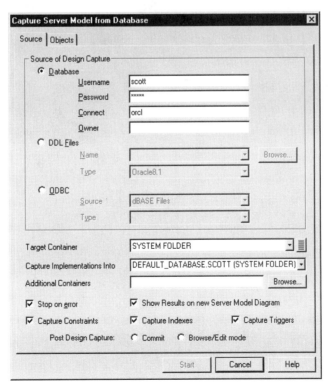

5. Enter the user name (**scott**), the password (**tiger**), and the connect string (**orcl**) at the top of the dialog box and then click the Objects tab. Designer connects as the specified Oracle user and retrieves a list of all database objects belonging to that user, as shown here:

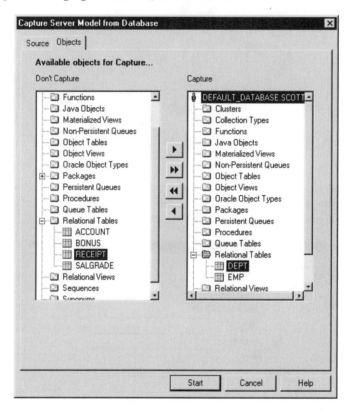

6. Choose the desired objects in the left pane and click the single arrow to move them to the right frame. In this simple example, just move the EMP and DEPT tables to the right frame and then click Start to capture them.

7. The message window appears and shows the progress of the capture, including any applicable warnings and errors. When capturing these two tables from the default database, you will probably see some warnings about "invalid tablespace references." These warnings can safely be ignored—they simply mean that these two tables and their primary-key indexes were stored in the SYSTEM tablespace in the database, but you did not select to capture that tablespace.

8. When the capture completes, the new objects appear in the Navigator in the left side of the window, and the Design Capture utility shows the new tables on a new diagram at the right, as shown in the next illustration. The elements of the Design Capture window are as follows:

■ **The Design Navigator**   Shows all objects in the repository that the Design Editor can work with. It has four tabs along the top: Server Model, Modules, DB Admin, and Distribution. While working with the table definitions, you need the Server Model tab.

■ **The Server Model Diagram**   Shows a diagram of one or more tables. A table can be included on one or more Server Model Diagrams but does not have to be. If you do not want to keep the actual layout of your diagram, you do not have to save it—the tables are stored in the repository whether you keep the diagram or not.

■ **The Message Window**   Shows the results of design capture or generation. In the following illustration, it shows some warnings from the design capture.

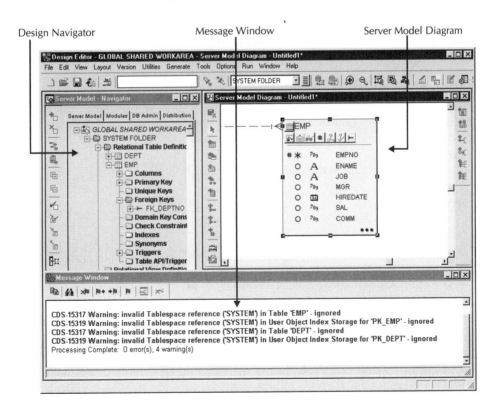

NOTE
After the capture, the Navigator has a gray background instead of the normal white. This means that you have to review the changes to the model and then choose either File | Save Uncommitted Data to accept the changes or File | Revert Uncommitted Data to roll back the changes. You can make Designer attempt to commit automatically by setting Post Design Capture to Commit in the Capture Server dialog box in Step 4. The capture can normally be committed, but it might fail if, for example, a table or column name contains a non-ASCII character.

9. Choose File | Save Uncommitted Data or press CTRL-S to save the changes. A progress bar appears while the data is committed to the Designer Repository. When the data is saved, the background of the Navigator pane turns white again.

Building the Application

A Designer PL/SQL Web application works just like the handwritten application described in the previous chapter. The application code is a PL/SQL package, and you need the Oracle HTTP Server and the PL/SQL module to pass the requests and responses back and forth between the Web browser and the PL/SQL code in the database.

The difference is that instead of coding the application following the four-step method in Chapter 7, you first build *modules* in the Design Editor and then *generate* code at the push of a button. The module definitions are stored in the Designer repository, and the generated PL/SQL code is stored in a file (and can be automatically installed in the database if you want).

NOTE
In addition to the HTML-generating PL/SQL code Oracle Designer generates, it can also generate JavaScript code to provide data validation and other features on the client side, in the Web browser. Refer to the Designer help for more information on using JavaScript in Designer.

In your module definitions, you can also define your own PL/SQL code that Oracle Designer will then merge into the complete application code at specific points. You can even add your own JavaScript code to your module—Designer will then also include this code together with the JavaScript it generates itself.

The Oracle Schemas Involved in a Designer Web Application

You might remember from Chapter 7 that a handwritten PL/SQL application is stored in some schema in the database. To send HTML back to the Web browser, you used the Oracle-supplied HTP (Hyper Text Procedures) package that was simply available. The default installation of the Oracle8i Release 3 database installs the HTP package and the other packages of the PL/SQL Web Developers Toolkit in the SYS schema, creates public synonyms, and grants execution rights to everyone.

A Designer-generated Web application needs a little more: it needs the packages of the Designer PL/SQL Web Library. If you followed the installation instructions in Chapter 4, you also installed these packages in the SYS schema. However, the default installation does not grant execution rights on these packages to anyone; you must do this by hand for every application user.

Preparing to Build an Application

To build a Web application in the SCOTT schema, you need to start SQL*Plus, log on as the user **sys** (password **change_on_install**, connect string **orcl**), and execute the script O:\oracle\des608\cgenw61\cvwetc\wsguser.sql. The script prompts you for the name of the application user (see Figure 8-2); enter the name **SCOTT** and press ENTER.

This script will probably show one error message—you can ignore that.

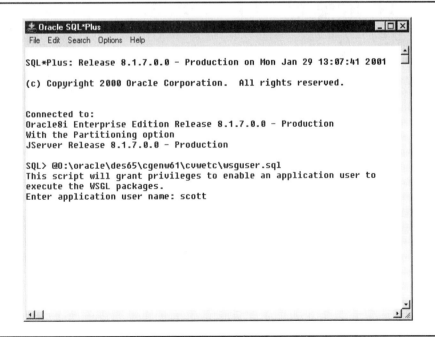

FIGURE 8-2. *Setting up an application user for Web applications*

Setting Up a Database Access Descriptor

If you did not already set up a Database Access Descriptor (DAD) in Chapter 7, you need to do so now to tell the Oracle HTTP Server how to translate the URL into a database connection.

If you did not change the **DocumentRoot** parameter in your Apache configuration file, you can enter the address **http://yourserver** in your browser, where *yourserver* is the name of the machine on which the Oracle HTTP Server is installed. This will show the Oracle HTTP Server introduction screen in Figure 8-3.

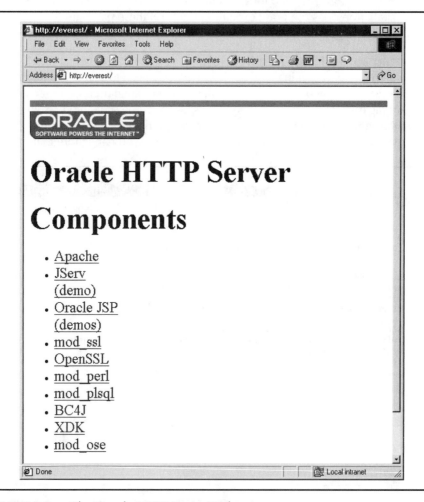

FIGURE 8-3. *The Oracle HTTP Server Welcome page*

To add or change Database Access Descriptors, configure the mod_plsql module. When you click the mod_plsql link, the Gateway Configuration Menu screen shown in Figure 8-4 appears.

Click the Gateway Database Access Descriptor Settings link. The Database Access Descriptors page shown in Figure 8-5 appears.

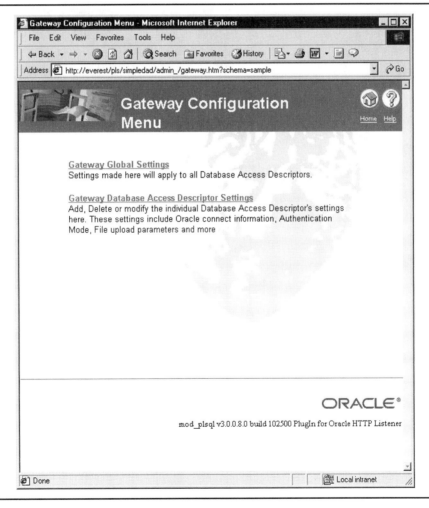

FIGURE 8-4. *Gateway Configuration Menu page*

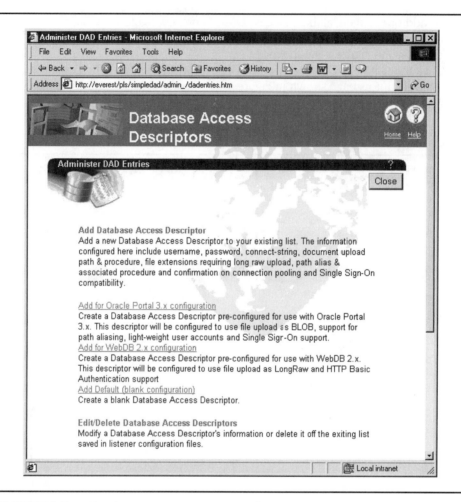

FIGURE 8-5. *Database Access Descriptor administration*

Click Add Default (Blank Configuration) to create a simple DAD suitable for the basic examples in this chapter. The Create DAD Entry page (see Figure 8-6) appears.

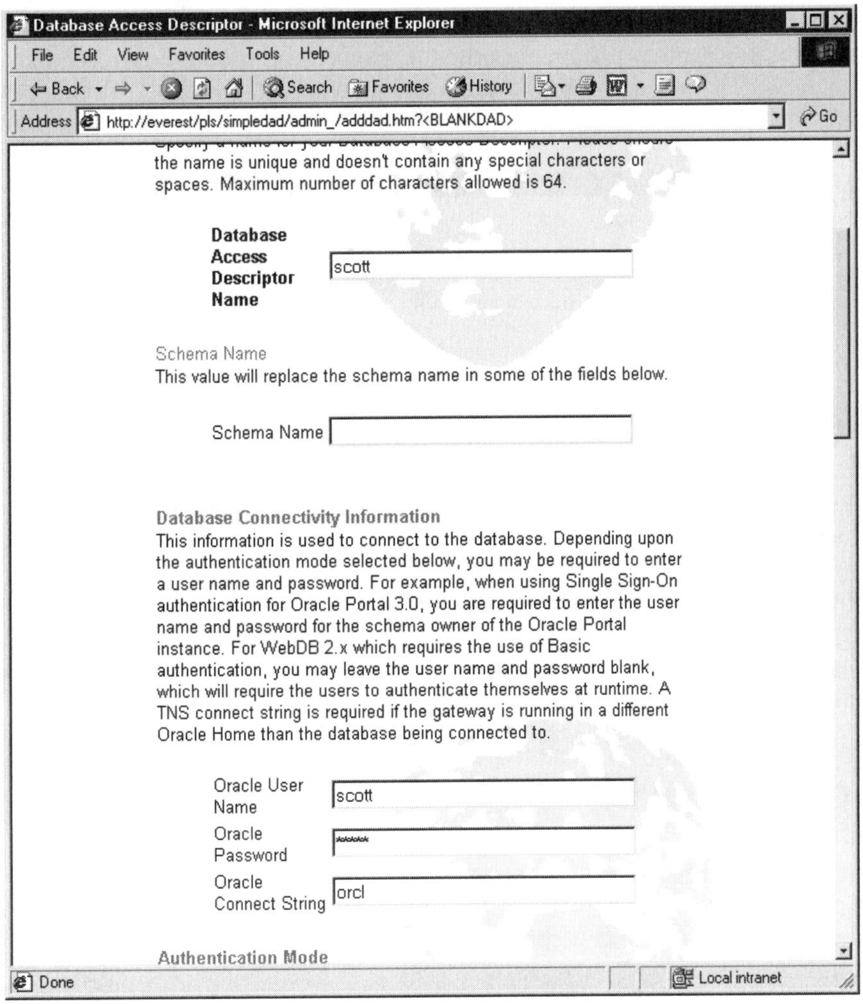

FIGURE 8-6.   *Creating a Database Access Descriptor*

Enter a name for your DAD (for example, **scott**), the Oracle user name (**scott**), the password (**tiger**), and the connect string (**orcl**, if you followed the installation instructions in Chapter 4). Then click the OK button. You should be returned to the Database Access Descriptor Administration page with the message "The changes have been successfully made!"

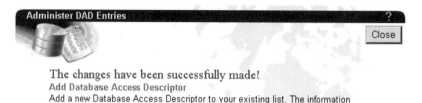

You can click the Close button to return to the previous screen or close your Web browser.

You will now be able to run your generated applications in the SCOTT schema through URLs like this:

http://*<yourserver>*/pls/scott/*<module>*$.startup

where *<yourserver>* is the name of the machine on which the Oracle HTTP Server is running and *<module>* is the name of your Designer module.

Hello World

The first example application is, as always, the Hello World application. This is trivial in Oracle Designer, but it does serve to show the basics of working with the Design Editor. You'll see how to use *User Text* in Designer and how to set a few of the *generator preferences* that control the application generated.

Creating the Module

To start creating the module, open the Design Editor from the Designer main page. When the Design Editor Welcome page appears (see Figure 8-7), choose Module Applications, leave the Use a Guide check box selected, and click OK to start the Module Application Guide. If the Welcome screen does not appear, you can choose Tools | Module Application Guide to start the Guide.

Using the Module Application Guide

On the first screen of the Guide (see Figure 8-8), choose SYSTEM FOLDER from the Context Container drop-down list and click the link Create and Edit Modules.

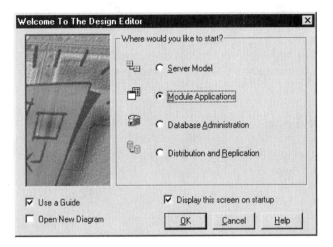

FIGURE 8-7.   *The Design Editor Welcome page*

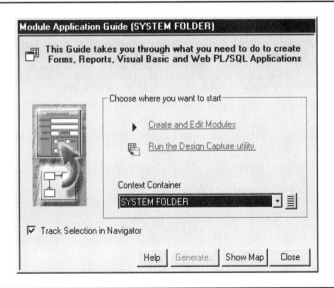

FIGURE 8-8.   *The Module Application Guide Start Screen*

On the next screen (see Figure 8-9), choose the Modules link. An empty Modules screen appears. Click Create to go to the first step in the module guide shown in Figure 8-10.

On this screen, enter a module short name, name, and purpose and choose Web PL/SQL as the language. Click Next three times to go to the User Text step (see Figure 8-11).

Adding User Text

In this dialog box, the Text Location list on the left shows all the places you can add text to the module, and the User Text box on the right shows the text you have entered. For the "Hello World" example, enter the following text:

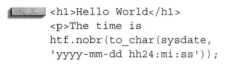
```
<h1>Hello World</h1>
<p>The time is
htf.nobr(to_char(sysdate,
'yyyy-mm-dd hh24:mi:ss'));
```

The <h1> and <p> Tags   These are normal HTML tags that Designer should just pass to the Web browser.

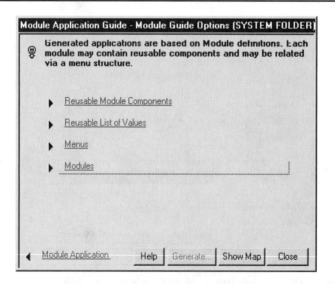

FIGURE 8-9.   *The Module Application Guide Options screen*

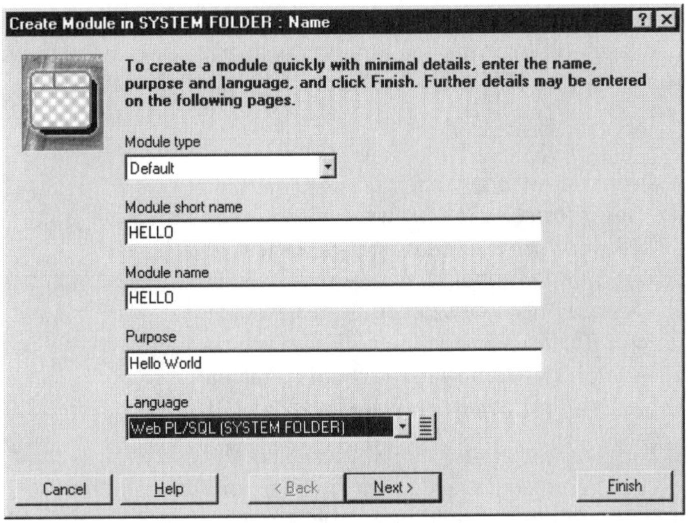

FIGURE 8-10. *Creating a module*

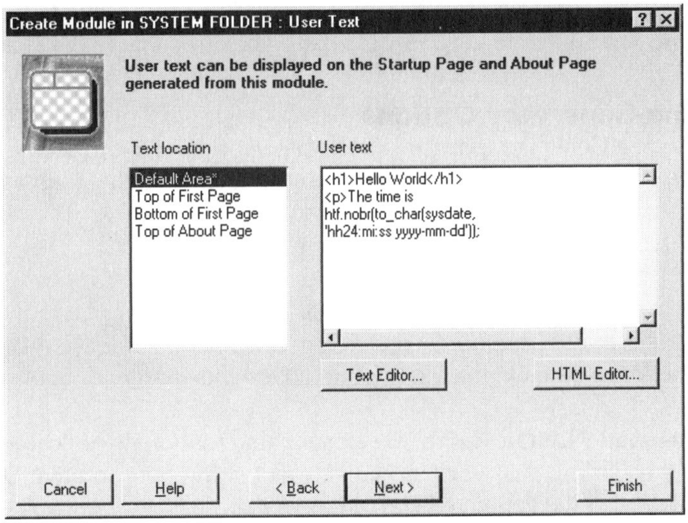

FIGURE 8-11. *Defining user text in a module*

The htf.nobr Function This is a call to the NOBR (no break) function in the HTF (Hyper Text Functions) package. Designer automatically recognizes calls to the HTF package and *executes* the function instead of displaying the name of the function.

NOTE
The NOBR function wraps the text in <NOBR> </NOBR> tags instructing the browser not to break the line. This is not strictly necessary; but unless you call a package that Designer generates (like the HTF package), Designer will not recognize and execute the TO_CHAR function. Instead, it will display "to_char(sysdate, 'hh24:mi:ss yyyy-mm-dd')" as part of the Web page—not what you want!

When you have entered the text, click Finish to end the definition of the module. Your Design Editor window should now look something like Figure 8-12 with your newly created module displayed both in the Module Navigator on the left and in the Module Application Guide on the right.

Generating the Module

OK, enough modeling—let's see the Oracle Designer generator in action! Right-click the HELLO module in the Navigator and choose Generate from the pop-up menu. The Generate Web PL/SQL dialog box (see Figure 8-13) appears.

Setting the Generator Options
Before you let the Generator loose, first click the Options button to set the Generator Options. The Web PL/SQL Generator Options screen in Figure 8-14 appears.

Source Leave this at the File System setting.

Target This section can be used to control where Designer places the PL/SQL source code files that it generates. You can provide a value or leave this section blank—if you leave it blank, the files go into a Designer system directory.

Install Generated PL/SQL Provide a user name (optionally followed by a slash and the corresponding password) and a connect string here to have Designer automatically install the generated code in the database.
If you don't provide a password, Designer will prompt you for it every time you attempt to install generated code in the database.

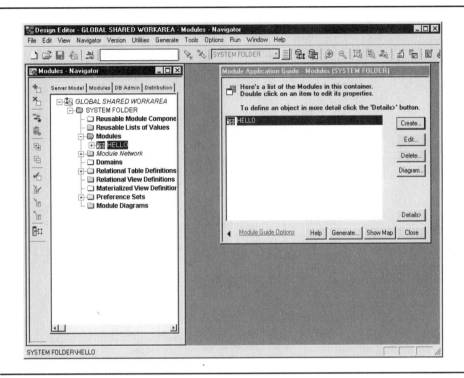

FIGURE 8-12.   *An empty module in Design Editor*

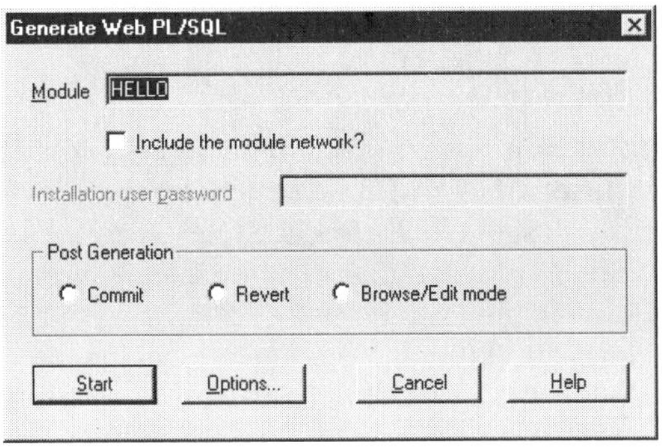

FIGURE 8-13.   *The Generate Web PL/SQL dialog box*

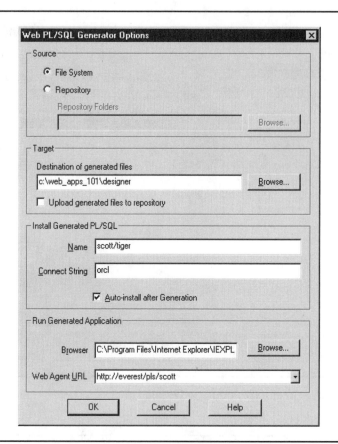

FIGURE 8-14. *The Web PL/SQL Generator Options screen*

Run Generated Application In this section, you can provide the path to your Web browser and the first part of a URL set up to correspond with the Oracle user mentioned earlier in the "Install Generated PL/SQL" section. If you fill in these fields, you can click a button in Designer to automatically view your generated application module through the Web browser.

In a default Windows 2000 installation, the Internet Explorer browser is found at C:\Program Files\Internet Explorer\IEXPLORE.EXE.

If you set up the DAD as described in the preceding section, the Web Agent URL is http://<*servername*>/pls/scott, where <*servername*> is the name of your Web server.

Running the Generator

When you have set the Generator options, click OK to close the Options dialog box and click Start to start the generator. If everything runs correctly, you will see some messages flash by in the Message window and then a command prompt where a SQL*Plus session automatically installs the generated packages in the database schema you specified. Finally, a "Generation is complete" message appears.

Looking at the Results

To see your new application module in action, choose Messages | Build Actions or click the Actions button (a small wrench icon) in the Message Window toolbar. The Build Action window appears:

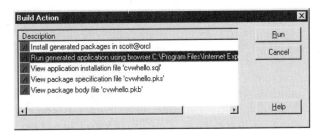

Choose the Run Generated Application option and click Run to start your Web browser and see the application. You should see something like the following illustration.

Well—not quite what we were looking for. You see that Designer did return the current date and time, but there are two problems with this module:

- It displays your HTML tags.

- It generates an extra About link that you did not ask for.

The HTML tags are shown because Designer, with the best of intentions, tries to protect you from having to know any HTML. After all, you got exactly what you typed in the User Text field!

The About link is automatically added so Designer has a page on which to brag that it built the page—you'll probably want to get rid of this as well.

Setting Generator Preferences

Fortunately, Designer offers a way to control the generated application: *generator preferences*. These preferences can be set at different levels—you need to work at the module level for now.

To access the generator preferences, right-click the HELLO module and choose Edit Generator Preferences from the pop-up menu. The Generator Preferences window opens inside the Design Editor window (see Figure 8-15).

There are many preferences that you can set, and being familiar with the most important ones is crucial to controlling Designer-generated applications. The Designer help explains them very well—simply select a preference and press F1 to look it up. The preferences are grouped together under headings that can be collapsed and expanded and each preference has a name (such as MODSUB) and a description (such as Substitute HTML Reserved Characters). To change between viewing the name and the description, you can click the Show Description/Show Name button (see Figure 8-15). This button is a toggle—while the descriptions are shown, it's the Show Name button; while the names are shown, it's the Show Descriptions button.

To solve the two problems with the Hello World application, you need to set two preferences:

- To tell Designer to leave the HTML tags in your user text alone, under the Test Handling group, set the MODSUB (Substitute HTML Reserved Characters) preference to No.

- To tell Designer not to generate the About page, under the Startup Page group, set the MODALR (Startup Page: About Page Hyperlink) preference to No.

When you have set these two preferences, click the Save button, generate the module again, and call it up in a Web browser. You should now see something like Figure 8-16.

Employee List

The next example application is the unrestricted list of all employees in the EMP table. You'll see how to use *module components* and *table usages* to retrieve data from the database, and how to customize the look of the application using an application-specific formatting package and a cascading style sheet (CSS) file.

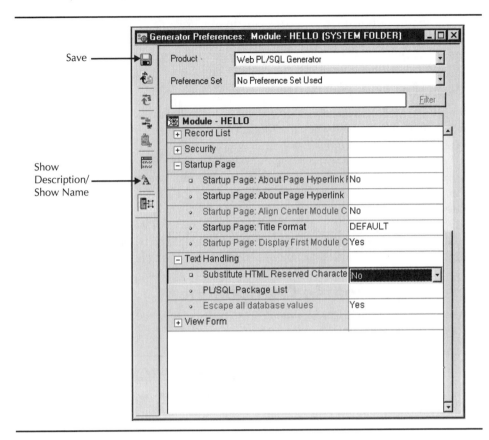

FIGURE 8-15.   *The Generator Preferences window*

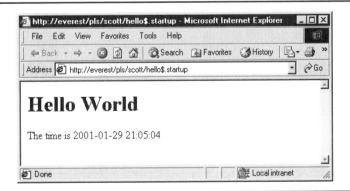

FIGURE 8-16.   *Hello World with the preferences set properly*

This and the following examples work on the EMP table, so the definition of this table must be stored in the Designer Repository. The easiest way to do this is by *design capture*, as described previously.

Creating the Module

To create the module, you can either use the Guide as before (choose Tools | Module Application Guide) or right-click the Modules branch in the Design Navigator and choose Create Module from the pop-up menu.

Provide a short name and a name (for example, EMPLIST), enter a purpose, and choose the language Web PL/SQL. Then click Next multiple times to step through the remaining steps of the wizard until you come to the Goodbye screen shown in Figure 8-17.

On this screen, select Create the Module Then Invoke a Wizard to Create a Module Component. This will start the next wizard with which you can add a module component and define the table that this module will work on. Then click Finish.

Creating a Module Component

As soon as the Module Wizard terminates, the first screen of the Module Component Wizard appears, as shown in Figure 8-18.

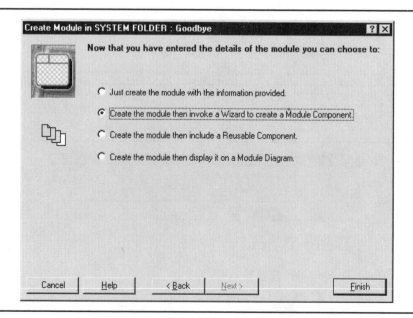

FIGURE 8-17. *The last step of the Create Module Wizard*

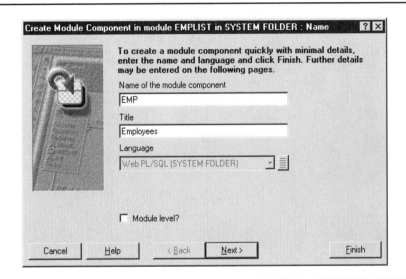

FIGURE 8-18.   *Naming the module component*

A module in itself doesn't really do anything—it serves mainly as a container for *module components.* These are the building blocks you use in your application and may again contain table usages.

Enter a name (EMP) and a title (Employees), and click Next. The Table Usage step of the wizard appears (see Figure 8-19).

On this screen, you can choose the *base table* that the module component must work on, and you can choose lookup tables as well. *Lookup* tables are used when supplementary information is found in an additional table related to the base table through a foreign-key relationship. For instance, if you want to display employees (from the EMP table) with the department name (found only in the DEPT table), you would use the EMP table as the base table and the DEPT table as a lookup table. Refer to the Designer help for more information on base tables and lookup tables.

In this case, choose the EMP table as a base table with no lookup. Click Next twice to proceed to the Operations step of the Module Component Wizard (see Figure 8-20).

This screen is a central one: it defines what operations are possible on the base table. In this first, simple case, you can leave everything at the default settings to create a query-only application. Click Next to go on to the Select Items step of the wizard shown in Figure 8-21.

Here you select the items that you are going to work with in the module component. It is not necessary to select every column in the table—to keep the module simple, just select the ones you need.

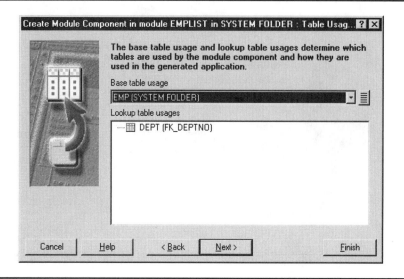

FIGURE 8-19. *Choosing a table for the module component*

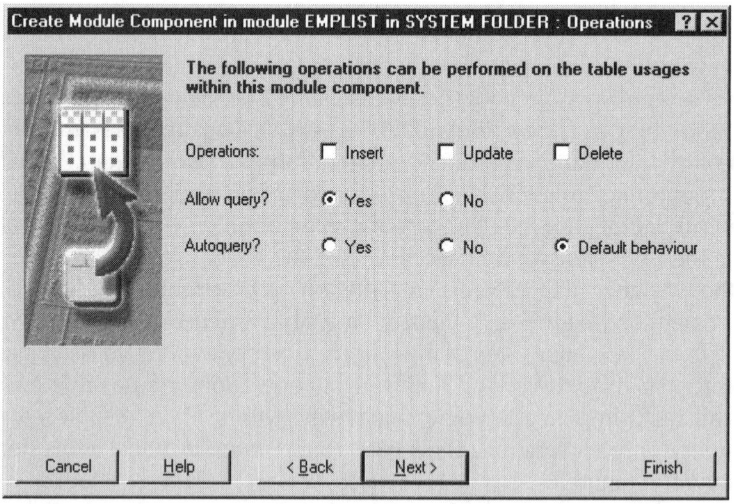

FIGURE 8-20. *Choosing operations for the module component*

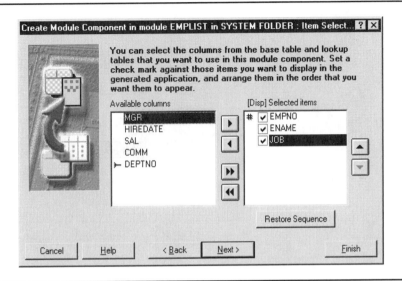

FIGURE 8-21. *Selecting items in the module component*

The check boxes next to each item determine whether they are displayed or not—you might use this to include but not display the primary key of a table.

For this example, choose the EMPNO, ENAME, and JOB columns and click Next twice to continue on to the Item Operations step in Figure 8-22.

Here you can specify in detail exactly on which *items* each operation is possible. For example, you might decide that a module component allows Update, but only on a specific column. To tell this to Designer, you would set the module component action to Update, but you'd only set some of the individual items to Update.

For this example, set all items to Query = No. When there are no queryable items in a module, Designer goes straight to the result, which is what you want in this example. If any items are queryable, Designer will automatically build a Search screen—you'll see this used in the next example. When you have finished click Next several times until you come to the last screen of the wizard, as shown in Figure 8-23.

On this screen, select Create the Module Component and Then Invoke the Display Wizard and click Finish.

Defining the Look of the Module Component

When the Module Component Wizard terminates, the first screen of the Module Component Display Wizard appears (see Figure 8-24). This is where you define how the items in the module component will be displayed in your Web application.

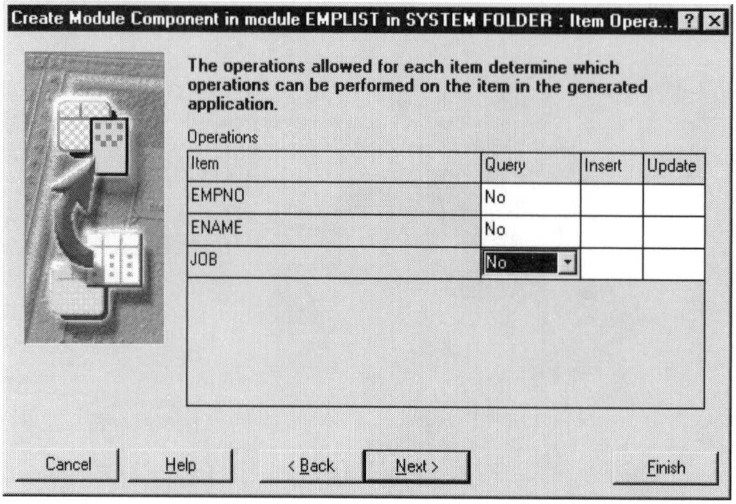

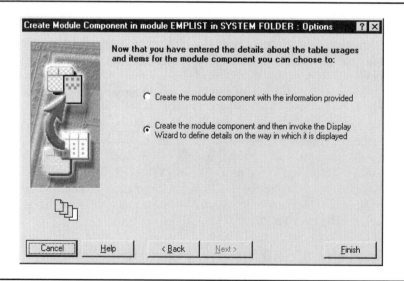

FIGURE 8-22. *Choosing item operations*

FIGURE 8-23. *The last step of the Module Component Wizard*

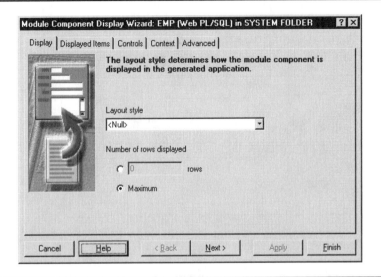

FIGURE 8-24. *The first screen of the Module Component Display Wizard*

The Layout Style setting determines which screens will be part of the Web application. For now, you can leave this at <Null> and click Next to go to the Controls tab shown in Figure 8-25.

On this screen, you can define the labels that Designer will place on the Web screens for the data items. Enter some values as shown in Figure 8-25 and click Next to get to the Context tab (see Figure 8-26).

Context items are used in the application to identify a record. This has nothing to do with the definition of the underlying table—it simply means that Designer will show these items whenever it is showing a list of records from a table.

There are three possible situations:

- **No context items are defined.** In this case, Designer shows the first (topmost or leftmost) item on the record list as a hyperlink, as shown next:

Employees

7369
7499
7521
7566

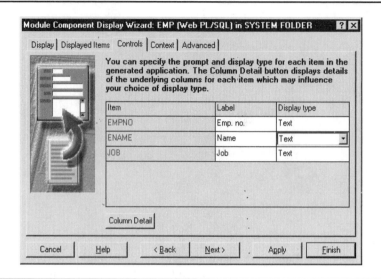

FIGURE 8-25. *Defining the item labels*

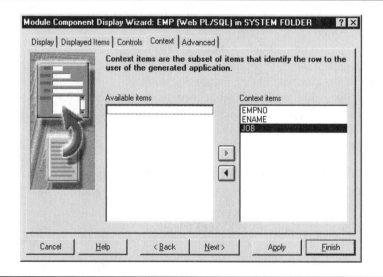

FIGURE 8-26. *Choosing the context items*

The user must then click one of the links to see the remaining items on a
screen, as shown next:

Employees

7521

Empno: 7521
Ename: WARD
Job: SALESMAN

- **Some, but not all, items are defined as context items.**   In this case, the context
  items appear on the record list and the first item is a hyperlink to the details.

- **All items are defined as context items.**   In this case, all the items appear
  on the record list and there is no details screen.

For this simple example, you want just a record list and no separate details screen.
Therefore, click the little arrow to move all the items from the left side (Available
items) to the right side (Context items). Then click Finish to close the wizard.

Generating the Module

To generate the module, right-click it in the Designer Navigator and choose
Generate from the pop-up menu. Designer remembers the generator options, so
you can just click Start in the Generate Web PL/SQL dialog box.

When the generation is complete, choose Messages | Build Actions, choose the
Run Generated Application . . . line, and click Run to start your Web browser and
see the new module. You should see something like Figure 8-27.

You'll notice that the About link appears again because you did not change
any generator preferences. In addition, Designer shows only ten results at a time
and automatically builds functionality to page back and forth in the result set.

Refining the Module

The module has the desired functionality, but it could still use a bit of polishing.
To do this, you'll need to create a preference set containing your preferences;
you'll also need to incorporate some standard formatting to make the generated
application look like the hand-built applications in Chapters 6 and 7.

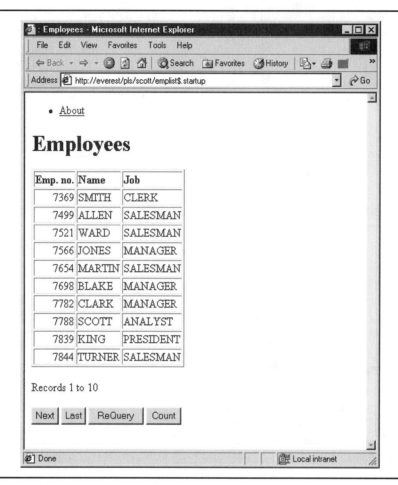

FIGURE 8-27. *Employee list, first attempt*

Creating a Preference Set

To make it easier to handle all the generator preferences that you need to set for an application, Designer offers the concept of a *preference set*.

To create a preference set, locate and expand the Preference Sets node in the Navigator. You'll see a node called Web PL/SQL Generator. Right-click this and choose Create Preference Set. Give the preference set a name (for example, WEB_APPS_101) and click the Save icon to save it. You'll see this preference set appear in the Navigator.

Right-click it, choose Edit Generator Preferences from the pop-up menu, and set the preferences as listed in Table 8-3.

Name	Description	Value	Comment
MODSUB	Substitute HTML Reserved Characters	No	To allow HTML tags in user text
MODALR	Startup Page: About Page Hyperlink	No	To remove the About link

TABLE 8-3.   *Initial Preferences for the Application Preference Set*

If you would like to show more than ten records per page, you can also set the ZONLRS (Record List: Record Set Size) property to a larger number.

When you've finished, save the preference set but do not close the window—there are a few more additions to make.

To use the preference set in the EMPLIST module, right-click the module and choose Edit Generator Preferences from the pop-up menu. In the Preference Set drop-down list at the top of the Generator Preferences window, select the WEB_APPS_101 preference set.

Using a Custom Formatting Package

In the handwritten applications in Chapter 7, the code to start and end pages was taken out and placed in a separate PL/SQL package; this approach can also be used in Designer-generated applications. A very simple format package could look like this:

```
CREATE OR REPLACE package format
as
  function pageStart(title in varchar2) return varchar2;
  function pageEnd return varchar2;
end format;
/
CREATE OR REPLACE package body format
as
  function pageStart(title in varchar2) return varchar2
  is
    retval varchar2(32767);
  begin
    retval := '<html>' || chr(10)
      || '<head>' || chr(10)
      || '<title>' || title || '</title>' || chr(10)
      || '<link rel="stylesheet" href="/webstart.css" '
      || 'type="text/css"/>' || chr(10)
      || '</head>' || chr(10) || chr(10)
      || '<body bgcolor="#FFFFFF">' || chr(10)
      || '<table width="550">' || chr(10)
```

```
            || '   <tr>' || chr(10)
            || '      <td>' || chr(10)
            || '         <h1>' || title || '</h1>' || chr(10)
            || '      </td>' || chr(10)
            || '         <td align="right">' || chr(10)
            || '            <img src="/Web_apps_101.gif" width="90" '
            || 'height="69"alt=Web Apps 101 logo"/> ' || chr(10)
            || '      </td>' || chr(10)
            || '   </tr>' || chr(10)
            || '</table>' || chr(10)
            || '<table width="550"><tr><td>'
      ;
      return retval;
   end pageStart;
   function pageEnd return varchar2
   is
      retval varchar2(32767);
   begin
      retval := '<p align="center">' || chr(10)
         || '<font size="-1">' || chr(10)
         || '  Comments, questions? Contact the ' || chr(10)
         || '  <a href="mailto:sten@vesterli.dk">webmaster</a>'
         || chr(10)
         || '</font> </p> ' || chr(10)
         || '</td></tr></table>' || chr(10)
         || '</body>' || chr(10)
         || '</html>'
      ;
      return retval;
   end pageEnd;
end format;
/
```

This package contains two functions: one returning the HTML to start a page (complete with calls to a Cascading Style Sheet to define fonts, for example) and one returning the HTML to end a page.

NOTE
This example depends on two files: the webstart.css Cascading Style Sheet and the web_apps_101.gif logo. If you followed the installation instructions in Chapter 4, you downloaded and installed both in the document root directory of the Web server.

Now you have to tell Designer to call these two functions; do this using the generator preferences shown in Table 8-4.

Name	Description	Value	Comment
PKGLST	PL/SQL Package List	format	The HTML-generating packages recognized by Designer
MODSFA	Standard Footer on All Pages	Yes	Instruction to use footer
MODSFT	Standard Footer	format.pageEnd	A call to the Format package
MODSHA	Standard Header on All Pages	Yes	Instruction to use header
MODSHD	Standard Header	format.pageStart ('Employee List')	A call to the Format package

TABLE 8-4. *Additional Generator Preferences for Standard Header and Footer*

Because the pageStart function returns the page header, you need to remove the Employees header from the module component. Expand the EMPLIST module and the module components node to see the EMP module component. Double-click the icon, clear the Title field, and click Finish.

Regenerating the Module

Regenerate the module and run it—you should now see something like Figure 8-28.

Searching for Employees

The next application builds on the Employee List you just built, adding a Web page for the user to enter query criteria.

Copying the Module

To create a copy of the EMPLIST module that was already built, right-click the module and choose Copy Object . . . from the pop-up menu.

The Extended Copy Wizard appears. Because of the many dependencies between objects, it can be a bit tricky to copy modules—until you are familiar with Designer, it is best to simply click Next all the way through this wizard without changing any of the default settings.

FIGURE 8-28. *Employee list, improved version*

When the Extended Copy Wizard ends, you probably will not see the new module right away—choose Edit | Requery All to refresh the display.

Editing the Module

The Extended Copy Wizard produced a new module called EMPLIST_1 that you must now give a new name. Double-click the module and provide a new name (e.g., SEARCHEMP) and a short name (e.g., SEARCHEMP).

Editing the Module Component

The next step is to make Designer produce a Web page where the user can enter a restriction on the employee name. This is actually very simple: all you need to do is to mark the ENAME item as queryable.

To find this item, you need to open the new SEARCHEMP module, then the EMP module component, and then the EMP table usage. When you have reached the item bound to the ENAME column, your Navigator pane should look like this:

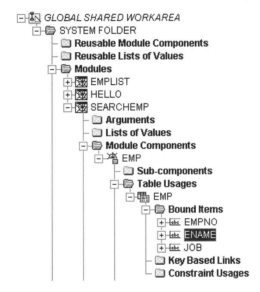

Double-click the ENAME node to see the Edit Bound Item dialog box shown in Figure 8-29.

Go to the Operations tab (see Figure 8-30), and set the Can This Item Be Queried . . . option to Yes. Then click Finish.

Since an item now can be queried, Designer will automatically build a Web page to enter the query conditions.

Generating the Module

Generate the module and run it. You should now see a first screen as shown in Figure 8-31.

Note the text Enter Query Criteria. This is automatically added by Designer, and there is no easy way to get rid of it. This is one of those places where you have to accept a rough edge on a building block that Designer makes available to you.

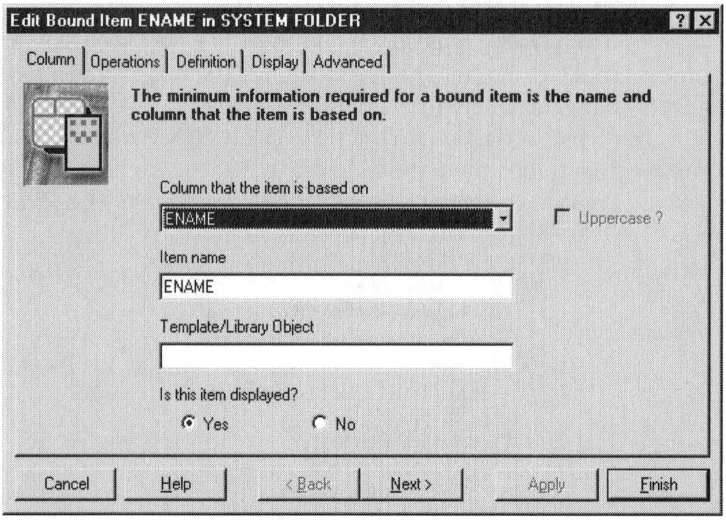

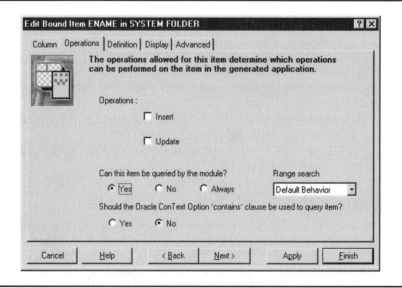

FIGURE 8-29. *Editing a bound item*

FIGURE 8-30. *The operations for a bound item*

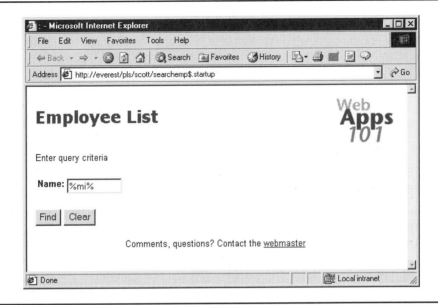

FIGURE 8-31. *The query form generated by Designer*

Maintaining Employees

The final example shows how to perform all the normal database operations on the EMP table: insert, update, and delete.

Copying the Module

First, create a copy of the SEARCHEMP module to work on. While you are learning to use Designer, it is a good idea to expand your application step by step so you can always go back a bit if something goes wrong. There are a lot of settings to change and a seemingly small change can have a dramatic impact on your module.

Right-click the SEARCHEMP module, choose Copy Objects . . ., go through the Extended Copy Wizard and choose Edit | Requery All to refresh the display to see the new module.

Editing the Module

First, rename the SEARCHEMP_1 copy to MAINTEMP (remember to change both the name and the short name).

The next step is to allow insert, update, and delete operations on the module component. To do this, open the module, navigate to the EMP module component, and double-click the module component icon to bring up the Edit Module Component Wizard. Choose the Operations tab and select the Insert, Update, and Delete check boxes (see Figure 8-32). Then click Finish.

The last step is to define exactly which items can be inserted and updated. To do this, navigate further down to the EMP table usage and double-click the table usage icon. The Edit Base Table Usage dialog box appears. Choose the Operations tab and allow Insert on EMPNO, ENAME, and JOB; allow Update on ENAME and JOB, as shown in Figure 8-33. Then click Finish.

Generating the Table API

Designer-generated PL/SQL Web applications do not go directly to the table when they need to change data (insert, update, or delete). Instead, the application module PL/SQL package calls a *Table API*. This is another PL/SQL package that handles all these operations and at the same time provides default values. You cannot generate a module that changes data in the database without first generating the Table API.

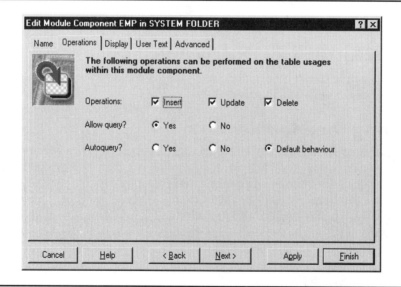

FIGURE 8-32. *Allowing all operations on the module component*

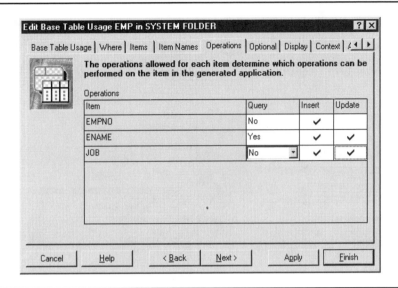

FIGURE 8-33. *Specifying operations at the item level*

Fortunately, this is easy with Designer:

1. In the Design Editor Navigator, select the Server Model tab at the top.

2. Choose the table or tables you need.

3. Choose Generate | Generate Table API.

4. Choose the database as Target for Generation and provide connection information.

5. Click Start.

Designer now generates the table access package and a number of triggers to intercept all insert, update, and delete statements.

Generating the Module

In the Design Navigator, change back to the Modules tab, right-click the MAINTEMP module, and choose Generate from the pop-up menu. Then run the generated application—you should see something like the screens shown in Figure 8-34.

FIGURE 8-34. *Maintain employees, list style*

Choosing a Layout Style

Designer supports three layout styles for PL/SQL Web Applications:

■ List (the default)

■ Form

■ List/Form

You can choose the layout at the module component level on the Display tab (see Figure 8-35).

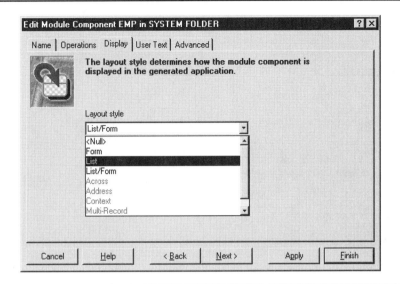

FIGURE 8-35. *Choosing a layout style for a module component*

Only Form, List, and List/Form apply to PL/SQL Web applications (the others are grayed out—they apply to Forms and/or Reports applications).

The List Layout
The screens you saw in Figure 8-34 show the List layout that Designer uses by default. This layout has four separate screens: a Query Form, a Record List (showing only the items marked as context items, remember?), a View Form to view and/or update a record, and an Insert Form to enter new records.

The Form Layout
There is also a Form layout (shown in Figure 8-36). This layout does away with the record list and uses only a Query Form, a View Form, and an Insert Form.

The Query Form and Insert Form are the same as for the List layout, but the View Form is a little different: it now has Next/Previous buttons to page through all the records one at a time, and to delete a record you now select a Delete check box.

The List/Form Layout
The final layout is the List/Form layout that places the Record List, View Form, and Insert Form in different frames on the same page, as shown in Figure 8-37. The Record List is normally placed to the left and the View or Insert Form to the right.

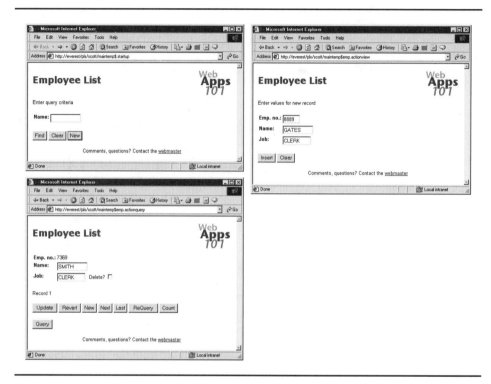

FIGURE 8-36. *Maintain employees, form style*

The Query Form by default appears on a separate page. By setting the generator preference LFQOSP (Query Form on Separate Page) to No, you can choose to include the Query Form on the same page as well (it goes into the top frame by default).

The way the screen is split into separate frames can be controlled with the generator preferences in the Frames, Frames—Custom, and Frames—Default groups. If you want to use this layout style, you'll need to read the help and experiment a bit with these preferences.

Since all modern browsers support frames, you have the option to use this layout if you wish. It provides a more compact way of displaying all the information; but because you are, in effect, viewing several different Web pages at the same time, the information in the different frames might get out of sync, potentially confusing the user. You'll need to try it out and show it to your users to decide whether this layout is useful in your application.

FIGURE 8-37. *Maintain employees, list/form style*

NOTE
Some versions of Windows NT 4 come with the very old Internet Explorer 2 Web browser that doesn't understand frames. Your Webmaster can probably tell you if you have any visitors with this browser.

Summary

You have seen some of the benefits of using Oracle Designer to create PL/SQL Web applications:

- **High productivity** Fully functional applications like these can be developed in less than an hour.

- **High quality** Oracle Designer builds all the code, so there is less room for programmer errors.

- **High maintainability** The application is stored in the Designer Repository, so it is easy to change.

Of course, there are limitations to the applications that Designer can build, and it takes time to learn the preferences that control how the application is generated. Designer has an excellent online help—the best in any Oracle product—but, unfortunately, there are few other resources. Refer to Chapter 13 for the names of two good books on Oracle Designer.

If Designer seems a bit too complicated, the next chapter explains a simpler approach with many of the same benefits: using Oracle Portal.

CHAPTER
9

Oracle Portal

f building an application with Oracle Designer is like using Lego bricks, using Oracle Portal is like using wooden building blocks. The blocks are bigger than the Lego bricks, so it takes less time to build; on the other hand, the result can be a bit clunkier, and the pieces do not interlock.

It is not quite fair to compare Oracle Designer, a tool specialized for modeling and building application systems, to Oracle Portal, because Oracle Portal is not a pure development tool. It is more a toolkit for building intranets with some application development capabilities. The topic of this book, however, is application development, and this chapter will describe how to use Oracle Portal to build applications.

What Is Oracle Portal?

As the name implies, you can use Oracle Portal to build portals. But as the old name for this product, Oracle WebDB, implies, it is also a tool for easily Web enabling a database.

Building Portals

A portal collects information from different sources to present a personalized view to each user containing only the information relevant to that user. In Oracle Portal, a portal administrator defines users, groups, and pages, and may allow users to create their own pages on which they can collect information.

Using Portlets

Each page is collected from information sources called *portlets*. Oracle Portal comes with a number of standard portlets, and third-party providers can develop additional portlets using a Portal Development Kit from Oracle.

You can also publish as portlets application components that you develop yourself.

Content Management

Oracle Portal comes with portlets to manage self-service content publishing. This allows authorized users to publish content (HTML files, word processing documents, or other types of content) for others to see.

Single Sign-On

Oracle Portal supports "single sign-on," where the user needs only to log on to Oracle Portal to be granted access to all applications integrated with Oracle Portal. These applications can be either *partner applications*, which delegate the user identification completely to Oracle Portal, or *external applications*, for which the user can allow Oracle Portal to store user names and passwords. This means that Oracle Portal authenticates the user in all external programs once the user logs on.

Web Enabling a Database

The other main feature of Oracle Portal is the ability to create simple applications based on a few tables. Since many applications do not need sophisticated features, Oracle Portal can be used for a large percentage of all applications. Even for those applications that do need more advanced functionality, it is possible to create all the basic parts in a simple tool like Oracle Portal.

Getting Started

Since Oracle Portal is purely browser based, you do not need any client-side development tools—a Web browser is enough.

On the server side, Oracle Portal consists of a number of tables, PL/SQL packages, and other database objects. If you followed the installation instructions for Oracle Portal in Chapter 4, this installation is already complete.

Users in Oracle Portal

There are three different types of user accounts associated with Oracle Portal:

- Oracle database user accounts (schemas)
- Single sign-on user accounts
- Oracle Portal user accounts

Oracle Database User Accounts

An Oracle database user account (also called a *schema*) is used to store tables, PL/SQL code, and other database objects. Database privileges are assigned to a database schema.

A DBA can create Oracle database schemas using SQL commands, or a tool like Oracle Enterprise Manager or the Schemas portlet in Oracle Portal.

Each Oracle Portal user account must be mapped to a database schema to determine the user's database privileges. If you want to use a database schema for this purpose, you must select the Use This Schema for Portal Users check box for the schema on the Edit Schema page in Oracle Portal.

Single Sign-On User Accounts

A single sign-on user account is used to access applications (including Oracle Portal) with a single user name and password so that the user does not have to remember many user names and passwords and log on to each application individually. Once a user has entered his single sign-on user name and password for one application, he can access other applications without having to log on again.

Single Sign-On user accounts can be created with the Users portlet in Oracle Portal.

Oracle Portal User Accounts

An Oracle Portal user account (also referred to simply as a user account or user) establishes user details, preferences, and privileges within Oracle Portal.

Oracle Portal user accounts do not have any direct privileges on the database. However, because Oracle Portal pages are displayed by executing procedures in the database, an Oracle Portal user account needs to have execute privileges on those procedures. This is achieved by associating each Oracle Portal user account with an Oracle database schema that has the appropriate privileges to display Oracle Portal pages.

Oracle Portal user accounts are created automatically when a portal administrator first attempts to edit the Portal user settings of a single sign-on user account, or when a user first attempts to log in to Oracle Portal using her single sign-on account.

Starting Oracle Portal

After performing the installation described in Chapter 4, you can access the Oracle Portal Welcome page by entering the following URL in your browser:

http://<servername>/ pls/portal30

The Oracle Portal public Welcome page appears (see Figure 9-1). This is the default page for the PUBLIC user, i.e., the start page that Oracle Portal shows to unidentified users. Click the Login link in the top right corner of this page to log in. On the Single Sign-On screen, enter **portal30** as both user name and password and click Login. The Oracle Portal home page for the PORTAL30 user appears (see Figure 9-2).

NOTE
The PORTAL30 user is installed by default. This user will be used for all the examples because it has the necessary privileges to build Oracle Portal applications.

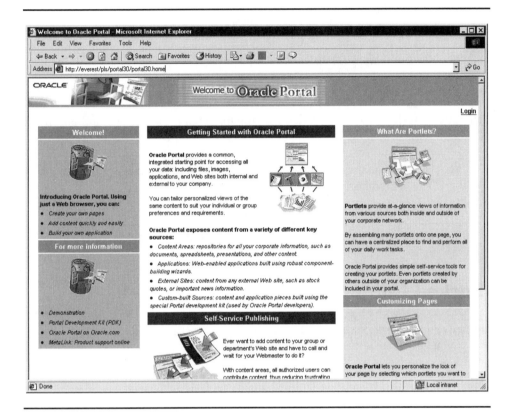

FIGURE 9-1. *Oracle Portal Welcome Page*

The right-hand side of the Oracle Portal homepage contains four tabs across the top:

■ **Build** Used to build pages, content areas, and applications. This tab is explained in more detail in the next section.

■ **Administer** Used to administer Oracle Portal. This involves maintaining Oracle Portal users and groups, and configuring Oracle Portal.

■ **Administer Database** Can be used to view a lot of information about the database and to create, change, and drop database schemas and objects.

This light-weight DBA functionality covers most of what a DBA needs to do in the day-to-day running of a database.

■ **Monitor**   Shows statistics about the use of Oracle Portal.

Building Things

The Build tab shown in Figure 9-2 shows the three main things you can build with Oracle Portal:

■ **Pages**   Containers that can contain content, applications, or other types of Oracle Portal objects.

■ **Content Areas**   Used to publish information.

■ **Applications**   Used to work with data in the database. The rest of this chapter describes how to build an application.

Locked Components

When working with Oracle Portal, it is important to click only the links and buttons on the Web pages themselves—do not use the browser Back button.

If you get an error message saying that a component is locked when you try to edit it, you probably accidentally used the browser Back button to leave a previous editing session.

To overcome this problem, use the Oracle Portal Navigator to open the component and click the Manage tab. On this tab, there is a Show Locks on This Component link. When you click it, you see who locked the component and when. If you have sufficient privileges, you will also see an Unlock link that you can click to unlock the component.

Hello World

As for every approach, the first example is a Hello World program showing the date and time. To build this, first log in as user PORTAL30, as just described.

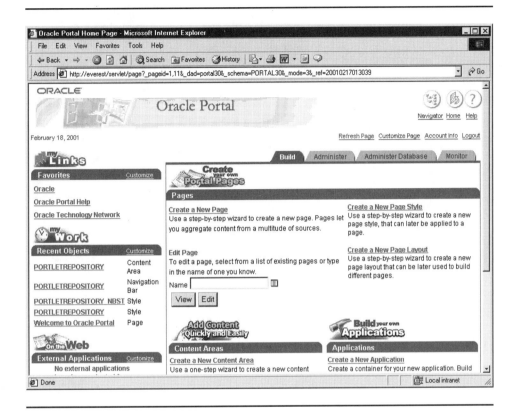

FIGURE 9-2. *Oracle Portal home page for user PORTAL30*

Building an Application

On the default page for the PORTAL30 user, click the Create a New Application link in the lower right part of the page. The application definition screen appears (see Figure 9-3).

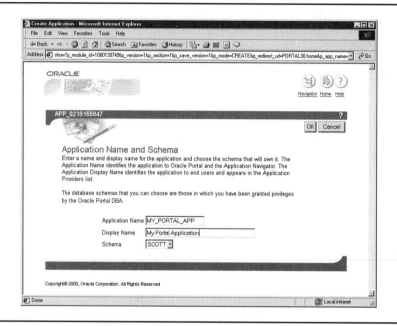

FIGURE 9-3. *Defining a Portal application*

Provide a name for the application (used internally in Oracle Portal) and a display name (shown to the users). You must also select a schema where the application code will be stored; if you followed the installation instructions, the SCOTT user is available on this list.

NOTE
The schemas shown on this drop-down list are not all schemas in the database—only the ones that have been marked as Oracle Portal application schemas in Oracle Portal are. So, even though you are logged in as user PORTAL30, you do not, by default, have rights to build applications in that schema.

When you have finished, click OK. The Manage Applications screen appears (see Figure 9-4).

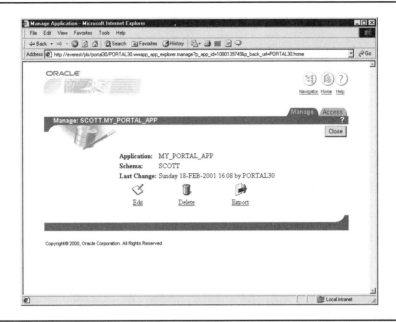

FIGURE 9-4. *Manage Applications screen*

From this screen, you can click the Edit link to change the application name, or you can use the Access tab to grant access to this application to other users. Click Close to return to the Portal home page for the PORTAL30 user.

Adding an Application Component

The next step is to add an application component to the application. Click the Navigator link in the top right corner of the page. The Oracle Portal Navigator page appears, as shown in Figure 9-5.

On this page, you can click the Applications tab to manage applications and their components. Click the MY_PORTAL_APP link to see the contents of this application (see Figure 9-6).

For the simple Hello World example, you need a dynamic page, so you must click the Dynamic Page link in the top half of the page next to the Create New . . . text. The first page of the Dynamic Page Wizard appears (see Figure 9-7).

Enter a name (for example, **HELLO_WORLD**), a display name (for example, **Hello World**) and choose the MY_PORTAL_APP application. Then click Next. The second step of the wizard appears, as shown in Figure 9-8.

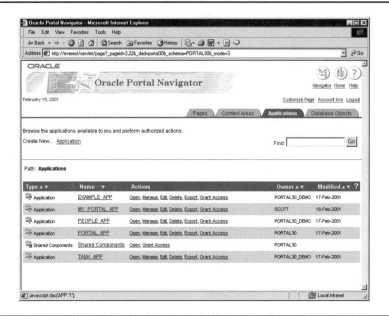

FIGURE 9-5. *The Oracle Portal Navigator, top level*

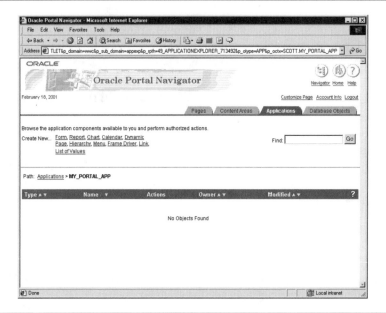

FIGURE 9-6. *The Oracle Portal Navigator showing the MY_PORTAL_APP application*

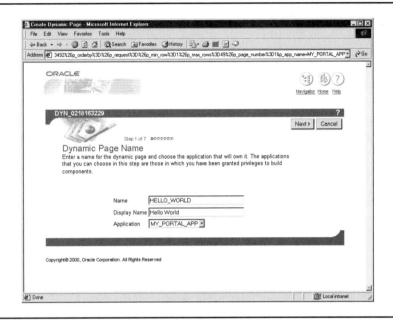

FIGURE 9-7. *The first page of the Dynamic Page Wizard*

In this step, you can enter HTML code interspersed with PL/SQL between
<oracle> and </oracle> tags. This is similar to PL/SQL server pages because there is
some static HTML and some dynamic content.

Between the <oracle> and </oracle> tags, you can write a SQL query or any
valid PL/SQL block. You must write a block of PL/SQL (starting with BEGIN and
ending with END)—you cannot write single lines of PL/SQL.

You can include *bind variables* that are assigned a value at runtime. To define
a bind variable, write a variable name preceded by a colon, like :deptno. You can
then assign a value to the bind variable on the *customization page* that you can
invoke before calling the page. However, this simple example does not use bind
variables and does not use a customization page.

For the Hello World example, enter the following HTML code:

```
<html>
<head>
<title>Hello World</title>
</head>

<body bgcolor="#FFFFFF">
<h1>Hello World</h1>
<p>The time is
<oracle>
```

```
begin
  htp.p(to_char(sysdate, 'hh24:mi:ss yyyy-mm-dd'));
end;
</oracle>
</p>
</body>
</html>
```

Then either click through the rest of the wizard or click Finished right away. The Develop page for this dynamic page component appears, as shown in Figure 9-9.

Here you can click the Run link to see your page in action. You should see something like Figure 9-10.

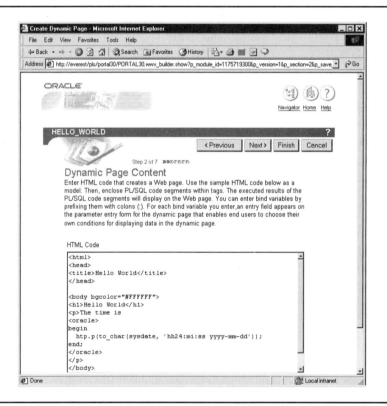

FIGURE 9-8. *The second page of the Dynamic Page Wizard*

FIGURE 9-9. *The Develop page of the Dynamic Page Wizard*

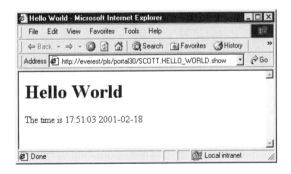

FIGURE 9-10. *The Hello World application*

Running the Application Outside Oracle Portal

Note the two texts under the Run Link heading in Figure 9-9. They show how you can invoke the dynamic page itself and the associated customization page outside of Oracle Portal:

Dynamic page	**http://<server>/pls/portal30/scott.hello_world.show**
Customization page	**http://<server>/pls/portal30/scott.hello_world.show_parms**

NOTE
The Portal-generated procedure must be executed through the dynamic page URL in the table, even though you would expect it to be possible to invoke it through a database access descriptor referring to the SCOTT schema. Unfortunately, this does not work.

List of Employees

The next example application you will build is an unrestricted list of employees created with an Oracle Portal Report component. But before you start building this component, you need to know a little about how to control the formatting of Oracle Portal components.

Controlling the Formatting

Components that are produced with Oracle Portal have a distinctive look that many users are not very happy with. However, it is not overly complicated to gain some measure of control over the look of the application.

Using a Style Sheet

Oracle Portal applications are HTML based, that is, all pages presented to the end user are normal Web pages. The fonts and colors used on the page, therefore, can to some extent be controlled with Cascading Style Sheets like the examples in the previous chapters.

Using a Format Package

You might remember that the applications in Chapters 7 and 8 used a PL/SQL package containing functions that return the HTML. One function returned the

HTML used at the beginning of every Web page; another returned the HTML used at the end of a Web page.

This approach can also be used in Oracle Portal applications, because many application components allow you to include a block of PL/SQL code that will be executed before and after the main content of each page.

Creating a Blank Formatting Template

Oracle provides a number of formatting templates that you can use in your applications; some application components require that you select a template. Inexplicably, Oracle neglects to provide a blank template and does not allow you not to select any template. This means that you have to define a blank template yourself to be able to build application components without any boilerplate images.

Templates vs. Format Packages   You can achieve almost the same formatting with an Oracle Portal template as with a custom formatting package. However, because a formatting package can be used in applications produced in other ways, this approach is more flexible.

Creating a Blank Template   In Oracle Portal terminology, a template is a *shared component*. Shared components are supporting elements (like colors, fonts, and templates) that can be used by user components (like forms and reports). To create a blank template, therefore, you must invoke the Oracle Portal Navigator by going to the Applications tab and going to the top level. To get to the top level, on the Applications tab, notice the Path line approximately in the middle of the screen (between the "Create New" links and the application component list:

This line always shows the path from the top level of the tab down to the current component. To navigate back up to the top of the Applications hierarchy, click the Applications link next to Path.

At the top level, you will see the MY_PORTAL_APP application you just created (as well as some sample applications that come with Oracle Portal) and the Shared Components link. Click this link to see the Shared Components page shown in Figure 9-11.

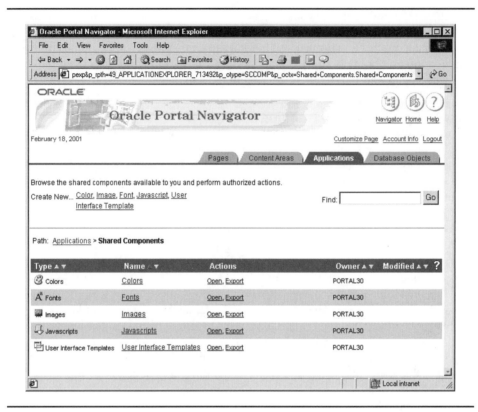

FIGURE 9-11. *The Shared Components page in the Portal Navigator*

Click the User Interface Templates link and then the Create New User Interface Template. The User Interface Templates page shown in Figure 9-12 appears. Here you have the option to create a *structured template* by filling in fields on a Web page or an *unstructured template* where you work directly with HTML code. Click the Unstructured UI Template link to see the Create Unstructured UI Template screen. Initially, this screen contains several HTML tags and placeholders—when you have finished, it should look like Figure 9-13.

On this page, you enter all the HTML code that you want to use in your template. This can be references to style sheets or images, or boilerplate text. Between the HTML tags, you then place a number of *placeholders*, like #BODY# (all the possible placeholders are listed at the bottom of the Web page). To create a blank template, delete all the sample HTML in the field except for the #BODY# placeholder. Then click Create to create the template.

FIGURE 9-12. *The User Interface Templates page*

FIGURE 9-13. *Creating an Unstructured UI Template*

Building a Report Component

To build a Report component in the MY_PORTAL_APP application, start from the default Oracle Portal home page for user PORTAL30, shown in Figure 9-2. Then click the Navigator icon at the top left corner to go to the Oracle Portal Navigator screen shown in Figure 9-5. If the Applications tab is not already selected, select it and open the MY_PORTAL_APP application if it is not already open. You should now see the application component screen shown in Figure 9-6.

Click the Report link in the top half of the page next to the Create a New . . . text. The report type selection page shown in Figure 9-14 appears.

For this example, choose Reports from SQL Query. The first step in the Report Wizard appears; enter a name (for example, **EMPLIST**) and a display name (for example, **Employee List**). You can leave the application drop-down at the default value MY_PORTAL_APP. When you have finished, click Next. The second step in the Report Wizard appears, as shown in Figure 9-15.

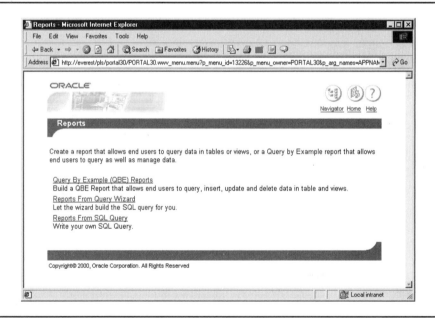

FIGURE 9-14. *Selecting a report type*

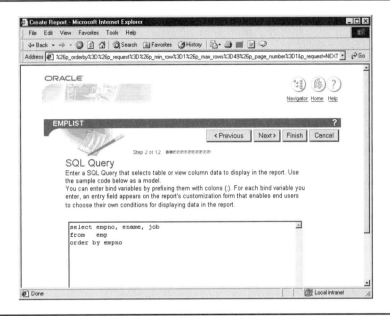

FIGURE 9-15. *Step 2 in the Report Wizard*

On this screen, enter the SQL query for the report, for instance:

```
select empno, ename, job
from    emp
order by empno
```

Then click Next to go to Step 3. In this step, leave the report layout at the default value of Tabular. Click Next again to proceed to Step 4.

In Step 4, you can define column labels and other column formatting. The default column labels are the column names—change these and any other column formatting as needed and click Next.

In Step 5, you can apply conditional formatting to format columns and/or rows if specific conditions are met. For instance, you could select that when the JOB column has the value MANAGER, the row should have a light blue background color (see Figure 9-16).

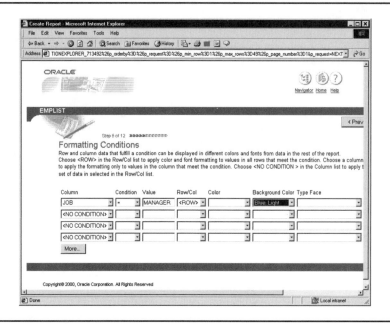

FIGURE 9-16. *Defining conditional formatting*

In Step 6, you can define display options that apply to the whole report. The section Full Page Options applies to the report when displayed as a normal Web page, whereas the section Portlet Options applies only when the report is included on a page in Oracle Portal. Notice the Table Row Color(s) box—if you scroll down this box, you will find that Gray, Light, and White are selected. The colors selected in this box are used by Oracle Portal to create a stripe effect in reports: Oracle Portal will alternate between all the selected colors in the report output. You cannot control the sequence of the colors—they appear in the same order in your Report as on this list, that is, alphabetically. If you do not want this effect, select only one color or choose the blank top line (it shows as light gray) in the list.

When you click Next in Step 6, the wizard automatically skips to Step 10. This step allows you to format the customization form where the user can assign values to any *bind variables* you have used in your query. Bind variables are variables whose value is defined by the user at runtime—they are indicated in a query by a colon prefix, for example, :deptno. Since the customization form will not be used for this unconditional list of employees, you do not have to change anything on this screen.

Step 11 allows you to select a template—select PUBLIC.BLANK (the template you created in the preceding section) and leave the remaining fields blank.

Step 12 (see Figure 9-17) allows you to specify some PL/SQL code that will be executed at specific points when the report is produced.

To use a format package like the one in Chapters 7 and 8, fill in the fields on this screen in both the Report and Customization columns:

Before displaying the page   htp.p(format.pageStart('Employee List'));

After displaying the page   htp.p(format.pageEnd);

NOTE
Even though you will not be using the customization form right now, it is a good idea to ensure that it is properly formatted. You might be using it in the future.

You can find a listing of an example format package in Chapter 7; the code can be downloaded from **www.vesterli.com**.

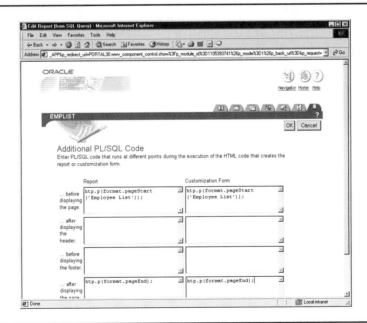

FIGURE 9-17. *Adding additional PL/SQL code*

When you have finished, click Finish. On the Develop tab of the application component page, you can now click the Run link to run the Employee List (see Figure 9-18).

Note that the three rows where the job title is MANAGER have a different background color because of the conditional formatting applied in Step 5.

As in the previous example, you can invoke this report and the associated customization page outside of Oracle Portal:

Report   **http://<server>/pls/portal30/scott.emplist.show**

Customization page   **http://<server>/pls/portal30/scott.emplist.show_parms**

FIGURE 9-18.   *Running the Employee List*

Search for Employees

The previous example needed only one Web page—the complete Employee List could be shown without asking the user for any input. In the next example, you will search for employees by name, so you need an extra screen to ask the user for the name to search for.

In Oracle Portal, this type of input screen is called a *customization screen.* All types of report components can have such a screen—in this example, you will use a *Query-by-Example (QBE)* report component with a customization screen to implement the employee search.

Building a QBE Report Component

To build a QBE Report component in the MY_PORTAL_APP application, use the Oracle Portal Navigator to open the MY_PORTAL_APP application, as in the previous example. Then click the Create New Report link to see the report type selection screen you already saw in Figure 9-14.

For this example, choose Query by Example (QBE) Reports. The first step in the QBE Report Wizard appears; enter a name (for example, **SEARCHEMP**) and a display name (for example, **Search for Employees**). You can leave the application drop-down at the default value MY_PORTAL_APP. When you have finished, click Next.

In the second step in the QBE Report Wizard, you must choose the table you want to work on. The SCOTT.EMP table is probably already selected—not because Oracle Portal can read your mind, but because this table is often used for demonstrations.

The third step in the QBE Report Wizard is shown in Figure 9-19 (don't worry that it says "Step 4" at the top of the screen—this is really Step 3). This screen shows all the columns in the selected table and allows you to select those you want included in your report.

Hold down the CTRL key and click the EMPNO, ENAME, and JOB columns to select them. Then click the > button to move them to the Selected Columns box and click Next.

In the fourth step, you can specify the format for each column. Change the column labels as needed; if you like, you can also apply some formatting. This

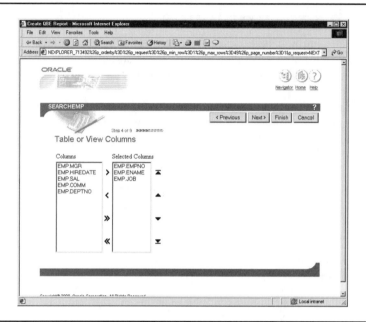

FIGURE 9-19. *Step 3 in the QBE Report Wizard*

screen also allows you to select a format mask for numeric columns and date columns using the normal Oracle format strings.

In the fifth step, you can apply conditional formatting, that is, display rows and/or columns with special fonts or colors when a condition is met.

In Step 6 (see Figure 9-20), you define display options for the whole report. This works just as in the previous example. Again, note that if you do not want your report output "striped," you need to select one color (for example, white) or the blank line at the top (which gives a light gray background) in the Table Row Color(s) box.

Notice the two check boxes Enable Update Link in the Report Output and Enable Delete Link in the Report Output. These options each produce a link in the record list that goes to an Update page and a Delete confirmation page, respectively. Unfortunately, the Update page does not execute any of the PL/SQL that provides formatting, and the delete confirmation screen has the Oracle Portal layout; so this feature is not very useful if you care about the look of the application.

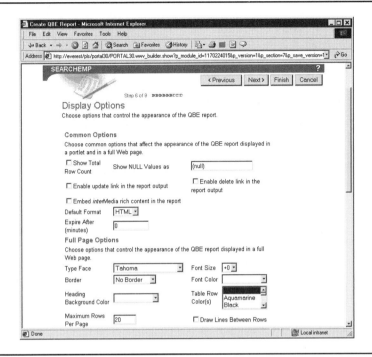

FIGURE 9-20. *Step 6 in the QBE Report Wizard*

Step 7 (shown in Figure 9-21) is used to define the features available to the end user on the Query form. All features are described in the Oracle Portal help—click the question mark in the blue bar (just above the Cancel button) to get help to the fields on this screen.

NOTE
Many screens in Oracle Portal have two help links in the top left corner. The top link (a question mark icon with the text "Help") invokes the general Portal help, while the lower one (the question mark in the blue bar) calls up specific help for the current screen.

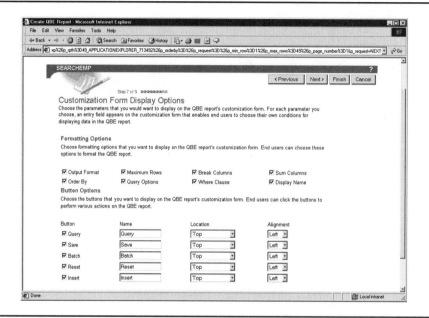

FIGURE 9-21. *Step 7 in the QBE Report Wizard*

If you want to offer the user the ability to create new records, you can select the Insert check box in this step. This setting produces a button on the customization screen that allows the user to create a new record with the values entered on that screen.

To keep the example simple, deselect all check boxes in the Formatting Options section and deselect all but the Query check box in the Button Options section. Then click Next to continue.

In Step 8, you can choose a template and provide user text that will be included in the report. Because you will be using a PL/SQL formatting package, choose the template PUBLIC.BLANK defined in the preceding example and leave the other fields blank.

In Step 9, you specify the custom PL/SQL that you want executed to achieve the desired formatting. Fill out the fields on this screen in both the Report and Customization sections with the values in the following table (similar to the example shown in Figure 9-17):

Before displaying the page   htp.p(format.pageStart('Search for Employees'));

After displaying the page   htp.p(format.pageEnd);

When you have finished, click Finish. On the Develop tab of the application component page, you can now click the Customize link to invoke the customization form (see Figure 9-22) or click Run to go directly to the search result without entering any parameters (see Figure 9-23).

Like the previous examples, this report and its customization page can be called directly:

Report **http://<server>/pls/portal30/scott.searchemp.show**

Customization **http://<server>/pls/portal30/scott.searchemp.show_parms**
page

As Figure 9-22 shows, a QBE Report customization form has a specific layout. Oracle Portal always displays all this information (and more, if you select more check boxes in Step 7 of the QBE Wizard); this inflexibility is the price you must pay for the ease of development that Oracle Portal offers.

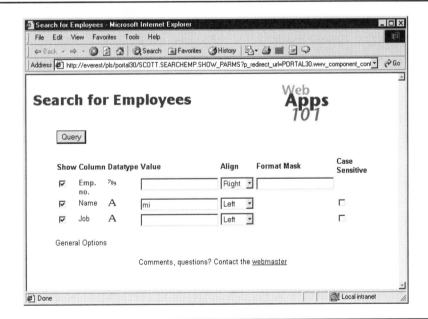

FIGURE 9-22. *Customization form for the search application*

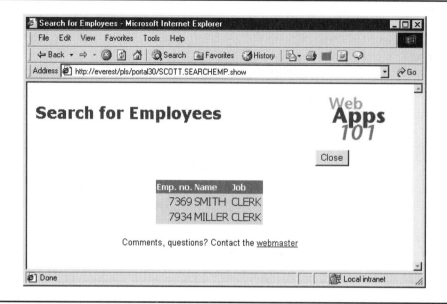

FIGURE 9-23. *Search result*

Maintaining Employees

The two preceding examples made use of two different types of Report application components; but for the final example, showing how to insert, update, and delete from the EMP table, you will use a Form application component.

> **NOTE**
> *You can, in fact, maintain data in one table with a report—as described in the previous example, the QBE Report offers the ability to insert, update, and delete.*

Building a Form Application Component

To build a Form component in the MY_PORTAL_APP application, use the Oracle Portal Navigator to open the MY_PORTAL_APP application, as in the previous example. Then click the Create New Form link to see the form type selection screen shown in Figure 9-24.

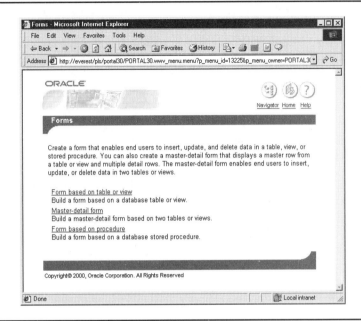

FIGURE 9-24. *Selecting a form type*

Oracle Portal has three options for creating forms:

- **A form based on a table or view**   Lets the user insert, update, and delete data in a database table or view.

- **A master-detail form**   Displays a master row and multiple detail rows within a single HTML page. The form contains fields for updating values in both database tables or views.

- **A form based on a procedure**   Lets the user call a stored procedure in the database.

Click Form Based on Table or View to start creating the form. The first step in the Form Wizard appears; enter a name (for example, **MAINTAINEMP**) and a display name (for example, **Maintain Employees**), and leave the application drop-down at MY_PORTAL_APP. When you have finished, click Next.

In the second step of the Form Wizard, you must choose the table you want to work on. Once more, the SCOTT.EMP table is already selected, so click Next.

In Step 3, choose Tabular form and click Next (custom forms are an advanced topic that is outside the scope of this book).

Step 4 (shown in Figure 9-25) is where you define most of the items on the Form.

The left side of this page shows a Navigator where you can select different items on the Form, and the right side shows the options you can set for the selected item. One item in the Navigator is marked with a yellow box—this is the *current item*. The right side of the window always shows the detailed information about the current item.

The standard items that Oracle Portal shows in the Navigator above the text TOP_SECTION are buttons that appear at the top of each page on the form; the items below the text BOTTOM_SECTION are buttons that appear at the bottom of the form. You can delete unwanted buttons by clicking the red X, and change the button order by clicking the arrows. While a button is selected, the right-hand side of the window shows the button properties that you can change—for instance, the button label.

Between the TOP_SECTION and BOTTOM_SECTION lines, Oracle Portal, by default, includes fields for all columns in the selected table. You can click the arrows next to an item to move it up and down the list, and click the red X to delete it.

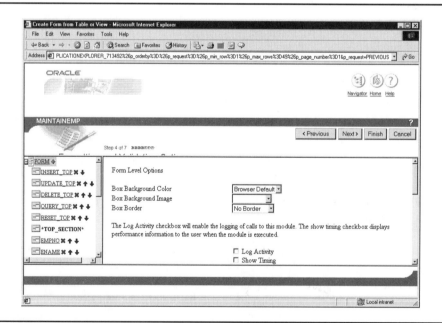

FIGURE 9-25. *Step 4 in the Form Wizard*

While a field is the current item (marked with a yellow box on the left), the right-hand side of the window shows the field properties for you to edit.

Notice the Begin on New Line check box in the Layout Options section. This setting allows you to control the appearance on the screen with more detail than Oracle Designer, which always places a specific number of items on a line through the whole form. This setting can be used together with the Row Span and Col Span options to create almost any layout that HTML allows. This is one place where Oracle Portal offers more flexibility than Oracle Designer, but you'll probably need to experiment a bit to get the results you want.

NOTE
If you have deleted the item corresponding to a specific column in the table and change your mind, you can add a new item using the green plus (+) at the top (next to the FORM node). If you type an item name that exists as a column in the base table, Oracle Portal automatically recognizes it and retrieves, inserts, or updates the corresponding column. You must know the exact spelling of the column name for this to work—there is no drop-down list available; and if you get one character wrong, Oracle Portal cannot associate the new item with any database column.

Because Oracle Portal, by default, places the field label very close to the field, you should include a bit of white space in the label. The way to do this in HTML is to include a *nonbreaking space*: type ** ** after each label. This HTML entity instructs the Web browser to follow the label with a bit of space.

To create an application to maintain the basic information about employees as in the previous chapters, make the following changes:

- **EMPNO**   Change the label to Emp. no. . Remove the check mark in the Updatable field.

- **ENAME**   Change the label to Name . Select the Mandatory check box.

- **JOB**   Change the label to Job .

- **MGR, HIREDATE, SAL, COMM, DEPTNO**   Delete.

When you have finished, click Next to continue.

In Step 5, you can choose a template and provide user text that will be included on the Form page. To use the PL/SQL formatting package, choose the template PUBLIC.BLANK defined previously and leave the other fields blank.

Step 6 is used to specify custom PL/SQL code. Fill out the fields on this screen with the values in the following table:

Before displaying the page   htp.p(format.pageStart('Maintain Employees'));

After displaying the page   htp.p(format.pageEnd);

When you have finished, click Finish. On the Development tab of the application component page, you can now click the Run link to see your application. The query form is shown in Figure 9-26, and the detail form is shown in Figure 9-27.

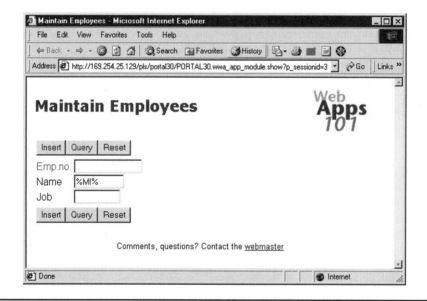

FIGURE 9-26. *Query form for maintaining employees*

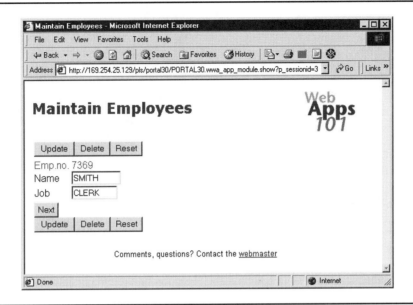

FIGURE 9-27. *Detail form for maintaining employees*

Summary

In this chapter, you learned about some of the application components that Oracle Portal offers: dynamic pages, Reports, and Forms. It is very easy to build application components with Oracle Portal, but the customization options are generally more limited than they are with Oracle Designer.

Application components that do not need to identify each user can easily be built with Oracle Portal and integrated with components built with other tools (and even in other programming languages); but if you want to authenticate the application users, you should use the single sign-on features in Oracle Portal.

The next chapter shows how to use Oracle Forms for Web applications with traditional login, just as in client/server.

CHAPTER
10

Oracle Developer

he previous four chapters explained how to use new tools and approaches to develop Web applications, but these are not your only options. If you come from the traditional client/server world, you do not have to throw all your existing applications and skills away; Oracle has actually made a big effort to allow you to "Web enable" your existing client/server applications without any changes.

The examples in this chapter are mainly intended to show how Reports and Forms look when deployed to the Web. They are kept simple to let you follow what happens, even if you are not familiar with Oracle Reports and Oracle Forms. If you are familiar with these tools, feel free to expand on the examples or use the guidelines to deploy your own existing Reports and Forms to the Web.

Report Builder and Form Builder are very capable development tools—this book only scratches the surface of what you can to with either of them. If you do not know these tools, you can refer to Oracle documentation for more information about using Forms and Reports to develop client/server and Web applications.

How Forms and Reports Work on the Web

Oracle Forms and Oracle Reports have a long heritage as client/server development tools, and many developers have experience with these tools.

As Web applications started to take off, Oracle created new tools especially for these new kinds of applications; but, at the same time, they also adapted the existing tools so they could be used for the Web as well.

Because it was clearly not feasible to require everybody to redevelop all of their existing applications in new tools, Oracle promised their customers that the existing applications developed with the "old" tools would be able to run unchanged as Web applications. It has taken a while for them to completely deliver on this promise, but today applications developed with Oracle Forms and Reports run well in many Web applications.

Web Forms

The traditional tool for building Oracle applications in the client/server world is Oracle Forms, and now it is possible to deploy the same form in either a client/server environment or a Web environment.

Forms in Traditional Client/Server Deployment

In a traditional client/server application developed with Oracle Forms, the client is the Oracle Forms Runtime. This is a piece of platform-dependent software that must be installed on each client machine; you need the Windows Forms Runtime for a Windows client and the Mac Forms Runtime for a Macintosh client.

The client reads the form definition from a form definition file that must also be installed on the client. This file is produced by the Forms developer and defines the user interface and probably quite a bit of the business logic. The Forms client then connects to the database (using an Oracle network protocol like SQL*Net or Net8) where it can retrieve, store, and change data.

Forms in Web Deployment

In a Web environment, everything is different. Because the client has a Java-capable Web browser, it is no longer necessary to have a specific Forms Runtime for each type of client—one common Java applet works on all platforms.

However, the Forms Runtime is many megabytes big, so it would clearly not be possible for each client to download all of this code before starting an application.

Oracle's solution is to isolate the part of the Forms Runtime software that actually paints pixels on the screen and interacts with the user, and to rewrite only that part in Java. This part became the Forms applet that the user downloads to the client; the rest of the Forms Runtime remains on the server as the Forms Runtime Engine. In this way, it is possible to create a reasonably slim Forms applet and let the majority of the code stay on the server side. At the same time, this approach makes it unnecessary to install the Forms definition files of the application on each client— they can remain on the server.

Refer to Chapter 3 for a more detailed description of the components that make up the Oracle Web Forms solution and to Chapter 4 for installation instructions.

Differences Between Client/Server and Web Deployment

You can deploy the exact same forms definition file in both a traditional client/server environment and in a Web environment. But there are a few things that you should pay special attention to when deploying to the Web environment.

Network Traffic   It is desirable to keep the network traffic down in a client/server environment, but it's even more important in a Web environment. Web clients are often connected via lower bandwidth connections, meaning that it takes longer to transfer a given amount of data. Even more important, Web clients are connected through more routers and other network hardware, so the *server roundtrip time*— the time it takes for a message to go from a client to the server and back—is much longer.

You can reduce the number of network messages by limiting the use of mouse triggers (WHEN-MOUSE-CLICK, and so on) and timers. Both types of events require that the Forms applet communicate with the Forms Service. As a matter of fact, Oracle has completely disabled the WHEN-MOUSE-MOVE triggers when a form is deployed to the Web.

Windows Components and Host Commands   You cannot use Windows components like ActiveX or OCX controls when you deploy your forms in a Web environment, since they would execute on the server (where the user cannot see them).

Similarly, it is not possible to use the HOST_COMMAND built-in function. In a traditional client/server environment, this function could be used to execute other programs on the client program, but in a Web environment it will attempt (and probably fail) to execute the other program on the application server instead.

Icons   If you create your own icons in a traditional client/server environment with a Windows client, these have to be in icon (.ICO) format. When deploying forms to the Web, they must be in .GIF format.

The Java Virtual Machine on the Client

Although Web browsers have contained Java Virtual Machines (JVMs) for a long time, they were often buggy in the past. In addition, the JVMs even in the latest browsers often lagged behind the development of the Java language. To overcome this problem, Sun offered a Java plug-in that end users could install in their Web browsers. By writing the HTML code that contains the applet in a special way, an application developer could then specify that the applet should not be executed by the browser's default JVM, but rather through the plug-in JVM.

Oracle decided that this was a good idea, but they were not satisfied with Sun's Java plug-in, so they created their own and called it *JInitiator*. This is another JVM that you can install in your browser; it is optimized especially for running the Forms applet.

Oracle supports the use of the built-in JVM in Microsoft Internet Explorer version 5 and above, but they still recommend that you install JInitiator.

Web Reports

Oracle Reports is Oracle's full-featured reporting tool. Like Oracle Forms, this powerful tool has been used for a long time, and it is now Web enabled.

Reports in Traditional Client/Server Deployment

When a user requests that a report be executed in a traditional client/server application, it is executed through the Oracle Reports Runtime. This is platform-dependent software that is installed on each client machine.

The report developer produces a report definition file that defines any parameters the report must request from the user, which data to retrieve, and how to format and present the data. This report definition is then placed on the client machine where the Reports Runtime reads it. The program then displays a screen where the user can enter any applicable parameters, connects to the database via an Oracle network protocol, and retrieves and formats the data.

Reports in Web Deployment

Because a report needs only limited interaction with the user, Oracle decided to do away with the Reports Runtime on the client in a Web deployment scenario.

Instead, the report definition file and the Reports Runtime are moved to the application server. A user then requests a report through a normal URL that the Web/application server passes to the Reports Runtime Engine. If applicable, this engine sends a basic HTML page back to the requesting browser where the user can enter any parameters. When the report request is complete, the Reports Runtime Engine then connects to the database, retrieves and formats the data, and writes the report in a file on the Web/application server. Finally, the Reports Runtime Engine instructs the browser to retrieve the report output.

Refer to Chapter 3 for a more detailed description of the Oracle Web Reports architecture and to Chapter 4 for installation instructions.

The Output Formats

Just like Forms developers, Reports developers were used to having very precise control over the appearance of the report. Since HTML does not offer this degree of precision, Oracle decided to offer three output options:

- Plain HTML

- HTML with Cascading Style Sheets (CSS)

- Portable Document Format (PDF)

Plain HTML   This output is formatted as a plain HTML table that will display in most browsers. It does not contain page breaks—the whole report is one long page.

HTML with Cascading Style Sheets   This output format is some rather messy HTML that attempts to control the layout as well as HTML version 4 allows. It provides explicit placement instructions for every element on the page and contains page breaks. This format will normally display correctly in fourth-generation browsers and above.

Portable Document Format (PDF)   This format is defined by Adobe and can only be displayed by the Adobe Acrobat Reader, which can be downloaded for free from the Adobe Web site and installed as a browser plug-in.

It provides complete control over the fonts, graphics, and layout—a report in PDF format looks exactly as it would when run through the Reports Runtime in traditional client/server deployment.

A Hello World Form

The first example is the familiar "Hello World" that you will build as a Web Form.

Start the Form Builder by choosing Start | Programs | Oracle Forms 6i – DevHome60 | Form Builder. The Oracle Form Builder Welcome screen shown in Figure 10-1 appears (unless you have already run Form Builder before and removed the check mark in the Display at Startup check box).

Building the Form

This simple example will not be based on a table, so choose Build a New Form Manually and click OK. The Form Builder main window appears with the Navigator in the left-hand side.

In Oracle Forms, the items displayed on the screen are placed on a *canvas.* To create a new canvas, click the Canvases node and then the green plus (+) button. This creates a new node under the Canvases node with a name like CANVAS2. Double-click the canvas icon to open the canvas. The Form Builder window should now look like Figure 10-2.

To place some static text on the canvas, use the Text tool: choose 18-point font size from the drop-down list and click the bold button to choose a bold font. Then select the Text tool, click the canvas near the top, and type **Hello World** as header on the page. Figure 10-3 shows the header along with some additional elements that you will add shortly.

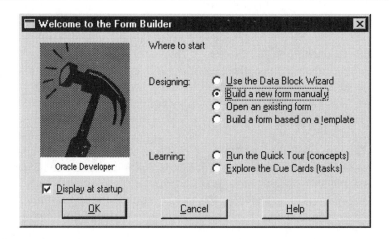

FIGURE 10-1. *The Form Builder Welcome screen*

Canvas icon

Run Form
Client/Server   Run Form Web

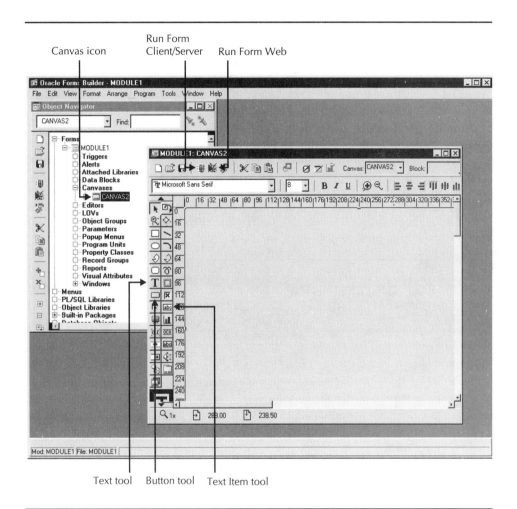

Text tool   Button tool   Text Item tool

FIGURE 10-2.   *An empty canvas in Form Builder*

The next step is to create a text item that will hold some text and the current date. First, change the font back to 12-point and click the bold button again to choose regular text. Choose the Text Item tool and drag the mouse cursor on the canvas to create a wide text item. Double-click the text item to bring up the property palette for the field, scroll down to the Data subheading, and set the Maximum Length property to 50. Then scroll further down to the Physical heading, find the Bevel property, and set it to the value None. (The *bevel* effect is the default three-dimensional look where the text field seems to be inset from the rest of the page.)

Next, choose the Button tool and drag the mouse cursor to create a button under the text field. Double-click the button to bring up the property palette for the button, scroll down to find the Label property, and set it to Update.

To set the background color of the canvas, right-click the canvas in the Navigator window and choose Property Palette from the pop-up menu. In the Property Palette window, scroll down to the Background Color property (in the Color section) and type **white**. Now your screen should look like Figure 10-3.

The final step is to add some code that will populate the text item you created. In Oracle Forms. This code is called a *trigger* because it is executed in response to a specific triggering event. There are many different triggers that can be associated with items at many levels; in this case, you need a WHEN-BUTTON-PRESSED trigger on the button you just created. To do this, expand the button in the Navigator pane by clicking the plus sign. Then select the Triggers node and click the green plus (+)

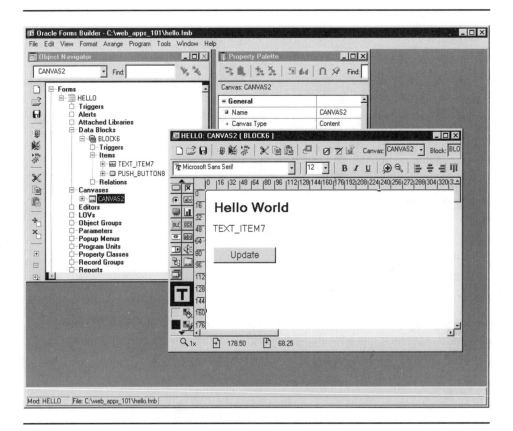

FIGURE 10-3. *The Hello World form*

button to add a trigger. In the trigger list that pops up, choose WHEN-BUTTON-
PRESSED and click OK. The PL/SQL Editor window then opens, as shown in
Figure 10-4, to let you enter the trigger code. Look in the Navigator to determine
what name the Form Builder has given to the text item you created (TEXT_ITEM7
in Figure 10-3). Then enter some code like the following:

```
:text_item7 := 'The time is '
    || to_char(sysdate, 'hh24:mi:ss yyyy-mm-dd');
```

Notice the colon in front of the name of the text item. This indicates that
text_item7 is an element on the form.

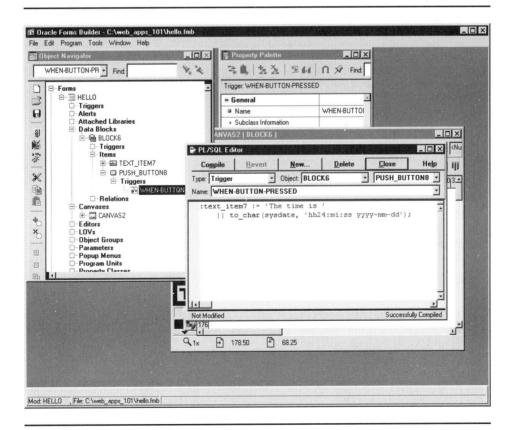

FIGURE 10-4.   *Entering the trigger code*

NOTE
For this simple example, you only have one block called BLOCK6, so a block reference is not necessary. In a real application, you might have many blocks and should include the block name in the item reference, for example, :block6.text_item7.

That's all you need to do to create this simple sample application.

Running the Form from Form Builder

You can run the form you built in several ways:

- As traditional client/server
- As a Web Form through the Appletviewer
- As a Web Form through the Forms Service

By default, all ways of running the form require that you connect to an Oracle database. If you run the form from within Oracle Form Builder, you will be prompted to log in the first time you run the form. Provide a user name, password, and connect string (for example **scott**, **tiger**, and **orcl**). The Oracle Form Builder establishes a database connection that lasts until you shut down the tool, so you will not be prompted again during the same session.

Traditional Client/Server

To run this form in traditional client/server mode, you can click the Run Form Client/Server button (a traffic light icon showing green—refer to Figure 10-2). If you have not already logged in, you will be prompted for a user name and password. The form then appears in the Forms Runtime, as shown in Figure 10-5 (you have to click the Update button to make the time appear).

Through the Appletviewer

You can also see how the form will work when deployed to the Web by clicking the Run Form Web button (a spiderweb icon). This will start the Appletviewer—a stand-alone Java Virtual Machine especially for running applets—and a Forms Service. The Appletviewer contacts the Forms Service to show your Form.

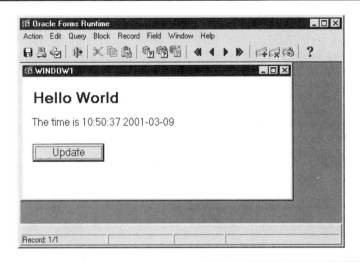

FIGURE 10-5.   *Running the Hello World form with the Forms Runtime*

NOTE
This doesn't always work if you have installed the Oracle9i Application Server and the Forms Service on the same machine. If you have performed the installation in Chapter 4, run the form through the Web browser as described in the following section.

Running the Form from a Web Browser

If you have followed the installation instructions in Chapter 4, you created a directory—c:\web_apps_101—and added this to the FORMS60_PATH value in the Windows Registry. This allows you to run your form in "true" Web fashion by opening your Web browser and entering a URL like this:

http://<servername>/cgi-bin/ifcgi60.exe?form=hello&userid=scott/tiger@orcl

The /cgi-bin/ part of this URL indicates to the Web/application server that the request is for a program to be executed; the ifcgi60.exe is the name of a program that delivers a Web page containing the right HTML tags to request the Forms applet and JInitiator. The last part, ?form=hello&userid=scott/tiger@orcl, contains the parameters that are passed to the Forms applet so that it can tell the Forms Service which form and which database connection it needs. The Forms Service will search for the form with the name "hello" in the directories listed in the Registry value FORMS60_PATH.

NOTE
If you want to use the built-in JVM in Internet Explorer, you can add the string &config=ie50native to the end of the URL to tell the Forms CGI program to produce a Web page that does not request JInitiator.

The first time you invoke the Forms applet, the JInitiator download prompt appears (see Figure 10-6). Click Yes and go through the wizard to install JInitiator.

NOTE
Your users do not have to install JInitiator themselves—it is a normal piece of software that the IT people can install on every client workstation to avoid a 9MB download. If you choose to do this, no user will ever see the screen in Figure 10-6.

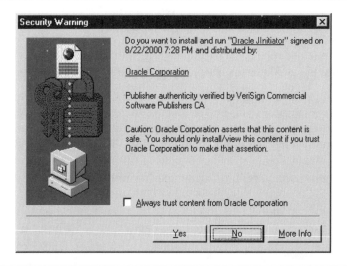

FIGURE 10-6. *Installing JInitiator*

When the JInitiator installation completes, the Forms applet is downloaded and your Web form appears, as shown in Figure 10-7.

NOTE
If you are using JInitiator, the Forms applet stays in cache, that is, it remains available to subsequent Web forms applications without a new download.

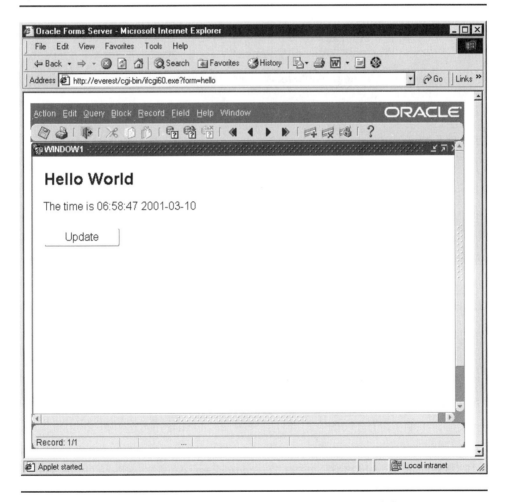

FIGURE 10-7. *The Hello World form running through the Web browser*

An Employee List Report

For the second example (the unrestricted list of employees), you will be creating a report.

Building the Report

Start the Report Builder by choosing Start | Programs | Oracle Reports 6i – DevHome60 | Report Builder. The Oracle Report Builder Welcome screen shown in Figure 10-8 appears (unless you have already run Report Builder and removed the check mark in the Display at Startup check box). Follow these steps:

1. Leave the radio button Use the Report Wizard selected and click OK. On the Welcome page of the Report Wizard, click Next.

2. Leave the title field blank, leave the radio button Tabular selected, and click Next.

3. Leave the radio button SQL Statement selected and click Next.

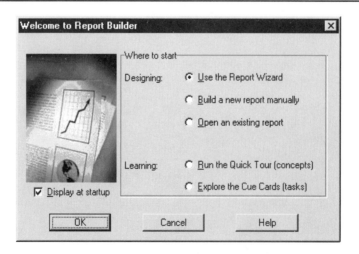

FIGURE 10-8. *The Report Builder Welcome screen*

4. Enter this query in the Query field (see the following illustration):

```
select empno, ename, job
from emp
order by ename
```

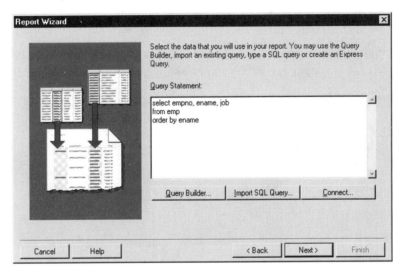

If you do not want to write the SQL statement directly—for example, if you do not remember all the column names—you can click the Query Builder button to start the Query Builder tool that lets you build your query visually. When you have finished, click Next to proceed to the next step shown here. (If you have not yet logged in to the database, you will be prompted for connection details now.)

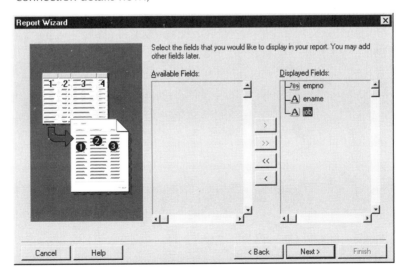

5. Since you want to display all three selected fields in the report, click the >> button to move all fields from the Available Fields box on the left to the Displayed Fields box on the right. Then click Next.

6. You can specify sums and other calculated values you might desire. For this simple report, click Next to continue without specifying any calculated fields.

7. You can specify the labels and width for each column, as shown in the following illustration. When you have finished, click Next to continue.

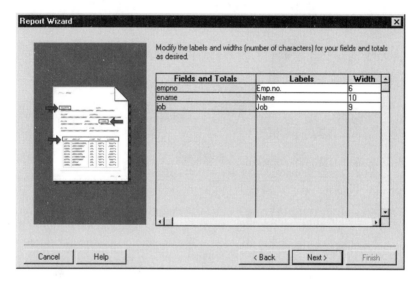

8. You can choose a template for your report. For this example, choose No Template (see the following illustration). Then either click either Next to proceed to the exit page of the wizard or click Finish to end the wizard right away.

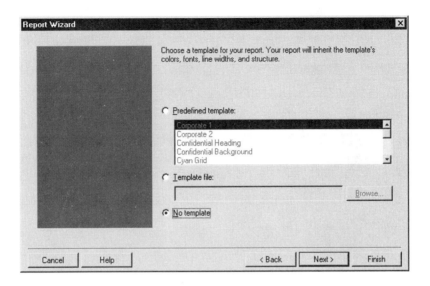

The Live Previewer window appears (see Figure 10-9) from which you can change fonts, column widths, and other aspects of your report.

NOTE
You cannot change the page margin in the Live Previewer. To change the margin, you have to open the Layout Model, choose View | Layout Section | Edit Margin, and drag the thick black page margin box.

Save your report definition with a name like EMPLIST in directory c:\web_apps_101.

If you want to execute the report from your Web browser, the directory where you save it must be specified in the REPORT60_PATH value in the Windows Registry. If you followed the instructions in Chapter 4, you created a directory c:\web_apps_101 and added it to this Registry value.

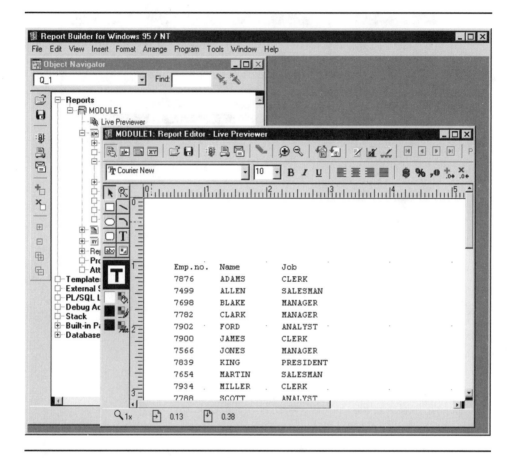

FIGURE 10-9. *The report shown in the Live Previewer*

Adding Formatting

If you want to use this report as part of an existing HTML-based application, you will, of course, want the report pages to look like the Web pages. Oracle Reports lets you use standard HTML code in different places in the report and provides default values.

Changing the HTML

The ugly gray bar that appears at the bottom of each page is a Reports default. To get rid of it, select the report node (EMPLIST) in the Navigator and press F4 to open the property palette. Scroll down to the section Report Escapes, find the After Page Value property, and clear it.

Using PL/SQL Formatting

A more flexible approach than modifying the HTML in every report is to use a PL/SQL package that produces standard HTML that will be used to start and end each page.

The example in the next section assumes that you have created a package called FORMAT package as shown in Chapter 7 with functions PAGESTART and PAGEEND that return the HTML to use at the top and bottom of every page.

Reports Triggers

In Oracle Reports, you can define PL/SQL triggers that will get executed at different times during the execution of the report. To define the formatting, you can use the BEFORE_REPORT trigger.

In the report, expand the Report Triggers node and click the icon next to BEFORE_REPORT. You must click the little gray dot itself, not just the text. This should open a PL/SQL editor window, as shown in Figure 10-10.

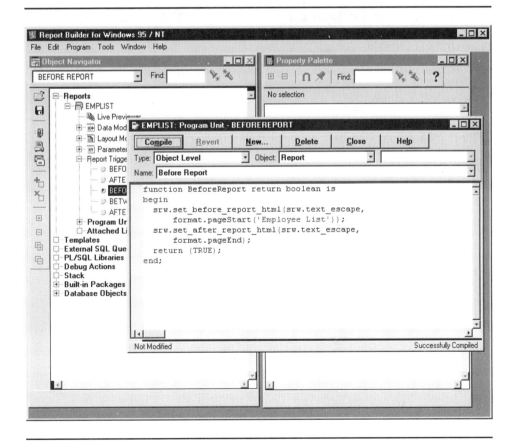

FIGURE 10-10. *Adding a report trigger*

Add some calls to the SRW package in the existing code so your trigger looks like this:

```
function BeforeReport return boolean is
begin
   srw.set_before_report_html(srw.text_escape,
      format.pageStart('Employee List'));
   srw.set_after_report_html(srw.text_escape,
      format.pageEnd);
   return (TRUE);
end;
```

The SRW package is a built-in PL/SQL package that comes with Oracle Reports, and it contains procedures to handle many tasks associated with reports. In this case, you just need to set the HTML to display at the top and bottom of the report.

Running the Report from Report Builder

When you are satisfied with the look of your report in the Live Previewer, you can run it by choosing from menu items on the View menu. First, select one of the Use . . . options, and then select the Generate to Web Browser option. For long reports, you can also use these menu items to choose whether to show all pages or only the current page.

While you are working on your report, you should deselect the Generate to Web Browser menu item so you can work in the Live Previewer without having Oracle Reports generate the report to your browser all the time.

Running a Traditional Client/Server Report

To run the report in the traditional client/server way, choose View | Runtime Preview. This invokes the Reports Runtime that shows the report as it will look when deployed in a client/server environment.

Running an HTML Web Report

To run the report in HTML format, choose View | Web Preview | Use HTML.

NOTE
This option generates reasonably clean HTML output with the data formatted in an HTML table. The report does not contain page breaks.

The report should look something like Figure 10-11.

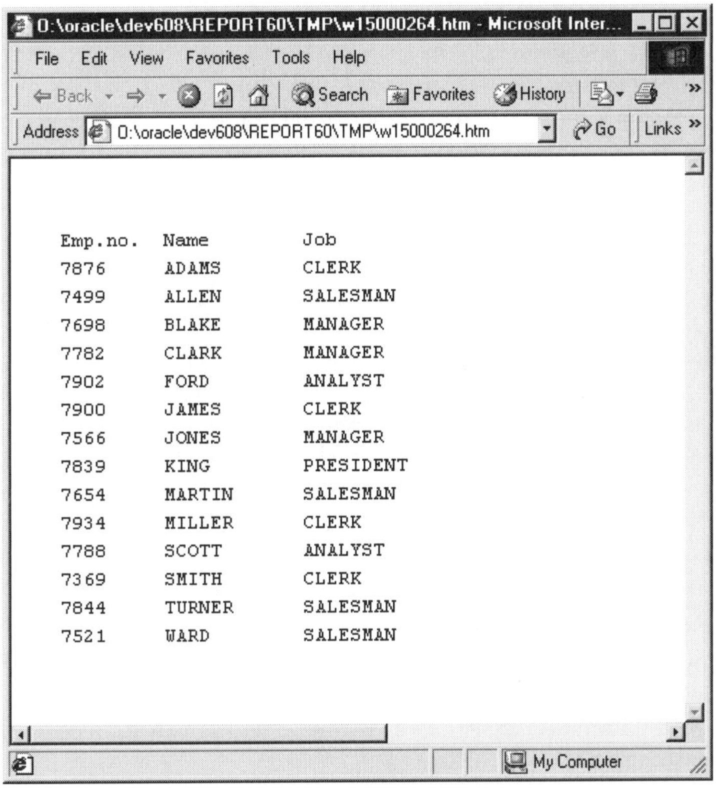

FIGURE 10-11. *An HTML Web report*

When you run a report from the Report Builder, it gets stored on the local file system before the Web browser shows it. Because the FORMAT package is intended to run from a Web browser, the references to images and style sheets will not work when viewing the report from Report Builder. They should work correctly when running the report from a Web browser, however.

Running an HTML Web Report with Style Sheets

To format your report for HTML output, including style sheet extensions (HTMLCSS), choose View | Web Preview | Use HTML Style Sheets.

NOTE
When you choose this option, the HTML code uses a lot of absolute positioning tags to place the individual elements on the page. The HTML code is messy and can only be understood by fourth-generation browsers and later; however, this option does ensure that the page breaks in the same places as a client/server or PDF report.

Running a PDF Web Report

The Portable Document Format (PDF) is a proprietary format invented by Adobe. It has the advantage over HTML that you can completely control the fonts, formatting, page breaks, and so on. To view PDF files, you need the Acrobat Reader that you can download for free from the Adobe Web site.

To send output to a PDF file, choose View | Web Preview | Use PDF. Depending on the settings in your browser and the Acrobat Reader, the PDF file might appear inside the browser window or in a separate window. The report should look something like Figure 10-12.

Running an XML Report

If you like, you can also produce the report in XML format by choosing View | Web Preview | Use XML. You will need an XML-capable browser (like Microsoft Internet Explorer version 5 or later) to see the XML file. Refer to the resources in Chapter 13 for more information about XML.

Running the Report from a Web Browser

If you followed the installation instructions in Chapter 4, you can also run your report through the Web browser. To see the report in Figure 10-13, you can enter a URL like the following:

> **http://<servername>/cgi-bin/rwcgi60.exe?module=emplist+
> userid=scott/tiger@orcl+destype=cache+desformat=html+server=repsrv**

The /cgi-bin/ part instructs the Web/application server that rwcgi60.exe is a program to be executed; after the question mark are parameters that get passed to the report engine on the server (see Table 10-1).

FIGURE 10-12.   *A PDF Web report*

Parameter	Meaning
module	Name of the report to execute
userid	The database connection to use
destype	Destination type (must be "cache" for a web report)
desformat	Destination format (must be "html," "htmlcss," or "pdf" for a Web report)
server	The name of the report server (specified during installation)

TABLE 10-1.   *Parameters for the Report Server*

FIGURE 10-13. *The Employee List run from a Web browser*

NOTE
You are not required to include the user name and password in the URL. If you leave them out, you will be prompted for them; you can also use a Key Map File (see the Reports documentation) to hide parameters from the URL.

Report with Parameters: Search for Employees

The third example shows how to limit the report based on a user-defined parameter value. In Oracle Reports, this is achieved by defining a user parameter, including it in the SQL statement, and defining a parameter form where the user can enter a value.

Building the Report

If you still have the EMPLIST report open in the Report Builder, you can create a copy by choosing File | Save As and providing a new name (for example, SEARCHEMP). If you no longer have the EMPLIST report open, create a copy in the file system, rename it, and open it from Report Builder.

Add a User Parameter

To add a user parameter, expand the Data Model node in the Navigator and choose the node User Parameters (see Figure 10-14).

Click the green plus (+) button to create a new user parameter. Give it the name **p_empname**, and change the data type to Character.

Include the Parameter in Your Query

To use the newly created parameter in your query, expand the Queries node and click the query to show the query properties in the property palette window. Then double-click the SQL Query Statement property to open the SQL Query Statement window, as shown in Figure 10-15.

Add a WHERE condition to the SQL statement so it looks like this:

```
select empno, ename, job
from emp
where upper(ename) like '%' || upper(:p_empname) || '%'
order by ename
```

Note that the colon before **p_empname** identifies it as a parameter. If you type a parameter name that does not already exist, Oracle Reports will automatically create another user parameter for you and show an information message.

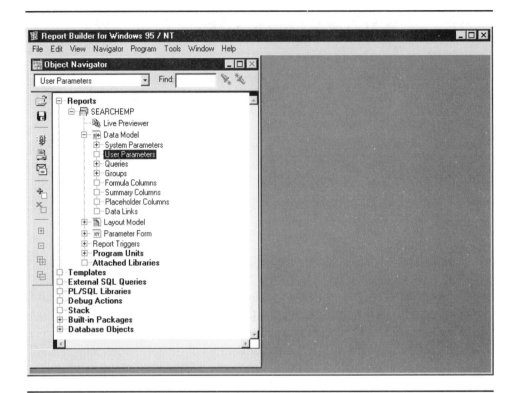

FIGURE 10-14. *Adding a user parameter*

Define the Parameter Form

The last step is to define the parameter form that will be shown to the user at runtime. Oracle Reports offers you a lot of possibilities to customize the parameter form, but you only need the basics here.

Double-click the Parameter Form node in the Navigator to see the Parameter Form window shown in Figure 10-16. This window is a small screen painter where you can add text and fields to get the layout you want.

First, use the Text tool to place a field label on the canvas. Then select the Field tool and drag the mouse to create a field on the parameter form. Notice that the new items you create automatically appear in the Navigator.

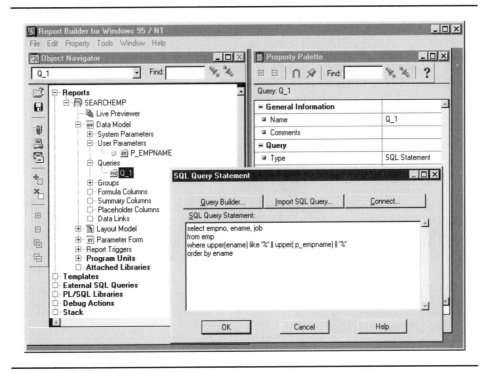

FIGURE 10-15. *Changing the SQL query*

Double-click the parameter field (either in the Navigator or on the parameter form) to call up the property palette for the field. Then set the Source property to the **p_empname** parameter you just defined.

NOTE
The list of possible values for the source property also contains all the System parameters that control things like format, orientation, and so on. For example, you could add a parameter field and associate it with the system parameter DESFORMAT to allow the user to choose between HTML and PDF format before running the report.

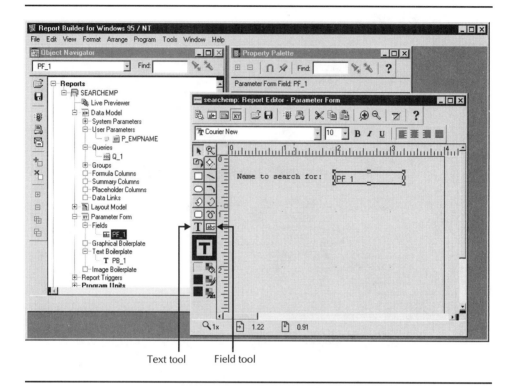

Text tool   Field tool

FIGURE 10-16. *Defining a parameter form*

Running the Report

You can run this report from the Report Builder by changing back to the Live Preview window (choose View | Live Previewer). Then use the commands on the View menu as in the preceding example to see your report in different formats.

If you have the Reports Server configured, you can also run the report from a Web browser like in the previous example. The URL would look like this:

> **http://<servername>/cgi-bin/rwcgi60.exe?module=searchemp+**
> **userid=scott/tiger@orcl+destype=cache+desformat=html+**
> **server=repsrv+paramform=yes**

If you like, you can customize the parameter form by changing the HTML in the report properties or by adding a trigger calling procedures from the SRW package, like in the previous example.

NOTE
You can also run the report without the
paramform=yes *attribute. If you do not display
the parameter form, all parameters take default
values that you can define.*

Maintaining Data in the Employees Table

The last example is a Web Form that can maintain (insert, update, and delete) data
in the EMP table.

Building the Form

If the Form Builder is not already open, you must open it now. If the Welcome
screen appears, choose Use the Data Block Wizard and click OK. If this screen does
not appear (or if you already have Form Builder open), you can choose File | New |
Form to create a new form and then Tools | Data Block Wizard to start the wizard.

   If the Welcome page of the wizard appears, just click Next to move on to the
first step of the wizard.

   Choose to base the data block on Table or View and click Next to proceed to
the next step, as shown in Figure 10-17.

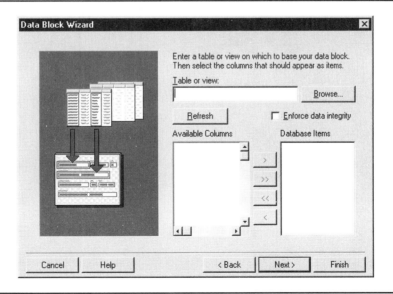

FIGURE 10-17. *Entering a table or view in the Data Block Wizard*

Click Browse to see a list of tables accessible to the current user. If you have not logged in to the Oracle database yet, a login prompt appears:

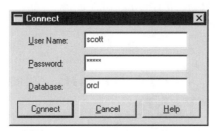

Enter user name **SCOTT**, password **TIGER**, and connect string **ORCL** and click OK. The list of tables in the SCOTT schema appears:

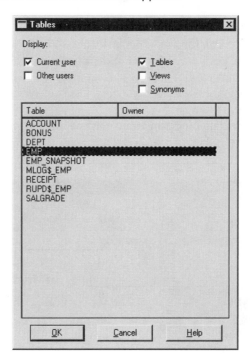

Choose the EMP table and click OK. The table list disappears and the Data Block Wizard appears again. Move the columns EMPNO, ENAME, and JOB from the Available Columns box on the left to the Database Items box on the right. Your screen should now look something like Figure 10-18. Click Next.

On the exit screen of the Data Block Wizard, leave the radio button Create the Data Block, Then Call the Layout Wizard selected and click Finish. The Data Block Wizard closes and the Layout Wizard starts.

If the Welcome screen of this wizard appears, click Next to proceed to the first step shown in Figure 10-19.

You do not have to change anything on this screen—just click Next to create a new canvas to place your items on.

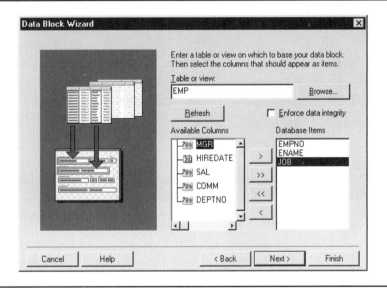

FIGURE 10-18. *Data Block Wizard with columns selected*

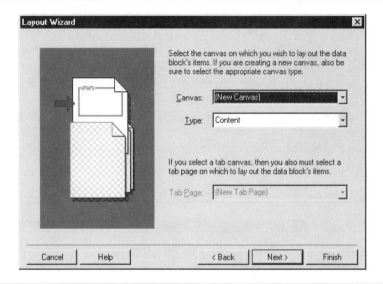

FIGURE 10-19. *First step in the Layout Wizard*

In the next step, click the **>>** button to move all the items from the Available Items box on the left to the Displayed Items on the right. Then click Next.

In the third step, you can change the column labels and widths. When you have finished, click Next to proceed to the fourth step, as shown in Figure 10-20.

In this step, you can choose either a Form layout, which normally shows one record at a time, or a Tabular layout, which shows many records at the same time in a spreadsheet-like format. When you change the setting, the picture in the left half of the wizard changes to show what each layout looks like. For this example, choose a Form layout and click Next.

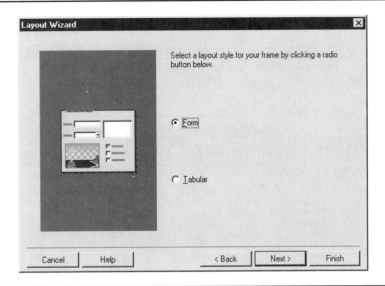

FIGURE 10-20. *Selecting a layout style in the Layout Wizard*

In the next step, you can provide a frame title. Type **Maintain Employees** in this field, and click Next to proceed to the exit page of the wizard or click Finish to leave the wizard right away.

The newly created canvas containing your items appears, as shown in Figure 10-21.

Save the form as MAINTAINEMP in directory c:\web_apps_101. (You created this directory if you followed the installation instructions in Chapter 4.)

Running the Form from Form Builder

You can change the form layout by selecting, changing, and moving the items on the canvas. When you are satisfied with your form, you can run it by clicking one of the buttons on the toolbar above the canvas.

Run Form Client/Server   Run Form Web

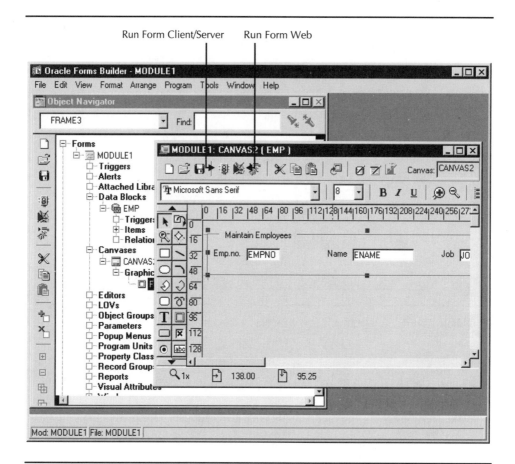

FIGURE 10-21. *The form to maintain employees*

Traditional Client/Server

To run the form in traditional client/server mode, click the Run Form Client/Server toolbar button (the green traffic light). The Forms Runtime starts, as shown in Figure 10-22.

In a Forms application, you can use the same screen for querying, inserting, updating, and deleting records. The following operations can be executed either by using the toolbar buttons or by choosing the corresponding menu items.

Querying   To query records, click Enter Query, fill in one or more fields with search criteria, and click Execute Query. The form then shows only the records that

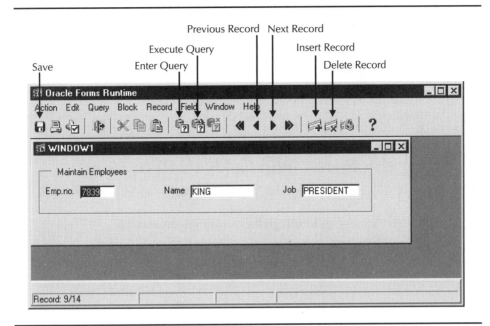

FIGURE 10-22. *Running the form as a traditional client/server*

satisfy the search criteria. You can click Next Record or Previous Record to page through the records that satisfy the search criteria.

For example, you can click Enter Query, type **%MI%** in the Name field, and click Execute Query. This retrieves two records (SMITH and MILLER) that you can go back and forth between with the Next Record and Previous Record buttons.

You can also click Execute Query without entering any search criteria to retrieve all records.

Inserting   In a Forms application, you can enter a new record any time. By default, the Forms Runtime will display a blank record after the last record that satisfies the search criteria. You can navigate to that record with the Next Record button, or you can click Insert Record to insert a blank record after the current record anywhere.

On this blank record, you can enter the values for the new record and then click Save.

Updating   To update a record, you must first find it (by querying) and then update it. When you have finished making changes, click Save to commit your changes.

Deleting   To delete a record, you must find it (by querying), click Remove Record, and then click Save.

Through the Appletviewer

To run the form as a Web form from the Form Builder, you can click the Run Form Web toolbar button, as in the previous Web form example.

All the buttons work the same way they do when you run the form in traditional client/server mode.

Running the Form from a Web Browser

As before, you can run the form in true Web fashion by entering a URL like this:

> **http://<servername>/cgi-bin/ifcgi60.exe?form=maintainemp &userid=scott/tiger@orcl**

In the Web browser, the form will look similar to Figure 10-23.

Summary

Most existing applications developed with Oracle Forms and Reports can be deployed to an intranet with little effort—as soon as you have the requisite server components installed, your application is ready to run through a Web browser. This allows you to add new features to existing applications without having to change to a different tool.

For developing new applications, you should carefully consider whether your users really need the complex user interface possible only with a Java applet application. If not, use an HTML-based application. But if your users do need a Java applet application, Oracle Forms is a viable way of building it.

For the reports you need in your Web applications, there are easier tools that can be used to build simple HTML-based reports. But if you need anything more than basic reports, Oracle Reports is an excellent choice for both HTML and PDF reports.

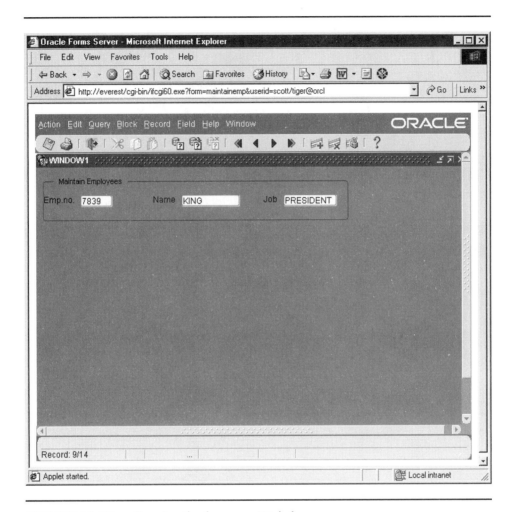

FIGURE 10-23. *Running the form as a Web form*

PART
III

Reference

CHAPTER
11

Tools of the Trade

his chapter describes some of the tools that can help you configure your Oracle Web environment and develop your applications. Some of the tools are specific to one or a couple of approaches (see Table 11-1).

If you are going to be hand-building PL/SQL Web applications, you should get yourself a PL/SQL development tool.

For the hand-built approaches (whether you use Java or PL/SQL), you need conversion and HTML tools if you are going to follow the approach described in this book.

If you will be using a code-generating tool like Oracle Designer or Oracle Portal, you do not need to convert any code, but you might want to use some HTML tools to create HTML code for headers and footers and other page elements.

Oracle Forms is a completely self-contained tool that does not really benefit from any additional utilities; but, if you are going to use Oracle Reports to develop reports in HTML format, you might want to use additional tools. You could use HTML tools to create standard page elements or even create HTML and convert it to PL/SQL for inclusion into reports, as shown in Chapter 10.

If you are going to write Java servlets, you should also look at the section on the Javadoc utility from Sun. This utility automatically generates documentation in HTML format, based on code comments following a specific format. It is a good idea to comment all your Java code in this format to ensure consistent, high-quality documentation.

Approach	PL/SQL Tool	Conversion Tool	HTML Tools	Javadoc	PSP Tool
Java servlets	No	Yes	Yes	Optional	No
Hand-built PL/SQL	Yes	Yes	Yes	No	Optional
Oracle Designer	No	No	Optional	No	No
Oracle Portal	No	No	Optional	No	No
Oracle Forms	No	No	No	No	No
Oracle Reports	No	Optional	Optional	No	No

TABLE 11-1. *Tools for Different Approaches*

If you want to write your PL/SQL applications by hand, you might also consider the third-party product for developing PL/SQL Server Pages (PSP) described at the end of this chapter. This product overcomes many of the limitations of the Oracle PSP implementation and is more similar to the elegant implementation of Java Server Pages.

General Utilities

Some general utilities are useful no matter what approach you choose:

- For editing configuration files, you need a standard editor (preferably a bit more powerful than Notepad).

- For adding virtual directories to your Web site, it can be useful to have a tool to create symbolic links in the NTFS file system.

- For being able to return your environment to a known state where everything works, you can use a disk image program.

- To establish a separate drive for your Oracle software on a disk that's already formatted and contains the operating system or other software, you can use a disk repartitioning program.

Text Editor

There are any number of programming file editors out there with special support for this or that—you can find literally hundreds on the big download sites, such as **www.download.com**.

For simple text editing, I like Programmer's File Editor for the following reasons:

- It's small, fast, and free.

- It offers a simple macro recording feature that can handle all the repetitive tasks involved in converting HTML to your language of choice.

The program was available from **http://www.lancs.ac.uk/people/cpaap/ pfe/default.htm** at the time of writing.

Symbolic Links

People who are used to working on Unix systems miss an important feature in Windows: the ability to create *symbolic links*. A symbolic link looks like a directory but is really just a reference to somewhere else in the directory structure.

Microsoft doesn't advertise it, but the NTFS file system does support symbolic links in the form of *NTFS junction points* (for more information, search the Microsoft Knowledge Base for this term). This is not a Windows shortcut—shortcuts work from the desktop—but you cannot use commands like cd to follow a Windows shortcut from the command line.

To create or delete junction points, you can use the junction utility from Sysinternals.

The small utility was available from **http://www.sysinternals.com/ntw2k/ source/misc.shtml#junction** at the time of writing.

Disk Images

When you are playing around with Oracle software, you will occasionally get into a situation in which suddenly nothing works anymore. An experienced DBA or developer might be able to help you out, but a much easier option on a development machine used just for experiments is to restore a complete *disk image* using the appropriate software.

Such software can write one big file containing a compressed image of one or more disks and later allow you to restore the complete content of those disks. Note that if you restore your database files in this way, you will lose all database changes made since you wrote the disk images. You will have to read from the latest database backup after restoring the disk image.

Two products that do this are DriveImage from PowerQuest or Norton Ghost from Symantec (see **http://www.powerquest.com/driveimage/** or **http://www.symantec.com/sabu/ghost/ghost_personal/**).

Disk Partitioning

If you want to change your disk partitioning after initially formatting the disk, you need a third-party tool. This can be useful, for example, if you want to establish a separate drive for your Oracle software and the hard disk on your machine has already been partitioned with just one hard disk partition.

A tool that makes it possible to repartition a disk without losing data is PartitionMagic from PowerQuest (**http://www.powerquest.com/partitionmagic/**).

PL/SQL Editor

A very powerful tool for PL/SQL developers is Tool for Oracle Application Developers (TOAD). This tool started life as free software and was built by a developer who was fed up with having to use SQL*Plus and Notepad for his own development.

It still exists in a time-limited version for free, as well as in a commercial version with a lot more features. The free version will run for a couple of months after you download it—you'll have to download a new version occasionally.

Note that the license conditions currently say that no more than five people in your organization may use the free version—but if you've got more than five PL/SQL developers, you can probably afford to pay for your tools.

At the time of writing, this program was available from **http://www.toadsoft.com/ downld.html**.

Conversion Tools

If you follow the four-step approach described in Chapters 5, 6, and 7 to hand-build Web applications in Java or PL/SQL, you will benefit from having some kind of tool to convert the HTML you create in an HTML tool into code in your chosen language.

HTML to Java

Converting HTML to Java involves two tasks:

1. *Escaping* all the double quotes; that is, placing a backslash \ before all the double quotes (")

2. Wrapping each line in out.println(); calls

With an Editor

You don't strictly need a tool to convert HTML to Java—if your editor of choice has a simple macro function, that will do.

For example, in Programmer's File Editor, to do a search and replace to escape all the double quotes, go to the first line, start recording a macro with SHIFT-F7, type some spaces for indentation, type **out.println(", press the** END key to go to the end of the line, type **");**, press LEFT ARROW to go to the start of the next line, and press CTRL-F7 to stop recording. Then press F7 repeatedly to execute the macro for every line in the file.

html2java

An easier way to convert HTML to Java is to use the html2java utility written by Morten Tangaa-Andersen. Simply type **html2java *filename*.html** to make this utility create a file *filename***.java**, where double quotes are escaped and every line is wrapped in an out.println() call.

If you want to indent with a different number of spaces, use the **–i** option, for example, **html2java –i8 *filename*.html**.

The html2java utility is available from **www.vesterli.com/tools**.

HTML to PL/SQL

Converting HTML to PL/SQL is even easier, because PL/SQL uses single quotes to delimit text, and you don't have to worry about the double quotes. Simply wrap every line of HTML in a call to **htp.p ();**.

With an Editor

To convert HTML to PL/SQL in Programmer's File Editor, go to the first line, start recording a macro with SHIFT-F7, type some spaces for indentation, type **htp.p(',** **press the** END key to go to the end of the line, type **');**, press LEFT ARROW to go to the start of the next line, and press CTRL-F7 to stop recording. Then press F7 repeatedly to step execute the macro for every line in the file.

html2plsql

You can also use the html2plsql utility written by Morten Tangaa-Andersen to convert HTML to PL/SQL. Simply type **html2plsql** *filename***.html** to make this utility create a file *filename***.pls**, where every line is wrapped in an htp.p() call.

   If you want to indent with a different number of spaces, use the **–i** option, for example, **html2plsql –i8** *filename***.html**.

   The html2java utility is available from **www.vesterli.com/tools**.

WebAlchemy

Another way to convert HTML to PL/SQL is to use WebAlchemy by Alan Hobbs. This free tool creates a complete stored procedure from an HTML file. It does not just wrap every line of HTML, but rather attempts to use the "correct" function or procedure from the Web PL/SQL Toolkit. It is several years old and does not quite understand XHTML (the latest version of HTML—see details in Chapter 7).

   The output from WebAlchemy is functionally identical to wrapping every line of HTML in a call to htp.p(). However, the code looks completely different— it is sometimes more, sometimes less readable than just wrapping the HTML.

   It also has some advanced features like the ability to automatically convert specially formatted HTML into PL/SQL cursor for loops.

   At the time of writing, this program was available from **http://www.users. bigpond.com/ahobbs/**.

HTML Tools

In all but the simplest HTML-based applications, you need to create HTML code for headers, footers, and other page elements. In addition, you might want to create images or use style sheets to improve the appearance of your pages.

HTML Editor

If you have any HTML editing to do—even if you just need a standard header and footer on every page—you should get yourself an HTML editor. These come in two main flavors:

- Code editors
- Visual editors

Allaire HomeSite

Many experienced HTML programmers prefer to work directly with the code to maintain full control over their HTML. If you are just starting out and intend to learn how to write HTML, you should do the same: use a code editor so that you can get to know the details.

One of the best code editors is HomeSite from Allaire. This is not free (but not unreasonably priced either), and might be bundled with Macromedia Dreamweaver.

At the time of writing, you could download a 60-day trial version from the Allaire Web site at **www.allaire.com**. Since Allaire is merging with Macromedia, you might have to look at the Macromedia site by the time you read this book.

Macromedia Dreamweaver

If you only need to produce a few headers and footers, and have no intention of learning the details of HTML programming, you should probably use a visual editor.

The clear winner in this category is Dreamweaver from Macromedia. Even though it is a visual tool, it does not mess up your code, and it allows you to work in either visual or code mode. This professional tool does cost money, but it is worth it.

At the time of writing, a 30-day trial was available for download from the Web site **http://www.macromedia.com/download**.

FrontPage

Another visual editor is Microsoft FrontPage. This tool is geared toward the home or casual user and is easy to use, but it tends to add unnecessary extra HTML tags to your code.

This tool is bundled with certain versions of the Office 2000 suite; and, at the time of writing, for a nominal fee you could order a 45-day trial version on CD at **http://www.microsoft.com/FRONTPAGE/officetrial/default.htm**.

Microsoft Word

Microsoft Word offers the option of saving your text as HTML, but this feature is not really useful for developing Web applications. Word is first and foremost a word processor, so it attempts to loyally reproduce the exact look of the document in HTML. The result is some rather convoluted and unreadable HTML that can be *very* hard for a programmer to understand.

Since the programmer needs to understand the HTML in order to add business logic, it follows that you should *not* use Word to develop HTML.

Style Sheet Editor

You might never need to edit a style sheet—many organizations already have standard style sheets developed by professional graphics artists that are used on the Internet or intranet Web site. If that is not the case, you can use a free style sheet from a Web site (for example, the style sheet that's used for the examples in this book, which is available at **www.vesterli.com**).

NOTE
Don't just grab a style sheet from any Web site—style sheets (like HTML code) are protected by copyright. Only use a style sheet from a Web site if you are explicitly allowed to do so by the site.

If you need to make more than trivial changes to a style sheet, however, it is a good idea to use some kind of tool. Your HTML tool might already be able to edit style sheets (Dreamweaver can), or you can use a tool especially for editing style sheets.

TopStyle from Bradsoft is an example of such a tool. It is available in several versions depending on your need—the Lite version might be bundled for free with HomeSite or other tools. At the time of writing, you could download this free version from **http://www.bradsoft.com/topstyle/download/index.asp**.

Image Editor

If you are creating HTML-based applications, you are most likely going to want to include some images—even if it's just colored bars or bullets. To create these images, you need some kind of image editing tool.

Many Web professionals use expensive, full-featured tools like Adobe Photoshop, but almost everything you can do with Photoshop, you can also do with inexpensive programs like Paint Shop Pro from JASC.

At the time of writing, you could download a trial version of Paint Shop Pro from **http://www.jasc.com/download_4.asp**.

Another good tool (though more expensive) is Fireworks from Macromedia. This is a professional product that costs real money, but you might be able to get it in a bundle together with Dreamweaver. It integrates well with Dreamweaver and makes it *very* easy to create some advanced effects like rollovers (where the Web page changes when you move the mouse over an area).

At the time of writing, you could download a trial version of Fireworks from **http://www.macromedia.com/downloads/**.

Javadoc

If you have looked at the Java documentation, you probably noticed that it is all in HTML format and has a distinctive style. This is not accidental—all the documentation for the Java language itself has been automatically produced using the Javadoc tool.

This tool interprets all comments that start with /** and end with the normal comment terminator */ as documentation that will be used to produce HTML files. You can use normal HTML syntax within these comments, and you can add specific Javadoc @ tags to the code.

You can invoke the Javadoc utility from the command line or in JDeveloper by choosing Wizards | Generate Javadoc.

The following code example taken from the DatabaseUtility package from the Web Application Toolkit (see Chapter 12) illustrates the most common tags. Figures 11-1 and 11-2 show part of the documentation that Javadoc produces based on this markup.

```
/**
 * The DatabaseUtility class contains methods to simplify the
 * handling of database-related operations
 * <p>
 * @author <a href="sten@vesterli.com">Sten Vesterli</a>,
 *         <a href="http://www.vesterli.com">www.vesterli.com</a>
 * <p>
 * @version 2.0, 2000-12-27
 */
public class DatabaseUtility extends Object {
  /**
   * This method formats a ResultSet as an HTML table
   * without column headers.
   *
   * @param rs    The ResultSet object to render as an HTML table
```

```
 * @return        An HTML-formatted table
 * @exception SQLException Passed to calling class to handle
 */
static String formatHtmlTable(ResultSet rs)
    throws SQLException {
```

Refer to the Javadoc reference page at **http://www.javasoft.com/javadoc** for more information, including an explanation of the possible Javadoc tags.

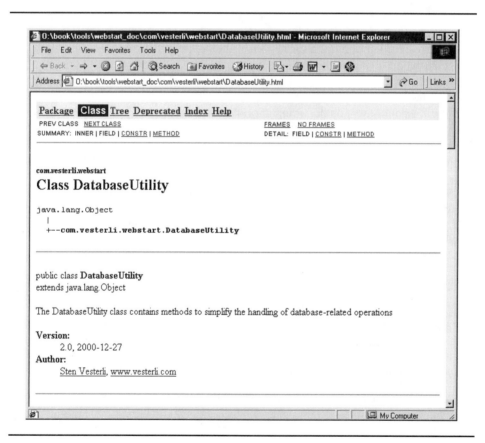

FIGURE 11-1. *Class documentation generated by Javadoc*

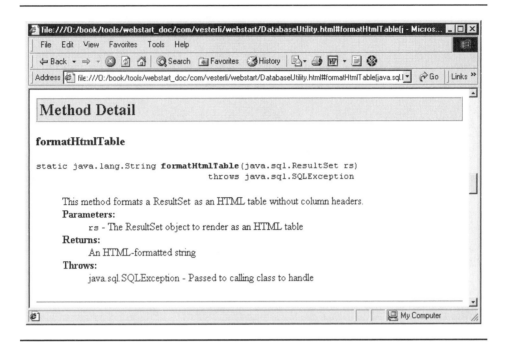

FIGURE 11-2. *Method documentation generated by Javadoc*

PL/SQL Server Pages

Oracle PL/SQL Server Pages (OPSP) is only remotely related to other server page technologies like Active Server Pages (ASP) or Java Server Pages. Other server page technologies allow the developer to simply place the server page file in a directory on a correctly configured Web/application server, and the server automatically compiles or interprets the page. But with Oracle PL/SQL Server Pages, you must use a command-line tool to translate the PL/SQL server page into a stored procedure in advance.

An alternative to OPSP is ChangeGroup PL/SQL Server Pages (CGPSP) that is compatible with OPSP. CGPSP offers automatic server compilation when the page is accessed through the browser, compilation and display in the browser directly from the HTML editor, the ability to build whole projects, visual error correction in the browser, and much more. For more information, see **www.changegroup.dk/en/cgpsp**. For a 45-day trial, send an e-mail to **info@changegroup.dk**.

CHAPTER
12

The Web Application
Toolkit

"Good as it is to inherit a library, it is better to collect one."

—Augustine Birrell

ost experienced computer professionals have a library of code—
a toolkit containing scripts, routines, and code templates that
solved a problem once and might do so again.

You can inherit a complete library from an experienced colleague or buy
off-the-shelf packages, but you should consider that only a starting point for building
your own toolkit. Pick up tools from experienced developers, Web sites, user
conferences, and books like this one, and feel free to adapt and expand them to fit
your situation and the challenges you face. And when you have built a new tool,
tell your fellow developers about it—write an article or publish it on a Web site—
so that someone else can pick it up and improve it again.

This is the philosophy that has made the open source movement great, and I
encourage you to always make available the source code for your improved tools.
Using wrapped PL/SQL or publishing only the compiled Java classes should be
limited to the few occasions when real business secrets are involved.

All the code described in this chapter is available for download from my Web
site at **www.vesterli.com**. This software is OSI Certified Open Source Software (OSI
Certified is a certification mark of the Open Source Initiative). Please read the
license in the README file on the Web site.

HTML Templates

Any toolkit for Web applications should contain templates for all the different
types of Web pages you will be using. The Web Application Toolkit presented here
contains only one page, but bigger Web sites will have many different types of
pages and, therefore, many different templates.

You should also have a standard Cascading Style Sheet (CSS) file that you can
use as a starting point for the application Web pages. This file defines colors, fonts,
and other visual attributes and quickly sets the tone for the entire Web site. The
style sheet presented in this book is simple, but it does show some of the most
important features.

The template file using the standard style sheet produces a page like the one
shown in Figure 12-1.

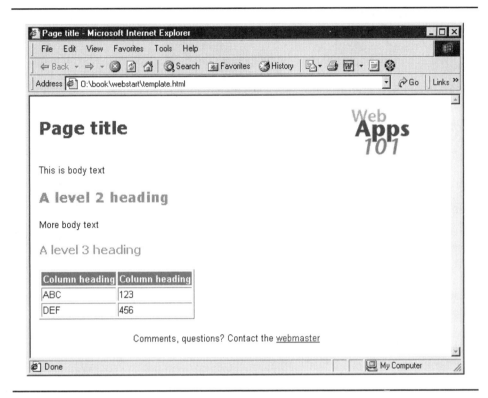

FIGURE 12-1.   *A template for your Web pages*

NOTE
If you use the sample HTML from this toolkit, please change the Webmaster e-mail address from the example (mine) to one that is relevant for your application—I am unlikely to be able to help your users.

JavaScript

As you probably remember, the HTML standard does not really offer any features for field validation—all data must be sent to the server before it can be checked. However, using JavaScript, it is possible to perform simple checks on data that the user enters into fields on forms.

To use JavaScript to validate the content of a field the moment the user leaves the field, you can include an onBlur attribute in the <input> tag, for example:

```
<input name="deptno" onBlur="checkNum(this)">
```

The Web Application Toolkit contains three simple JavaScripts, as shown in Table 12-1. You can include them in your page by placing the webstart.js file in the root directory on your Web server and placing the following tag in the header of your page:

```
<script src="/webstart.js">
```

Java Tools

The following Java classes implement commonly used functionality like project-specific HTML formatting, handling HTML forms, and presenting data from a query as an HTML table.

All three classes are *static* classes. This means that you do not create instances of these objects, but rather use the static methods (or *class methods*) that each class offers.

The documentation in Javadoc format is available on **www.vesterli.com**.

Sample Format Class

As you saw in Chapter 6, using a project-specific Format class makes your code easier to read, and it's easier to ensure a consistent look of your application across tools. The example that is part of the Web Application Toolkit contains the methods in Table 12-2. Every function returns the HTML as a String object.

Function	Arguments	Description
isNumber	this	Shows an alert box if the value entered in the field is not a number.
isValidEmail	this	Shows an alert box if the value entered in the field is not a valid e-mail address.
minLength	this, minLength	Shows an alert box if the value entered in the field does not have the required minimum length.

TABLE 12-1.   *The Web Application Toolkit JavaScript Functions*

Method	Arguments	Description
pageStart	(String title)	The standard page header.
introText	(String text)	The lead text on each page. Normally used for a one-sentence description of what the user is expected to do on the page.
errorText	(String error)	Formats an error message in a special font (normally with fixed spacing) to clearly set it off from the rest of the page.
pageEnd	–	The standard page footer.
message	(String text)	Formats some message in a special way (in this case, between horizontal lines) to set it off from the rest of the page. Typically used for messages confirming insertion or deletion of records shown as part of the following page.
warningPage	(String warningMessage)	A complete page with a warning and a link to go back to the application.
errorPage	(String errorMessage)	A complete page showing some fatal error. Includes error message and an instruction to the user to contact the help desk.

TABLE 12-2. *Methods in the Sample Format Java Class*

HtmlForm Class

Chapter 6 also described how you could use generic HtmlForm class to produce the HTML tags for common elements of HTML forms. All of the methods described in Table 12-3 return the HTML in a String object.

Many of these methods are *overloaded*, that is, they exist is different versions that you can call with different combinations of arguments. Based on the arguments you pass, the Java Virtual Machine (JVM) will automatically invoke the right version.

Method	Arguments	Description
formStart	(String action) (String action, int border)	Starts an HTML form with the specified destination, and at the same time starts an HTML table to align all the form elements. One argument creates a borderless table; two arguments create a table border with the given width in pixels.
formEnd	–	Ends an HTML form and the associated HTML table.
textField	(String label, String name) (String label, String name, String value) (String label, String name, int maxlength, int fieldSize) (String label, String name, String value, int maxlength, int fieldSize)	Creates a row in an HTML table containing a cell with the field label and a cell with the text input field. If a value argument is provided, it is used as the default value for the field, that is, as the value attribute of the <input> tag. If maxlength and size are provided, produces the corresponding HTML attributes.
passwordField	(String label, String name) (String label, String name, int maxlength, int fieldSize)	Creates a row in an HTML table containing a cell with the field label and a cell with a password-type text input field. If maxlength and size are given, produces the corresponding HTML attributes.
keyField	(String label, String name, String value)	Creates a row in an HTML table containing a cell with the field label and a cell with the field value. Also creates a hidden HTML field with the value. Normally used when you want to display a value without letting the user change it, for example, to show the primary key in an update screen.

TABLE 12-3.   *Methods in the HtmlForm Java Class*

Method	Arguments	Description
updateField	(String label, String name, String value) (String label, String name, String value, int maxlength, int fieldSize)	Creates a row in an HTML table containing a cell with the field label and a cell with the text input field. The value argument is used as the **value** attribute of the <input> tag, that is, shown in the field as the initial value. The method also creates a hidden HTML field with the old value. If maxlength and size are given, produces the corresponding HTML attributes. Normally used to allow the user to change an existing database value.
hiddenField	(String name, String value)	Creates a hidden HTML field with the specified name and value.
buttonsStart	–	Opens an HTML table row and a cell spanning two columns. Used to create a row that is not subdivided into a label cell and a value cell, normally for buttons.
buttonsEnd	–	Closes a table cell and row.
submitButton	(String label) (String label, String name)	Creates a Submit button with the specified label (the label is the value attribute of the <input> tag). If the name argument is given, a name attribute is also produced.
button	(String label, String destination)	Creates a normal button with an associated JavaScript that goes to the page URL specified in the destination argument.
submitButtonRow	(String label)	Creates a row that contains only a Submit button. A shortcut for calling buttonsStart, submitButton, and buttonsEnd in sequence.

TABLE 12-3.   *Methods in the HtmlForm Java Class* (continued)

Method	Arguments	Description
selectStart	(String label, String name) (String label, String name, int listSize) (String label, String name, int listSize, boolean multiple)	Creates a row in an HTML table and a cell with the label. Starts a table cell and produces a <select> tag to start a select list. The label/name version produces a default <select> tag, displayed to the user as a drop-down list box. The label/name/listSize version produces a <select> tag with a size attribute, displayed to the user as a list box showing the specified number of items and allowing multiple selection with CTRL or SHIFT-CLICK. The version taking all four arguments is similar to the previous version, but you can disable the multiple selection capability by setting the multiple argument to false.
selectOption	(String text) (String text, String value)	Creates an <option> tag, that is, one option in a select list. Only valid within a <select> tag, so a call to the selectOption method must be preceded by a call to selectStart and followed by calling selectEnd. One argument produces a plain <option> tag where the value passed to the handling module is the same as the value shown to the user. A text and a value argument produce an <option> tag with a value attribute, that is, the text argument is displayed to the user, but the value argument is passed to the module handling the input on the form.

TABLE 12-3. *Methods in the HtmlForm Java Class* (continued)

Method	Arguments	Description
selectEnd	–	Ends the select, the HTML table cell, and the table row.
selectTable	(String label, String name, String tableName, String textCol) (String label, String name, String tableName, String textCol, String valueCol) (String label, String name, String tableName, String textCol, int listSize) (String label, String name, String tableName, String textCol, int listSize, String valueCol) (String label, String name, String tableName, String textCol, int listSize, boolean multiple) (String label, String name, String tableName, String textCol, int listSize, boolean multiple, String valueCol)	Creates a row in an HTML table containing a table cell for the label and a table cell with a <select> tag showing the result of a database query. The textCol and no valueCol arguments produce one plain <option> tag for every result row in the query; the textCol and valueCol arguments produce <option> tags with a value attribute. The listSize argument without multiple argument produces a <select> tag with a size attribute and a multiple attribute. This displays to the user as a list box showing the specified number of items where the user can select multiple values. The multiple argument can be used to create list boxes where the user can only select one value by setting the multiple argument to false.

TABLE 12-3.   *Methods in the HtmlForm Java Class* (continued)

Method	Arguments	Description
selectQuery	(String label, String name, String query varchar2) (String label, String name, String query varchar2 int listSize) (String label, String name, String query varchar2, int listSize, boolean multiple)	Creates a row in an HTML table containing a table cell for the label and a table cell with a <select> tag showing options resulting from the given database query. Produces one <option> tag for every result row in the query. If the select list of the query contains only one item, this value is displayed to the user and passed to the module handling the form input; if it contains two items, the first is used as value attribute of the <option> tag and passed to the handling module, and the second is displayed to the user. The listSize argument without the multiple argument produces a <select> tag with a size attribute and a multiple attribute. This displays to the user as a list box showing the specified number of items where the user can select multiple values. The multiple argument can be called to create list boxes where the user can only select one value; this is achieved by passing the value false as the multiple argument.
checkbox	(String label, String name) (String label, String name, String value) (String label, String name, boolean checked) (String label, String name, String value, boolean checked)	Creates a row in an HTML table containing a cell with the field label and a cell with a check box input field. The value argument produces a corresponding value attribute in the <input> tag. With the boolean argument checked, you can specify whether the check box is initially checked or not.
radiobutton	(String name, String[] labels, String[] values) (String name, String[] labels, String[] values, int selectedValue)	Creates a row in an HTML table containing a number of radio buttons with corresponding labels. In the selectedValue argument, you can choose which radio button is initially selected (1 is the first radio button).

TABLE 12-3. *Methods in the HtmlForm Java Class* (continued)

Method	Arguments	Description
textarea	(String label, String name) (String label, String name, String value) (String label, String name, String value, int rows, int cols)	Creates a row in an HTML table and a cell spanning two columns. In the cell, produces a label and, below that, a \<textarea\> tag. The value argument is used as the default value (initial content) of the text box. The rows and cols arguments produce corresponding attributes in the \<textarea\> tag to control the size of the text box.

TABLE 12-3. *Methods in the HtmlForm Java Class* (continued)

NOTE
If there is a problem with the parameters passed to these methods, they will return HTML that includes an HTML format comment containing the string FIXME, like this: <!--   -->

DatabaseUtility Class

The final example in Chapter 6 used a support class to avoid having to include all the code needed to establish a database connection, execute a query, and present the result as an HTML table. This is what the DatabaseUtility class shown in Table 12-4 does.

It contains one public method called htmlTable in three different versions that take different combinations of parameters. The method returns an HTML table: a String object containing valid HTML tags for starting a table, and producing a row of table headers (\<th\> tags) and one row of HTML table cells (\<td\> tags) for each row of data in the data set.

In addition to this public method, it contains a nonpublic method that returns a String object containing valid HTML tags for one row of HTML table cells (\<tr\> and \<td\> tags) for each row of data in the data set. The method is defined without an *access modifier* like public, protected, or private—this means that the method is accessible from other classes in the com.vesterli.webstart package, but not from classes outside this package.

Method	Parameters	Description
htmlTable	(Connection conn, String query)	Returns the result of an HTML query as an HTML table using the column names as headers.
htmlTable	(Connection conn, String query, String[] labels)	Returns the result of a SQL query as an HTML table using the provided labels as column headers.
htmlTable	(Connection conn, String query, String[] labels, int linkCol, String linkURL)	Returns the result of a SQL query as an HTML table containing the specified links and using the provided labels as column headers. This version is used when you want to create an HTML table where one column contains links to detail records. You must provide the URL of the link, including parameter name, and indicate which column contains the link value. The following column is automatically used as the link text. See the example following this table.
formatHtmlTable	(ResultSet rs)	Formats a ResultSet as rows in an HTML table. Does not produce <table> start or end tags, nor <th> tags for column headers.
formatHtmlTable	(ResultSet rs int linkCol String linkURL)	Formats a ResultSet as rows in an HTML table. One of the columns in the result set will contain a hyperlink <a href> tag, where the hyperlink destination consists of the linkURL string concatenated with the value of the column number indicated by linkCol. The hyperlink text is the column following the linkCol in the order of the columns in the result set.

TABLE 12-4. *Methods in the DatabaseUtility Java Class*

An Example of Using the htmlTable Java Class

You can call the htmlTable method like the following snippet of Java code shows.

```
Connection conn = null;
// code to establish connection not shown
String queryString = "select empno, ename, ename, job";
String[] labels = { "Name", "Job" };
int linkCol = 1;
String linkURL = "showEmpDetail?empno=";
String page = DatabaseUtility.htmlTable(conn, queryString,
     labels, linkCol, linkURL);
```

This would produce HTML code like this:

```
<table>
  <tr>
    <th>Name</th>
    <th>Job</th>
  </tr>
  <tr>
    <td>
      <a href="showEmpDetail?empno=7369">SMITH</a>
    </td>
    <td>CLERK</td>
  </tr>
  <tr>
    <td>
      <a href="showEmpDetail?empno=7499">ALLEN</a>
    </td>
    <td>SALESMAN</td>
  </tr>
[snip]
</table>
```

Note that if you want to use a column value as both link value and link text (for example, to display the empno and use it in a hyperlink at the same time), you must select it twice in your query.

PL/SQL Tools

The following PL/SQL packages implement functionality equivalent to the Java classes described in the preceding section.

Sample Format Package

In Chapter 7, you saw how to use a project-specific Format class to make your code easier to read and to ensure a consistent look of your application. The example PL/SQL package that is part of the Web Application Toolkit contains the functions in Table 12-5. Every function returns the HTML in a VARCHAR2 return value.

HtmlForm Package

Chapter 7 also described how you could use generic HtmlForm packages to produce the HTML tags for common elements of HTML forms. All of the functions described in Table 12-6 return the HTML in a VARCHAR2 return value.

Function	Parameters	Description
pageStart	(title in varchar2)	The standard page header.
introText	(text in varchar2)	The lead text on each page. Normally used for a one-sentence description of what the user is expected to do on the page.
errorText	(error in varchar2)	Formats an error message in a special font (normally with fixed spacing) to clearly set it off from the rest of the page.
pageEnd	–	The standard page footer.
message	(text in varchar2)	Formats some message in a special way (in this case, between horizontal lines) to set it off from the rest of the page. Typically used for messages confirming insertion or deletion of records shown as part of the following page.
warningPage	(warningMessage in varchar2)	A complete page with a warning and a link to go back to the application.
errorPage	(errorMessage in varchar2)	A complete page showing some fatal error. Includes error message and an instruction to the user to contact the help desk.

TABLE 12-5. *Functions in the Sample Format PL/SQL Package*

Function	Parameters	Description
formStart	(action in varchar2, border in number default 0)	Starts an HTML form with the specified destination and at the same time starts an HTML table to align all the form elements. The value of the border parameter specifies the table border width in pixels.
formEnd	–	Ends an HTML form and the associated HTML table.
textField	(label in varchar2, name in varchar2, maxlength in number default null, fieldSize in number default null) (label in varchar2, name in varchar2, value in varchar2, maxlength in number default null, fieldSize in number default null)	Creates a row in an HTML table containing a cell with the field label and a cell with the text input field. If a value parameter is provided, it is used as the default value for the field, that is, as the value attribute of the <input> tag. If maxlength and/or size is provided, produces the corresponding HTML attributes.
passwordField	(label in varchar2, name in varchar2, maxlength in number default null, fieldSize in number default null)	Creates a row in an HTML table containing a cell with the field label and a cell with a password-type text input field. If maxlength and/or size is given, produces the corresponding HTML attributes.
keyField	(label in varchar2, name in varchar2, value in varchar2)	Creates a row in an HTML table containing a cell with the field label and a cell with the field value. Also creates a hidden HTML field with the value. Normally used when you want to display a value without letting the user change it, for example, to show the primary key in an update screen.
updateField	(label in varchar2, name in varchar2, value in varchar2, maxlength in number default null, fieldSize in number default null)	Creates a row in an HTML table containing a cell with the field label and a cell with the text input field. The value parameter is used as the value attribute of the <input> tag, that is, shown in the field as the initial value. The function also creates a hidden HTML field with the old value. If maxlength and/or size is given, produces the corresponding HTML attributes. Normally used to allow the user to change an existing database value.

TABLE 12-6.   *Functions in the HtmlForm PL/SQL Package*

Function	Parameters	Description
hiddenField	(name in varchar2, value in varchar2)	Creates a hidden HTML field with the specified name and value.
buttonsStart	–	Opens an HTML table row and a cell spanning two columns. Used to create a row that is not subdivided into a label cell and a value cell, normally for buttons.
buttonsEnd	–	Closes a table cell and row.
submitButton	(label in varchar2, name in varchar2 default null)	Creates a Submit button with the specified label (the label is the value attribute of the <input> tag). If the name parameter is given, a name attribute is also produced.
button	(label in varchar2, destination in varchar2)	Creates a normal button with an associated JavaScript that goes to the page URL specified in the destination parameter.
submitButtonRow	(label in varchar2)	Creates a row that contains only a Submit button. Shortcut for calling buttonsStart, submitButton, and buttonsEnd in sequence.
selectStart	(label in varchar2, name in varchar2) (label in varchar2, name in varchar2, listSize in number, multiple in boolean default true)	Creates a row in an HTML table and a cell with the label. Starts a table cell and produces a <select> tag to start a select list. If a value is provided for listSize, produces a <select> tag with a size attribute, displayed to the user as a list box showing the specified number of items and allowing multiple selections with CTRL or SHIFT-CLICK. If the multiple parameter has the value false, multiple selections are not allowed.
selectOption	(text in varchar2, value in varchar2 default null)	Creates an <option> tag, that is, one option in a select list. Only valid within a <select> tag, so a call to an option must be preceded by a call to selectStart and followed by calling selectEnd. If a value is provided for the value parameter, generates a value attribute in the option tag.
selectEnd	–	Ends the select, the HTML table cell, and the table row.

TABLE 12-6. *Functions in the HtmlForm PL/SQL Package* (continued)

Function	Parameters	Description
selectTable	(label in varchar2, name in varchar2, tableName in varchar2, textCol in varchar2, valueCol in varchar2 default null) (label in varchar2, name in varchar2, tableName in varchar2 textcol in varchar2, listSize in number, multiple in boolean default true, valueCol in varchar2 default null)	Creates a row in an HTML table containing a table cell for the label and a table cell with a <select> tag showing the result of a database query. The function produces one <option> tag for every result row in the query. The value of the textCol parameter is displayed to the user; and if a value is given for the valueCol parameter, the value of this column is used as the value attribute of the <option> tag. The listSize parameter produces a <select> tag with a size attribute and (controlled by the multiple parameter) a multiple attribute. If the listSize parameter is not given, the select list displays to the user as a drop-down box; if the listSize parameter *is* given, displays as a list box showing the specified number of items. If the multiple parameter is true (the default), the user can select multiple values.
selectQuery	(label in varchar2, name in varchar2, query in varchar2, listSize in number default null, multiple in varchar2 default null)	Creates a row in an HTML table containing a table cell for the label and a table cell with a <select> tag showing options resulting from the given database query. Produces one <option> tag for every result row in the query. If the select list of the query contains only one item, this value is displayed to the user; if the select list contains two items, the first is used as the value attribute of the <option> tag, and the second is displayed to the user. If a value is provided for the listSize parameter, produces a <select> tag with a size attribute and (controlled by the multiple parameter) a multiple attribute. Displays to the user as a list box showing the specified number of items instead of the drop-down otherwise shown. If the multiple parameter is true (the default), the user can select multiple values.

TABLE 12-6. *Functions in the HtmlForm PL/SQL Package* (continued)

Function	Parameters	Description
checkbox	(label in varchar2, name in varchar2, value in varchar2 default null, checked in boolean default false) (label in varchar2, name in varchar2, checked in boolean)	Creates a row in an HTML table containing a cell with the field label and a cell with a check box input field. If a value parameter is provided, it is used as the value attribute of the <input> tag. If the checked parameter is true, produces a check box that is initially checked.
radiobutton	(name in varchar2, label1 in varchar2, value1 in varchar2, label2 in varchar2, value2 in varchar2, selectedValue in number default null) (name in varchar2, label1 in varchar2, value1 in varchar2, label2 in varchar2, value2 in varchar2, label3 in varchar2, value3 in varchar2, selectedValue in number default null) (name in varchar2, label1 in varchar2, value1 in varchar2, label2 in varchar2, value2 in varchar2, label3 in varchar2, value3 in varchar2, label4 in varchar2, value4 in varchar2, selectedValue in number default null) (name in varchar2, label_arr in owa.vc_arr, value_arr in owa.vc_arr, selectedValue in number default null)	Creates a row in an HTML table containing a number of radio buttons with labels. If a value is provided for the selectedValue parameter, produces a checked attribute for the corresponding radio button. The version taking two PL/SQL tables of the type owa.vc_arr (defined in the OWA package that is part of the PL/SQL Web Toolkit) will produce any number of radio buttons in one row, but you need to create two PL/SQL table variables of the correct type to invoke it.
textarea	(label in varchar2, name in varchar2, value in varchar2 default null, rows in number default null, cols in number default null)	Creates a row in an HTML table and a cell spanning two columns. In the cell, produces a label and, below that, a <textarea> tag. If a value parameter is provided, uses this as default value (initial content) of the text box. If a value is provided for the rows and/or cols parameter, produces the corresponding attributes in the <textarea> tag to control the size of the text box.

TABLE 12-6. *Functions in the HtmlForm PL/SQL Package* (continued)

NOTE
If there is a problem with the parameters passed to these methods, they will return HTML that includes an HTML format comment containing the string FIXME, like this: <!-- -->

DatabaseUtility Package

This package contains one public function called htmlTable in two different versions that take different parameters—see Table 12-7. The function returns an HTML table: a VARCHAR2 value containing valid HTML tags for starting a table, and producing a row of table headers (<th> tags) and one row of HTML table cells (<td> tags) for each row of data in the data set.

Function	Parameters	Description
htmlTable	(query in varchar2, labels in owa.vc_arr default empty_vc_arr) (query in varchar2, linkCol in number, linkURL in varchar2, labels in owa.vc_arr default empty_vc_arr)	Returns the result of a SQL query as an HTML table. If the labels parameter (a PL/SQL table type) is provided, the values in the table are used as column headers; if no labels are provided, the column names are used as headers. If a linkCol and linkURL parameter is supplied, an HTML table is produced where one column contains hyperlinks to detail records. You must provide the URL of the link, including parameter name, and indicate which column contains the link value. The following column is automatically used as the link text. See the example following this table.

TABLE 12-7.   *Functions in the DatabaseUtility PL/SQL Package*

NOTE
owa.vc_arr is a PL/SQL table type defined in the OWA package that is part of the PL/SQL Web toolkit. empty_vc_arr is an empty table of this type; it's defined in the DatabaseUtility package and used only as a default value.

An Example of Using the htmlTable PL/SQL Function

You can call the htmlTable procedure like the following snippet of PL/SQL code shows.

```
declare
  query varchar2(250) := 'select empno, ename, job from emp';
  linkCol number := 1;
  linkURL varchar2(250) := 'showEmpDetail?empno=';
  label_arr owa.vc_arr;
  page varchar2(32767);
begin
  label_arr(1) := 'Name';
  label_arr(2) := 'Job';
  page := DatabaseUtility.htmlTable(query, linkCol,
      linkURL, label_arr);
end;
```

This would produce HTML code like this:

```
<table>
  <tr>
    <th>Name</th>
    <th>Job</th>
  </tr>
  <tr>
    <td>
      <a href="showEmpDetail?empno=7369">SMITH</a>
    </td>
    <td>CLERK</td>
  </tr>
  <tr>
    <td>
      <a href="showEmpDetail?empno=7499">ALLEN</a>
    </td>
    <td>SALESMAN</td>
  </tr>
[snip]
</table>
```

Note that if you want to use a column value as both link value and link text (for example, to display the empno and use it in a hyperlink at the same time), you must select it twice in your query.

CHAPTER
13

Useful Books
and Web Sites

his book helped you get started with Oracle Web applications by showing you how to install the necessary software and by leading you step by step through developing some simple applications. This last chapter shows you how to find more information to let you continue on your way to becoming an expert on Oracle Web applications. It contains some general tips on finding information, explains the information choices available from Oracle, and lists some books and Web sites that provide additional information about the topics covered in this book.

Finding What You Need

With so much information out there, it's no wonder you can't find what you're looking for. I recommend the following strategy:

1. Build a library of reference books. The reference titles in this section could form a starting point—all of them are part of my library, but you probably don't need each title.

2. Learn to use a general search engine. If I have a problem, I normally throw a couple of terms at AltaVista and let it work its magic. Since most search engines charge for a listing these days, this approach will not find every page, but there are so many Web sites out there with Oracle information that it is impractical to search each of them.

3. If the Internet didn't provide a result, try Oracle. Search the Oracle Technology Network (OTN) Web site and Oracle Metalink (see the next section for more information).

4. Ask someone. Post a question in a Technical Forum on OTN or Metalink, or ask in a discussion group or mailing list. The ODTUG-WEBDEV-L hosted by the Oracle Development Tools User Group (ODTUG) is full of knowledgeable and helpful people (sign up at **http://www.odtug.com/subscrib.htm**).

Oracle Technology Network

The Oracle Technology Network (OTN) is Oracle's developer program, and membership is free. This program is your number one source for Oracle software, manuals, white papers, code examples, and much more. If you are not already a member, go to **http://otn.oracle.com** and sign up now!

Software

All the latest software is available for download from the OTN Web site at **http://otn.oracle.com/software/index.htm**. Since many packages run well into the hundreds of megabytes, you'll need a fast connection if you want to download everything.

If you don't feel like downloading everything, for a reasonable fee, you can sign up for one or more OTN Technology Tracks at the URL just mentioned. Oracle will regularly send you a bundle of CDs with the latest software.

NOTE
The software available from OTN is provided under a developer license. This basically means that you are allowed to play around with the software but not to use it in production. You can read the fine print on the OTN Web site.

Oracle Documentation

Even though your organization has a whole bookshelf full of Oracle manuals, the one you are looking for never seems to be there, right? The solution to this is also found on OTN—you can find all the manuals for individual download at **http://otn.oracle.com/docs/index.htm**.

Most of the manuals are available in both HTML and PDF format.

You can also find documentation for older versions here. This can be useful, for example, when Oracle forgets to include the documentation for the PL/SQL Web Toolkit in the Oracle9i Application Server documentation set. To get a copy, look under Archived Product Documentation, OAS.

Oracle Support

These days, Oracle prefers that you use the Web to help yourself solve any problems you might have with Oracle software. Even if you are paying for a support contract, the basic support level from Oracle probably doesn't include the privilege of talking to someone from Oracle Support—you are supposed to use the Web-based Oracle MetaLink at **http://metalink.oracle.com**.

Fortunately, this does work pretty well. If you don't already have an account, you need to sign up first. You need to provide a valid *support identifier* to prove that you have paid for Oracle support.

NOTE
If your organization has several support identifiers, remember to add them all to your profile. You can only see information about the products you have proven you have a support contract for.

Following is a list of some of the features that MetaLink offers:

- A *search* feature that lets you search part of the Oracle bug database. This occasionally provides an answer to your questions.

- The possibility to download the latest *patches*. These are really useful.

- The ability to open a Technical Assistance Request (TAR) when you can't find a solution to the problem in the bug database.

- A Product Lifecycle section showing the certified combinations of development tools and databases, which is useful, and an availability matrix showing available software versions, which is frequently outdated and, therefore, useless.

Books

Table 13-1 lists some reference books that I use or have read and enjoyed while learning about some aspect of Web applications. This list is not definitive—you can go to amazon.com or any other large online bookshop and find a wide variety of books on all the following topics. I encourage you to read the online reviews of each of these books to find out if it is appropriate for your level of expertise.

NOTE
The ISBN numbers in the table apply to the latest edition at the time this book was printed. Remember to check whether a new version of a book has come out in the meantime.

You can also find an up-to-date version of this list with links to amazon.com on **www.vesterli.com/books**.

Topic	Description	Title, Author, ISBN
Apache	A serious reference that explains all the configuration options you need (and more). Doesn't cover Windows especially, but that should not be a problem. Also contains all the information you will need for more advanced Apache configurations.	*Professional Apache*, Peter Wainwright, 1861003021

TABLE 13-1. *Books on Developing Web Applications*

Topic	Description	Title, Author, ISBN
HTML	A great tutorial introduction to HTML programming with lots of examples.	*Teach Yourself Web Publishing with HTML and XHTML in 21 Days*, Laura Lemay, 0672320770 **Note:** This is the latest version—I haven't read it, but the HTML 3.2 and 4 versions were good.
HTML	The title says it—this is the definitive reference book to turn to for the authoritative explanation of every HTML tag and option. If your HTML doesn't come out the way you wanted in a specific browser, this book will tell you why (and often how to solve the problem with browser-compatible code).	*HTML & XHTML: The Definitive Guide,* Chuck Musciano and Bill Kennedy, 059600026X
HTML	A first-class HTML tutorial. Also available for free on the Internet at **http://www.htmlgoodies.com**.	*HTML Goodies*, Joe Burns, 0789718235
Java	A tutorial for learning Java. Very beginner oriented with simple examples and a lot of focus on the object-oriented way of thinking. The whole book is also available for free on the Internet at **http://www.eckelobjects.com/TIJ2/**.	*Thinking in Java*, Bruce Eckel, 0130273635
Java	A comprehensive Java tutorial with larger examples for experienced programmers wanting to learn Java.	*Core Java 2, Volume 1: Fundamentals*, Cay Horstmann and Gary Cornell, 0130894680
Java	An indispensable reference to the Java language.	*Java in a Nutshell*, David Flanagan, 1565924878
Java	A good collection of real Java programs that illustrates all language features.	*Java Examples in a Nutshell*, David Flanagan, 0596000391
Java	Everything you need to know about writing Java servlets. With lots of good examples, including advanced features.	*Java Servlet Programming*, Jason Hunter and William Crawford, 156592391X **Note:** A second edition should be out by the time you read this book

TABLE 13-1. *Books on Developing Web Applications* (continued)

Topic	Description	Title, Author, ISBN
JavaScript	Though somewhat dated (from 1998), this book is a good JavaScript reference. It is not a tutorial, but it explains all the features of the JavaScript language.	*JavaScript: The Definitive Guide*, David Flanagan, 1565923928
JavaScript	Also rather old (from 1998), this book is a good reference for how to manipulate Web pages using JavaScript. It describes the Document Object Model that defines the hierarchy of objects on a Web page.	*Dynamic HTML: The Definitive Reference*, Danny Goodman, 1565924940
Oracle Designer	A complete description of the CASE Application Development Method (CADM). For each step in the method, the book provides a thorough explanation followed by a chapter describing how to use the Designer tools to support that phase. Covers the old version 2.1 of Designer; but even though some of the tools have changed a bit, the method and most of the tool descriptions remain valid.	*Oracle Designer Handbook*, Peter Koletzke and Dr. Paul Dorsey, 0078824176
Oracle Designer	How to use Designer to its full potential, generating databases, forms, and reports from Designer.	*Oracle Designer Generation*, Kenneth Atkins, Paul Dirksen, Zikri Askin Ince, 0078824753
Oracle Web Applications	A thorough reference with many tips and tricks for Oracle Web applications with different tools. Written in 1999, some of the content is outdated by now (especially the stuff on the Oracle Application Server), but much of the material is still relevant.	*Oracle8i Web Development*, Brad Brown, 0072122420 **Note:** Stay tuned for an updated version
Web Graphics	Explains what you need to know about creating graphics for the Web and uses Paint Shop Pro to demonstrate. Works as a Paint Shop Pro tutorial as well. Rather old (1998) and covers an old version of the software (version 5), but holds up well.	*Creating Paint Shop Pro Web Graphics*, Andy Shafran and Brad Castle, 0966288904
XML	Thorough coverage of the XML features in the Oracle servers and tools—Steve Muench really knows what he's talking about. If you are not familiar with XML, you might need a more beginner-oriented book in addition to this one.	*Building Oracle XML Applications*, Steve Muench, 1565926919

TABLE 13-1. *Books on Developing Web Applications* (continued)

Web Sites

Books and Web sites complement each other. In a book you can be sure to find the information you read yesterday in the same place today; on the Web everything is changing constantly. The latest information is almost always going to be found on a Web site somewhere, and Table 13-2 lists some sites where you can download tools or get more information about topics covered in this book.

Just like the book list in Table 13-1, this list is just a starting point; you'll be adding and removing sites to your personal Web reading list constantly.

Topic	Description	URL
Apache	The home page for the Apache Software Foundation, the people who brought us the excellent Apache HTTP Server. Contains whole subsites about the Apache HTTP Server, Apache JServ, and many other interesting things. Lots of news, information, and FAQs.	**http://www.apache.org**
Conversion	Download page for the WebAlchemy tool to convert HTML pages into PL/SQL stored procedures. Uses all the functions and procedures in the Oracle PL/SQL Web Toolkit.	**http://www.users.bigpond.com/ ahobbs**
Conversion	Download page for a small utility to convert an HTML file into a snippet of Java servlet code.	**http://www.vesterli.com/tools**
Conversion	Download page for a small utility to convert an HTML file into a snippet of PL/SQL code.	**http://www.vesterli.com/tools**
General utilities	A general download site offering a lot of tools (HTML editors, image editing programs, HTML validation, and lots more).	**http://www.download.com**
General utilities	Download page for Programmer's File Editor.	**http://www.lancs.ac.uk/people/ cpaap/pfe/default.htm**
General utilities	Download page for the junction utility.	**http://www.sysinternals.com/ ntw2k/source/misc.shtml#junction**

TABLE 13-2. *Useful Web Sites*

Topic	Description	URL
General utilities	Information about the Norton Ghost disk image tool for saving and restoring the contents of one or more disks. Also contains a link to buy online.	**http://www.symantec.com/sabu/ ghost/ghost_personal/**
General utilities	Information about the DriveImage disk image tool for saving and restoring the contents of one or more disks. Also contains a link to buy online.	**http://www.powerquest.com/ driveimage/**
General utilities	Information about the PartitionMagic tool that can be used to resize partitions without destroying the content. Also contains a link to buy online.	**http://www.powerquest.com/ partitionmagic/**
HTML	Great online tutorials on HTML, JavaScript, CSS, and much more. If you like online tutorials, this is as good as it gets!	**http://www.htmlgoodies.com**
HTML	A list of all the MIME types (long).	**ftp://ftp.isi.edu/in-notes/iana/ assignments/media-types/media-types Note:** That's ftp, not http—don't worry; even if you don't know ftp, your browser does
HTML	A list of the most common HTML entities.	**http://htmlgoodies.earthweb.com/ tutors/&command.html**
HTML	The official source XHTML specification.	**http://www.w3.org/TR/xhtml1**
HTML	How to write XHTML that shows correctly in fourth-generation browsers.	**http://www.w3.org/TR/xhtml1 #guidelines**
HTML	Upload an HTML file for validation. This page accepts any Web page you upload and produces a report showing any errors the page has.	**http://validator.w3.org/ file-upload.html**

TABLE 13-2. *Useful Web Sites (continued)*

Topic	Description	URL
HTML	Validation of a Web page anywhere on the Internet. Produces a report showing any errors the page has.	**http://validator.w3.org/**
HTML	Download page for Paint Shop Pro, a powerful and inexpensive image editing program.	**http://www.jasc.com/download.asp**
Java	The complete book *Thinking in Java* for download.	**http://www.eckelobjects.com/TIJ2/**
Java	The official source for Java information.	**http://www.javasoft.com/**
Javadoc	Information about the Javadoc utility and how to format comments for Javadoc.	**http://www.javasoft.com/j2se/javadoc**
JavaScript	Great online tutorials on JavaScript, HTML, CSS, and much more. One of the best online tutorials I have found.	**http://www.htmlgoodies.com**
Oracle Web Applications	The companion site to this book. All the examples and the Web Application Toolkit available for download. Also an updated list of books and Web sites.	**http://www.vesterli.com**
PL/SQL tools	Information about ChangeGroup PL/SQL Server Pages, a development tool for HTML-based Web projects. A 45-day trial can be ordered from the Web site.	**http://www.changegroup.dk/en/cgpsp.htm**
PL/SQL tools	Download page for TOAD—a powerful SQL and PL/SQL development environment that exists in a free version.	**http://www.toadsoft.com/downld.html**
XML	The official XML specification.	**http://www.w3.org/XML/**

TABLE 13-2. *Useful Web Sites* (continued)

Index

483

INTERNATIONAL CONTACT INFORMATION

AUSTRALIA
McGraw-Hill Book Company Australia Pty. Ltd.
TEL +61-2-9417-9899
FAX +61-2-9417-5687
http://www.mcgraw-hill.com.au
books-it_sydney@mcgraw-hill.com

CANADA
McGraw-Hill Ryerson Ltd.
TEL +905-430-5000
FAX +905-430-5020
http://www.mcgrawhill.ca

GREECE, MIDDLE EAST,
NORTHERN AFRICA
McGraw-Hill Hellas
TEL +30-1-656-0990-3-4
FAX +30-1-654-5525

MEXICO (Also serving Latin America)
McGraw-Hill Interamericana Editores S.A. de C.V.
TEL +525-117-1583
FAX +525-117-1589
http://www.mcgraw-hill.com.mx
fernando_castellanos@mcgraw-hill.com

SINGAPORE (Serving Asia)
McGraw-Hill Book Company
TEL +65-863-1580
FAX +65-862-3354
http://www.mcgraw-hill.com.sg
mghasia@mcgraw-hill.com

SOUTH AFRICA
McGraw-Hill South Africa
TEL +27-11-622-7512
FAX +27-11-622-9045
robyn_swanepoel@mcgraw-hill.com

UNITED KINGDOM & EUROPE
(Excluding Southern Europe)
McGraw-Hill Education Europe
TEL +44-1-628-502500
FAX +44-1-628-770224
http://www.mcgraw-hill.co.uk
computing_neurope@mcgraw-hill.com

ALL OTHER INQUIRIES Contact:
Osborne/McGraw-Hill
TEL +1-510-549-6600
FAX +1-510-883-7600
http://www.osborne.com
omg_international@mcgraw-hill.com

Get Your FREE Subscription to *Oracle Magazine*

Oracle Magazine is essential gear for today's information technology professionals. Stay informed and increase your productivity with every issue of *Oracle Magazine*. Inside each **FREE,** bimonthly issue you'll get:

- Up-to-date information on Oracle Database Server, Oracle Applications, Internet Computing, and tools
- Third-party news and announcements
- Technical articles on Oracle products and operating environments
- Development and administration tips
- Real-world customer stories

Three easy ways to subscribe:

1. Web Visit our Web site at **www.oracle.com/oramag/.** You'll find a subscription form there, plus much more!

2. Fax Complete the questionnaire on the back of this card and fax the questionnaire side only to **+1.847.647.9735.**

3. Mail Complete the questionnaire on the back of this card and mail it to P.O. Box 1263, Skokie, IL 60076-8263.

If there are other Oracle users at your location who would like to receive their own subscription to *Oracle Magazine*, please photocopy this form and pass it along.

Knowledge is power. To which we say,

crank up the power.

Are you ready for a power surge?

Accelerate your career—become an **Oracle Certified Professional (OCP)**. With Oracle's cutting-edge *Instructor-Led Training*, *Technology-Based Training*, and this *guide*, you can prepare for certification faster than ever. Set your own trajectory by logging your personal training plan with us. Go to **http://education.oracle.com/tpb**, where we'll help you pick a training path, select your courses, and track your progress. We'll even send you an email when your courses are offered in your area. If you don't have access to the Web, call us at 1-800-441-3541 (Outside the U.S. call +1-310-335-2403). **Power learning has never been easier.**